GRAMMAR AND MEANING
papers on syntactic and semantic topics

GRAMMAR AND MEANING

papers on syntactic and semantic topics

James D. McCawley University of Chicago

ACADEMIC PRESS   1976

New York   San Francisco   London

A Subsidiary of Harcourt Brace Jovanovich, Publishers

Preface

This volume contains essentially my complete works on syntax and semantics up to December 1971. The only works of mine in that area which do not appear here are term papers done while I was a student, a couple of short papers whose contents duplicate portions of later longer works, a couple of minor book reviews, and my long contribution to the Fifth International Seminar on Theoretical Linguistics, 'Syntactic and logical arguments for logical structures', which will appear either after the other speakers at the Seminar have submitted their manuscripts or posthumously, whichever comes first. The texts that appear here are lightly edited and heavily annotated. Rather than rewriting those papers which do not reflect my current thinking (i.e. most of them), I have confined myself to making stylistic improvements, making some changes of terminology (e.g. replacing 'intended referent' by 'purported referent', which is less liable to misunderstanding), introducing a uniform method of bibliographical citation, and replacing certain examples by others that are better suited to making the points in question, but have added copious annotations (in the form of footnotes designated [a,b,c] . . .; the original footnotes are designated [1,2,3] . . .). The annotations contain retractions, criticism of the arguments presented, additional facts of relevance, and references to subsequent work on the topic under discussion.

The papers are arranged roughly in the order in which they were written, which bears little relationship to the order in which they were published. In cases where the writing of a paper was spread over a long period of time, I have inserted it into the chronology by estimating the date on which it was ' essentially finished ', which generally involves a decision as arbitrary as that of theologians as to when a human fetus becomes a person and as capricious as those which a parole board makes. Since all bibliographical references are made in terms of a single bibliography, which appears at the end of the volume, in which published works (many of which were not yet published when the papers in which I cite them first appeared) are listed according to the year of publication, the reader should not be distressed if he finds a reference to Ross (1970) in a paper which

I wrote in 1967 and was published in 1968.   ' Forthcoming ' works which have not come forth are listed in the bibliography as G. Lakoff (abortion *a*), etc.

There are many persons who deserve my thanks for helping to make it possible for me to produce the works contained in this volume, of whom the following are those especially deserving of mention: Noam Chomsky and Morris Halle, who took me in as a student at MIT when I was suffering from an advanced case of intellectual malnutrition and constipation and who rapidly provided a cure for those maladies, George Lakoff and Haj Ross, who provided me with a post-doctoral course on the structure of English during many long telephone conversations in my first few years of teaching, and my students at the University of Chicago, who are intellectual gourmets who have no hesitation in sending improperly prepared fare back to the kitchen.

Acknowledgements

Permission to reprint these articles from the following sources is gratefully acknowledged :

"Concerning the Base Component of a Transformational Grammar," *Foundations of Language* 4. 243–69.

"The Role of Semantics in a Grammar," *Universals in Linguistic Theory*, edited by Emmon Bach and Robert T. Harms (New York : Holt, Rinehart and Winston, 1968).

"Meaning and the Description of Languages," *Kotoba no Uchû*, vol. 2, nos. 9, 10, and 11 (Tokyo : TEC Co. Ltd., 1967).

"Where Do Noun Phrases Come from?" *Readings in English Transformational Grammar*, edited by Roderick Jacobs and Peter S. Rosenbaum (Boston : Ginn and Company, 1970).

"Lexical Insertion in a Transformational Grammar without Deep Structure," *Papers from the Fourth Regional Meeting, Chicago Linguistic Society* (Chicago : Linguistics Dept. of the University of Chicago).

"Review of *Current Trends in Linguistics*, vol. 3 : Theoretical Foundations," *Language* 44. 556–93.

"English as a *VSO* Language," *Language* 46. 286–99.

"Review of Otto Jespersen, *Analytic Syntax*," *Language* 46. 442–9.

"On the Applicability of *Vice Versa*," *Linguistic Inquiry* 1. 278–80.

"Semantic Representation," *Cognition: a multiple view*, edited by Paul M. Garvin (New York : Spartan Books, 1970).

"Tense and Time Reference in English," *Studies in Linguistic Semantics*, edited by Charles J. Fillmore and D. T. Langendeon (New York : Holt, Rinehart and Winston, 1971).

"*Similar in that S*," *Linguistic Inquiry* 1. 556–9.

"On the Deep Structure of Negative Clauses," *Eigo Kyoiku* vol. 19, no. 6 (Tokyo : Taishukan Publishing Co. Ltd., 1970).

"A Program for Logic," *The Semantics of Natural Language*, edited by Donald Davidson and Gilbert H. Harman (Dordrecht : Reidel, 1972).

"William Dwight Whitney as a Syntactician," *Papers in Linguistics in honor of Henry and Renee Kahane*, edited by Braj Kachru et al. (Champaign : University of Illinois Press).

"Interpretative Semantics Meets Frankenstein," *Foundations of Language* 7. 285–96.
"Prelexical Syntax," *Monograph Series on Languages and Linguistics* 24 (Washington: Georgetown University).
"Notes on Japanese Potential Clauses," *Studies in Descriptive and Applied Linguistics*, Bulletin of the Summer Institute in Linguistics (Tokyo: International Christian University, 1972).

Table of Contents

1. Quantitative and Qualitative Comparison in English[*]

This paper is concerned with the English sentence types exemplified respectively by the sentences

    (1) John is more stupid than Harry.
    (2) John is more stupid than ignorant.

I propose to demonstrate that the identity of shape of these two constructions is only superficial and that they are derived through the action of different transformations and from radically different deep stuctures.

    There are a number of differences between these two types of comparative structures. First, it is possible for the adjective to be followed by the ending -*er* instead of being preceded by *more* in the first type of structure:

    (3) John is sicker than Harry.

but not in the second type: one cannot say

    (4) *John is sicker than depraved.

but only

* An earlier version of this paper was read at the winter meeting of the Linguistic Society of America, New York, Dec. 29, 1964. It is published here for the first time.

(5) John is more sick than depraved.

Secondly, in the first type, the *more* & Adj combination can precede a noun:

(6) John is a more stupid man than Harry.

but not in the second type:

(7) *John is a more stupid man than ignorant.

Third, it is possible to have a structure of the second type which does not involve an adjective at all, for example,

(8) John is more a philosopher than a linguist.;

however, there is no corresponding adjective-less structure of the first type.[a] Fourth, the two types of structure do not occur as answers to the same types of questions. Thus, one could have a dialogue:

(9) How stupid is John?
     Answer: He's very stupid; he's more stupid than Harry.

but not a dialogue such as

(10) How stupid is John?
      *Answer: He's very stupid; he's more stupid than ignorant.

These facts show that there are transformations whose structural descriptions are met by structures of the one type but not those of the other. Thus there must be some difference between the shapes of the deep structures of the two types of comparatives which will cause one but not the other to meet the structural descriptions of these transformations. The question of what the difference is is answered in part by the fact that one structure but not the other can be used as an answer to the question ' How stupid is John? '. From this I conclude that one but not the other belongs to the syntactic category of *how* in the question, namely to the category of adverbs of degree. I thus hypothesise that (1) has a deep structure of the form.[1]

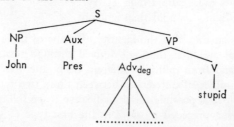

---

[1] George Lakoff (1965) argues convincingly that ' verbs ' and ' adjectives ' as traditionally understood differ only in certain very superficial respects and are thus best regarded as two subcategories of a single syntactic category, here called *V*. The principal differences between verbs and adjectives are that adjectives but not verbs must be preceded by the copula *be* when serving as the head of a verb phrase, that adverbs of degree precede adjectives (*John is very stupid*) but follow verbs (*John works a lot*), and that adjectives do not form passives (*This fact is known by all* but not *This fact is been aware of by all*). The copula is inserted by a transformation at the beginning of any *VP* which begins with a [−Verbal] element, where ' verbs ' are specified as [+Verbal] and adjectives as [−Verbal].

Note now that the *than* can be followed by a wide variety of rather complex items, for example,

(11)   John is more stupid than Harry used to be when they were in the third grade.

The total range of ' *than* phrases ' can best be described as the structures which arise from ' *than S* ' by the deletion of certain omittable items. I thus propose that the Adv$_{deg}$ position in the deep structure of (1) is filled by ' *er than S* ', where the S is the structure corresponding to the sentence *Harry is stupid*:[2]

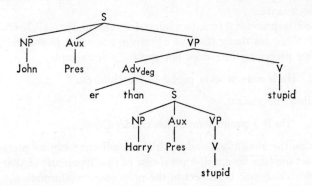

(2) must now be assigned a deep structure, and moreover, one of a different type from that assigned to (1). I propose that (2) is simply a conjoined sentence, derived in exactly the same way as is

(12)   John is stupid and ignorant.,

that is, that the deep structure is a conjunction of the sentences *John is stupid* and *John is ignorant*, only with *more than* instead of *and* for the conjunction:

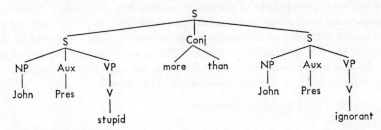

[2] One interesting question about which I have nothing cogent to say at present is the question of why *John is more stupid than Harry* implies that Harry is stupid but *John is more intelligent than Harry* does not imply that Harry is intelligent. Evidently the term corresponding to the ' positive ' end of a scale of evaluation is taken as ' unmarked ' and must be used when a comparison simply specifies the relative position of two items on the scale without indicating how close either comes to the extreme values of the scale. I have no idea what implications this fact has for the deep structure of comparatives.

I will now show that this assignment of deep structures is sufficient to account for the differences I have observed between the two types of comparison. Since the crucial problem will be the possibility of putting the one kind of *more &* Adj combination before the noun but not the other kind, let me digress into a discussion of the conditions under which an adjective can precede a noun. Following Smith (1961), I will treat attributive adjectives as being derived from the same deep structures as relative clauses[3,b]. Thus, *John is a tall man* has the same deep structure as does *John is a man who is tall.* There is a transformation which optionally eliminates the *who is* of this structure, leaving *tall* immediately preceded by *man;* another transformation then moves the adjective in front of the noun.

The adjective-preposing transformation does not apply to all Noun-Adjective sequences: there are many cases of adjectives belonging to complex modifiers to which the preposing rule does not apply. For example,

(13)   He is man who is proud of his children.

does not allow the variant

(14)   *He is a proud man of his children.

To determine the conditions under which an adjective can be placed in front of a noun, let me take up a well-known case of two apparently similar constructions, of which only one is subject to the preposing transformation. I refer to the case of *John is easy to please* and *John is eager to please*: one can say

(15)   John is an easy man to please

but not

(16)   *John is an eager man to please.

Let me recapitulate the discussion given by Chomsky (lectures at MIT), modified slightly in accordance with the result of Lakoff's noted in footnote 2. The word *John* not only is the subject of the entire sentence but also bears a grammatical relation to the word *please* in each of the two sentences: in *John is easy to please*, *John* stands in the object relation to *please*, whereas in *John is eager to please*, it stands in the subject relation to *please*. This is evidenced by the fact that in the one case only a noun phrase which can be the object of the included verb can be the subject of the entire sentence. For example,

(17)   *We pleased the liverwurst.

is odd, and

(18)   *The liverwurst is easy to please.

[3] Except for certain classes of adjectives which can not be used predicatively. Thus, *John's former wife* has no corresponding relative *John's wife who is former* and is derived from a structure involving the adverb *formerly*, a structure which can be paraphrased as *the (person) who formerly was John's wife.* Such modifiers are treated in detail in Annear (1964).

is odd in exactly the same way. Similarly, in the second case, only a noun-phrase which can be the subject of the contained verb, or rather, verb-phrase, can be the subject of the entire sentence. Thus, since

(19)   *My uncle equals the square of the hypotenuse.

is odd, so also is

(20)   *My uncle is eager to equal the square of the hypotenuse.

To account for these facts,[c] it is necessary to assign these two sentences deep structures having embedded sentences in which *John* is respectively the object and subject of the verb *please*. Chomsky proposes for *John is easy to please* a deep structure representable as

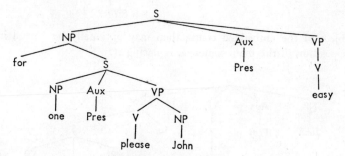

which if no optional transformations were applied would yield the sentence

(21)   For one to please John is easy.

John is easy to please is derived from this structure by the following transformations. First, an optional transformation of ' extraposition ' moves the clause *for one to please John* to the end of the sentence, leaving *it* in the subject position[4]:

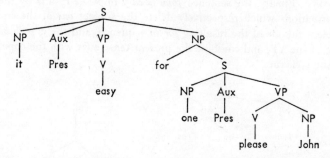

---

[4] More precisely, this transformation adds a copy of the embedded clause at the end of the sentence and ' pronominalizes ' the first occurrence of it. Since a sentence counts as neuter singular, the resulting pronoun is *it*. Note that this transformation differs from the ' extraposition ' manifested in *A man was here who wanted to talk to you*, which is a true movement of a clause rather than duplication plus pronominalization.

If no further optional transformations were applied, the result would be

(22)   It is easy for one to please John.

An obligatory transformation replaces the auxiliary of the embedded clause by *to:*

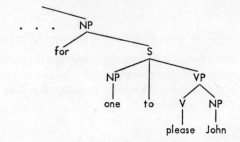

The object of the embedded clause then may optionally be moved into the subject position of the main sentence, replacing *it:*

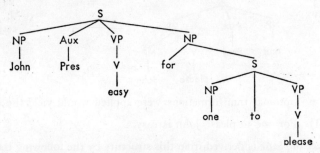

If no further optional transformations were applied, the sentence

(23)   John is easy for one to please.

would result.   Finally, the sentence *John is easy to please* results by the action of transformations which respectively delete the subject *one* of the embedded clause, delete the *for* of the resulting *for to* sequence, add the copula *be* at the beginning of the VP, and combine the present tense affix with the copula, thus yielding the structure[d]

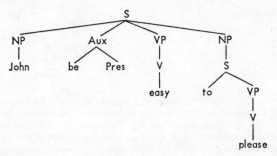

In the case of *eager to please*, it is impossible to assign a deep structure of the above shape, since it is impossible to get such parallel sentences as

(24) *For one to please John is eager.
(25) *It is eager for one to please John.

Since the *easy to* construction is derived by a series of rules, one of which moves the object of the embedded sentence to the beginning, *easy to* can not be followed by an entire verb phrase but only by a transitive verb phrase minus its object. However, not only can *eager to* be followed by a full verb phrase, transitive or intransitive, but indeed, *eager* can be followed by any *for NP to VP* combination in which the NP can function as the subject of the VP in an independent sentence, for example,

(26) John is eager for Mary to please his parents.
(27) John is eager for the Orioles to win the pennant.
(28) John is eager for his friend to be acquitted by the jury.

Note, however, the following constraint on the semantic interpretation of this class of sentences: if the subject of the infinitive has the same form as the subject of the whole sentence:

(29) John is eager for John to be acquitted by the jury.

then the two occurrences of that NP must be interpreted as referring to two different individuals. This fact plus the fact that

(30) John is eager to be acquitted by the jury.

has precisely the meaning excluded in (29), namely that it is himself rather than another person called John that John wants to be acquitted, suggests that the basic form of this construction is *John is eager for S* and that *John is eager to please* arises from a structure of the shape *John is eager for John to please* via a deletion transformation which is operative when the subject of the infinitive is identical to the subject of the whole sentence. Note that 'identical' must be interpreted as meaning 'identical both formally and semantically'. Each noun phrase in a deep structure must be supplied with an 'index' corresponding to its 'purported referent'. *A man killed a man* and *A man killed himself* will each have two occurrences of *a man* in their deep structures. In the one case the two occurrences of *a man* will have different indices and thus the reflexive transformation will be inapplicable since the two noun phrases will not be 'identical'; in the other case the identity condition of the reflexive transformation will be met and it will convert the second noun phrase into a reflexive pronoun. Note also that 'subject of the infinitive' means the element which is subject of the embedded sentence after the transformations have applied to that sentence. The transformational component applies 'cyclically',[e] first affecting the innermost clause, then the clause containing it, etc. Thus the deep structure of (30) involves an embedded sentence *The jury acquits John*. The transformational component applies first to that embedded sentence, converting it into the passive

(*John is acquitted by the jury*), and then the transformations are applied to the entire sentence.

Instead of having a clause with *to* in place of the auxiliary, it is possible to have an ordinary noun phrase:

(31) John is eager for adventure.

I will treat *adventure* in (31) and *for the Orioles to win the pennant* in (27) as standing in the same grammatical relationship to the rest of the sentence, namely, they are each the object of a prepositional phrase which is part of a verb phrase. I thus assign *John is eager to please* the deep structure[5]

The deep structure of (31) would be exactly the same except that instead of *for S*, *adventure* would appear under the *NP* node of the prepositional phrase. The derivation of the surface structure of this sentence from its deep structure involves replacing the auxiliary of the embedded sentence by *to* via the same transformation as before, deleting the repeated subject *John* in the embedded clause, deleting *for* before *to* by the same transformation as above, and deleting the object *one*, which is permissible after certain verbs such as *please*. The resulting structure is

Note now one important detail of the derivation of *John is easy to please* and *John is eager to please*. The derivation of the former involves a rule shifting a clause to the end of the sentence. This rule creates an extra branch emanating from the upper S node. Thus at the end of the derivation, *to please*, which the embedded clause has been reduced to, and the adjective *easy* go back to the S node by separate branches. On the other hand, the derivation of *John is eager to please* does not involve any shifting of whole clauses; thus, at the end of the derivation the adjective *eager* and the reduced clause *to please* still remain part of the same verb phrase which they had belonged to from the beginning. Can one ascribe the fact that the *easy* of *easy to please* can be put in front of a noun but the *eager* of *eager to please* can not to this difference in derived constituent structure? One indeed can, in view of the fact that one likewise can not place in front of a noun the adjective of a verb phrase which consists of adjective and prepositional phrase. As I noted above, *a man who is proud of his children* does not allow the variant **a proud man of his children*. Similarly, *a man who is interested in politics* does not allow **an interested man in politics*, *a book which is yellow with age* does not allow **a yellow book with age*, and *a man who is filthy with money* does not allow **a filthy man with money* as a variant.[6] It is thus necessary to impose on the adjective preposing rule the restriction that it only applies to an adjective which is at the end of the verb phrase, thus excluding adjectives which are followed by other elements of the verb phrase, such as the *eager* of *eager to please* or the *proud* of *proud of his children*.[7,f]

Let me now return to the two types of comparatives. I propose to show that the transformations required to convert the deep structures of *John is more stupid than Harry* and *John is more stupid than ignorant* into their surface structures will yield structures of such a shape that the condition I have just imposed on the adjective preposing rule will be met by the *more* & Adj of the first structure but not that of the second.

The derivation of (1) from the deep structure hypothesized above is as follows. First the transformations apply to the embedded sentence, the only effect here being to insert *be*. Then the transformations apply to the 'outer' sentence. The comparative morpheme *-er* is adjoined to the adjective:

---

[5] The deep structure must contain the complementizer *for* in addition to the preposition *for*, since *for* shows up regardless of what preposition the adjective takes: *John is afraid* **of** *the dark* but *John is afraid* **for** *you to go out alone.* Prepositions are always deleted before complementizers: *John is afraid* **that** *you will dislike him.* The term 'complementizer' is due to Rosenbaum (1965).

[6] Sentences such as *He is a prudent man in money matters* do not contradict this assertion, since *prudent in money matters* is not a verb phrase. Note that *in money matters* is preposable: *In money matters he is prudent*, whereas prepositional phrases within the verb phrase can not be preposed: English speakers generally would not say ✡*Of his children he is proud* or ✡*With age the book is yellow* (the ✡ indicates that the sentence has a Yiddish flavor to it).

[7] Lakoff (1965) points out that the 'adjective preposing rule' is really a 'verb phrase preposing rule' which applies to a verb phrase that ends in a verb. Note his examples: *a soundly sleeping child* but **a sleeping soundly child*.

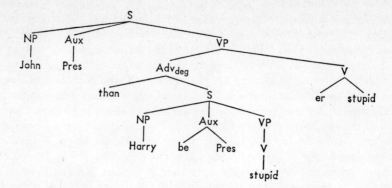

Then the embedded *than S* is shifted to the end of the sentence:[g]

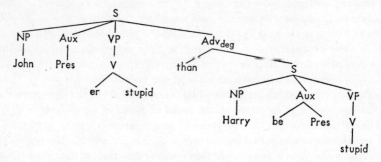

Deletion transformations then apply which eliminate the verb phrase of the embedded clause and optionally any repeated elements such as the copula here:

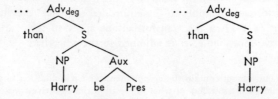

Because *than Harry is* or *than Harry* got where it is by a transformation shifting it to the end of the sentence, exactly the same situation obtains here as in the case of *easy to please: er & stupid* (=*more stupid*) is an adjective at the end of the verb phrase, *than Harry* (*is*) is a separate constituent, and *er & stupid* is thus preposable:

(32)   John is a more stupid man than Harry (is).

Now consider the deep structure which I hypothesized for (2). If (2) is indeed a conjoined structure, then it will be subject to the same rule ('conjunction reduction ') by which a conjoined sentence whose conjuncts are identical except for one constituent can be collapsed into a simple sentence which has a conjoined element for that constituent.   Thus, from a conjoined structure of the form

(33) John knows the answer and Harry knows the answer.

in which the two conjuncts are identical except for the subject noun phrase, one can form the sentence with conjoined subject

(34) John and Harry know the answer.

This transformation is peculiar in that it involves the creation of a new syntactic node. Specifically, the structure

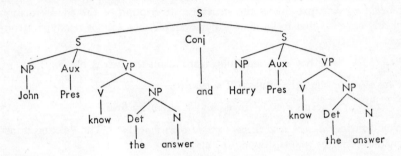

is converted into

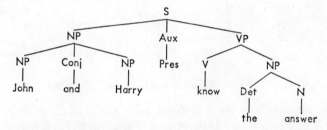

The new node created is the NP node which dominates the two NP nodes.   It is necessary for this node to be created since the conjoined subject behaves like a noun phrase in that it plays the NP role in the application of any transformation which calls for an NP (see Schane 1964).   Since, further, *John* and *Harry* do not cease being noun phrases when they are conjoined, the resulting structure must be as shown above: an NP node dominating two NP nodes separated by a conjunction.   Applying this transformation to the deep structure of (2), the result will be

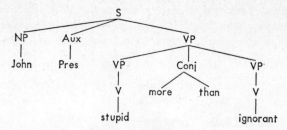

An optional transformation moves the *more* in front of the first adjective. The impossibility of applying the adjective preposing rule to *more stupid* here follows from the general principle that a transformation does not pull an item out of a coordinate structure unless the structural description of the transformation explicitly calls for that to be done. For example, one cannot relativize a conjunct:

(35) *The boy who and John just got on the bus is my brother.

nor make a conjunct the subject of a passive:

(36) *Chicago was destroyed and London by fires.

Now consider *a man who is more stupid than ignorant*. The deletion transformation removes *who is*, leaving the structure

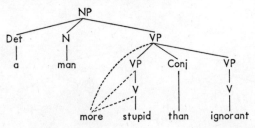

The dotted lines indicate my uncertainty as to which of the three nodes the *more* should be attached to. Only when it is attached to the lowest or middle node would *more stupid* be a VP which ends in an adjective. However, it woud then still be a conjunct of a conjoined VP and thus not available for the preposing rule. While *more stupid* thus is not preposable, the entire conjoined structure *more ignorant than stupid* is available for preposing, corresponding to the fact that one can say

(37) John is a more stupid than ignorant man.

although not

(7) *John is a more stupid man than ignorant.

ᵃ I suspect that this is wrcng and that the following should be regarded as the comparative of a predicate noun:

> John is more of a philosopher than Bill.

ᵇ See Bolinger (1967 a) for further such examples and for observations which cast serious doubt on the correctness of the derivation of prenominal modifiers from relative clauses.
ᶜ This is fantastically little evidence to serve as the basis for drawing such a conclusion. I should have at least mentioned (cf. Chomsky 1964: 66–7) that in *John is easy to X*, the X must be a VP minus one NP, e.g.

> John is easy to talk to.
> That knife is easy to slice salami with.
> *John is easy to talk to Frank.
> *That knife is easy to slice salami with a hacksaw.,

whereas in *John is eager to X* the X is a whole VP, e.g.

> *John is eager to talk to.
> *John is eager to slice salami with.
> John is eager to talk to Frank.
> John is eager to slice salami with a hacksaw.

I eventually did refer to those facts, but this is the place where I should have brought them up.
ᵈ At the time when I wrote this paper, few linguists ever thought of testing the correctness of the derived constituent structure implied by their rules, even in cases (such as this paper) where that constituent structure played a central role in the argument being presented. Subsequently several linguists (e.g. Ross 1967 a: 419) have noted that there is considerable evidence that *easy to please* is a constituent, contrary to the implicit claim of the following diagram, e.g. it can be pronominalized or serve as an instance of a quantified variable:

> Frank is easy to please, and he has always been that.
> Frank is easy to please, which he wasn't until recently,
> Frank is something that I have never been, namely easy to please.

These facts indicate that (21) is converted directly into (23), without any intermediate stage such as (22).
ᵉ For an argument that the transformations do not make up one big cycle and that there are in addition postcyclic transformations, see ' English as a VSO language '.
ᶠ However, this restriction is not stringent enough. Note that *who is easy to please* generally can be reduced to *easy . . . to please* only in a predicate NP, and moreover, if the head noun is not something as meager in content as *man*, the result differs in meaning to the extent of suggesting that individuals of that type are harder to please than ordinary people:

> *Give this book to the easy man to please.
> *Seven easy men to please bought encyclopedias from me.
> ?Arthur is an easy ornithologist to please.

ᵍ I gave no justification of the claim embodied in this tree that the Adv_{deg} is moved out of the VP. Note that according to one test given above, it should remain within the VP:

> *Than Harry, John is more stupid.

If *than Harry* is still part of the VP, then *more stupid* should not undergo adjective preposing. It turns out that there is reason for believing that *John is a more stupid man than Harry (is)* in fact does not involve preposing of *more stupid*, indeed that it does not involve the comparative of *stupid* but rather the comparative of *stupid man*.   For example,

  (i)   Jack is a shorter midget than Sam.
  (ii) Jack is a midget who is shorter than Sam.

differ not only in that Sam is assumed to be a midget in (i) but not in (ii) (this observation appears in Chomsky 1965: 234; Chomsky attributes it to Brandon Qualls) but also with respect to how tall Jack is claimed to be: in (i), Jack is claimed to be a short midget (i.e. significantly shorter than midgets usually are), whereas in (ii) there is nothing to preclude Jack's being a tall midget (e.g. 4'6'' tall).   These facts are explained if (ii) involves a comparison of degrees of being short but (i) involves a comparison of degrees of being a short midget.   I conjecture that they must be analyzed as having underlying structures like

  (i') The extent to which Jack is a short midget exceeds the extent to which Sam
        is a short midget.
  (ii') Jack is a midget such that the extent to which he is short exceeds the extent
        to which Sam is short.

This conjecture would also shed light on the relative acceptability of

    Mike is a craftier lawyer than Jonathan.
    ?Mike is a taller lawyer than Jonathan.

It makes sense to speak of the extent to which one is a crafty lawyer, but not of the extent to which one is a tall lawyer, since there is no special scale or type of tallness for lawyers.

2. Review of Owen Thomas, *Transformational Grammar and the Teacher of English**

If the volume under review, a not very thick paperback, sold for $1.25 instead of for $5.00, my review of it would contain much praise about how much better it explains transformational grammar to the uninitiated than do books costing several times the price, even if it happens to be rather sloppily put together. However, the price being asked for it leads me to temper my praise of it and to devote a good deal of space to listing its shortcomings—shortcomings, I might add, most of which could have been avoided if the author had explored the available literature a little more thoroughly and had reread his manuscript reasonably carefully and if the publisher had had the manuscript read and criticized by someone who is well up on current work on English syntax. These failings would have been more forgivable if the book were being sold at normal paper-back prices but are hardly tolerable at $5.00 a copy.

The book's most serious shortcoming is the almost total lack of evidence presented to the reader in justification of the various analyses proposed. Sketches of ' deep structures ' are presented with no explanation of why they rather than other equally (if not more) plausible analyses are chosen, and little consideration

* x+240 pp., Holt, Rinehart, and Winston, New York, 1966.
  This review appears here for the first time. It was rejected for publication on the grounds of being too long, and I never got around to shortening it.

is given to the question of what kind of facts would confirm or disconfirm a particular analysis.

Its most irritating shortcoming is its lack of internal consistency.   For example, throughout the book Thomas oscillates between a version of transformational syntactic theory in which the notion ' kernel sentence ' plays a crucial role and complex sentences are derived from structures underlying ' simple ' sentences, and the more modern conception of syntax in which the notion ' kernel sentence ' plays no role, the ' base component ' specifies the class of ' deep structures ' which underlie the sentences of the language, and two sentences may have the same ' deep structure ' only if they are stylistic variants of one another and have the same ' cognitive meaning '.   The deep structures which Thomas presents exhibit an amazing type of fence-straddling on this point : he always constructs the deep structure of a complex sentence in such a way that the structure minus embedded sentences always underlies a sentence of English.   To accomplish this he has to resort to such absurdities as representing virtually all nounphrases with embedded sentences as the word *something* plus a relative clause. On p. 50 he uses the term ' generalized morpheme ' and on p. 53 the term ' basic morpheme ', both evidently meaning what he elsewhere simply calls ' morpheme ', except on p. 51, where he uses ' morpheme ' in the sense usually attached to the word ' morph '.   His ' sample grammars ' are rarely self-consistent.   For example, in his ' second model grammar ', the phrase structure rules have the symbol V used to denote the combination of verb and objects or complements :

$$
\text{PS3.4} \quad V \rightarrow \begin{Bmatrix} V_i \\ V_t + NP \\ V_c + Adj \end{Bmatrix}
$$

(p. 64), whereas the ' morphographemic rules ' of this grammar use V to denote ' verb '.   On p. 76 he for no apparent reason replaces the term ' noun phrase ' by ' nominal ' and restates his phrase structure rules with *Nom* wherever *NP* had occurred before, but then on p. 100 he states two transformations in terms of *NP* rather than *Nom*, although another transformation on the same page refers to *Nom* rather than to *NP*.   On both p. 100 (' third model grammar ') and p. 141 (' fourth model grammar '), he places a ' transformation ' which replaces ' *be+Pas* ' by *was* or *were* before two transformations which refer to the *be* which this transformation has eliminated.

Thomas's first chapter, ' New terms and old ideas ', is a brief and thus necessarily sketchy survey of linguistics and the history of linguistics.   One section of this chapter is quite misleading, namely the description of ' competence ' and ' performance '.   After correctly drawing the distinction between ' competence ' (the tacit ' knowledge ' of one's language which one uses in speaking and understanding it) and ' performance ' (observed behavior), Thomas states ' . . . on the basis of being exposed to almost random and arbitrary linguistic data, every child develops a certain degree of linguistic " competence " '.   The word ' degree ' here suggests that Thomas is not using ' competence ' in the sense in which he has defined it but rather in the popular sense of 'adeptness'. 'Competence', as Thomas (following Chomsky) has defined it, is an entity rather than a quality or a quantity. Later on the same page, Thomas states '. . . linguistic competence generally increases, up to a point, as the speaker grows older. But this competence [change in competence?—J. McC.] may be different from a change in performance which is brought about, for example, when a child moves from one part of the country to another and abandons the pronunciation common in the old area for that common in the new'. The first sentence of this passage repeats the error of treating 'competence' as a quantity or quality rather than an entity. The second sentence appears to treat phonology as if it were not part of a speaker's tacit knowledge of his language. It is hard to decide which is the more incredible assertion: Saussure's claim that only phonology and morphology are *langue* ('competence') and syntax is merely *parole* ('performance') or Thomas's apparent assumption that it is just the other way round.

The second chapter, 'The English sentence', begins with an admirably lucid discussion of the proposition that sentences which have similar surface structures may have totally different structures underlying them. The examples are taken from Chomsky: *John is eager to please* vs. *John is easy to please* and *I expected John to be examined by the doctor* vs. *I persuaded John to be examined by the doctor*. However, the deep structures which Thomas alludes to in his discussion of these examples are not exhibited in this section, nor, indeed, anywhere else in the book. There then follows a page of examples and discussion relating to the profusion of sentence shapes in English and to the notion of relatedness between sentences. Next comes 3/4 of a page about the fact that languages are constantly changing. This passage, which by all rights should have been in the preceding chapter, suffers from confusion between the terms 'language' and 'languages'; indeed, it begins with the sentence 'Language is constantly changing' and has near its end the sentence 'Language has rules'. The rules that Thomas is talking about are clearly rules of an individual language rather than rules of language (whatever that might mean), a fact which could easily escape the uninitiated reader.

The next topic which Thomas takes up is the point that a language contains infinitely many sentences and that a grammar of a language will have to specify what are and what are not among the infinitely many sentences of the language. Included is a cogent discussion of the point that a science typically does not come up with operational definitions of its more fundamental concepts but rather takes them as undefined primitives and establishes relationships between them. Here Thomas does an excellent job of softening the shock which many English teachers will undoubtedly experience at the thought of discussing sentences other than on the basis of a definition of the term 'sentence'. This generally excellent section is marred by some of the howlers which the book regrettably contains quite a few of: 'Thus, we cannot define the axioms of Euclidean geometry . . .'; 'The definition, of course, is semantic; that is, it assumes that the reader knows the *meaning* of the phrase "a complete thought". Certainly this notion has defied philosophers for thousands of years. Plato wrote an entire book, *The*

Republic, trying to define not a complete thought but a single word : *justice* '.

The next section, ' Basic English sentences ', introduces the notion of phrase structure rule, discusses several hypothetical phrase structure rules of English and several sentences which illustrate them, introduces the tree diagrams (redundantly called ' branching tree diagrams ' by Thomas) which correspond to derivations in a phrase structure grammar, and presents a ' first model grammar ' consisting of four phrase structure rules and a lexicon.   In connection with the tree diagrams, he castigates authors of American high school textbooks for the profusion of systems of ' diagraming ' sentences which they give.   Thomas fails to note that this profusion relates to two mutually unrelated questions : the notational system used in the diagram and the grammatical analysis which is represented in the diagram.   In chapter 8, where he illustrates eight different diagrams of the sentence *We asked for whoever might be there*, some of the diagrams are merely notational variants of one another (e.g. diagrams *b* and *f*), whereas others involve different judgements as to the immediate constituent structure of the sentence (for example, diagram *c* treats *asked for* as a single constituent, whereas diagram *e* assigns *for* to a constituent *for whoever might be there* and diagrams *d* and *h* assign it to a constituent *for whoever* ; in diagram *d*, *whoever might be there* is not a constituent, but in most of the other diagrams it is).   Thomas's assertion that ' such disagreement is impossible in transformational grammar ' is misleading, since it relates only to the question of notation rather than to the substance of the analyses ; it is quite easy to find transformational descriptions in which *asked for* is treated as a constituent and others in which it is not.

Chapter 3, ' Words and Morphemes ', begins with a five-page discussion of the notion ' morpheme ' which effectively explains the concept to the uninitiated despite the terminological inconsistencies noted above.   In the process, Thomas states that the symbols $\{Z_1\}$, $\{Z_2\}$, and $\{Z_3\}$ are ' generally employed by transformational grammarians ' to indicate ' 3rd sg. pres.', ' plural ', and ' genitive ' respectively, a remark which I find baffling in that I can find no instance of these symbols in any works of Chomsky or Lees or Postal or anyone else, for that matter.   Next comes a section on ' form words and structure words ' which includes one good point often missed by transformational grammarians[1], namely that ' well-formed nonsense ' of the Jabberwocky variety must not only involve morphemes which are phonologically admissible in the language in question but must involve the ' structure words ' and bound morphemes which actually occur in the language, rather than phonologically admissible substitutes for them, as is illustrated by Thomas's example of a sentence in which ' structure words ' have been replaced by phonologically admissible substitutes and which is decidedly not ' Jabberwocky ' :

Che boys gill sebe toap sitting pe chup wall.

Thomas now gives a ' second model grammar ', which involves two transformations : an agreement transformation and a transformation which puts affixes

[1] For example, myself.   See McCawley (1968a : 44).

after the item to which they are attached. The concept of 'transformation' would have been put across better if this 'model grammar' had also included a couple of transformations which exemplify better what transformations normally do, which is to rearrange the elements of a tree according to a formula expressible in terms of the labels on the nodes of a tree; the 'particle separation rule', which optionally moves a 'particle' past the noun phrase which follows it, as in *He looked all of those people up*, would have been an excellent example to give at this point. While the structure of English forces one to discuss those two highly atypical transformations at an early point in one's exposition, that fact does not prevent one from making clear from the beginning how atypical they are. The 'model grammars' given by Thomas close not with a phonological component but with 'morphographemic rules' which convert the surface syntactic representation into orthographic form. In presenting these rules, Thomas conceals (perhaps wisely) from the reader the fact that much less is understood about the relation of orthography to a grammar than about the relation of phonetics to a grammar. Indeed, no one to my knowledge has presented any concrete proposals as to what the 'morphographemic component' of a transformational grammar would look like. It should be pointed out in this connection that Thomas uses the term 'surface structure' in a totally novel sense, namely the output from rather than input to the 'morphographemic rules'. Thomas evidently did this so that 'surface structure' in his framework would be something analogous to the 'diagram' of American high school texts, in which the written word is the minimal unit represented; but he has provided for confusion on his readers' part by redefining a well-established term without informing his readers that he has done so rather than simply creating a new term such as 'orthographic surface structure'. An examination of the trees with which he illustrates the output of his morphographemic rules shows that Thomas's formulation of them is incomplete, in that when a rule coalesces two constituents into a single constituent (e.g. *can* and *Past* into *could*), the rules he formulates do not indicate what is to happen to the nodes which dominate the two constituents. The trees on pp. 66–9 suggest that he wants the nodes which dominate one of the input constituents to remain and dominate the resulting constituent (e.g. a node labeled *Modal* dominates *could* in the tree on p. 67), but the rules give no indication of which nodes are to be kept. Moreover, he occasionally indulges in such inconsistencies as writing the double label $Tn+$ *Modal* on a node (p. 181).

Chapter 4, 'Nouns and Nominals', covers a large amount of material relating to the structure of the noun phrase. It suffers from the fact that topic of relative clauses, which is intimately connected with much of the material discussed, is relegated to a small subsection of the chapter and totally ad-hoc rules are given for many constructions which arise (although the reader is not told this) from the a deletion of relative pronoun and copula in a relative clause (see e.g. Smith 1961).[a] For example, there is a transformation (T4.4) which turns an embedded sentence with $be+Adj$ into a prenominal adjective and a totally different transformation (T4.6) which turns an embedded sentence with $be+$

Loc into a postnominal locative. The question of noun-phrases such as *an easy man to please* is ignored entirely, even though Thomas is clearly familiar with the literature in which it is shown that the ' relative clause reduction transformation ' and ' adjective preposing transformation '[2] involved in *the tall man* and *the man in the garden* automatically yield *an easy man to please* if formulated correctly.   Thomas's failure to discuss *an easy man to please* is especially perplexing in view of the fact that such a discussion would provide the answer to the question which he raised at the beginning of chapter 2 regarding the deep structures of *John is easy to please* and *John is eager to please*.   Even though there are several places where this could have been discussed profitably (the treatment of prenominal modifiers on pp. 91–2, the treatment of ' infinitival nominals ' on pp. 112–3, the discussion of ' adjectives [which] can be followed by ' infinitival nominals ' on p. 159), the reader is never given any indication of how the deep structures of *John is easy to please* and *John is eager to please* differ.

Chapter 4 begins with a brief discussion of the fact that English has numerous devices for creating noun phrases out of underlying sentences.   Thomas's statement that ' . . . we might replace the $T+N+N^\circ$ by an entire nominalization . . .', which characterizes his policy on agentive and action nominalizations, conflicts with the fact that the underlying determiner and number of noun phrases containing these nominalizations may show up in surface structure, as in *all violations of this law will be punished*.   Thomas is evidently misled by the commonness of the genitive of e.g. *John's refusal to come surprised me* into thinking that the nominalization transformation simply replaces an entire noun phrase by a sentence with the subject in genitive form.   Actually, the genitive is created by a totally separate transformation which replaces an underlying *the* by the genitive expression (cf. *the refusal by John to come surprised me*) ; this transformation may well be the same one which creates the genitives of *John's house*, etc., where again a genitive replaces an underlying *the* (cf. *a house of John's, those houses of John's*).

Next follows a page concerning selectional restrictions and the subclasses of the category *Noun*.   Of the three selectional restrictions which Thomas states, two are given a hopelessly inadequate statement : ' The verb *to elapse* can never take a *concrete* subject ' (actually, it can only take a quantity expression of time as subject : one cannot say **That John loves Mary elapsed* or even **the day when I arrived elapsed*) ; ' transitive verbs of the senses cannot have *abstract* nouns as subjects ' (the restriction actually has to do with animateness rather than abstractness : **the trombone tasted the wine*).   Thomas makes the puzzling assertion that ' Instead of the usual distinction between concrete nouns and *abstract nouns* found in most school grammars, transformationalists prefer to make a distinction between count nouns, on the one hand, and mass/abstract nouns, on the other '.   A glance at such works as Lees's *Grammar of English*

---

[2] Lakoff (1965) has shown that the ' adjective preposing transformation ' is really a ' verb phrase preposing transformation ' which is applicable when the verb phrase ends in a verb or adjective ; thus *the soundly sleeping child* but not **the sleeping soundly child*.

Nominalizations will show the authors making the count vs. mass/abstract dinstiction in addition to rather than instead of the concrete vs. abstract distinction; indeed, only four lines before the passage just quoted, Thomas himself introduces ' N_{ab}=abstract noun ' as one of ' the standard symbols that are used '. It is difficult to say for sure what Thomas means by ' concrete noun ' in view of his description of the noun *honesty* as ' certainly concrete '.

Thomas next takes up determiners, stating that each noun phrase contains a ' regular determiner ', which may be preceded by a predeterminer and/or prearticle and may be followed by a postdeterminer. He splits up ' regular determiners ' into three subclasses : articles, demonstratives, and genitives. By listing genitives as ' my, our, your, his, her, its, their, $Nom+Z_3$ ' (Z_3 is Thomas's symbol for the genitive morpheme), Thomas obscures the fact that all of the items in this list consist of a noun phrase and a genitive morpheme, a fact which must be recognized in order for *His singing of the aria was magnificent* to be derived in the same way as *John's singing of the aria was magnificent*. In chapter 7, Thomas returns again to the question of genitives and for the first time in the book suggests that genitives do not appear as such in deep structures but are derived from embedded sentences ; however, the two examples which he gives there :

Sentence 7.41   The boy has a bike. → The boy's bike . . .
Sentence 7.42   The table has a leg. → The leg of the table . . .

are given without any indication that the genitive is an underlying relative clause which may replace *the* (i.e. *the bike* [*the boy has a bike*]$_S$ → *the bike* [*which the boy has*]$_S$ → *the bike of the boy's* → *the boy's bike*), and the deep structures of the relevant sentences are not shown. Thomas indicates dissatisfaction with that analysis on the grounds that the genitives of *the man's rudeness, the king's picture, an hour's work*, and *Nestle's chocolate* cannot be derived from an embedded sentence with *have*. However, that is hardly an objection, since no one has to my knowledge proposed that the incredibly heterogeneous uses of the English genitive all come from the same source. Thomas has actually discussed the source of the genitive of *the man's rudeness* earlier in the book, namely in the section on ' action nominals ' on pp. 108–110 ; however, in view of the fact that all of his examples of nominalizations involve nominalized verbs rather than nominalized adjectives, it may be that he does not realize that the nominalization transformations operate regardless of whether the included verb phrase has a verb or an adjective as head.[3] *An hour's* in *an hour's work* is some kind of measure adverb, and *the king's picture* (in the sense of ' the likeness of the king ') is, as Thomas suggests in a footnote, derived from a nominalization in which *the king* is the underlying direct object.

The existence of Thomas's class of ' prearticles ' is doubtful, since the four

[3] Lakoff (1965) cites convincing evidence that adjectives and verbs are merely two subclasses of the same underlying category, differing only in such superficial respects as whether they are preceded by a copula and where a degree adverb is positioned relative to them.

words which he cites as belonging to this class cannot be so analysed: *all* and *both* are simply predeterminers and *only* and *just* are not part of the determiner system at all (cf. *John works only at night*, where *only* has exactly the same function as in Thomas's example *only that boy*).　Thomas's inclusion of *all* and *both* in this putative class is a consequence of his unfortunate definition: ' pre-articles . . . as their name suggests can precede articles (or demonstratives or genitives) '.　The appearance of *all* and *both* directly before an article or demonstrative in *all the boys* or *both those girls* is due to a peculiarity of those two words whereby they allow the optional deletion of a following *of*.　*All of the boys* and *all the boys* must be treated as arising from the same deep structure through an optional deletion (or optional insertion) of *of*, since *all* and *both* may not be preceded by a predeterminer: **each of all boys, *one of both girls*.

The next section, entitled ' Nouns ', begins with a revision of an earlier phrase structure rule so as to accomodate ' pro-determiners ' and pronouns:

$$4.7a \quad \text{Nom} \rightarrow \begin{Bmatrix} \text{PRO}_D + \text{PRO}_N \\ \text{Det} + \text{N} + \text{N}^\circ \end{Bmatrix}$$

One unfortunate consequence of this rule is that according to it, a *PRO*$_D$ is not a *Det* and a PRO$_N$ is not an *N*, so that the *some* of *someone* and the *any* of *anywhere* are different from the *some* of *some man* and the *any* of *any Tuesday*. Another is that by omitting the number constituent from PRO$_D$+PRO$_N$, Thomas makes it impossible for his number agreement rule to apply when such a noun phrase is in the subject position.　He then states ' With PRO forms available to us, we can now make the important statement that *no transformation ever deletes an irrecoverable item* ' and gives as an example the sentence *For want of a nail, the battle was lost*, which he claims to be derived from an underlying *SOMEONE lost the battle for want of a nail*.　The significance of the capitalization is unclear.　Thomas states that ' the morphographemic rules will combine [SOME +ONE and SOME+THING] to form SOMEONE and SOMETHING ', which can hardly be taken literally, since Thomas's ' morphographemic rules ' elsewhere give as output ordinary orthography with ordinary capitalization conventions.　If Thomas intends his SOMETHING and SOMEONE to represent ' unspecified inanimate NP ' ' unspecified animate NP ' rather than (as I had assumed at first) the words *something* and *someone*, his analysis is unimpeachable, although his reference to ' morphographemic rules ' is confusing, since the items in question would in that case always be deleted by some transformation.　However, for clarity's sake he should have told the reader that the very example which he gives shows that *someone* cannot be taken as the underlying subject of ' agentless passives ': *for want of a nail, the battle was lost* has a quite different meaning from *for want of a nail, the battle was lost by someone* and thus cannot be derived from the same deep structure.

Thomas then turns to pronominalization and states ' PRO forms are obviously related to pronouns in English ', an assertion which is hardly intelligible, let alone obvious, after the confusion which Thomas has just created regarding what ' PRO ' means.　His statement that ' . . . in one sense, the determiner

SOME is built into the PRO form from which the pronoun is derived ' compounds the confusion: while many scholars (e.g. Postal 1966) treat personal pronouns (which Thomas is discussing in the passage just quoted) as involving an underlying definite determiner, Thomas may be the only person ever to propose that they have an underlying indefinite determiner, a hypothesis for which he offers no evidence. He describes pronominalization as follows: ' Repeated items (which are easily recoverable) are either deleted completely or else are replaced by the pronoun form of PRO forms '. Thomas confuses the issue by saying ' easily recoverable ' instead of merely ' recoverable ', since the ease with which the input to a transformation can be recovered from its output is totally irrelevant to the admissibility of the transformation. Indeed, pronominalization may be obligatory even in cases where it creates an ambiguity: *John told Harry to go to his room*, but **John told Harry to go to John's room*, **John told Harry to go to Harry's room*.

In the next section, 'Adjectives ', the phrase structure rule cited above is modified so as to add an optional *S* at the end of *Nom*. Nowhere in this section is the reader told that this *S* is a relative clause, which may be deformed in various ways. Instead the reader is simply given ad-hoc rules such as that cited earlier for creating prenominal adjectives:

T4.4 $Det + N_{matrix} + N^\circ (+Det + N_{const} + N^\circ + be + Adj)$
$\rightarrow Det + Adj + N_{matrix} + N^\circ$, where $N_{matrix} + N^\circ = N_{const} + N^\circ$.

This transformation not only is unnecessary, as pointed out above, but is also formulated in a most questionable fashion, since N_{matrix} and N_{const} are not names of syntactic categories, and the transformation irrecoverably deletes the determiner of the constituent sentence.

The next section, ' Subordinate clauses ', begins with a revision of the phrase structure rule for determiners, which is now made to allow ' *wh-* ' as a determiner. He treats both relative pronouns and interrogative pronouns as arising from an underlying noun phrase whose determiner is ' *wh-* '. His treatment ignores such well-known differences as the fact that interrogatives but not relatives allow adjuncts such as *else*: *Who else did you see?* but not **The boy who else I saw*. Thomas is inconsistent about the inclusion of *wh-* in the deep structures of relative clauses: when he restates T4.4 later in the chapter (the ' third model grammar '), no *wh-* appears in the embedded sentence.

Next comes a section entitled 'Appositives and Locatives '. Thomas derives appositives from a structure which would also underlie a restrictive relative clause; however, the source of the appositives which Thomas discusses would have to be non-restrictive rather than restrictive clauses since they can appear only with those noun-phrases which allow non-restrictive clauses:

My mother-in-law, who is a telephone operator, . . .
My mother-in-law, a telephone operator, . . .
*Every American, who is an intelligent person, . . .
*Every American, an intelligent person, . . .

In this section Thomas presents a peculiar proposal regarding the intensifying pronoun:

> 'the name intensifying pronoun is a good one; it indicates that the constituent sentence is identical to the entire matrix sentence. Thus we have:
>
> Sentence 4.13a Rupert (Rupert drank the coffee) drank the coffee. In this case the entire constituent sentence is replaced by the intensifier *himself*'.

It is unclear what facts Thoms intended this analysis to explain: he cites no facts whatever about intensives, even though they have many interesting properties, for example, the fact that only definite NP's allow an intensifier: *Some man himself drank the coffee*. Thomas's analysis appears to allow such non-sentences as *Rupert himself himself drank the coffee*, which would result from embedding sentence 4.13a within itself.

Next comes a 'third model grammar', which for no apparent reason omits much of the material which has just been discussed (e.g. predeterminers, post-determiners, intensifying pronouns). The sample derivations which follow suggest confusion on Thomas's part as to how a transformational grammar is organized. His derivation of the sentence *Those witches who dance at midnight will become hungry* begins with a phrase-structure derivation, in the process of which Thomas says

> 'Line no. 9 is the terminal string of the phrase structure derivation of the matrix sentence. By substituting words from the lexicon and applying the appropriate transformations and morphographemic rules we get:
>
> 10. those+witches (+S)+will+become+hungry.
>
> Line no. 10 is the surface structure [sic] of the matrix sentence. We now need to embed a sentence that has the shape: *wh-witches dance at midnight*'.

Taken literally, this means that the matrix sentence undergoes the entire system of transformations and even 'morphographemic rules' before anything is embedded in it, and that the 'embedding transformations' such as those cited above apply to a sentence in orthographic form. Not only is this inconsistent with the embedding transformations given by Thomas, which refer to constituents such as N^o which his 'morphographemic' rules eliminate altogether, but it is a conception of the organization of a grammar which no one has ever seriously proposed. The most widely accepted conception (Fillmore 1963, Chomsky 1965) is that the transformational component applies cyclically (first the transformations are applied to the 'innermost' sentence of the deep structure, then to the next 'innermost' sentence in the resulting structure, etc. until the 'outermost' sentence is reached)[b], that a matrix sentence accordingly will not have undergone *any* transformations at the point where transformations combining it with an embedded sentence apply, and that it is the output from the entire transformational component which forms the input to the phonological (and presumably also the 'morphographemic') component. The reason why the transformational component must apply cyclically is that the possibility of applying a given transformation to a given sentence is generally contingent on the effect that transformations have had on the sentences embedded within it. For example, *The bagel is believed by Irving to have been eaten by John* has a deep structure which may be represented informally as [Irving believes [John ate the bagel]$_S$]$_S$. Only if the inner sentence is passivized can *the bagel* be converted into the subject of the entire sentence by further passivization.[c]

The next section, 'Nominals Revisited', covers part of the material of Lees (1960). Thomas, in a not very well thought out attempt to translate Lees's results into the framework of Chomsky's *Aspects*, describes all the nominalizations he treats as arising from his ubiquitous *SOMETHING* plus an embedded sentence. This analysis is wrong since in reality the determiner and number of the matrix sentence may be anything at all rather than just 'SOME' and 'singular': Thomas's (not explicitly formulated) rules yield his sentence 4.30d, *George is the admirer of Marge*, but not *George is an admirer of Marge* or *Several admirers of Marge visited her*. On p. 113 Thomas enters another digression on 'recoverability', this one even more confused and confusing than that quoted earlier. He states

> 'the subjects of infinitival nominals may be deleted, although in doing so we must be particularly careful to avoid ambiguity. That is, we can say:
>   Sentence 4.38b. I bought this corsage to wear.
> In this case we have deleted the former subject of the embedded sentence but, in contrast with sentence 4.38 [*I bought this corsage for you to wear*], we no longer know the " person " (i.e. *I, you, he, she, we, they*) of the subject'.

This discussion is triply muddled: (a) sentence 4.38b is completely unambiguous, the only possible underlying subject of the embedded sentence being *I*, (b) ambiguity has nothing to do with recoverability, since (as noted earlier) a pronominalization or deletion may be obligatory even in cases where it creates an ambiguity, and (c) 'recoverability' relates not to the 'person' of a deleted or pronominalized item but to its *identity*.

Chapter 5, 'Verbs', begins with a section, 'The main verb', which deals primarily with the classification of verbs according to the different adjuncts which accompany them. Among the topics he treats are particles and such verb-plus-preposition combinations as *fight with* and *think about*. The discussion would have been more valuable if Thomas had formulated explicitly the rules to which he refers: he points out that a particle can either follow or precede a noun phrase (*look the word up* vs. *look up the word*) but never exhibits the deep structure of such verb phrases nor does he formulate the transformation which gives rise to the variant word orders. He asserts that verb-plus-particle and verb-plus-preposition are both of the category 'transitive verb' but never gives the corresponding phrase structure rule and never discusses the difference between these constructions with respect to interposed adverbial elements: *he fights often with his friends* but not **he looks often up words*.

The following sections, entitled 'Auxiliary verbs' and 'Yes/no questions and preverbs', consist of a fairly adequate sketch of what *Syntactic Structures* and *The Grammar of English Nominalizations* say about these topics. The next section, 'Fourth model grammar', begins with a confusing digression on boundary symbols. Thomas first introduces the symbol # to denote sentence boundary (he says that it is 'sometimes also called a *boundary juncture*', presumably a reference to the usage of linguists who also say 'cash money') and asserts that it 'is actually a morpheme' and is realized phonetically as the 2–3–1 terminal pitch contour. He then presents the tree

which would appear to involve a new symbol #S# and presumably a new rule #S# → # S # ; however, in the rest of the book he reverts to the normal practise of treating # as a boundary marker rather than a morpheme and draws trees in which the topmost node is labeled S rather than #S#. He then states that # is also used to represent word boundary but does not indicate whether he regards this also as a morpheme. Clarity would have been served if he had adopted two different symbols for sentence boundary and word boundary rather than perpetuating Chomsky's peculiar practise of writing # for both. He then takes up the rules for inserting word boundary and the rule which inserts *do* when an affix is preceded by word boundary.[4] This leads into a reconsideration of the rule which permutes an affix with a following verb or auxiliary. In the discussion, Thomas adopts the somewhat objectionable formulation given to the rule by Chomsky (1957) and adds some commentary which is guaranteed to give the reader an incorrect conception of the way a transformational grammar is organized. Thomas states,

> 'we can now remove the restriction on the affix transformation by rewriting the transformation in the following form:
> T5.2 $Af+v \rightarrow v+Af\#$ '

The restriction to which Thomas refers is the words 'applies only once for each *S*', which appear in the earlier formulation of the rule. What does this restriction mean? The obvious interpretation of 'affects only one $Af+v$ per *S*' is not what Thomas means, since he gives examples (e.g. p. 139) in which several $Af+v$ combinations in the same *S* are affected. However, the only other conceivable interpretation that can be put on the 'restriction': 'applies to all $Af+v$ combinations present at some point in the derivation but does not apply after

---

[4] Thomas formulates this rule so that it inserts *do* before an affix which is preceded AND FOLLOWED by #. However, that formulation is incorrect, since in cases where an affix is followed by the contracted negative morpheme (e.g. *John doesn't know*), *do* is inserted even though the affix is not followed by a word boundary.

that ', is not a restriction, since that is the way that transformations normally work: the transformations have a fixed order (a point which Thomas never states explicitly), each affects all combinations of elements which meet the structural description of the transformation, and the resulting structure serves as input to the next transformation.[5,d]   There is no reason for the affix permutation transformation to make reference to a word boundary, as it does in Thomas's and Chomsky's formulations; however, there would be a reason for it if the transformations applied in unordered fashion.   Thus the combination of Chomsky's incorrect formulation of the rule and Thomas's ' restriction ' on his earlier formulation of it could well mislead a reader into thinking that the transformational component of a grammar is an unordered system.

The ' fourth model grammar ' (the last one which Thomas gives) which follows is even less comprehensive than the ' third model grammar '.   Rather than tabulating all the rules which he has presented so far, which would have been a distinct service to the reader (to say nothing of the author), Thomas presents a system of rules which differs from his ' third model grammar ' only in that the phrase structure rule for *Aux* is more complete, that for ' *MV* ' is less complete, the rule for inserting word boundary is included, and two of the transformations of the ' third model grammar ' are omitted.

Chapter 6, 'Adjectives and adverbs ', contains a review of work by Lees and Carlota Smith on ' complex adjective constructions ', a survey of the various things traditionally called ' adverbs ', and some remarks about comparative and superlative constructions.   Despite the large amount of material covered in this chapter, not a single transformation is explicitly formulated, and the reader is only rarely told what deep structures underlie the various sentences discussed.

The section on adjectives suffers from too heavy reliance on the classification given in Lees (1960).   Lees classified adjectives according to whether they must or may or may not take a ' complement ' and according to whether that complement is *that*+*S* or an ' infinitival nominal '.   Since all ' infinitival nominals ' arise from an underlying embedded *S* with the ' complementizer '[6] *for . . . to*, the latter dimension of the classification is simply the choice of complementizer:

---

[5] This same use of ' restriction ' reappears later in the book: ' There is one restriction on [the passive] transformation: it must be applied *before* the transformation that guarantees agreement between the subject and verb'.   These and several other passages suggest that Thomas may subscribe to a conception of the transformational component of a grammar as an unordered system of rules; indeed, such an impression is hard to escape in the case of such passages as the following statement about ' tags ' after imperatives: ' Since the auxiliary, to which *Ng* [= ' negation'] would normally be attached, is deleted in the transformation, we have the alternative of both positive and negative tags'.   The only interpretation which I can put on this passage is that Thomas is saying that the tag-formation transformation may apply either before or after the imperative transformation (which deletes the auxiliary) and that a negative tag (*close the door, won't you?*) or a positive tag (*close the door, will you?*) arises depending on whether the auxiliary is deleted first or the tag is formed first.   However, it is difficult to say for sure what Thomas intends here, since his tag formation rule would not yield *Close the door, will you?* unless *Close the door* had an underlying *Ng* in it, which I am sure he does not intend.

[6] This term is due to Rosenbaum (1965).

that or *for . . . to.* The subject of an embedded sentence with the *for . . . to* complementizer is deleted if identical to a certain noun phrase in the matrix sentence; thus

> She is eager to win the prize.
> She is eager for the Orioles to win the pennant.

both have embedded sentences with the *for . . . to* complementizer, and the difference between their shapes arises from the fact that the former but not the latter meets the conditions for deletion of the subject of the embedded sentence; in both cases the deep structure is like that of *she is eager for excitement*, with complementizer+*S* in place of the noun phrase *excitement*. Thomas correctly observes that these sentences involve an underlying preposition which is deleted before the complementizer but incorrectly asserts that ' both the preposition and the repeated nominal are deleted by the transformation '; the deletion of the preposition and the deletion of the repeated nominal are the effects of two totally different transformations, since the preposition is deleted regardless of whether the conditions for the deletion of the nominal are met.

The section on adverbs leaves unclear whether Thomas believes that the myriad words and expressions traditionally labeled ' adverbs ' constitute a single syntactic category. He speaks of ' subcategories of adverbs ' or ' subclasses of adverbs ' but never exhibits any common property shared by sentence adverbs (*probably, clearly*), ' preverbs ' (*hardly*), and locative, time, manner, and degree ' adverbs '; it is doubtful that any common feature unites them. This section contains some worthwhile observations on the relation between adjectives and manner and sentence adverbs (*probable* and *probably*; *quick* and *quickly*). Thomas proposes that sentences with sentence adverbs are optional variants of sentences of the form *that S is Adj* (e.g. *Certainly the semester is over* is to have the same deep structure as *That the semester is over is certain*). He also proposes a relation between action nominalizations and sentences with manner adverbs, noting that only verbs which allow action nominalizations may be accompanied by a manner adverb; however, he makes no explicit proposal as to the deep structure of these sentences.

The section on ' Comparative and superlative degrees ' begins with the observation that comparative expressions (*more . . . than S, as . . . as S*) and superlative expressions (*most . . . of NP*) are of the same syntactic category as simple degree adverbs such as *very*. This observation is undoubtedly true of comparatives, although so little is known about superlatives that no one is in much of a position to say where they come from syntactically. In describing the transformations which affect the word order of comparative expressions, Thomas several times makes statements such as ' the transformation places the adjective of the matrix between the discontinuous elements *as . . . as* '. If this is to be taken literally, the transformation will convert[7]

---

[7] Since Thomas draws no trees and gives no phrase structure rule to introduce the constituent he calls *Deg*, the tree that I give represents my best guess as to his intentions.

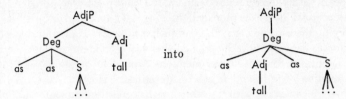

thus yielding the absurd result that in the surface structure of the sentence *John is as tall as Harry* the phrase *as tall as Harry* is a degree adverb. The fact that Thomas describes the transformation as one which puts the adjective between the *as*'s rather than as one which puts the *as S* after the adjective is symptomatic of the fact that (like Chomsky in *Syntactic Structures* and Lees in *The Grammar of English Nominalizations*) he expresses transformations by formulas which indicate the order into which things are rearranged but not the resulting constituent structure. For example, the affix permutation transformation $Af + v \rightarrow v + Af$ (I omit the superfluous # of Thomas's and Chomsky's formulation) does not make clear whether it would convert Thomas's

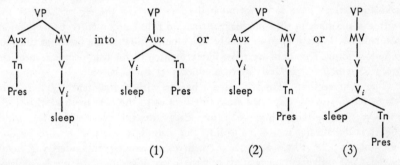

To distinguish between the three possibilities, a notation like the following is needed:

(1)		(2)		(3)	
Af	v	Af	v	Af	v
1	2	1	2	1	2
→ 2+1	0	→ 2	1	→ 0	2+1

Presumably (3) is what Thomas intended. Thomas's disregard for derived constituent structure is also exhibited in the many places where he speaks of a transformation as 'rewriting a string'. Transformations, of course, do not operate on strings of morphemes but on trees which happen to terminate in occurrences of those morphemes.

Chapter 7, 'Rearranging the basic sentence', is devoted to a discussion of a variety of topics in English syntax (interrogatives, negatives, passives, imperatives, conjoined sentences, etc.) which have not been treated in chapters 2 through 6. The section on questions treats all questions as arising from deep structures which begin with a 'presentence' element, the 'interrogative morpheme' Q. The discussion would have been more enlightening if Thomas had devoted some space to justifying the assertion that there is such a thing as a 'question morpheme'; for example, he could have mentioned that his Q is identical with the *whether* of dependent questions (he never mentions dependent questions) and the question intonation of independent yes/no questions. However, the rules he formulates are inconsistent with the assertion that question intonation is a phonetic realization of Q, since his auxiliary attraction rule replaces the Q by the auxiliary rather than attracting the auxiliary towards the Q (i.e. it converts *Q John Pres drink* into *Pres John drink* rather than *Q Pres John drink*). While he mentions question intonation, he leaves totally unclear how the grammar would put it into the sentence.

In the following section, 'Negative and emphatic sentences', the phrase structure rules are revised so as to allow optional negative and emphasis morphemes: S → (Ng) (Emph) (Q) Nom+VP, and it is stated that transformations move those elements to a position after the Tense morpheme and the {Modal, *be, have*} (if any) which immediately follows it. The discussion would have been more valuable if it had been related to the discussion of interrogatives: the transformations have to be formulated so as to allow the *Ng* or *Emph* to move with the auxiliary in the 'auxiliary attraction rule', and a correct formulation of the rule would have been especially welcome in view of the fact that the source which Thomas's readers are most likely to turn to for the formulation of these rules (*Syntactic Structures*) gives an incorrect formulation.

The next section, 'Passive voice', begins with the sentence 'There is still some debate among transformation linguists as to the best method of introducing the passive morpheme [sic] {*by+Psv*} into the phrase structure rules'. There is debate not merely as to how but also as to whether it is to be done: not only is Chomsky's analysis of passives as having an underlying manner adverb[8] not universally accepted, but there are several competing formulations of passivization which can claim distinguished adherents. In some, passives are taken as having the same deep structure as actives; in others, passives are taken as having a deep structure in which an active sentence is embedded in a sentence whose subject is what will appear as subject of the passive sentence. Lakoff (1965) argues against Chomsky's formulation, noting that the principal reason which Chomsky advances for it (the assertion that the verbs which allow passivization are simply the transitive verbs which allow manner adverbs) is false: 'verbs of cognition' such as *know* and *believe* allow passivization (*This fact is known by everyone*) but not manner adverbs (**John knows this fact carefully*).

Regarding the two possibilities for passivizing sentences with indirect objects (*The money was given to John*; *John was given the money*) Thomas observes, 'Notice that we must include a direction to drop the *to* when the indirect object is

---

[8] *Aspects*, pp. 103ff. Thomas does not indicate what category the '*by+Psv*' constituent is supposed to belong to, nor does he give any reasons for having such a constituent in the deep structure.

moved into the subject position', which is simply false. The absence of *to* in sentences such as *John was given the money* is simply a consequence of the rule (Fillmore, 1965) which deletes the underlying *to* and *for* of *He gave John the money* and *He bought John a present* (cf. *He gave the money to John* and *He bought a present for John*). The passive transformation moves into subject position the first noun phrase which follows the verb. Thus *The money was given to John* corresponds to the active sentence *He gave the money to John* and *John was given the money* corresponds to *He gave John the money*. The three transformations involved here: movement of indirect object, deletion of *to/for*, and passivization, apply in precisely that order. When passivization applies, either the indirect object has been moved to the end, so that *The money was given to John* arises, or it has remained after the verb and the *to* has been deleted, so that *John was given the money* arises.

The section on imperatives is a brief summary of Klima's analysis, which treats imperatives as having an underlying subject *you* and an underlying auxiliary *will* which are both deleted by the imperative transformation. One problem in this analysis which Thomas oversimplifies is that of negative imperatives. His statement

> ' we could add the negative morpheme (which would automatically trigger the *do* transformation):
> Sentence 7.35 m   John, don't close the door!'

does not show what is going on, since the *do* transformation inserts *do* only when an affix is preceded by word boundary, and *Ng* is not an affix in Thomas's analysis. It is necessary to have the imperative transformation leave a present tense morpheme before the verb. If there is no *Ng*, the present tense morpheme simply combines with the verb; if a negative morpheme is present, the present-tense morpheme remains unattached and the *do*-insertion transformation adjoins *do* to it. It is not clear how this analysis can be extended in any natural way to dependent imperatives: *I said to close the door, I said not to close the door*.

The chapter concludes with a four-page survey of several topics which Thomas

John works and Harry loafs   John works while Harry loafs

has not chosen to go into in detail.   His treatment of the first of these topics,
' Conjunctions ', makes coordination and subordination look as if they were the
same thing : ' we can say, however, that all conjunctions, that is, both subordinat-
ing and coordinating, are introduced into a matrix sentence from a constituent '.
Thomas appears unaware that coordination and subordination correspond to
two totally different deep structures, given on the preceding page.   The fact
that these sentences have deep structures differing as above is evidenced by the
fact that the latter but not the former can form a ' gerundive nominalization ' :
John's working while Harry loafs amazes me but not **John's working and Harry*
loafs amazes me.   Just what Thomas envisions as the deep structure of a
conjoined sentence is unclear, since he gives no examples of conjoined sentences.
The treatment of subordinate clauses in this section can only be termed atro-
cious :

> ' The exact details have yet to be worked out, but it seems to the author
> that there is a connection between certain pairs of words : *when* and
> *after* (Sentence 7.38), *why* and *because* (sentence 7.39), *whether* and *if*
> (sentence 7.40) and so on.   Consequently there is probably a non-*wh*
> transformation that corresponds to the *wh*-transformation :
>
> Sentence 7.38a   He came when we were ready to leave.
> Sentence 7.38b   He came after we were ready to leave.
> Sentence 7.39a   I know he was there for SOME REASON (+S).
> (matrix)
> Sentence 7.39b   SOME REASON is SOMETHING (+S). (first
> constituent)
> Sentence 7.39c   I saw him. (second constituent)
> Sentence 7.39d   SOME REASON is (that I saw him). (new first
> constituent)
> Sentence 7.39e   I know he was there for SOME REASON (SOME
> REASON is that I saw him). (new matrix)
> Sentence 7.39f   I know he was there because I saw him. (derived
> sentence)
> Sentence 7.40a   I don't know whether I will go.
> Sentence 7.40b   I don't know if I will go.'

Actually there is no more a relation between *when* and *after* than there is between *when* and *before* or *when* and *while*.   *When* and *why* are interrogative elements corresponding to the categories ' time adverb ' and ' reason adverb ';
after, *before*, and *while* (which may be considered a suppletive variant of *during*)
are prepositions which have an embedded sentence for their object[e]; the *when*
and *where* of subordinate clauses correspond to the preposition *at* of temporal
and locative prepositional phrases.   The *whether I will go* and *if I will go* of 7.40a
and 7.40b are dependent questions which function as the direct object of *know ;*
whether and *if* are simply two variants of the question morpheme *Q* discussed
above.   In the case of sentences 7.39, it is a total mystery why Thomas includes 7.39b (which can hardly be called a sentence) as one of the underlying

constituents of 7.39f.   All that is going on is that the preposition *because* (which takes the form *because of* when an ordinary noun-phrase follows) has the sentence *I saw him* as its object.

Next follow a few observations on genitives, which I have already commented on, and a paragraph on subjunctive mood, which consists in essence of the observation ' The grammar would indicate that such verbs as *prefer*, *suggest*, and *insist* may be followed by factive nominals in which the verb is in the subjunctive mood ';   no indication is given of how Thomas would incorporate this observation into a grammar.   Finally, there is a page of discussion of prepositions which correctly emphasizes that prepositions as traditionally understood do not constitute a very homogeneous class, so that e.g. the *at* of *at four o'clock*, the *with* of *the man with the beard*, and the *of* of *all of the men* function quite differently from each other.   However, he draws no conclusions relating this observation to a grammar of English.

The final chapter, ' Grammar and the school ', presents Thomas's views on the teaching of English language and literature in elementary and secondary schools.   He pleads for a sane and realistic view of language on the part of textbook writers and presents a liberal sample of the horrors to be found in current elementary school readers (for example, ' I see the kitten.   I will get the white kitten.', which violates English pronominalization rules).   He criticizes the profusion of modes of ' diagraming ' sentences to be found in current high school texts, although he would have done better to criticize not their profusion but the fact that none of them is in any way systematic: the information contained in the various diagrams is in part immediate constituent structure, in part category information, and in part head/modifier information, all combined into a hodgepodge in which none of these types of information is represented in full. The chapter closes with a brief discussion of linguistics and literary analysis.

In summary, Thomas is a talented popularizer, who puts across ideas lucidly and readably to the extent that he has understood them in the first place.   The book suffers from the fact that his understanding of its subject matter is often superficial, vague, or erroneous.   There is enough worthwhile material on linguistics and the structure of English in the book that, despite its many serious faults, a reading of it would probably be beneficial and instructive to the average highschool teacher.[f]   But it would have been much more so if the author had devoted to it the care which it deserved.

[a] See Bolinger (1967a) for important observations that cast serious doubt on the derivation of prenominal adjectives from relative clauses.
[b] See McCawley (1970a) for a discussion of the conception of cycle which I currently hold, in which there are postcyclic transformations in addition to a cycle.   Note *b* of that paper contrasts that with the quite different conception of cycle held by Chomsky in which there are no postcyclic transformations but some transformations of the cycle are marked as ' last cyclic ', i.e. as applying only when the cycle applies to non-subordinate clauses.

[c] This example actually does not establish that there is a cycle.   For example, as noted by G. Lakoff (abortion *a*), it is perfectly consistent with the hypothesis that there is no cycle and all applications of passive precede all applications of subject-raising.   The input to subject-raising in that case would be

[[the bagel was eaten by John]ₛ is believed by Irving]ₛ,

and subject-raising would have the same effect as in a sentence such as

The bagel seems to Irving to have gone moldy.

which has an underlying structure with a sentential subject.   See McCawley (1970a) for a real argument for a cycle in syntax.

[d] I am no longer as convinced that transformations are ordered as I was when I wrote this review. Koutsoudas (1972) has shown many popular arguments for ordering of transformations to be fallacious, and Lakoff's (1970b) notion of 'global rule' makes it possible to insure proper interaction of transformations in many cases where it had previously been thought that an ordering had to be imposed on them.

[e] Geis (1971) provides evidence that *after S* comes from a structure of the form *after the time at which S*, which in turn comes from *at a time which is later than the time at which S*.

[f] In saying this, I was assuming the state of affairs that prevailed in 1966, in which there were virtually no elementary introductions to transformational grammar available.   With the appearance of Langacker's (1968) excellent introductory text, I retracted my suggestion that a reading of Thomas would be beneficial to a high-school teacher.

3. Concerning the Base Component of a Transformational Grammar[*]

1. Introduction

The *base component* of a transformational grammar, which specifies what structures are available for the transformations to operate on, has hitherto been regarded by Chomsky and others as involving *rewriting rules*. In Chomsky's most recent treatment (Chomsky, 1965, henceforth *Aspects*), the base component consists of two subcomponents: a *constituent structure* subcomponent, consisting of rewriting rules and rules of another type which will be discussed below, and a *lexicon*. In earlier treatments by Chomsky (Chomsky, 1957, 1962), the lexicon is itself considered to consist of rewriting rules and the base component is regarded as a single system of rewriting rules rather than something consisting of two subcomponents. The term 'rewriting rule' is borrowed from the mathematical theory of rewriting systems. A *rewriting system* is a finite set of rules $\varphi \rightarrow \psi$, where φ and ψ are strings of symbols, and a *derivation* in a rewriting sys-

* This paper originally appeared in *Foundations of Language* 4-243-69.—I am grateful to Noam Chomsky, Erica García, David Hays, T. R. Hofmann, George Lakoff, Barbara Hall Partee, Paul Postal, John Robert Ross, and William S.-Y. Wang for reading a prepublication version of this paper and making valuable suggestions for its improvement. This acknowledgement does not imply that they approve of all that I say here.

tem is a sequence $x_1, x_2, \ldots, x_n$ of strings of symbols such that the first string (or 'line') x_1 of the derivation consists of the single symbol S and each subsequent line can be obtained from the preceding one by substituting a string of symbols ϕ for a string φ, where $\varphi \to \phi$ is a rule of the rewriting system. A derivation is said to be *terminated* if its last line consists only of symbols from a preassigned set called *terminal symbols* (the other symbols which appear in the rules are called *non-terminal symbols*). The last line of a terminated derivation is said to be *generated by* the rewriting system, and the *language generated by* the rewriting system is the set of all strings generated by it.

It should be emphasized that even though the base component of Chomsky's earlier versions of syntactic theory consists entirely of rewriting rules, it is not a rewriting system, since Chomsky imposes an ordering on the rules of the constituent structure component, whereas the term 'rewriting system' refers to an unordered system of rewriting rules (Chomsky, 1963). Thus, while in a rewriting system any derivation is permitted in which each line is obtained from the preceding one by 'applying a rule', i.e. by replacing the string of symbols on the left half of the rule by that on the right half, in the constituent structure component of a grammar as conceived of by Chomsky, only those derivations are allowed in which the sequence of rule applications accords with the ordering imposed on the rules: if rule A precedes rule B in the ordering, then all applications of rule A must precede all applications of rule B in any derivation. I note in passing that while there is an extensive literature on the mathematical properties of rewriting systems, very little work has been done on the mathematical properties of ordered systems of rewriting rules.[1]

In this paper I will discuss certain inadequacies of the position that the base component of a grammar should involve rewriting rules and will propose an alternative conception of the base component which is free from these inadequacies and which in addition involves neither ordering nor rewriting rules.

2. Derivations and Trees

Chomsky's conception of constituent structure component involves rewriting rules of a special type called *phrase structure rules :* rules of the form $\varphi_1 A \varphi_2 \to \varphi_1 \omega \varphi_2$, where A is a single non-terminal symbol and φ_1, φ_2, and ω are strings of terminal and/or non-terminal symbols, of which at least ω is non-zero. For the remainder of this section I will confine myself to the special case of *context-free* rules, i.e. rules in which the φ_1 and φ_2 are zero and which thus have the form $A \to \omega$. In the next section I will return to the general case of arbitrary φ_1 and φ_2.

From a derivation that involves only phrase-structure rules one can construct a set of objects called *nodes* with relationships which define the mathematical object known as a *tree* (more precisely, a *rooted, labeled, oriented tree ;* the adjectives will be omitted below). Before giving the procedure for construct-

---

[1] See, for example, Zwicky (1966), Peters (1966).

ing a tree from a derivation, it will be necessary to give a definition of the notion ' tree '.   A tree is a finite set of objects (called ' nodes ') with three relationships ρ ' directly dominates ', λ ' is to the left of ', and α ' bears the label ', satisfying the following axioms : (1) there is a node x_0 such that for no node x does $x\rho x_0$ (x_0 is called the ' root ' of the tree) ; (2) if x is a node distinct from x_0, then $x_0\rho^*x$, where ρ^* is the relationship which holds between two nodes a and b if there is a chain of nodes $a_1, \ldots, a_n$ such that $a\rho a_1, a_1\rho a_2, \ldots, a_n\rho b$ (ρ^* can be read ' dominates ' ; this axiom asserts that a tree is ' connected ') ; (3) if $x\rho y$ and $x'\rho y$, then $x=x'$ (i.e. a tree contains no ' loops ') ; (4) λ is a partial ordering on the nodes (i.e. if $x\lambda y$ and $y\lambda z$, then $x\lambda z$; if $x\lambda y$, then it is false that $y\lambda x$) ; (5) for any two nodes x and y, if $x\neq y$, then either $x\rho^*y$ or $y\rho^*x$ or $x\lambda y$ or $y\lambda x$; (6) if x is non-terminal (i.e. if there is a z such that $x\rho z$) and $x\lambda y$, then there is an x' such that $x\rho x'$ and $x'\lambda y$; if y is non-terminal and $x\lambda y$, then there is a y' such that $y\rho y'$ and $x\lambda y'$; (7) every node bears the relation α to exactly one element (its ' label '), the possible labels being a set of objects distinct from the nodes.

Given a derivation involving only phrase structure rules, a tree can be constructed as follows.   If the last line of the derivation is $a_1a_2 \ldots a_k$, construct nodes $x_1, x_2, \ldots, x_k$ and let $x_1\lambda x_2, x_2\lambda x_3, \ldots, x_{k-1}\lambda x_k$ and $x_1\alpha a_1, x_2\alpha a_2, \ldots, x_k\alpha a_k$ (N.B. $x_1, \ldots, x_k$ must be distinct from each other but $a_1, \ldots, a_k$ need not be).   This associates to the last line of the derivation a sequence of nodes $x_1, \ldots, x_k$.   Each higher line of the derivation is made to correspond to a sequence of nodes by comparing it with the line below it.   By the assumption that only phrase structure rules are involved, any two consecutive lines can be divided into a common beginning, a common end, and a residue in the middle which for the upper line will consist of a single symbol :

(1)

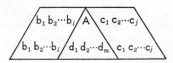

Suppose that the b's of the lower line correspond to nodes $y_1, \ldots, y_i$, the d's to nodes $x_1, \ldots, x_m$, and the c's to nodes $z_1, \ldots, z_j$.   Construct a new node x, let $x\rho x_1, \ldots, x\rho x_m$, let $y\lambda x$ for every y which either is one of the y_n's or is dominated by one of them, and let $x\lambda z$ for every z which either is one of the z_n's or is dominated by one of them, and let $x\alpha A$.   The upper line of the derivation will then correspond to the sequence of nodes $y_1, \ldots, y_i, x, z_1, \ldots, z_j$.   This process of associating each line with a sequence of nodes continues until all the lines of the derivation have been exhausted.   It is easy to verify that the set of nodes and the relations thus constructed satisfy axioms (1) to (7).   They in addition satisfy the axiom of ' continuity ' : (8) if $w\rho^*x$, $w\rho^*z$, $x\lambda y$, and $y\lambda z$, then $w\rho^*y$; a tree not possessing this property would be ' discontinuous ' : there would be a node w which dominated two nodes x and z without dominating all the nodes that were between them.

A tree may be represented graphically by a set of points (representing the nodes) arranged so that one point is higher than and connected by a line to another point if the node corresponding to the former point is in the ρ-relation to the node corresponding to the latter point, with the left-to-right arrangement of the points matching the λ-relation and with labels corresponding to the α-relation. For example, from the derivation

(2)   *S*
                        AB
                        APQ
                        MNPQ
                        MNRSQ
                        mNRSQ
                        mNRSq
                        mnRSq
                        mnRsq
                        mnrsq

one can construct the tree which may be represented graphically as

(3)

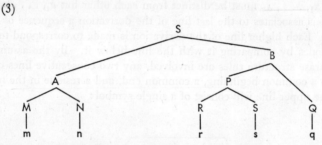

A tree whose *terminal nodes* (i.e. nodes which dominate no other nodes) are labeled by morphemes and whose non-terminal nodes are labeled by syntactic category names is called an *immediate constituent structure tree* or *IC-tree*. In a transformational grammar, all syntactic representations of a sentence are in the form of IC-trees[a]: the 'deep syntactic representation' of a sentence is an IC-tree and is converted by the transformational component into the 'surface syntactic representation', which is also an IC-tree, as are all intermediate stages between deep and surface representation; each individual transformation is an operation which converts a class of IC-trees into a class of IC-trees.

One difficulty with considering the deep IC-tree of a sentence to be constructed from a derivation involving rewriting rules is the fact noted early by Chomsky that two or more IC-trees may correspond to the same derivation. Specifically, to a derivation involving two consecutive lines

(4)   ...*AB*...
                ...*ACB*...[2]

can correspond equally well either of the two trees

(5)   (6)

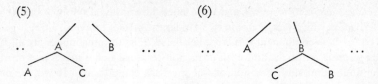

Tree (5) would be appropriate to represent the fact that a rule $A \to AC$ had applied, tree (6) to represent the fact that a rule $B \to CB$ had applied.   There are three situations under which a pair of consecutive lines such as (4) could arise: (i) the grammar contains the constituent structure rule $A \to AC$ but not $B \to CB$; (ii) it contains $B \to CB$ but not $A \to AC$; (iii) it contains both. In case (i) only tree (5) should be admitted as an IC-tree, in case (ii) only tree (6), and in case (iii) both trees.   Consequently, a derivation (sequence of lines) may not be sufficient to determine what tree should correspond to it, so that one must have recourse to information not in the derivations to determine what trees should be admitted.

This difficulty could be obviated if the base component operated directly in terms of IC-trees rather than through the intermediate stage of a rewriting rule derivation.   I know of exactly two proposals for the nature of the base component in which rules operate directly in terms of trees.   In the one proposal, which is implicit in such works as Stockwell, Bowen, and Martin 1965 (pp. 8ff), the base component consists of *tree formation rules*: a rule is interpreted not as an instruction to, say, replace a symbol A by a sequence of symbols BC but rather as an instruction to put two nodes labeled B and C under a hitherto terminal node labeled A.   In place of a rewriting rule derivation (sequence of strings of symbols), this proposal substitutes a tree derivation: a sequence of trees, each a part of the following one, the first tree of the sequence consisting of a single node labeled S and the last tree of the sequence being a full IC-tree. I will symbolize a tree formation rule thus: $A{>}BC$.   In the other proposal, to my knowledge first suggested by Richard Stanley (personal communication July 1965), the notion of 'derivation' is dispensed with entirely: the base component is a set of *node admissibility conditions*, for example, the condition that a node is admissible if it is labeled A and directly dominates two nodes, the first labeled B and the second labeled C.   I will formulate a node admissibility condition thus: $<A;\ BC>$.   Under the first proposal, a tree is generated by the

[2] It has been proposed in several works (Postal, 1964; Bach, 1964) that grammars be constrained so as to exclude the rules which would give rise to configurations such as (4), i.e. that rules of the form $A \to \varphi A$ or $A \to A\varphi$ be excluded.   However, Lakoff and Peters (1969) have recently presented convincing evidence that an adequate grammar of English requires rules of those types, specifically the rule NP $\to$ NP S and the rule schema NP $\to$ *and* NP[n].   The former rule relates to relative clauses, the latter rules to conjoined noun phrases, at least some of which (Lakoff and Peters argue) must be present as such in deep structure rather than derived from conjoined sentences by a transformation of 'conjunction reduction'.   The constraint proposed by Postal and Bach in order to insure unique convertability of derivations into IC-trees thus appears to exclude rules which actually must be available in linguistic description.

base component if its terminal nodes are labeled by terminal symbols and if there is a derivation which terminates in it.   Under the second proposal, a tree is generated by the base component if its root is labeled S, its terminal nodes are all labeled by terminal symbols, and each of its non-terminal nodes meets one or other of the node admissibility conditions of the base component.   It will be noted that each of these proposals avoids the difficulty referred to above: a tree formation rule $A > AC$ or a node admissibility condition $<A; AC>$ will give rise to trees such as (5) but not to trees such as (6).

The tree formation rule proposal resembles the rewriting rule proposal in that both involve the notion of ' derivation ' and, accordingly, both allow subproposals in which only a certain class of derivations is considered to generate admissible deep structures.   In particular, both allow the subproposal in which the rules have a pre-assigned ordering and only those derivations are admitted in which the steps of the derivation which arise through the application of any particular rule precede the steps which arise through the application of any ' later ' rule.   They likewise allow the more frequently encountered subproposal that imposes an ordering on the rules but allows one to return to the first rule of the ordering whenever a tree is reached in which S is the only ' unexpanded terminal symbol ' present.   On the other hand, node admissibility conditions are by nature unordered: the admissibility of a tree is defined in terms of the admissiblity of all of its nodes, i.e. in the form of a condition which has the form of a logical conjunction.   Accordingly, the question of the ordering of rules of the base component will be of interest in connection with choosing between these proposals.

Chomsky, in all the works of his with which I am familiar, treats constituent structure rules as ordered.   One fact which casts some doubt on the hypothesis of ordered constituent structure rules is the fact that no examples have been found of dialects differing merely in the ordering of their constituent structure rules, whereas there are numerous examples of adjacent dialects in which the same phonological rules or the same transformational rules apply but in a different order (Klima, 1964; Kiparsky, 1965).   There is thus considerable evidence that in acquiring a language not only the transformational and phonological rules of the language must be learned but also the order in which they apply, whereas there is a conspicuous lack of evidence that any ordering of constituent structure rules must be learned.   Note further that in the fragments of grammars which have been written using ordered constituent structure rules, little if any work is done by the ordering.   The fragments of constituent structure components given in Chomsky (1957) and Chomsky (1962) yield exactly the same IC-trees as they would if interpreted as unordered rather than ordered rules.   The ordering of the constituent structure rules in Lees (1960) plays a role only to the extent that it enables one to avoid saying ' elsewhere ' in conjunction with certain context-sensitive rules; for example, by placing the first of the following rules before the second:

(7) $N_m + N^0 \rightarrow N_m + Sg$

$$(8) \quad N^0 \to \begin{Bmatrix} Sg \\ Pl \end{Bmatrix}.$$

Lees is able to state rule (8) without any indication that N^0 can be rewritten as Pl only when the conditions for rule (7) are not met, i.e. only when it is not preceded by an occurrence of the symbol N_m. However, if one accepts the view of the constituent structure component presented in *Aspects* (p. 139), according to which only context-free constituent structure rules are needed, the context sensitivity of earlier versions of the theory being incorporated into the lexicon rather than the constituent structure component, even this not particularly convincing reason for imposing an ordering on constituent structure rules loses its relevance entirely.   In *Aspects*, Chomsky introduces a use of ordering of constituent structure rules which had not appeared in grammars written in the earlier framework, a use which relates to the rules creating ' complex symbols '.   I will argue in Section 4 that there is no real reason for having such rules in the grammar at all.   If this conclusion is accepted, it will mean that here there is likewise no particular reason for imposing an ordering on constituent structure rules.

I thus conclude that nothing currently in print gives any valid reason for preferring a theory with ordered constituent structure rules to one with unordered constituent structure rules.   However, it is of interest to consider not merely the question of whether constituent structure rules *must* be ordered but also the question of whether they *may* be ordered : Chomsky points out (personal communication) that since not all unordered sets of constituent structure rules can be ordered in such a way that the ordered system of rules generates the same language as did the unordered system, an affirmative answer to the question of whether the constituent structure rules of all languages may be ordered would further delimit the class of ' possible natural languages ' and thus be of interest to linguistic theory.   Lakoff and Peters (1966) provides some rules which bear crucially on the question of whether constituent structure rules may be ordered. If the rules NP → NP S and NP → *and* NP^n are part of an unordered system of rules, then both the configurations

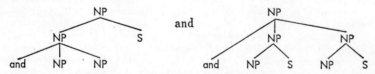

would appear in deep structure, whereas imposing an ordering on the rules would exclude one or other of these two configurations.   I maintain that both of these configurations do in fact appear in deep structures of English, specifically in the deep structures of

(9)   A man and a woman who met in Vienna live upstairs.

(10)   The man who I saw and the boy who you met are similar.

respectively. If this analysis is correct, it would imply that the constituent structure rules of English not only do not have to be regarded as ordered but indeed must be regarded as unordered.

3. Context-sensitive Rules

Since the notion of context-sensitive rewriting rule will be crucial to a discussion of the history of certain matters relating to the lexicon of a transformational grammar, I will at this point digress briefly into that topic. Consider first the mathematical object known as a *context-sensitive grammar*, i.e. a rewriting system whose (unordered) rules are of the form $\varphi_1 A \varphi_2 \rightarrow \varphi_1 \omega \varphi_2$, where A is a non-terminal symbol and φ_1, φ_2, and ω are strings of terminal and/or non-terminal symbols, of which at least ω must be non-zero. A rule $\varphi_1 A \varphi_2 \rightarrow \varphi_1 \omega \varphi_2$ may be interpreted as an instruction ' rewrite A as ω when it is in the environment $\varphi_1\_\varphi_2$ '. However, that interpretation may not be unique: from the formula $AB \rightarrow ACB$ one cannot tell whether he is to rewrite A as AC in the environment $\_B$ or to rewrite B as CB in the environment $A\_$. Thus the procedure for constructing an IC-tree fails even more than in the context-free case: in the case of context-free rewriting rules, the derivations did not contain enough information to determine what trees were to be admitted and it was necessary to look at the rules to obtain the additional information needed, whereas in the context-sensitive case, even if one examines the rules he may not find the information needed to characterize the admissible trees. One can again do as before and replace rewriting rules by either tree formation rules or node admissibility conditions. However, it is important to note that there are several possible interpretations of the terms ' context-sensitive tree formation rule' and ' context-sensitive node admissibility condition ', and under most of these interpretations the system of rules will not always generate the same language as the original system of rewriting rules did.[3] The one interpretation of the term ' context-sensitive tree formation rule ' under which the same language is generated as by the corresponding rewriting system is the interpretation of a

---

[3] A system F of tree formation rules generates a tree if there is a terminated derivation in F whose last ' line ' is that tree. The set of trees generated by F may be denoted by T(F). A system G of node admissibility conditions generates a tree if its terminal nodes are labeled with terminal symbols, its root is labeled S, and each of its non-terminal nodes meets a condition of G. T(G) may be used to denote the set of trees generated by G. The language L(F) or L(G) generated by a system of tree-formation rules F or a system of node admissibility conditions G is the set of all strings of terminal symbols spelled out by the terminal nodes of the trees of T(F) and trees of T(G) respectively. Many of the familiar results about languages (sets of strings) and their grammars are not true of sets of trees and their grammars. For example, while the intersection of two context-free languages may fail to be context-free, the intersection of two context-free sets of trees is context-free (a set of trees is called context-free if it is generated by a system of context-free node admissibility conditions). While the union of two context-free languages is always context-free, the union of two context-free sets of trees may fail to be context-free. While a finite language is always context-free, a finite set of trees (even a one-member set) may fail to be context-free.

rule ' $A{>}BC$ in env. $D{\_}E$ ' as meaning ' put nodes labeled B and C under a hitherto terminal node labeled A if that node is immediately preceded and immediately followed by *hitherto terminal* nodes (i.e. nodes which at this point of the derivation do not dominate any other nodes) labeled D and E respectively. If the emphasized condition were not imposed, the tree formation rules could generate trees which terminated in strings of symbols that were not generated by the original rewriting rules.   For example, if the rewriting system also had rules $DA \rightarrow dA, B \rightarrow b, C \rightarrow c, E \rightarrow e$, then a string of symbols of the form . . . *dbce* . . . could be generated by the tree formation rules without the emphasized condition but would not be generated by the rewriting system or by the tree formation rules with the emphasized condition.   The reason is that in the latter two systems, once the symbol A has been rewritten as BC or nodes labeled B and C added under a node labeled A, the definition of derivation would not permit one to (respectively) rewrite D as d or add a node labeled d under the node labeled D, since (respectively) the current line of the derivation would not contain the sequence of symbols DA or in the evolving tree the terminal node immediately to the right of the node labeled D would be labeled B rather than A, as illustrated below.

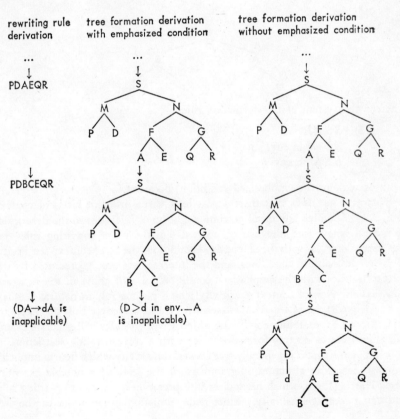

rewriting rule derivation   tree formation derivation with emphasized condition   tree formation derivation without emphasized condition

It should be clear from this example that a context-sensitive rewriting rule whose non-terminal symbols are interpreted as grammatical categories, e.g. $V \to V_t$ in env. __NP, cannot be interpreted as 'a verb is transitive when followed by *a noun phrase*' but only as 'a verb is transitive when the occurrence corresponding to it of the symbol V is followed by *the symbol NP* at some point in the derivation'. The latter interpretation corresponds to tree formation rules with the emphasized condition and to rewriting systems, the former to node admissibility conditions. The former might seem at first glance to correspond alternatively to tree formation rules without the emphasized condition. However, it turns out that, unlike the context-free case, a set of tree-formation rules (with or without the emphasized condition) may generate a smaller set of trees than would the same formulas interpreted as node admissibility conditions. To cite an obvious example, the set of node admissibility conditions

(11) $<S; AB>$
      $<A; mn$ in env.__$p>$
      $<B; pq$ in env. n__$>$

generates the tree

(12)

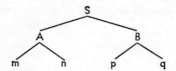

whereas the system of tree-formation rules

(13) $S>AB$
      $A>mn$ in env.__p
      $B>pq$ in env. n__

(with or without the emphasized condition) does not.

What this means is that there are at least three different kinds of context-sensitivity, of which any or all or none might be of relevance to the description of natural languages: the 'string context-sensitivity' of rewriting rules and tree formation rules with the emphasized condition, the 'tree context-sensitivity' of node admissibility conditions, and the intermediate type represented by tree formation rules with the emphasized condition. I will argue in the next section that the type of context sensitivity which plays a role in natural language is a restricted type of tree context-sensitivity and moreover that the restricted type of node admissibility conditions which I will consider will generate exactly the same trees as do tree formation rules with a corresponding restriction. I note in passing that it is generally tree context-sensitivity which figures implicitly in most American structuralist grammars of the 1940's,[4] a notable exception being Harris (1946), which has a clear interpretation in terms of rewriting rules and string context-sensitivity. Since node admissibility conditions can be used

equally well to define classes of discontinuous trees as to define classes of continuous trees, this framework provides a ready way of interpreting the discontinuous structures which figured in these grammars.

4. The Lexicon in a Transformational Grammar

The grammatical theory of *Syntactic Structures* treated the lexicon as consisting simply of those constituent structure rules which rewrite a non-terminal
symbol as a specific morpheme or string of morphemes. Next to nothing was
said in *Syntactic Structures* about the mode of representation of those morphemes; a morpheme appears in the rules either in ordinary orthography or
written as a sequence of (presumably atomic) phonological segments or in the
form of a special symbol such as *Past* which is given its phonological shape by
later rules of the grammar. Soon after the appearance of *Syntactic Structures*,
Chomsky adopted Halle's proposal (Halle 1959) that a morpheme (except for
'grammatical morphemes', which could still be denoted by a special symbol
such as *Past*) should appear in the constituent structure rules in the form of a
matrix of +'s, −'s, and blanks, which represent the underlying values of phonological features, the blanks corresponding to feature specifications whose
value of + or − can be predicted.

Note that in this conception of the base component, each 'dictionary entry'
provides exactly two pieces of information about each lexical item: its underlying phonological shape and the syntactic category to which it belongs, the
category being denoted by the symbol which appears to the left of the arrow
in the rule which introduces the lexical item in question. With the advent of
Katz and Fodor's programmatic sketch of a semantic theory (Katz and Fodor,
1963), the 'dictionary entry' was enlarged to include also a semantic representation. After this (obviously necessary) revision of the theory, the 'dictionary'
of a transformational grammar was regarded as consisting of rewriting rules
whose left half is the name of a syntactic category and whose right half is a complex entity consisting of a matrix of phonological features and a semantic representation. Alternatively, such a dictionary entry could be viewed simply as a
single complex of three types of information (syntactic, semantic, phonological)
which characterize the way the lexical item behaves, subject to the constraint
that the syntactic information be in the form of a single unanalyzable category
symbol.

A large part of *Aspects* is devoted to showing that this last constraint is responsible for several inadequacies in the earlier theory and to exploring the questions of what syntactic information each dictionary entry must contain and
what is an appropriate formalism for representing that information. The earlier

---

⁴ For example, Bloch (1946). Postal (1964), to my mind incorrectly, interprets Bloch's
references to contexts as string context-sensitivity. The one example which Postal cites
of context-sensitivity in Bloch's paper cannot be reformulated as a rule of a context-
sensitive grammar, since the context is a node which dominates the node in question
rather than a node which precedes or follows it.

theory allowed a category to be subdivided only through creating a proliferation
of category symbols via constituent structure rules such as

$$(14) \quad N \rightarrow \begin{Bmatrix} N_{common} \\ N_{proper} \end{Bmatrix}$$

$$N_{common} \rightarrow \begin{Bmatrix} N_{com-human} \\ N_{com-nonhuman} \end{Bmatrix}$$

$$N_{proper} \rightarrow \begin{Bmatrix} N_{prop-human} \\ N_{prop-nonhuman} \end{Bmatrix}$$

Even with this proliferation of category symbols, there is often no symbol available for a category implicit in the rules, as will prove the case any time sub-
classifications crosscut each other, as in (14), where the rules have introduced
no symbol for the category ' human noun ', which can only be designated by the
disjunction $\{N_{com-human}, N_{prop-human}\}$; if nouns had first been subdivided into
human and non-human and then those categories subdivided into proper and
common, then the rules would provide no symbol for the category ' common
noun '.　What is needed to avoid this defect is a mode of representation involv-
ing ' complex symbols ' such as $\begin{bmatrix} N \\ +Human \\ -Common \end{bmatrix}$, which represent a syntactic
category by a set of simultaneous components rather than by a single unanaly-
zable symbol.　In *Aspects* Chomsky explores such componential representations
in detail.

　　The constituent structure rules which divided syntactic categories into subcategories in works such as Lees (1960) were of three types: (i) rules such as
(14), which are generally context-free, and two types of context-sensitive rules;
(ii) rules which subclassify members of a category according to what adjuncts
they take (e.g. classify ' verb ' into ' transitive verb ', ' verb with directional
complement ', etc.), and (iii) rules which subclassify members of a category
according to what kinds of lexical items may co-occur with them (e.g. ' verb
with human subject ', ' verbs with abstract object ', etc.).　In *Aspects*, these
three types of rules are replaced by rules which add three types of features to
complex symbols: (i) ' inherent ' features such as [+Animate]; (ii) ' strict
subcategorization ' features such as [+__NP] (i.e. occurs followed by NP in
deep structure, i.e. is transitive); and (iii) ' selectional ' features such as
[+[−Animate]__[+Abstract]] (i.e. takes inanimate subject and abstract object).
The syntactic information in a dictionary entry will then be in the form of a
category symbol such as N or V plus a set of specifications for syntactic features
of these three types.[5]

_____

[5] Lakoff (1965) has shown that a fourth type of syntactic feature must be allowed to appear
in dictionary entries, namely features which mark a morpheme as having exceptional
behavior with respect to some transformation or other (a morpheme would be exceptional, e.g. by virtue of causing a transformation not to apply even though the conditions
for it are otherwise met, by causing a normally inapplicable transformation to apply, or
by being allowed to appear only in environments where the conditions for a certain trans-

Chomsky's conception of the base component of a grammar, as presented in *Aspects*, is accordingly as follows:

(I) (a) The base component consists of two subcomponents; (i) a constituent structure subcomponent, consisting of an ordered system of rules of two types, context-free rewriting rules and rules which create ' complex symbols '; and (ii) a lexicon subcomponent, which is a set (unordered) of ' dictionary entries ', each dictionary entry being a complex of syntactic, phonological, and semantic information, as sketched above.

(b) The constituent structure subcomponent defines a set of ' skeleton ' trees, whose terminal nodes are labeled by ' complex symbols ' rather than by lexical items.

(c) The deep IC-trees generated by the base component are those which can be obtained by applying the *lexical insertion rule* to the above ' skeleton ' trees: under each complex symbol one may insert a morpheme (i.e. a copy of its dictionary entry) if the feature specifications in the dictionary entry are consistent with the feature specifications in the complex symbol (e.g. under a complex symbol with the specifications V and $[+[+\text{Animate}]\_]$ one may insert a verb which is specified as taking an animate subject or a verb which is unspecified as to the animateness of permitted subjects but not a verb which is specified as not allowing an animate subject).

I turn my attention now to the rules of the constituent structure component which create complex symbols. Consider first the rules which add ' inherent ' features to a complex symbol. The following are taken from *Aspects* (p. 83):

(15)   (i) N → [+N, ±Animate, ±Common]
        (ii) [+Common] → [±Count]
        (iii) [−Count] → [±Abstract, −Animate]
        (iv) [+Animate] → [±Human]

These rules are suspicious, since they duplicate information about the language which is already present in the lexicon: the content of rule (i) is that nouns may be animate or inanimate, and common or proper, a fact which the grammar already indicates by containing dictionary entries such as those for *boy*, *book*, *John*, *Egypt* which contain the four combinations of values for the features [Animate] and [Common]. Chomsky points out (*Aspects*, p. 165) that rules such as (15) may be reformulated as rules predicting certain values of features which need not be specified in dictionary entries (*redundancy rules*). For example, if the rules (15) only allow + for the coefficient of [Animate] in complex symbols which contain the specification [+Human], then animateness need not be specified in the dictionary entries of [+Human] nouns and is predictable by

---

formation will be met). Lakoff notes that such features are implicit in the categories set up in Lees 1960; for example, Lees' V_{t32} consists of those verbs which are subject to deletion of indefinite object (*eat*, *steal*, etc.), a transformation which verbs are not normally subject to (a different and much preferable analysis of these verbs is given in Gruber (1965)). In addition, there will have to be features corresponding to grammatical gender, inflectional type, etc. (cf. *Aspects*, pp. 170ff.).

a rule [+Human] → [+Animate].   However, it is highly questionable that rules such as (15) rather than the corresponding redundancy rules should be considered part of the grammar.   Note that such a treatment of redundancy would be the direct opposite of that normally adopted in phonology (see Stanley, 1967), where only the impossibility of a feature specification need be the subject of a rule (namely a rule predicting the opposite value for that feature) and the possible segment combinations are simply those which are not specifically excluded by such rules.   Moreover, a grammar with rules such as (15) has the peculiar property of making the sentence

(16)   My neighbor is tall.

appear ambiguous: due to the male/female distinction in personal pronouns, Chomsky's approach would require the base component to contain a rule

(17)   [+Human] → [±Female]

and (16) would be derivable in two different ways: one with the specification [+Female] and one with [−Female].[6]   Furthermore, while semantically distinct lexical items count as different for the purposes of the ' conjunction collapsing ' transformation, the occurrence of *neighbor* which Chomsky would derive

---

[6] The rules which I ridicule here are not totally unreasonable, since they account for the two possible reflexivizations in

(a)   My neighbor hurt himself.
(b)   My neighbor hurt herself.

The description of sentences as these raises the question of whether the choice between himself/herself/itself is made on the basis of linguistic properties of the antecedent noun phrase or on the basis of one's knowledge about the purported referent of that noun phrase. Chomsky's treatment demands the former conclusion, mine the latter.   According to Chomsky's treatment,

(c)   *The waitress hurt himself.

is ungrammatical, according to mine merely semantically anomalous.   Some support for the latter view is given by Postal's observation (personal communication, July 1966) that in cases of semantic anomaly, either of the two incompatible elements may be interpreted metaphorically; this test is passed here, since either *the waitress* or *himself* may be interpreted metaphorically, indicating respectively the effeminacy of a waiter or the masculinity of a waitress.   In discussing sentences such as these, it is worthwhile to draw a distinction between ' meaning ' and ' presupposition '.   The information that my neighbor is a woman would be classified as part of the presupposition rather than the meaning of (b), corresponding to the fact that one would not utter such a sentence in order to convey the information that the neighbor is a female but only to convey the information that that individual has suffered an injury.   This distinction is supported by the fact that (b) is more correctly paraphrased by

(d)   My neighbor suffered an injury.

than by

(e)   My neighbor, who is a woman, suffered an injury.

One does not use a sentence like (b) to inform his listener of his neighbor's sex unless he is being rather devious.

with specifications of [+Female] and [−Female] do not:

    (18)   *The balls were well-attended and wooden respectively.

    (19)   John's neighbors are a man and a woman respectively.

Consider now the rules for introducing the other two types of features (*Aspects*, pp. 94, 97; Chomsky later shows the environment of rules (20) to be fully predictable):

$$
(20) \quad V \rightarrow CS \text{ in env. } \_ \begin{cases} \text{NP} \\ \# \\ \text{Adjective} \\ \text{Predicate-Nominal} \\ like \text{ Predicate-Nominal} \\ \text{Prepositional-Phrase} \\ that \text{ S}' \\ \text{NP} (of \text{ Det N}) \text{ S}' \end{cases}
$$

$$
(21) \quad V \rightarrow CS \text{ in env. } \begin{cases} \alpha \text{ Aux } \_ \\ \_ \text{ Det } \alpha \end{cases}, \text{ where } \alpha \text{ is a N.}
$$

Rule (20) adds the feature [+_NP] to an occurrence of the symbol V which is in the environment_NP, the feature [+_#] to an occurrence of the symbol V which is in the environment _#, etc.; rule (21) adds the feature $\left[+[+\text{Anim}] \right.$ _] to a V complex symbol which is in the environment $\begin{bmatrix} \text{N} \\ +\text{Anim} \end{bmatrix}$ Aux_, etc. These rules are also suspect since the information which they mark in the evolving structure is completely redundant, and since the lexical insertion rule, which is the only device in the grammar which makes any use of this redundant information, could perfectly well be formulated in such a way as to avoid reference to these two kinds of features: to determine whether a morpheme specified as $\begin{bmatrix} \text{V} \\ +[+\text{Anim}]\_ \\ +\_\text{NP} \end{bmatrix}$ may be inserted under a V node in a skeleton tree, one need not look at the complex symbol which Chomsky sets up there but could instead simply examine the preceding NP to see whether its head is [+Anim] and examine the 'right sister' of the V node to see whether it is labeled NP. This loosely described procedure of examining adjacent pieces of a tree can be made precise by saying that it amounts to treating each dictionary entry as a context-sensitive node admissibility condition, the context-sensitivity being expressed by the selectional and strict subcategorization features.

    I accordingly propose the following alternative to Chomsky's conception of the base component:

    (II) (a) The base component is a set (unordered) of rules of two types, constituent structure and lexical.

    (b) Both types of rules are node admissibility conditions, the former being context-free and the latter context-sensitive.

(c) The form of the rule is $<A;\ \omega>$ (ω being a non-zero string of non-terminal symbols) for constituent structure rules and $<A;\ x$ in env. $y>$ (where x is a complex of phonological and semantic information[7] and y is expressed in terms of selectional and strict subcategorization features) for lexical rules; the rule asserts that a node in a tree is admissible if it bears the label to the left of the semicolon, directly dominates nodes labeled as indicated to the right of the semicolon, and (in the case of lexical rules) meets the environment condition.

Before discussing the relative merits of proposals (I) and (II), it would be worthwhile to take up Chomsky's comparison of proposal (I) with a third alternative (henceforth, proposal (III)), which is virtually identical with proposal (II) except that it treats trees as constructed from rewriting rule derivations rather than described directly. Specifically, proposal (III) treats the constituent structure component as consisting entirely of rewriting rules (i.e. there are no rules creating complex symbols); lexical items are inserted into an evolving deep IC-tree by means of a revised version of the lexical insertion rule, according to which a lexical item having a strict subcategorization feature $[+A_1A_2 \ldots A_r\_\_ B_1B_2 \ldots B_s]$ may be inserted for a category symbol which is preceded by a string of symbols $\alpha_1\alpha_2 \ldots \alpha_r$, where $\alpha_1, \alpha_2, \ldots, \alpha_r$ are strings of symbols belonging respectively to the categories $A_1, A_2, \ldots, A_r$, and followed by a string of symbols $\beta_1\beta_2 \ldots \beta_s$, where $\beta_1, \beta_2, \ldots, \beta_s$ are strings of symbols belonging respectively to the categories $B_1, B_2, \ldots, B_s$. Chomsky suggests that (I) may be superior to (III) by virtue of the fact that (I) would impose on any language sharp restrictions on the set of strict subcategorization and selectional features available, whereas (III) would allow in any language the full gamut of conceivable strict subcategorization and selectional features: " It is an interesting question whether the greater flexibility by [proposal (III)] is ever needed. If so, this must be the preferable formulation of the theory of the base. If not, then the other formulation . . . is to be preferred " (*Aspects*, p. 123).

The two cases of ' greater flexibility ' in (III) which Chomsky discusses relate to the place of strict subcategorization rules in the ordering of the constituent structure rules and the question of ' single ' and ' double ' selectional features. On pp. 99–100, Chomsky asserts that the environment of rules such as (20) is completely predictable, so that the only thing which must be specified in a rule A → CS is its position in the ordering: the environment can only be ' $\alpha\_\_\beta$, where $\alpha A\beta$ is a σ, where, furthermore, σ is the category symbol that appears on the left in the rule $\sigma \to \varphi A\phi$ that introduces A . . . If this condition is adopted as a general condition on the form of a grammar, then the strict subcategorization rules can simply be given in the form A → CS, the rest being supplied automatically by a convention. In other words, the only characteristic of these rules that must be explicitly indicated in the grammar is their position in the sequence of rules. This position fixes the set of frames that determine subcategorization.'[8]

---

[7] x will also have to contain the other types of information mentioned in footnote 5.

[8] *Aspects*, p. 99. The A would have to be constrained to be the head of the item dominated by the σ, so that, e.g. verbs would be subcategorized according to whether they may precede two noun phrases but noun phrases would not be subcategorized according

Consider the various possible places where a rule V → CS could appear in a grammar of English which conformed to proposal (I). The rule could directly follow the rule which expands VP, in which case the verb node would be sub-categorized in terms of the labels on its *sisters* (two nodes are said to be sisters if they are directly dominated by the same node); another possibility consistent with proposal (I) would be for V → CS to follow the rules which expand some of the constituents of the verb phrase, in which case the verb would be subcate-gorized not in terms of its sisters but in terms of various nodes dominated by those sisters. Thus, in the first case V → CS would create features such as [+__NP], whereas if V → CS followed the rule NP → (Det) N (S), features such as [+__Det N] would be created instead. Proposal (I) presumably would also allow V → CS to appear in both positions, in which case both sets of strict subcategorization features would be created.

However, it is not clear that strict subcategorization of a node other than in terms of its sisters is ever actually necessary. Chomsky (*Aspects*, p. 102) suggests one possible case of such subcategorization: "a verb could be strictly subcategorized with respect to particular types of PrepP's introduced by PrepP expansion rules". But this case is dubious since there is grave doubt that 'PrepP' exists as a deep structure category in English. According to attractive proposals by Postal and Fillmore[9], all English noun phrases have a preposition, which in certain circumstances is deleted (any preposition is deleted when it is in the subject position; *of* is deleted when it follows an unnominalized verb (with a few exceptions such as *approve of*). The preposition can be considered to originate as a feature of the verb and become attached to the noun phrase by a transformation. Under this proposal, deep structures no longer involve the category PrepP. If, as I conjecture, there are no real cases of strict subcategoriza-tion of a node in terms of nodes dominated by its sisters, then not only the environment of the rule but also its place in the ordering is completely predicta-ble: it must directly follow the rule which introduces the category being sub-categorized. But if both the content of the rule and its place in the ordering are completely predictable, then everything about the rule is predictable, which means that there is no reason for it to appear at all in a grammar.

Suppose that indeed a node need only be subcategorized in terms of its sisters. Then the constraint quoted above on the environment of strict subcategoriza-tion rules can be sharpened to an assertion that a strict subcategorization feature can only be a specification of the labels on the sisters of a node. If the con-stituent structure rules were interpreted as tree formation rules rather than rewriting rules, other things being the same as in proposal (I) (call this soon to be dismissed proposal (IA)), there would no longer be any need for an ordering of the constituent structure rules: regardless of what sequence the rules applied in, the sisterhood relation would remain the same throughout the derivation, so that the same strict subcategorization features would be added to each com-

---

to whether they may occur between a verb and another noun phrase.
[9] Fillmore (1966); Postal's proposal is summarized in Lakoff (1965).

plex symbol by $V \to CS$, etc. even if the rules were treated as unordered. Consequently, even if the grammar is to contain rules creating complex symbols, no ordering need be imposed on the constituent structure rules. Of course, as indicated above, there is no need to have rules such as $V \to CS$ at all: proposal (II) allows one to do away with such rules without introducing any extra complexity elsewhere in the rules. The sharpened version of the constraint on strict subcategorization features can be incorporated into proposal (II) by making specific the kind of context-sensitivity referred to in clause (c) of proposal (II): a condition $[+A_1 \ldots A_r\_\_B_1 \ldots B_s]$ is met by a node if its left sisters are labeled $A_1, A_2, \ldots A_r$ (in that order) and its right sisters $B_1, B_2, \ldots, B_s$ (in that order). This, of course, creates a different kind of node admissibility than that thus far considered, since sisterhood rather than mere adjacency is the relationship on which it is based.

Consider now the matter of 'single' and 'double' selectional features. Chomsky compares two alternatives within proposal (I) for the rule adding selectional features to the verb complex symbol in English[10]:

$$(22) \quad [+V] \to CS \text{ in env. } \begin{Bmatrix} \alpha \text{ Aux } \_\_ \\ \_\_ \text{ Det } \beta \end{Bmatrix}$$

which adds two features such as $[+[+\text{Human}]\_\_]$ and $[+\_\_[+\text{Abstract}]]$ to a transitive verb, one marking a selectional restriction between verb and subject and the other between verb and object, and

$$(23) \quad [+V] \to CS \text{ in env. } \alpha \text{ Aux } \_\_ \text{ (Det } \beta).$$

which adds one feature such as $[+[+\text{Human}]\_\_[+\text{Abstract}]]$, which marks a single restriction between subject, verb, and object. Chomsky notes that he has no clear cases upon which to base a preference for one of these alternatives over the other but suggests that the latter type of features may be necessary to account for the occurrence of the verb *command* in sentences (i), (ii), and (iii), but not (iv):

(24)   (i) John commanded our respect.
        (ii) John commanded the platoon.
        (iii) John's resignation commanded our respect.
        (iv) *John's resignation commanded the platoon.

Chomsky notes that *command* admits both human and abstract[11] subjects ((i) and (iii)) and admits both human and abstract objects ((i) and (ii)), so that if

---

[10] *Aspects*, p. 118. Presumably (23) is to be interpreted as adding to the $[+V]$ complex symbol all features of the form $[+[x]\_\_[y]]$, where x is a feature of the α and y a feature of the β, although Chomsky does not explicitly say so.
[11] The inadequacy of this formulation is discussed in section 5. I suspect that (24 iii) must actually be derived from the structure which also underlies
   (a) John commanded our respect by the fact that he resigned.
or perhaps
   (b) John commanded our respect by the way in which he resigned.,
in which case the problem in question here would not arise.

the dictionary entry simply listed what kinds of subjects it allows and what kinds of objects it allows, it would fail to indicate that the combination of abstract subject with human object (iv) may not occur.   Chomsky accordingly interprets the sentences (24) as giving some evidence that the double selectional features of (23) rather than the single selectional features of (22) are required. Chomsky does not take up the possibility that there might be languages which lacked items such as *command* and for which rules such as (22) would be admissible.   If there are such languages, then a child in acquiring its native language would have to learn whether the language categorized verbs in terms of ' double ' or ' single ' selectional features.   Either way, proposal (I) would force the constituent structure component to have rules corresponding to only one type of selectional feature, whereas, Chomsky argues, proposal (III) would allow both kinds of features to appear side by side in the dictionary of a single language, thus allowing each language a much wider class of features than are needed to describe it.

However, Chomsky's analysis of *command* can not be accepted.   Lakoff (1965, p. E–2) argues that since *command* has a different meaning in (ii) than it does in (i) and (iii), the above problem would not arise: the one meaning (assuming for sake of argument Chomsky's incorrect formulation of the restriction) would have a restriction that subject and object both be human, the other a restriction that the object be abstract.   Since the lexicon must in any case indicate which meanings go with what phonological and syntactic information, the one meaning could simply be associated with the ' single ' selectional features $[+[+$ Human]__] and $[+\_[+$Human]] and the other with $[+\_[+$Abstr]] ;   no need for ' double ' selectional features would arise, since (i), (ii), and (iii) would be generated and correlated with the proper meaning and (iv) would be excluded.   Until a clear case of something requiring double selectional features can be found[12], it would seem worthwhile to propose as a linguistic universal that only single selectional features are needed to characterize co-occurrence restrictions between lexical items.   This proposed universal would have to be

---

[12] A possible case of double selectional restrictions is given by verbs such as *marry*, which one might analyze, following Katz (1967, p. 168) as requiring subject and object to have opposite values for the feature [Female].   However, a consideration of this selectional restriction leads one to doubt that it is in any way a linguistic constraint.   A treatment such as that of Katz (1967) would require every lexical item having to do with marriage (e.g. *divorce, adultery, engaged, spouse*) to be marked with such a selectional restriction. However, these lexical items would all have semantic representations which made reference to marriage, and the supposed selectional restriction would be predictable from that reference to marriage and thus (contrary to Katz's treatment) would not have to be part of the dictionary entry.   However, the prediction of this selectional restriction from the semantic representation of these morphemes would actually be an application of factual information, namely that in our culture marriage is entered into only by two persons of opposite sex.   In a culture in which a woman of high status was allowed to assume the male role in a marriage and take women as wives (as Oswald Werner informs me is the case in parts of Dahomey and Nigeria), the lexical items relating to marriage would undoubtedly exhibit ' selectional restrictions ' which accorded with this different factual situation.   However, that is merely to say that sentences such as *My sister is that woman's spouse* are factually rather than linguistically odd.

imposed on grammars regardless of whether the base component is regarded as conforming to proposal (I), (II), or (III). Once this constraint is imposed, exactly the same selectional features are available in all three cases, which would mean that the rules which attach selectional features would no longer be a way in which languages might differ from each other according to the predictions from any of the three theories.

Thus, the imposition of the highly plausible universal constraints on grammars that strict subcategorizations be only in terms of sisters and that there be only ' single ' selectional features eliminates the ' greater flexibility ' of proposal (III) which led Chomsky to conjecture that proposal (III) (and by implication, proposal (II)) would allow a wider class of grammars than corresponded to the possible diversity of natural languages. Rather, with these constraints imposed, proposal (I) requires grammars to contain a large number of rules whose content is completely predictable and a rule ordering on the constituent structure component which is predictable to the extent that it plays any role in the operation of the rules. Proposal (II) does without these superfluous rules and this superfluous dimension of organization, as well as doing away with the *ad hoc* devices which proposal (I) requires to predict the predictable rules and predictable ordering.

Since the extra machinery present in proposal (I) would be needed only if one or other of the two universal constraints proposed above is incorrect, it is proposal (II) and not proposal (I) which makes the stronger claim about language. As a result of the specific way in which I have formulated clause (c) of proposal (II), there is yet another way in which it makes a stronger claim about language than proposal (I) does. Clause (c) asserts that lexical rules are of the form $<A; \ x$ in env. $y>$, interpreted as meaning that a node labeled A is admissible if it dominates the complex of information x and satisfies the environmental condition y. This specific form of the proposal implies that the environmental conditions y are not part of the complex of information by which the morpheme is represented in the trees generated by the base component. On the other hand, proposal (I) gives rise to trees which contain selectional and strict subcategorization features. Accordingly, while proposal (I) does not exclude a transformation from making reference to these types of features, proposal (II) does. Proposal (II) thus entails a host of predictions about natural languages such as, for example, the prediction that whenever a transformation deletes the object of a transitive verb leaving no trace such as an agreement marker, then all subsequent transformations will treat the verb exactly the same way as they would treat an intransitive verb[13].

---

[13] It has occasionally been claimed (e.g. Lees; 1960, p. 33) that the English adjective-preposing transformation must make reference to strict subcategorization features on the grounds that the -*ing* form of a transitive verb may not be preposed even if its object has been deleted :
    (a)   There are sleeping children upstairs.
    (b)   *There are eating men upstairs.
But this generalization does not cover the facts, as is shown by examples such as
    (c)   Visiting relatives are a nuisance.

It should be noted that if the environments in context-sensitive rules are restricted to specifications of the sisters of the node in question, then an unordered set of tree formation rules generates exactly the same set of trees as does the corresponding set of node admissibility conditions. As was noted above, this is not true if a wider class of environments is admitted. Proposal (II) with the above restriction on environments is thus fully equivalent to the proposal obtained by replacing node admissibility conditions by unordered tree formation rules.

5.   Selectional Restrictions

In this section I will dispute a point which I assumed to be true in the last section: that 'selectional restrictions' have to do with the base component of a grammar.

Most of the discussion of selectional restrictions which has appeared in print is misleading in that it suggests to the reader that selection has to do with only a small set of very general features such as 'Animate', 'Human', 'Male', 'Physical object', etc. While the selectional restrictions stated in works such as *Aspects* are all in terms of this small range of features, it is important to note that very few of those restrictions have been stated correctly. For example, Chomsky's description of *command* in sentence (24 iii) as taking an abstract subject and abstract object does not correctly capture the restriction, since a wide variety of combinations of 'abstract' noun phrases violate the selectional restriction in question:

(25)   *Our respect commanded John's decision to resign.
(26)   *The fact that 2+2=4 commanded our respect.

In reality, an enormous range of features would be needed to express the full range of selectional restrictions to be found in English, as is clear from a consideration of the selectional violations in

(27)   *That verb is in the indicative tense.
       *Bernstein's theorem is non-denumerable.
       *John diagonalized that differentiable manifold.
       *That electron is green.
       *I ate three phonemes for breakfast.
       *He pronounces diffuseness too loud.
       *My hair is bleeding.
       *That unicorn's left horn is black.

I maintain that selectional restrictions are actually semantic rather than syntactic in nature, that the full range of properties which figure in semantic representations can figure in selectional restrictions and that only semantic properties figure in selectional restrictions, and that it is the semantic representation of an entire syntactic constituent such as a noun phrase rather than (as implied by the proposals of *Aspects*) merely properties of the lexical item which constitutes its 'head' that determines whether a selectional restriction is met or violated. Lakoff and Ross (1967) have observed that paraphrases satisfy the same selectional restrictions, e.g. that there is no verb with a selectional restriction which would be met if *a bachelor* were used as its subject but violated if *an unmarried man* were used as its subject. There are also clear cases of pairs of sentences in which the same selectional restriction is violated by (in the one case) material introduced by the head noun and (in the other case) by material introduced by a modifier, for example,

> (28) a. *My sister is the father of two.
> b. *My buxom neighbor is the father of two.

and in which different adjuncts to a given head produce selectional violation and non-violation respectively:

> (29) a. *The arm of the statue is bleeding.
> b. My arm is bleeding.

Moreover, despite Chomsky's assertion that " *every* [original emphasis] syntactic feature of the Subject and Object imposes a corresponding classification on the verb " (*Aspects*, p. 97), no clear case has been adduced of a selectional restriction which involves a non-semantic feature. For example, while one might suggest that *name* has a selectional restriction involving the feature ' proper ' (vs. ' common '):

> (30) a. They named their son John.
> b. *They named their son the redheaded boy over there.

or that *count* has a selectional restriction involving the feature ' countable ' (vs. ' mass '):

> (31) a. I counted the pigs.
> b. *I counted the sand. (in the sense of ' enumerate ', as opposed to the sense ' include in an enumeration '),

the restrictions actually involve the semantic properties of designating a proper name:

> (32) They named their son something absurd.

and designating a set:

> (33) *I counted the pig.
> (34) I counted the crowd.

In McCawley (1970b), I argue that the selectional restrictions imposed by a lexical item can be predicted from its meaning and that the supposed counterexamples to this assertion, i.e. items which supposedly have the same meaning but different selectional restrictions, actually have different meaning.[b] For example, the various Japanese verbs which may be glossed ' put on (said of headwear) ' (*kaburu*), ' put on (said of gloves) ' (*hameru*), ' put on (said of coats, shirts, etc.) ' (*kiru*), etc. actually mean the specific manner of putting on, as is shown by the fact that when one puts on an article of clothing in an unnatural manner (e.g. puts a pair of socks on his hands, uses a necktie to hold up his trousers), it is not the garment but the manner in which it is put on that determines the choice of verb : putting socks on one's hands would demand the use of *hameru* rather than *haku* and putting a shirt on top of one's head would demand the use of *kaburu* rather than *kiru*.   Note that according to this analysis, the sentence

> (35)   kutu o kabutta. (*kutu*=' shoes ', *o*=acc. case, *kabutta*=past tense of *kaburu*)

is not linguistically odd but will almost always be token-odd : there is nothing wrong with the sentence per se but only with using it to refer to putting on shoes in the way that people normally put them on.   Thus *kaburu, hameru*, etc. probably have identical selectional restrictions.

Fillmore (personal communication) has proposed that selectional restrictions are not restrictions imposed by a lexical item on other syntactic constituents but rather presuppositions about the purported referents of those constituents, e.g. that the selectional restriction imposed by *diagonalize* is not that its object have a semantic representation consistent with the semantic features that characterize matrixhood but rather the presupposition that the purported referent of the object be a matrix, and that selectional violation consists not in a semantic representation violating a condition imposed by some lexical item but rather in a contradiction between the assertions and presuppositions made about the various entities to which the sentence refers.   I regard this as the most worthwhile proposal which has yet been made about selectional restrictions.   First of all, it explains why under the earlier proposals a selectional restriction could require the absence but could not require the presence of a ' semantic marker ',[14] e.g. that a restriction ' requires female subject ' was met equally well by a noun phrase unspecified as to sex (e.g. *my neighbor*) as by one specified as female (e.g. *my sister*).   Secondly, Fillmore's proposal (unlike the earlier proposals) requires no modification to make it consistent with the conclusion (McCawley, 1970b) that the lexical material of a noun phrase may originate in a ' higher ' sentence than the one in which it appears, e.g.

> (36)   John denies that he kissed the girl who he kissed.,

which is most normally interpreted with *the girl who he kissed* not being part of John's denial but being the speaker's description of the girl who John was talking about.   Third, as pointed out by Fillmore, this proposal allows an item to impose a selectional restriction ' on itself ' in the sense that *bachelor* may be regarded not as meaning ' human, male, adult, unmarried ' but rather as having

---

[14] Katz (1966, p. 160) asserts that a restriction may require the presence of a marker : " the reading for ' burn up ' will have the selectional restriction ⟨(Physical Object)⟩ which permits a reading for the nominal subject of an occurrence of ' burn up ' to combine with it just in case that reading has the semantic marker (Physical Object) ".   However, Katz gives no justification for this formulation.

the meaning 'unmarried' and the 'selectional restriction' (presupposition concerning purported referent) 'human, male, adult', which fits well the fact noted by Fillmore that one may apply the word *bachelor* to someone known to be a male adult human in order to express that he is unmarried but may not apply *bachelor* to someone known to be an unmarried adult human in order to express that he is male.

The reader will have undoubtedly noticed that the last sentence is inconsistent with what I said earlier about the selectional restrictions imposed by an item being predictable from its meaning: 'male' surely is not predictable from 'unmarried'. I can maintain my earlier assertion only by revising the representation of *bachelor* to the extent of replacing 'unmarried' by 'not having a wife'. If I assert that the selectional restriction imposed by a property is that the item to which the property is applied be a 'candidate' for having the property[15] and assert that candidacy for not having a property is the same as candidacy for having the property, then 'human', 'male', and 'adult', which are necessary to make one a candidate for having a wife, will be imposed as 'selectional restrictions' by *bachelor*. This approach is confirmed by the fact that the other conditions which are involved in candidacy for having a wife also play a role in the applicability of *bachelor*; for example, one would not call a Roman Catholic priest a bachelor, even though he is human, male, and adult, and has no wife.

[a] This statement accords with the practice of virtually all transformational grammarians, though not with the official policy of Chomsky, who in numerous lectures at M.I.T. (though not in any published work that I am aware of) described transformations as operations on 'P-markers', where a P-marker was taken to be the set of all strings that, roughly speaking, could be obtained by moving left-to-right through a tree, e.g. {S, AB, MNB, mNB, . . .} in the case of (3).
[b] Leisi (1967) contains many examples that may very well be of the type that I claimed here not to exist, e.g. German *schwanger* 'pregnant (said of a woman)', *trächtig* 'pregnant (said of an animal)'.

[15] While this discussion is confined to 'properties', i.e. one-place predicates, it can be extended in an obvious fashion to multiple-place predicates.

4. The Role of Semantics in a Grammar[*1]

My conscience demands that I begin by pointing out that I am writing under false pretenses. I do not purport to have any universals in semantics to propose and indeed feel that linguists at present are as ill-equipped to propose universals of semantics as pre-Paninian linguists would have been to propose universals of phonology. Accordingly, let me for the bulk of this paper forget that this is a conference on language universals and simply talk about semantics as it relates to English.

There is an uncomfortable similarity between the way that semantics has

* This paper was read at the conference on language universals at the University of Texas at Austin, April 13–15, 1967, and was published in Emmon Bach and Robert T. Harms (editors), *Universals in linguistic theory* (New York: Holt, Rinehart and Winston, 1968), pp. 124–169.
[1] I am grateful to Noam Chomsky, Jerrold Katz, George Lakoff, Leonard Linsky, Lester A. Rice, and John Robert Ross for valuable discussions of some of the topics treated in this paper. Needless to say, none of them swallows whole everything I have to say.

A portion of this paper was read under the title ' The syntax and semantics of plural noun phrases' at the annual conference of the Linguistic Circle of New York, March 19, 1967.

I wish to dedicate this paper to the memory of Uriel Weinreich, whose untimely death has taken from linguistics one of its most productive scholars; his influence will be apparent at many places in this paper.

generally been treated in transformational grammar and the way that syntax was treated in the 'phonological grammar' of Trager and Smith. In either case the subject was treated as a nebulous area which cannot be dealt with on its own ground but is accessible only through the more manageable field of syntax or phonology. This similarity is made especially clear in Katz and Fodor's dictum (1963) that 'linguistic description minus grammar equals semantics', which in effect asserts that semantics is (by definition) the hairy mess that remains to be talked about after one has finished with linguistics proper. Both phonology and syntax have progressed immeasurably as a result of the realization by linguists that phonology and syntax are two interrelated areas, each of which leads its own kind of existence and neither of which can be defined in terms of the other with a minus sign in front of it. I will present evidence in support of my belief that the corresponding realization regarding the roles of syntax and semantics may have an equally great effect on the progress of both these areas of linguistics.

As a prerequisite to the rest of what I will say about semantics, I must take up one aspect of the notions 'dictionary entry' and 'lexical item'. Katz and Fodor (1963) treat a polysemous item such as *bachelor* as a single lexical item with a single dictionary entry containing four subentries, one for each of the four meanings of *bachelor* which they recognize ('1. A young knight serving under the standard of another knight; 2. one who possesses the first or lowest academic degree; 3. a man who has never married; 4. a young male fur seal when without a mate during the breeding time'). Katz and Fodor's position, like that of most professional lexicographers, is to group together in a single dictionary entry all the readings which can be associated with a given phonological shape and belong to a single syntactic class. However, there is no a priori reason why the information in the dictionary must be grouped together on the basis of phonological identity rather than on the basis of some other identity, say, identity of semantic representation or (to take an absurd case) identity of the list of transformations and phonological rules which the item is an exception to. Moreover, there is no a priori reason for grouping items together in a dictionary at all: one could perfectly well take the notion 'lexical item' to mean the combination of a single semantic reading with a single underlying phonological shape, a single syntactic category, and a single set of specifications of exceptional behavior with respect to rules. Under this conception of 'lexical item', which was proposed by Weinreich (1966), there would simply be four lexical items pronounced *bachelor* rather than a single four-ways ambiguous lexical item. There are a number of compelling reasons for believing that language operates in terms of Weinreich lexical items rather than Katz-Fodor lexical items, the chief reason being that transformations which demand the identity of a pair of lexical items demand not merely the identity of their Katz-Fodor dictionary entries but indeed the identity of the specific readings involved. An instructive example of this is the following problem, which is discussed inconclusively in Chomsky (1965). What is the source of the anomaly of the following sentences (Chomsky, 1965, p. 183)?

(1)   *John is as sad as the book he read yesterday.
(2)   *He exploits his employees more than the opportunity to please.
(3)   *Is Brazil as independent as the continuum hypothesis?

Since each of these sentences is a comparative construction arising from a deep
structure which Chomsky would represent along the lines of Fig. 1 through a
transformation which deletes in the embedded sentence an adjective identical
to that of the main sentence, the obvious place to look for the source of the
anomaly is the identity condition on the adjectives.   If different readings associated with the same phonological shape are considered to be different lexical
items, the problem is immediately solved.   There are, then, two different lexical
items: sad_1, meaning ' experiencing sadness, said of a living being ', and sad_2,
meaning ' evoking sadness, said of an esthetic object '.   This means that the
diagram in Fig. 1 could represent any of four conceivable deep structures, depending on whether the two items labeled sad are occurrences of sad_1 or sad_2.[a]   Of
these four deep structures, the two having sad_1 in the embedded sentence would
be anomalous because of a selectional violation in which sad_1, which requires a
living being as subject, is predicated of *that book;* the structure having sad_1
in the main sentence and sad_2 in the embedded sentence could not undergo the
comparative transformation because the two adjectives are not identical; and
finally, the structure which has sad_2 in both places would be anomalous because
of a selectional violation in the main sentence, in which sad_2, which requires an
' esthetic object ' as subject, is predicated of *John.*   However, this solution
to the problem of why Sentences 1 to 3 are anomalous is not available to a linguist who, like Chomsky (1965),[2] considers the terminal nodes in deep structures

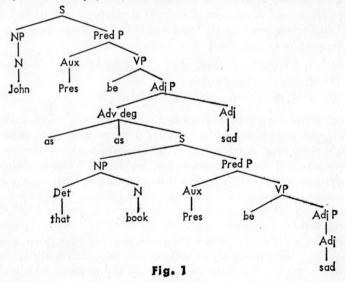

Fig. 1

[2] Chomsky has since modified his conception of ' lexical item ' (see fn. 6 of Chomsky,
1966).

to correspond to single polysemous items such as Chomsky's undifferentiated *sad*. I thus will henceforth assume that each terminal node in a deep structure has exactly one semantic reading attached to it.

I should say a word here about the relation of the 'disambiguation' of polysemous lexical items in Katz and Fodor's theory to Weinreich's notion of lexical item. Katz and Fodor's semantic projection rules are of the following type: if an item consists of two constituents, one which has a set of *m* readings attached to it (that is, is *m*-ways ambiguous) and one which has a set of *n* readings attached to it, the *mn* combinations of one reading of each constituent are formed, those combinations in which a reading for one constituent violates a selectional restriction in the reading for the other constituent are discarded, and from each of the remaining combinations a reading for the whole item is constructed in a manner specified by the projection rule. By applying the projection rules to successively larger constituents in the deep structure, one eventually ends up with a set of readings for the whole sentence. Disambiguation in Katz and Fodor's theory is effected solely by means of the discarding of combinations of readings which violate a selectional restriction. If Katz and Fodor's notion of lexical item is replaced by Weinreich's, disambiguation will consist in eliminating a certain subset of a set of deep structures which terminate in homophonous Weinreich lexical items; the projection rules would apply separately to each of these deep structures, each application of a rule consisting in attaching to a node a reading which is obtained by combining in some way the single readings attached to the nodes it directly dominates, and the entire deep structure would be judged anomalous or nonanomalous rather than combinations of readings discarded whenever a selectional violation is encountered.

There are several advantages of such an approach over Katz and Fodor's. First of all, certain sentences are nonanomalous even though they have a selectional violation in an embedded sentence, for example,

(4)   It is nonsense to speak of a rock having diabetes.
(5)   Rocks can't have diabetes.
(6)   John said that the rock had diabetes.

This means that the procedure given in Katz and Fodor (1963) whereby a pair of readings for two constituents is discarded if one violates a selectional restriction in the other must be refined so that a decision as to the anomalousness of a deep structure will require examination of the semantic representation of the whole deep structure. An assertion that something anomalous is anomalous is a tautology and thus semantically impeccable, and there is nothing anomalous about reporting that someone has said something anomalous. The latter facts are recognized by Katz, who states (1966, p. 161): ' We may observe that the occurrence of a constituent without readings is a necessary but *not* sufficient condition for a sentence to be semantically anomalous. For the sentence *We would think it queer indeed if someone were to say that he smells itchy*, which contains a constituent without readings—which is semantically anomalous—is not itself semantically anomalous '. However, the position that the constituent in question has no readings is untenable, since that would mean that

    (7)   He says that he smells itchy.
    (8)   He says that he poured his mother into an inkwell.
    (9)   He says that his toenail sings five-part madrigals.

would be synonymous.   Moreover, if the embedded sentence in something like (4) contains a polysemous item only one reading of which makes the sentence anomalous, then throwing away anomalies whenever they arise would give an incorrect reading to the sentence.   For example, if *king* is assumed to have the two readings ' monarch ' and ' chess piece ', Katz's procedure would mark

    (10)   It is nonsense to speak of a king as made of plastic.

as unambiguously meaning ' it is nonsense to speak of a chess king as made of plastic ' and would exclude the normal interpretation, ' it is nonsense to speak of a monarch as made of plastic '.

Secondly, disambiguation actually involves not merely linguistic competence but also the language user's factual knowledge ; indeed, it is merely a special case of the judgment of a speaker's intentions.   In support of these contentions, I observe first that whether a speaker judges an expression such as Ziff's example ' the shooting of the elephants '[3] to be ambiguous depends on his knowledge of physics and biology and the strength of his imagination.   Evidently my imagination but not Ziff's is up to the task of imagining a gun with a trigger so large that an elephant could pull it ; I suspect that the difference between my judgments and Ziff's may be the result of my having read *Babar* as a little boy and his not having done so.   Similarly, Katz (1966, p. 158) states that the word *priest* has the semantic marker (Male) in its dictionary entry.   However, this marker relates solely to factual information as to who current regulations allow to be priests, since the discussion going on in liberal Catholic circles as to whether women should be allowed to become priests relates to the changing of the regulations and not to whether women should be allowed to undergo sex-change surgery so as to qualify them to become priests.   Thus the disambiguation of the sentence

    (11)   The innkeeper knocked the priest up.

in favor of the reading, ' The innkeeper awakened the priest by knocking on his door ', is based on factual information rather than purely on meaning.   Finally, there are many situations in which a sentence which Katz and Fodor's theory will disambiguate in favor of a certain reading will be understood as meaning something which their disambiguation procedure will reject as a possible reading. For example, Katz and Fodor's theory would mark *bachelor* in

    (12)   My aunt is a bachelor.

as unambiguously meaning ' holder of the bachelor's degree ', since the other

[3] The example but not the interpretation of it is taken from Ziff (1965).

three readings of *bachelor* would require a male subject. However, one can easily imagine situations in which this sentence would immediately be interpreted as meaning that the aunt is a spinster rather than that she holds an academic degree.[b] I conclude from these considerations that the violation of selectional restrictions is only one of many grounds on which one could reject a reading as not being what the speaker intended and that it moreover does not hold any privileged position among the various criteria for deciding what someone meant.

The term 'lexical item' should not mislead one into thinking that every 'lexical item' of a language must appear in the lexicon of that language. On the contrary, probably all languages have implicational relationships among their lexical items, whereby the existence of one lexical item implies the existence of another lexical item, which then need not be listed in the lexicon. For example, Lester A. Rice has called to my attention the fact that in many languages the words for temperature ranges (*warm*, *cool*, and so forth) may be used not only to represent those temperature ranges but also to represent the temperature sensation produced by wearing an article of clothing. Thus, the English sentence

(13)   This coat is warm.

is ambiguous between the meaning that the coat has a relatively high temperature and the meaning that it makes the wearer feel warm. There is exactly the same ambiguity in the Hungarian sentence

(14)   *Ez a kabát meleg.*

I propose then that English has two lexical items *warm*, of which only one appears in the lexicon, the other being predictable on the basis of a principle that for each lexical item which is an adjective denoting a temperature range there is a lexical item identical to it save for the fact that it is restricted to articles of clothing and means ' producing the sensation corresponding to the temperature range denoted by the original adjective '.[c] Note that while the derived lexical item involves the notion of causation, it is not derivable by the usual causative transformation because that transformation would not give rise to the restriction of the derived item to articles of clothing[d] and because the causative transformation yields sentences in which the underlying subject of the ' basic ' lexical item is present as the object of the ' derived ' item (as in ' John opened the door ', which is a causative in which the structure underlying ' The door opened ' is embedded), whereas the derived adjective *warm* does not allow the overt presence of a noun phrase corresponding to the person or thing which is made warm.

A second example of lexical items whose presence in a language is predictable from other lexical items is given by the process which Lakoff calls *reification*. Note the difference in meaning between the two occurrences of *the score* in the sentences (based on examples of Lakoff's)

(15)   John has memorized the score of the Ninth Symphony.
(16)   The score of the Ninth Symphony is lying on the piano.

and similarly between the two occurrences of *John's dissertation* in

(17)   John's dissertation deals with premarital sex among the Incas.
(18)   John's dissertation weighs five pounds.

In the first member of each pair the noun phrase refers to a work of art or scholarship, in the second case to its physical embodiment.   In this connection, note the difference in normalness between:

(19)   I am halfway finished with writing my dissertation, which deals with premarital sex among the Incas.
(20)   *I am halfway finished with writing my dissertation, which weighs five pounds.

Another case of reification is pointed out in Wierzbicka (1967a), namely the difference in meaning between the proper names in

(21)   John thinks that the world is flat.
(22)   John weighs 200 pounds.

In (21) the proper name refers to the person, in (22) to his body.   The distinction between these two meanings is made clear by Lakoff's example (1968a)

(23)   *James Bond broke the window with himself.

Note that *James Bond* referring to the person and *James Bond* referring to that person's body do not count as identical for the purposes of reflexivization.[4] Here also one may say that the existence of one set of lexical items implies the existence of a parallel set of lexical items : that each lexical item denoting a person implies the existence of an otherwise identical lexical item denoting that person's body, and only the former lexical items need appear in the lexicon.   Rules of a similar nature to these lexical prediction rules figure in Weinreich's treatment of metaphor (Weinreich 1966, Section 3.5).   Weinreich's ' construal rules ' amount to rules which create a new lexical item by modifying the semantic representation of an already existing lexical item so as to make it compatible with the semantic representation of a sentence in which the original lexical item would be anomalous in some way.   However, rules of this type, which create lexical items that are all in some way ' deviant ' and whose use is restricted to highly specialized poetic ends, must be distinguished sharply from the rules creating the derived senses of *warm, dissertation*, and *John*, which give rise to lexical items that are no more ' deviant ' than the items they are derived from.

I turn now to the question of selectional restrictions.   In most of the published literature on transformational grammar, selectional restrictions are treated as within the domain of the base component of a grammar.   For example, the

[4] However, the ' person ' appears to include the body, as is shown by examples such as:
(24).   James Bond hurled himself through the window.

treatment of selectional restrictions in Chomsky (1965) goes roughly as follows: the base component contains rules which add 'inherent' features such as [+ animate] or [−animate], [+human] or [−human], to each noun node; those rules are followed by rules which mark each verb node with features such as [animate subject], [nonhuman subject], and so on, depending on what features have been added to the noun node of the subject, and similarly for direct object, and other constituents, and then under each complex of features is inserted a lexical item whose feature composition does not contradict any of the features in the feature complex under which it is inserted. One important point to note is that Chomsky treats a selectional restriction as a restriction between two *lexical items*, say, a verb and the noun which is the head of its subject. An alternative conception of selectional restrictions appears in Katz and Fodor (1963), where the fulfillment or violation of selectional restrictions is determined in the semantic component of the grammar rather than the base component and selection is treated as operating not between two lexical items but rather between a lexical item and an entire syntactic constituent, say, between a verb and the entire noun phrase which serves as its subject. Specifically, the dictionary entry of the verb specifies a property which the semantic representation of its subject noun phrase must possess, and one determines whether the condition is met or violated by determining the semantic representation of that noun phrase and checking whether it possesses the required property. Katz and Fodor do not make clear whether they believe that these 'semantic selectional restrictions' would appear in the grammar instead of or in addition to 'syntactic selectional restrictions' such as appear in Chomsky (1965).

Remarkably little attention has been devoted to the question of whether an adequate theory of language requires only syntactic selectional restrictions or only semantic selectional restrictions, or both. Chomsky (1965, pp. 153–154) mentions the question briefly and dismisses it as if it were merely a matter of notation, which is surprising in view of the fact that the different answers to this question in fact have radically different empirical consequences. I will now present an argument that an adequate account of selection must be in terms of semantic selectional restrictions such as those of Katz and Fodor (1963) and that there is no reason to have the 'syntactic selectional features' of Chomsky (1965) nor the complicated machinery for creating 'complex symbols' which the use of such features entails.

Consider first the question of whether a selectional restriction imposed by a verb or adjective is a restriction on the entire noun phrase which serves as its subject, object, or what have you, or rather a restriction on the head of that noun phrase. The former appears to be the case in view of the fact that examples can readily be constructed of noun phrases which violate a selectional restriction because of a modifier rather than the head. For example, the sentence

(25)   *My buxom neighbor is the father of two.

violates the same selectional restriction as does

(26)   *My sister is the father of two.

but the violation of the selectional restriction in (25) has nothing to do with the head noun, since

(27)   My neighbor is the father of two.

contains no selectional violation. Moreover, there are no cases on record of a verb which will exclude a lexical item as the head of its subject but allow the subject to be a noun phrase which splits the same semantic-information between the head and a modifier; for example, there are no verbs on record which exclude *a bachelor* as subject but allow *an unmarried man*.[5]

This establishes that one must look at a representation of an entire constituent rather than its ' head ' lexical item to determine whether it meets or violates a given selectional restriction. Consider now the question of just what information about a constituent is involved in determining whether it meets a selectional restriction. I maintain first that any piece of information which may figure in the semantic representation of an item may figure in a selectional restriction and secondly that no other information ever figures in selectional restrictions. As evidence for the former assertion, I will point out that on any page of a large dictionary one finds words with incredibly specific selectional restrictions, involving an apparently unlimited range of semantic properties; for example, the verb *diagonalize* requires as its object a noun phrase denoting a matrix (in the mathematical sense), the adjective *benign* in the sense ' noncancerous ' requires a subject denoting a tumor, and the verb *devein* as used in cookery requires an object denoting a shrimp or prawn. Regarding my second assertion, that only semantic information plays a role in selection, I maintain that the various non-semantic features attached to nouns, for example, proper versus common, grammatical gender, grammatical number, and so on, play no role in selection. All the verbs which have suggested themselves to me as possible counterexamples to this assertion turn out in fact to display selection based on some semantic properties. For example, the verb *name* might at first glance seem to have a selectional restriction involving the feature [proper]:

(28)   They named their son John.
(29)   *They named their son that boy.

However, there are in fact perfectly good sentences with something other than a proper noun in the place in question:

(30)   They named their son something outlandish.

The selectional restriction is thus that the second object denote a name rather than that it have a proper noun as its head. Regarding grammatical number, verbs such as *count* might seem to demand a plural object:

(31)   I counted the boys.

[5] This fact and the example were suggested by Lakoff and Ross (personal communication).

(32)   *I counted the boy.

However, there are also sentences with grammatically singular objects:

(33)   I counted the crowd.

The selectional restriction on *count* is not that the object be plural but that it denote a set of things rather than an individual.   Similarly, there is no verb in English which allows for its subject just those noun phrases which may pronom- inalize to *she*, namely noun phrases denoting women, ships, and countries.[e] I accordingly conclude that selectional restrictions are definable solely in terms of properties of semantic representations and that to determine whether a con- stituent meets or violates a selectional restriction it is necessary to examine its semantic representation and nothing else.   Since if the base component were then to contain any machinery to exclude structures which violate selectional restrictions, that machinery would have to duplicate what already must be done by the semantic projection rules, I conclude that the matter of selectional restrictions should be totally separate from the base component and that the base component thus be a device which generates a class of deep structures without regard to whether the items in them violate any selectional restrictions.

    Before leaving the topic of selectional restrictions I would like to comment briefly on something which appears at first glance to be a counterexample to what I said above.   Specifically, the different vocabulary items used in sentences of different politeness levels in languages such as Japanese and Korean seem at first glance to exhibit selectional restrictions based on nonsemantic features of lexical items rather than on semantic features of larger constituents.   For example, the Japanese verbs *aru* and *gozaru* both mean ' there is ', but the latter is restricted to situations demanding honorific language.   In such situations the informal pronouns are excluded, so that while

(34)   *Watakusi wa zidoosya ga gozaimasu.*

is a permissible way of saying ' I have a car ' in a situation demanding honorific language and

(35)   *Ore wa zidoosya ga aru.*

is a permissible way of saying the same thing in a situation where highly informal language is allowed, *ore* and *gozaru* cannot be used together:

(36)   **Ore wa zidoosya ga gozaimasu.*

It should be noted that there are many respects in which these co-occurrence restrictions differ radically from what has hitherto been understood by ' selec- tion '.   First, there appears to be no nonarbitrary way of deciding which of the elements in question determines the choice of the other.   Second, rather than relating to a specific pair of constituents, say, a verb and its object, the restriction here applies globally: the presence of an honorific verb such as *gozaru* pre- cludes the presence of informal pronouns such as *ore, boku,* or *kimi* anywhere in the sentence, and indeed, anywhere in the entire discourse, for that matter. Third, unlike all other selectional restrictions that have ever been discussed, which remain the same regardless of whether the constituents belong to a main clause or to an embedded clause, some co-occurrence restrictions relating to politeness levels apply differently in independent clauses than in subordinate clauses. For example, the politeness morpheme *mas*, which is attached to verbs of the main clauses in formal and honorific discourses but not in informal speech, is absent from relative clauses regardless of the politeness level[f] and thus regardless of what pronoun forms appear in the relative clause. I thus conclude that this phenomenon is of a different formal nature from either what is described by a theory of semantic selectional restrictions such as I have sketched above or a theory of syntactic selectional restrictions such as described in Chomsky (1965). As my choice of words in describing this phenomenon suggests, I believe that what is going on here is that the choice of pronouns and verbs is dependent on features attached to the entire discourse rather than to individual lexical items and that the politeness morpheme *mas* is attached by a transformation to the appropriate verbs if the relevant discourse features are present.

If the position I take here on selectional restrictions is adopted, most of the discussion which has appeared in print on the question of the ' delicacy ' of syntactic subcategorization becomes totally vacuous. The dictionary entry of a lexical item must specify all semantic information needed to characterize exactly what it means and must contain a full specification of what transformations it is an exception to; nothing more is needed and in neither area does the linguist have any choice as to how finely lexical items are to be subcategorized.

I turn now to the topic of indices and their relation to syntax and semantics. The discussion here will be complementary to that of Bach's paper (1968): his paper dealt primarily with indices used as variables, whereas this paper will deal primarily with indices used as constants. Chomsky (1965, p. 145) observes that transformations which are contingent on the identity of two noun phrases require not merely that the noun phrases be syntactically identical but also that they purport to refer to the same thing. Thus,

(37) A man killed a man.
(38) A man killed himself.

are both English sentences, and in the former the speaker is understood as referring to two different persons by the two occurrences of *a man*. Chomsky's proposal for the incorporation of these observations into a formal description of English syntax is that the base component of the grammar supply each noun phrase[6] with an ' index ' which marks its purported referent and that identity

---

[6] Chomsky's actual proposal attaches the index to the head noun rather than to the entire noun phrase. However, the index must be attached to the noun phrase since transformations which require the identity of nouns rather than of noun phrases do not require coreferentiality: note the pronominalization of a repeated noun by *one* in sentences such as ' John has a blue hat and I have a brown one ' even though two different hats are re-referred to.[g] In Chomsky (1965), indices are only referred to informally; no rules are

between constituents be interpreted as meaning identity of everything, indices included.   Thus, (37) and (38) will each have a deep structure containing two occurrences of the noun phrase *a man*[7] and will differ only in that these two occurrences will have different indices in the case of (37) but the same index in the case of (38) (tense is ignored in these diagrams):

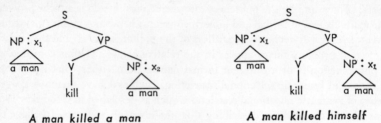

A man killed a man   **A man killed himself**

Fig. 2

Since these two sentences differ not only syntactically but also in meaning, this difference in index will have to be part of not only their syntactic representation but also their semantic representation.   An obvious proposal in this regard is that the semantic representation of sentences should involve not the feature-like 'markers' of Katz and Fodor (1963) but rather predicates (in the symbolic logician's sense of the term).   I thus propose that the most common reading of the word *man* be represented not as a set of markers {human, male, adult} but rather as an expression such as ' $human(x) \wedge male(x) \wedge adult(x)$ ', where x is a variable, and that the semantic projection rule which assigns a reading to a noun phrase containing that lexical item substitute the index of the noun phrase for that variable.   Such a rule formalizes the notion that in a noun phrase such as *that man* the properties 'human', 'male', and 'adult' are not merely being referred to but are being predicated of the individual to which the noun phrase purports to refer.

Some comments are in order here relating to both the status of indices and my use of the word *refer*.   Throughout this paper I will use *refer* in connection with the 'purported referent' of a noun phrase rather than its 'actual referent', that is, indices will correspond to items in the speaker's mental picture of the

given to provide the NP's with indices, and no indices appear overtly in any diagrams. Chomsky (personal communication) indicates that he did not intend indices to mark purported referents *per se* but only that sameness of index mark sameness of purported referent, that is, he wishes ' John shot himself ' to have the same deep structure regardless of who the speaker means by ' John '.   I argue below against the autonomy of linguistics from psychology which Chomsky's position presupposes.

[7] I do not mean to imply that the article *a* will be present in deep structure.   In fact, articles are to a large extent (though not completely) predictable on the basis of indices. However, since a full treatment of articles requires an adequate account of deixis, a subject which has so far been dealt with only in a fragmentary way, and since the points I am making here are not affected by the question of how articles are chosen, I will simply write *a man* to indicate a noun phrase which could be realized as *a man* and not commit myself as to whether its article would be present in deep structure.

universe[8] rather than to real things in the universe. This approach to indices is necessary if a theory of semantic representation is to cover such things as sentences dealing with imaginary objects and sentences based on misconceptions about the facts. It is of no relevance to linguistics whether a person has correctly perceived and identified the things he talks about; thus one need not know whether there are such things as guardian angels and heaven in order to assign a semantic representation to the sentence

(39) My guardian angel is helping me to get to heaven.

With this understanding of 'purported referent', one could perfectly well say that the index does not represent the purported referent but indeed *is* the purported referent: one's current knowledge and beliefs about the world involve his having available for use in his thinking certain terms which he identifies (rightly or wrongly) as corresponding to individual entities in the world, and it is those terms to which the expression 'purported referent' applies and which function as indices in the semantic representation of the sentences that person uses. One consequence of this point of view would be that when one learns a proper name, the semantic information he has learned is an index, namely the term corresponding to the individual who he has learned possesses that name. The learning of proper names appears to be of the same nature as the learning of a wide range of nonlinguistic knowledge: when one sees a person for the first time, he adds a new item to his conceptual repertoire and adds to his set of knowledge and beliefs a set of predications about that item which correspond to the things he has (correctly or falsely) observed about that person; in learning a name, one has simply added one more fact to his knowledge about the person. Thus indices are nonlinguistic units which happen to play a role in linguistic representations. Since in English many proper names can equally well be given to a girl as to a boy and there is no name which in principle could not be given to a member of either sex or to a horse or a boat for that matter, a sentence such as

(40) Gwendolyn hurt himself.

cannot be regarded as anomalous in itself, although it will be token-odd if applied to virtually any of the persons who actually happen to bear the name Gwendolyn; however, this token-oddity is in no way different from the token-oddity of *My neighbor hurt himself* when it is said of a person who is actually a woman. A somewhat different situation holds in Japanese, where not only may most first names be given only to a boy or only to a girl, but indeed many names may only be given to a first son, only to a second son, and so forth.[9] It is thus appropriate in this case (although not in English) to speak of personal names

---

[8] This remark of course applies only to constant indices and not to the variable indices of sentences such as ' No men have three ears '.

[9] Occasionally other uses of these personal names are found. For example, in Miyadi (1964) the names Taroo, Ziroo, Saburoo, and so on (normally reserved for first son, second son, third son) are attached to the chief (Taroo) of a troop of monkeys which Miyadi studied, the next highest monkey in the ' pecking order ' (Ziroo), and so on.

as having a semantic representation which includes information such as ' male '
and ' firstborn '.

Indices and the knowledge in which they figure play a role in the choice of
pronominal forms.   In English the choice between *he, she,* and *it* or between
who and *which* depends on one's knowledge of the intended referent of the noun
phrase rather than on the lexical items involved in the antecedent noun phrase.
Note the difference in relative pronoun in the sentences

> (41) Fafnir, who plays third base on the Little League team, is a fine
>   boy.
> (42) They called their son Fafnir, which is a ridiculous name.
> (43) *They called their son Fafnir, who is a ridiculous name.

The difference in pronoun choice relates to the different indices which the noun
phrases will have and the fact that the one index corresponds to a person whereas
the other corresponds to a name.   Similarly, the different choice of pronouns in

> (44) My neighbor hurt himself.
> (45) My neighbor hurt herself.

corresponds to whether the speaker's knowledge about the index of the token
of *my neighbor* in the sentence contains the information that that individual is
male or is female.   An alternative analysis of these sentences, proposed by
Chomsky (1965), would have the base component of the grammar supply each
noun with a full complement of specifications for the features which play a role
in any syntactic or morphological rule (for example, pronoun choice), so that
(44) and (45) would differ in deep structure by virtue of the noun *neighbor* having
the specification [+male] in the one deep structure and [−male] in the other.
However, that proposal is highly suspicious, since it would make sentences such
as

> (46) My neighbor is tall.

appear ambiguous, since they could be derived with either [+male] or [−male]
on the noun *neighbor*.   Moreover, the transformation which yields sentences
such as

> (47) The neighbors are respectively male and female.

would have to ignore the specifications of [+male] and [−male] which would

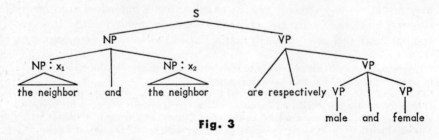

Fig. 3

be attached to the two occurrences of *neighbor* in the structure which would serve as input to that transformation (see Fig. 3 on the last page).

In view of these defects in the only alternative analysis with which I am familiar, I conclude that the difference between (44) and (45) corresponds not to a difference in deep structure but to a difference between the circumstances surrounding different tokens of the same deep structure. In support of this contention, I might mention that the sentence

(48)   My neighbor is a woman and suffered an injury.

ought to be a paraphrase of (45) according to the analysis in which a feature of [—male] is attached to the occurrence of *neighbor* in the deep structure of (45).[h] However, it does violence to the notion of paraphrase to say that (48) is a paraphrase of (45). While both convey the information that the individual named by *my neighbor* has suffered an injury, (48) but not (45) could be used to convey to the information that that person is female. Sentence (45) is what one would say simply in order to convey the information that the person in question suffered an injury, and in saying it one assumes that his hearer has prior information about that individual, among other things the information that she is a woman. To distinguish between the ways in which (48) and (45) convey information, it will be necessary to make a distinction between ' meaning ' and ' presupposition ': the information that the individual in question has suffered an injury is part of the meaning of both (45) and (48); however, the information that that individual is female is part of the meaning of (48) but only a presupposition of (45).

Actually, pronoun choice in English is not completely determined by presuppositions, since one feature which plays a role in pronoun choice, namely number, is not completely predictable from knowledge about the purported referent. Note that there are cases where one and the same thing may be referred to by either a singular noun phrase or a plural noun phrase, and anaphoric pronouns must have the same number as the noun phrase actually used:

(49)   John gave me the scissors; I am using them now.
(50)   *John gave me the scissors; I am using it now.
(51)   John gave me the two-bladed cutting instrument; I am using it now.
(52)   *John gave me the two-bladed cutting instrument; I am using them now.

In languages having lexical gender, anaphoric pronouns generally must agree in that feature with the head noun of the antecedent noun phrase. In some languages (for example, German) the anaphoric pronoun always agrees in gender with the head of the antecedent noun phrase, whereas in other languages (for example, French and Yiddish) there is agreement with the head of the antecedent noun phrase except when it refers to a human being, in which case the pronoun form corresponds to the sex of that person regardless of the gender of the head of the antecedent noun phrase. In the case of nonanaphoric (that is, deictic) pronouns, the choice of gender is always made on the basis of presupposition concerning the intended referent: when a girl enters a room one may nudge his companion and ask ' *Wie heisst sie?* ' even though later in the conversation he may refer to the same girl with the noun phrase *das Mädchen* and then refer anaphorically to that noun phrase with the pronoun *es*. What is common to pronoun choice in German, French, and English is the attachment of certain grammatical features to a noun-phrase node on the basis of the noun (if any) which that node dominates (in French, this is done only for noun phrases which do not refer to a human being). Pronominalization consists in wiping out everything except the index and those grammatical features; the specific form of the pronoun is determined on the basis of the grammatical features on the NP node, with presupposition concerning the index providing any information needed for pronoun choice which is not contained among those grammatical features. In the case of a deictic pronoun, no grammatical features of number or gender will be attached to the node in question and the choice of pronoun will be made entirely on the basis of knowledge in which the index figures.[1]

I have spoken so far as if an index could only be an item in a speaker's conceptual apparatus which he identifies as an individual. This is proper in the case of a singular noun phrase.[j] However, a plural noun phrase usually refers not to an individual but to a set of individuals. Moreover, plural noun phrases will have to bear indices since they, just like singular noun phrases, may meet or fail to meet identity conditions by virtue of what their purported referents are. Since a plural noun phrase generally refers to a set, it can be expected that its index will behave like a set, and indeed there are syntactic phenomena which show that it must in fact be possible to perform set-theoretic operations on indices and that syntactic rules must be able to make use of the results of such operations.

Consider conjoined modifiers of the type illustrated by

(53)   the male and female employees
(54)   new and used books
(55)   the string quartets of Prokofiev and Ravel

Note that (53) refers not to employees who are simultaneously male and female but rather to an aggregate consisting of some employees who are male and some who are female. It may thus be paraphrased by

(56)   the male employees and the female employees

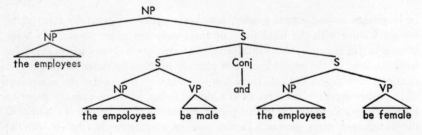

Fig. 4

I maintain that conjoined modifiers of this type arise from deep structures which (neglecting tense) are of the form in Fig. 4 (on the last page), in which the two occurrences of *the employees* under the S node have different indices, say *A* and *B* respectively.   The sentence which is adjoined to the noun phrase meets the conditions for the *respectively* transformation, yielding

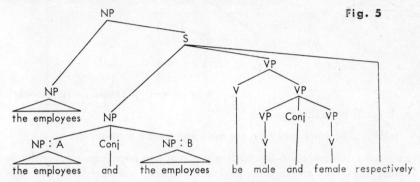

Fig. 5

The material under the S node of this tree would appear to underlie the non-sentence

    (57)   *The employees and the employees are male and female respectively.

There is a transformation which obligatorily collapses the conjoined subject *the employees and the employees* into a single occurrence of *the employees*.   This collapsing transformation is necessary in a grammar of English because sentences such as

    (58)   These boys are respectively Polish and Irish.

fill the semantic gap left by the nonoccurrence of *respectively* constructions with formally identical conjoined subjects.   The resulting structure

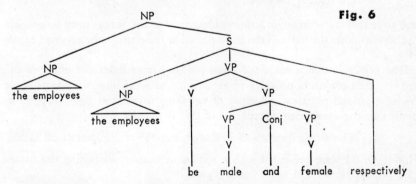

Fig. 6

is subject to the relative clause transformation, which converts the occurrence of *the employees* in the embedded sentence into a relative pronoun, thus yielding a structure

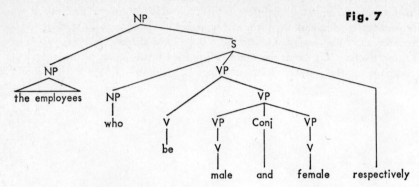

Fig. 7

which could be realized as

(59)   The employees who are male and female respectively.

The word *respectively* and the relative pronoun and copula may optionally be deleted, and if they are, then the conjoined predicate *male and female* is obligatorily placed in front of the noun by the well-known rule for forming prenominal modifiers (Smith, 1961 ; Lakoff, 1965), thus yielding (53).

The *respectively* transformation creates a conjoined noun phrase, which must have an index attached to it since it participates in transformations requiring identity of index ; for example, it may have a nonrestrictive clause attached to it. I propose that the index of a conjoined noun phrase be the set-theoretic union of the indices of its conjuncts.   This principle would attach the index $A \cup B$ to the noun phrase *the employees and the employees* in the second tree, and $A \cup B$ would remain the index of that noun phrase after the collapsing rule applies to it. Since the nonrestrictive clause transformation can attach a nonrestrictive clause to (53):

(60)   The male and female employees, who say they are dissatisfied, are actually very well paid.

and since that transformation requires identity of index, it thus must be possible to check whether the index of the noun phrase in the clause to be adjoined equals $A \cup B$.

The principle that a conjoined noun phrase has as index the union of the indices of its conjuncts provides an explanation of some interesting facts about conjunction and plurality.   Because of extralinguistic knowledge I happen to know that the appropriate paraphrase of (55) is

(61)   The string quartets of Prokofiev and the string quartet of Ravel.

However, if I were presented with a similar expression containing the names of two composers I had never heard of, say,

(62)   The string quartets of Eierkopf and Misthaufen.

I would be at a loss to say which of four conceivable paraphrases was the appropriate one :[k]

(63) The quartet of Eierkopf and the quartet of Misthaufen.
(64) The quartets of Eierkopf and the quartet of Misthaufen.
(65) The quartet of Eierkopf and the quartets of Misthaufen.
(66) The quartets of Eierkopf and the quartets of Misthaufen.

However, it is noteworthy that regardless of whether the appropriate paraphrase has two singulars, a singular and a plural, or two plurals, (62) has the plural noun *quartets*. This fact provides evidence that the plural morpheme is not present in deep structure but is rather inserted by a rule that is sensitive to whether a noun phrase has a set or an individual index, that is, a rule by which the plural morpheme is adjoined to any noun directly dominated by a noun-phrase node having a set index. This rule must apply later than the collapsing rule, so that when it applies *quartet* in (62) will always be directly under a noun-phrase node that has an index that is derived through the operation of union and is thus a set rather than an individual, which means that the plural morpheme will always be inserted. It should be remarked parenthetically that the notion of ' set ' that functions in English syntax and semantics is not exactly the same as the ' set ' of mathematics, since the mathematical notion admits an empty set and one-member sets, whereas only sets of two or more members count for the purposes of the rules in question here. The ' set theory ' involved here is one which ignores the difference between an individual and a one-member set and thus allows individuals to be combined by the union operation: $x_1 \cup x_2 = \{x_1, x_2\}$. The distinction between set and individual, thus understood, also allows a uniform treatment of number agreement. In published transformational descriptions (for example, Lees, 1960, p. 44), number agreement has generally been formulated as a rule that marks a verb as plural or singular depending on whether it is or is not preceded by the plural morpheme, with an extra clause whereby conjoined subjects require plural number agreement regardless of whether they contain the plural morpheme. However, what determines number agreement is clearly not the presence of the plural morpheme but rather something which may be called plurality of the whole subject and which corresponds very closely to the set/individual distinction. The correspondence is not exact because of *pluralia tantum* such as *scissors*, which take a plural verb even when they have an individual index. The following system of ordered rules is thus needed to derive number agreement:

(a) Mark a noun-phrase node [+plural] if it has a set index and [−plural] otherwise.
(b) Mark a noun-phrase node [+plural] if it directly dominates a noun marked as belonging to the class ' *pluralia tantum* '.
(c) Mark a verb [+plural] or [−plural] depending on whether its subject is marked [+plural] or [−plural].

Note that creation of a set index by the principle mentioned earlier is needed to derive the plural agreement of

(67)   John and Harry are Polish and Irish respectively.

and of the especially interesting example

(68)   John and Harry like the play and are disappointed by it respectively.

Here the two verbs take plural number agreement even though each of them applies semantically to a singular subject, but the conjoined subject created by the
respectively transformation still demands plural number agreement.   Note the
ungrammaticality of

(69)   *John and Harry likes the play and is disappointed by it respec-
       tively.

One interesting consequence of these facts is that the rule making the verb agree
in number with the subject cannot be formulated by any formula of the type
presently used to represent transformations, since it must attach the agreement
feature simultaneously to all the finite verbs of a conjoined verb phrase rather
than to a single verb : the transformation which creates the source of the plurality
(the conjoined subject) simultaneously creates a conjoined verb phrase.

So far I have considered conjoined noun phrases which arise through the
respectively transformation.   What about other conjoined noun phrases ?   Chomsky (1957, pp. 35–37) proposed that all conjoined constituents are derived from
pairs of simple sentences, so that

(70)   John and Harry are erudite.

would be derived by a conjoining transformation from structures which underlie
the two sentences ' John is erudite ' and ' Harry is erudite '.   This idea appears
in slightly revised form in Chomsky (1965, p. 225), where it is suggested that
(all ?) conjoined elements are derived from underlying conjoined sentences, so
that (70) would arise through a ' conjunction reduction ' transformation from a
structure which also underlies

(71)   John is erudite and Harry is erudite.

It has been long recognized (e.g. Whitney 1877 : 240) that some conjoined constituents cannot plausibly be derived from underlying conjoined sentences, for
example,

(72)   John and Harry are similar.
(73)   John and Mary embraced.

Note the deviance of the putative source sentence

(74)   *John is similar.

except when it arises through ellipsis as in

(75)   Max is a fool ; John is similar.

and the total inadmissibility, ellipsis or not, of

(76) *John embraced.

Lakoff and Peters (1969) have proposed that (70) has a conjunction of sentences as its deep structure but (72) has as deep structure a simple sentence with a conjoined subject:

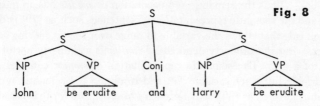

Fig. 8

John and Harry are erudite.

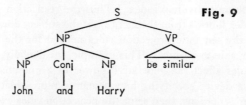

Fig. 9

John and Harry are similar.

Noting that the sentences to which they assign deep conjoined subjects admit variants in which one of the conjuncts appears in the verb phrase, for example,

(77) John is similar to Harry.
(78) John embraced Mary.

Lakoff and Peters propose that the latter sentences arise from the same deep structures as (72) and (73) through the application of a 'conjunct movement' transformation which optionally shifts one of the conjuncts of a conjoined subject into the verb phrase.[1]

In both types of sentences, a simple noun phrase may appear in place of the conjoined noun phrase, as in

(79) Those men are erudite.
(80) Those men are similar.

Consider what restriction must be placed on the subject of *similar* to exclude *John is similar*. An obvious suggestion would be that *similar* demands a plural subject, whether it be conjoined as in (72) or simple as in (80). However, that formulation of the restriction is not correct, since *pluralia tantum* may not function as the subject of *similar* unless interpreted as referring to a set:

(81) These scissors are similar.

is admissible only when *these scissors* is paraphrasable by *these pairs of scissors* and not when it is paraphrasable by *this pair of scissors*.   Evidently the restriction is that the subject must have a set index rather than an individual index.   However, that restriction is a logical consequence of the semantic representation of *similar* as contrasted with *erudite*.   The meaning of (79) is that each of the men in question has the property denoted by *erudite*; that is, eruditeness is a property of an individual.   Thus the semantic representation of *erudite* has an individual variable in it and the semantic representation of sentences such as (79) is derived by a projection rule that allows the variable to range over the set serving as index of the subject.   But the property denoted by *similar* is a property not of an individual but of a set.   The semantic representation of *similar* contains not an individual variable but a set variable,[10,m] and to obtain the semantic representation of a sentence such as (80), it is necessary to substitute for that variable the set which functions as index of the subject noun phrase.   But to carry out that operation it is necessary that there be such a set, and there is not in the case of a subject with an individual index.   Thus the restriction of *similar* to subjects with a set index follows from the fact that if the subject does not have a set index then one of the semantic projection rules needed for the interpretation of the sentence is unable to operate.   This example, incidentally, shows that semantic projection rules affect the generative power of a grammar.   If a grammar is taken to be a device specifying how semantic representations are paired with phonetic representations, then semantic projection rules exclude from this pairing any structure on which their functioning is blocked.

I wish now to reconsider the deep structure of (70).   In light of the above discussion, there is no longer any reason to consider (70) to be derived from an underlying conjoined sentence.   The differences between (70) and (72) are accounted for by the difference in the semantic representation of the adjective, and the

---

[10] The set variable in the semantic representation of *similar* is necessary for the following reasons.   *Similar* may be followed by *in that S*, as in

(82)   Those men are similar in that they play tennis well.

The meaning of this sentence can be represented as $\bigvee_{x \in M}$ [x plays tennis well], where M is the set of men in question.   Thus *similar in that* can be viewed as an operation performed on a set and a propositional function.   *Similar* when used without *in that S* appears to be identical in meaning to *similar in that S* except that the respect in which the items are similar is not expressed.   This will correspond in some cases to the semantic representation having a 'pro-propositional function' in place of the S of *similar in that S*; however, I conjecture that a sentence such as 'John is a fool; Max is similar' should be derived from a structure paraphrasable as 'John is a fool; Max and John are similar in that they are fools' and that *similar* results through ellipsis from *similar in that S*. Note that in this sentence the similarity must be interpreted as relating to their both being fools rather than, say, to their both having mustaches.   One important problem about *similar* is that of specifying what propositional functions may combine with it; it is odd to say

(83)   John and Harry are similar in that I met their respective sisters on a primenumbered day of the month.

This problem appears to be identical to that of specifying when a sentence can be said to express a property of a particular thing mentioned in it.

conjunct movement transformation could perfectly well be made contingent on that difference rather than on the presence of a deep, rather than a derived, conjoined subject. Since there is good reason why (72) may not be derived from a conjoined sentence and no reason for the deep structure of (72) to differ in shape from that of (70), I propose that in both cases the deep structure is a simple sentence with a conjoined subject and thus that no rule of conjunction reduction is needed to derive either conjoined noun phrase.

The evidence which has been adduced for saying that (70) is derived by the conjoining of two sentences is rather slight, namely, the facts that conjuncts have the same selectional restrictions as do simple constituents and that sentences such as (70) are paraphrasable by sentences such as (71). These two facts are just as easily explainable under my proposal. Let x_1 be the index of *John* and x_2 the index of *Harry* in the sentence ' John and Harry are erudite '. Then *John and Harry* has for its index their union, that is $\{x_1, x_2\}$. By exactly the same semantic projection rule which gave the semantic representation of ' Those men are erudite ', ' John and Harry are erudite ' will receive the semantic representation $\bigvee_{x \in \{x_1 x_2\}}$ [erudite x]. If semantic representations are assumed to be subject to the principle of symbolic logic that a universal quantifier over a finite set is equivalent[n] to the conjunction of the formulas obtained by substituting each of the members of that set,[11] this formula will be equivalent to ' erudite(x_1) $\wedge$ erudite(x_2) '. But that is simply the semantic representation of ' John is erudite and Harry is erudite ', which explains why it is a paraphrase of ' John and Harry are erudite '. If my earlier conclusion that selection is based on the semantic representations of the relevant constituents is accepted, then this also explains why the conjuncts in a sentence such as (70) have the same selectional restrictions as a simple subject, as in ' John is erudite '. Note also that conjuncts are all subject to the same selectional restrictions, even in cases like (72) or (73) where the sentence cannot be derived from conjoined simple sentences.

Consider now another class of sentences which has been proposed as an argument for deriving some conjoined noun phrases from conjoined sentences, namely sentences such as

(84) John and Harry went to Cleveland.

This sentence is ambiguous, allowing the two paraphrases

(85) John and Harry each went to Cleveland.
(86) John and Harry went to Cleveland together.

The former reading of (84) could plausibly be assigned the deep structure of a conjoined sentence and the latter of a simple sentence with conjoined subject.

---

[11] Russell (1920) points out that this principle, strictly speaking, is not correct: ' The apostles all had beards ' is not equivalent to ' Peter had a beard, and John had a beard, and . . . , and Judas Iscariot had a beard ', since the former cannot be deduced from the latter without the additional information that that is all the apostles there are. However, that observation does not affect the argument here, since the condition that ' that's all there are ' holds by definition if the set is defined by enumerating its elements.

However, there is a strong argument against that proposal, namely the fact that sentences such as

(87)   Those men went to Cleveland.

have exactly the same ambiguity as (84), and the Lakoff-Peters proposal allows no obvious way of letting the two readings of (87) differ in a fashion parallel to the two readings of (84). The only way I know of assigning deep structures to these sentences in such a way as to make the ambiguity of (87) parallel to that of (84) is to subcategorize noun phrases which have set indices into two types, which I will call joint and nonjoint. Joint noun phrases allow adjuncts such as *together ;* nonjoint noun phrases allow adjuncts such as *each.* Attached to each set index in deep structure will be a specification of [+joint] or [−joint].° Some verbs allow only a nonjoint subject, for example, *erudite :* some allow either a joint or a nonjoint subject, for example, *go ;* and some allow only a joint subject, for example, *similar.* Semantically, the distinction between joint and nonjoint relates to the order to quantifiers. In the one reading (joint) of (87), the meaning is that there was an event of ' going to Cleveland ' in which each of the men participated ; in the other reading (nonjoint), the meaning is that for each man there was an event of ' going to Cleveland ' in which he participated ; symbolized very roughly,

$$\text{Joint:} \quad \underset{y}{\exists} \; \underset{x \in M}{\forall} \text{ ' go to Cleveland ' } (x, y)$$

$$\text{Nonjoint:} \quad \underset{x \in M}{\forall} \; \underset{y_x}{\exists} \text{ ' go to Cleveland ' } (x, y_x)$$

The notion of joint and nonjoint is involved in the problem of the semantic interpretation of the sentence

(88)   These men and those boys are similar.

or alternatively,

(89)   These men are similar to those boys.

In the deep structure which I have proposed for this type of sentence, a noun-phrase node would dominate two noun-phrase nodes which had the indices A of *these men* and B of *those boys*, respectively :

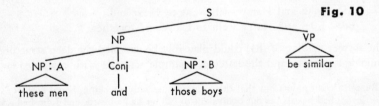

Fig. 10

This ought to mean that the whole subject has index $A \cup B$ and that the meaning of (88) and (89) is that the property *similar* applies to the set $A \cup B$. However, that is incorrect, since ' similar $(A \cup B)$ ' means that the men are similar not only to the boys but also to each other, which is in fact not part of the meaning of (88).   What is going on here is that, as mentioned in the last paragraph, the quantifier corresponding to a nonjoint NP takes the ' outside ' position in the semantic representation.   The meaning of (88) is actually that ' similar ($\{x_1,$ $x_2\}$) ' is true, where x_1 ranges over A and x_2 over B.   This example shows English to have at least two kinds of universal quantifier: if $\forall$ is interpreted as in symbolic logic, then ' $\underset{x_1 \epsilon A}{\forall} \underset{x_2 \epsilon B}{\forall}$ similar ($\{x_1,\ x_2\}$) ' would represent not the meaning of (88) but that of

(90)   Every one of the men is similar to every one of the boys.

The meaning of (88) involves two ' universal quantifiers ' whose combination implies not that the predicate holds of all pairs of an element of A and an element of B but rather that the pairs of elements for which the relation holds exhaust or almost exhaust A and B.   I will call this quantifier the ' set exhaustion quantifier ' and write ' $\underset{x \epsilon_1 A}{X} \underset{x_2 \epsilon B}{X}$ similar ($x_1,\ x_2$) ' to symbolize the meaning of (88).[p]   The set exhaustion quantifier is also involved in such sentences as

(91)   The men courted the women.

which does not imply that every man courted every woman but rather that every (or almost every) man courted one or more women and that every (or almost every) woman was courted by at least one man.

Recall my assertion that *similar* requires a [+joint] subject.   All apparent counterexamples to this restriction appear to arise through ellipsis from a deep structure with a [+joint] subject, for example,

(92)   John is stupid and Bill and Harry are similar.

Here *similar* has a nonjoint surface subject, but the clause arises through ellipsis from ' Bill and Harry are similar to John ', which has a deep structure in which *Bill and Harry* is not the whole subject but merely one conjunct of the [+joint] noun phrase *Bill and Harry and John*:

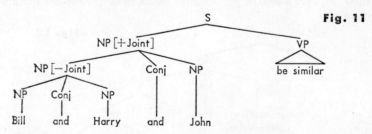

Fig. 11

A consideration of the restriction that *similar* have a [+joint] subject provides the death blow to the theory which derives conjoined noun phrases from conjoined sentences by a conjunction reduction transformation.   According to that theory it ought to be possible to reduce the conjoined sentence

(93)   These men are similar and those boys are similar.

into (88).   However, (88) in fact does not permit the paraphrase in (93), which
it ought to permit if conjunction reduction applied to conjoined sentences differing only in subject.   Thus there appears to be no non-ad-hoc way in which the
theory with conjunction reduction could prevent (88) from being analyzed as
having an ambiguity which it in fact does not have.

Another matter in which set operations and set relations play a role is person.
To discuss this topic it will be necessary for me first to summarize a recent proposal by John Robert Ross.[q]   Various descriptions of English have involved
elements such as a ' question formative ' which is to be present in the deep
structures of all questions and an ' imperative formative ' which is to be present
in the deep structures of all imperatives (Katz and Postal, 1964 ; Thorne, 1966).[r]
The meaning of these formatives can be paraphrased as ' the speaker asks the
person addressed whether . . .', ' the speaker asks that the person addressed
do . . .'.   They thus have the meaning of a verb with first person subject and
second person indirect object.   Ross proposes that these items indeed be analyzed as verbs and that the deep structures of not only questions and imperatives
but indeed all sentences have in their topmost S a first person subject, a second
person indirect object, and a verb of the type which J. L. Austin (1962) called
' performative verbs ' :   a verb that specifies the illocutionary force of the sentence it heads, that is, a verb that specifies the relationship the utterance mediates
between speaker and person spoken to.   Examples of overt performative verbs
are found in the sentences

(94)   I *promise* to give you ten dollars.   (This sentence is a promise by
       the speaker to the addressee)
(95)   I hereby *order* you to open the door.   (This sentence is an order
       by the speaker to the addressee)
(96)   I hereby *declare* that I will not pay this bill.   (This sentence is
       a declaration by the speaker to the addressee)

In Ross's proposal, all sentences which do not have an overt performative verb,
as these do, have a deleted performative which in deep structure appears in the
topmost S :

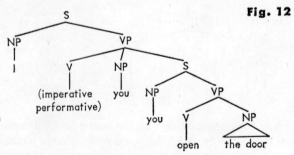

Fig. 12

Open the door!

There is a fairly large body of facts which support Ross's proposal. Consider first the fact that imperatives behave as if they had a subject, *you* (for example, NP's are reflexivized in imperatives if and only if they are in the second person: *wash yourself*, *wash himself, *wash you), and that that *you* is absent from the surface form of the sentence. If Ross's proposal is accepted, then these facts, rather than requiring ad hoc rules, as in all previous descriptions, become consequences of some very general mechanisms which the grammar must have anyway. Specifically, all verbs of ' ordering ' must be followed in deep structure by a noun phrase and an embedded sentence, and the subject of that sentence must be identical with the preceding noun phrase; furthermore, the equi-NP-deletion transformation of English deletes the subject of an embedded sentence if it is preceded by an identical noun phrase. These principles are needed to explain the syntax of sentences such as

(97) I ordered John to open the door.

Since the performative verb which Ross sets up in the deep structures of imperatives is a performative, its indirect object must be *you ;* since it is also a verb of ' ordering ', the subject of the embedded sentence must also be *you ;* and just as with other verbs of ' ordering ', the subject of the embedded sentence will be deleted by the equi-NP-deletion transformation. Thus the loss of the subject in imperatives is simply a special case of equi-NP-deletion and requires no special transformation. A second fact which supports Ross's analysis is the defective distribution exhibited by some of the overt performative verbs: certain verbs may appear as overt performatives when accompanied by the word *hereby* but not without it:

(98) I hereby tell you to open the door.
(99) *I tell you to open the door.
(100) I hereby ask you where you were last night.
(101) *I ask you where you were last night.
(102) I hereby tell you that Lyndon Johnson is an imperialist butcher.
(103) *I tell you that Lyndon Johnson is an imperialist butcher.

(there are of course also performatives which may appear without *hereby*, as in Sentence (94)). Moreover, with one exception which I will discuss below, for each of the deleted performatives that Ross's analysis demands, I have been able to find a verb that has this hole in its distribution. Temporarily leaving aside the one exception I mentioned, one could explain this hole in the pattern by proposing that the deleted performatives in Ross's analysis are not the abstract bundles of features he initially treated them as but, indeed, are real lexical items such as *tell* and *ask*, that the performative deletion rule is a minor rule which these items are marked as undergoing, and that that rule is formulated so as to apply when the sentence consists of subject, verb, indirect object, and embedded sentence (that is, the rule is inapplicable when there is any additional item such as *hereby*). Thus, (99), (101), and (103) correspond to deep structures which actually yield

(104) Open the door!
(105) Where were you last night?
(106) Lyndon Johnson is an imperialist butcher.

via the performative deletion transformation.   The exception to which I referred above is the performative verb which would be needed as the topmost
verb in 'echo questions' such as

(107) You saw *who?*

by Ross's analysis.   There is no lexical item overtly occurring in English which
has the above hole in its paradigm and which is synonymous with the echo-
question performative.   But there is no verb in English by which one can report
echo questions at all; that is, there is no verb such as **bnick* which could be used
in a sentence

(108) *John bnicked me what I beat my wife with.

which would be a report of John's having asked me the echo question

(109) You beat your wife with *what?*

Thus, this discrepancy from the correspondence noted above between deleted
performatives and overt performatives which may not appear alone does not
impair the above analysis; what it means is that the echo-question performative
is constrained so that it may only appear in the environment in which it will be
deleted.

    In Ross's analysis the deep structure of any sentence must have a performative
verb as its topmost verb and that verb must have *I* for its subject and *you* for its
indirect object.   Thus the person of the noun phrases in the topmost sentence
is predictable.   Accordingly, one could simply not specify these noun phrases
for person and have a rule which would add the specifications 'first person'
and 'second person' to them; that is, one could take the configurations 'subject of performative' and 'indirect object of performative' as *defining* the notions
'first person' and 'second person.'[12]   If this approach is adopted, then person
specifications need not appear in deep structures at all.   One undifferentiated
personal pronoun type will become specified for person on the basis of its index
and the indices of the subject and indirect object of the performative.   However,
the conditions for specifying a noun phrase as first or second person relate not
to identity of indices but rather to the subset relation between indices.   If the
index of the subject of the performative is contained in the index of a given noun
phrase, that noun phrase is marked 'first person'; then if the index of the
indirect object of the performative is contained in the index of a given noun
phrase which has not yet been specified for person, that noun phrase is marked
'second person'.   The effects of these rules can be seen in sentences such as

---

[12] This treatment is a generalization of an idea of Jakobson. Cf. Thorne's remark (1966 : 76)
' *You* is not a different pronoun from *he*, *she*, and *they* but a different form—the vocative
form—of them '.

(110)   You and I like our work.
(111)   You and John like your work.
(112)   John and Harry like their work.

where *our, your, their* correspond to indices containing respectively that of *I*, that of *you* but not *I*, and neither.

This treatment of person makes unnecessary some totally ad hoc restrictions on person which would otherwise be needed. Note what happens when an echo question corresponds to something with an overt performative and *hereby*. One may respond to the sentence ' I hereby order you to open the door ' with either of the echo questions

(113)   You hereby order me to do *what?*
(114)   *Who* hereby orders me to open the door?

Hereby appears in these questions with the subjects *you* and *who* but may not otherwise take such subjects:

(115)   *You hereby order me to open the door.
(116)   *Who hereby orders me to open the door?

The echo-question performative verb is unique in that the sentence embedded below it must be of the form which would correspond to the deep structure of a whole sentence, right down to the performative; this corresponds to the fact that what an echo question asks relates to the utterance which has just been produced rather than to its content. The noun phrase which is the subject of the clause containing *hereby* is marked for person by the above rules, and in the normal situation where one asks an echo question of the person who has supposedly just uttered the stimulus to it, it will be identical in index to the indirect object of the performative and thus will be marked ' second person ', thus yielding (113). Except in the case of echo questions it is impossible for the subject of a clause with *hereby* to meet the conditions for being labeled ' second person '. For another example, consider sentences such as

(117)   Shall I open the door?

This is to my knowledge the only type of question in English to which the appropriate answer is an imperative rather than a declarative sentence.[13]

(118)   Yes, open the door.
(119)   No, don't open the door.
(120)   *Yes, you shall open the door.

---

[13] The frequently encountered argument that imperatives must have an underlying auxiliary *will* because of ' tag imperatives ' such as ' Open the door, won't you ? ' is invalid, since the tag of the ' tag imperative ' is totally different in meaning from the tag of the tag question (while ' Mary is pretty, isn't she ? ' requests an answer such as ' Yes, she is ', the tag imperative does not request an answer such as ' Yes, open it ') and thus is probably the result of quite different rules. Further evidence for this conclusion is given in Bolinger (1967b).

Note that the question has a first person subject and the answer a (deleted) second person subject. In the case of a first person plural subject whose index includes the index corresponding to the hearer (that is, an inclusive first person plural), the answer is a first person plural imperative with *let's*:

(121) Shall we go to dinner now?
(122) Yes, let's go.
(123) No, let's not go yet.
(124) *Yes, we shall go.

These facts are explained if (117) and (121) are in fact analyzed as interrogated imperatives. A first person plural results in (121)–(123) since the noun phrase in question will have the index $\{x_1, x_2\}$, where x_1 and x_2 are the indices corresponding to the two persons involved. In (121) this noun phrase will be marked 'first person' because its index contains x_1, and in (122) and (123) it will be marked 'first person' because its index contains x_2. If *we* had been used in an exclusive sense in (121), that is, if the index of *we* there had included the index of the speaker but not that of the listener, the appropriate answers would have been

(125) Yes, please go.
(126) No, don't go yet.

since in the answer the index of the noun phrase in question would now contain the index corresponding to the person addressed but not that corresponding to the speaker. *Let's* requires an inclusive first person subject, as is shown by Lakoff's examples

(127) Let's you and me go to the movies.
(128) *Let's John and me go to the movies.

The Hungarian equivalent of 'Shall I go?' is *Menjek?*, that is, a first person singular imperative with question intonation; here an analysis as an interrogated imperative is unavoidable. The treatment of person proposed above again makes it unnecessary to state person restrictions that would otherwise be needed to exclude sentences such as *Menjek* (with declarative intonation). Note, however, that an uninterrogated first person singular imperative occurs in dependent imperative constructions such as

(129) *János azt mondta, hogy menjek.* 'John told me to go.'

Finally, there are a small number of examples (all to my knowledge obscene)[s] of idioms which require both an imperative and a reflexive.[14] These exhibit only a second person reflexive when used in independent sentences but are not restricted to second person in embedded imperatives such as 'I told John to ...'. The treatment of person which I propose makes it unnecessary to im-

[14] An idiom that has the surface appearance of belonging to this category but in fact does not belong to it is discussed in Quang (1966).

pose any person restriction on these idioms.   They are simply required to have a subject identical to the indirect object of the next higher sentence, and if the next higher sentence happens to be the topmost sentence, then the conditions for introducing the ' second person ' specification will always be met.

I will conclude by repeating the moral which I hinted at earlier, that a full account of English syntax requires a fairly full account of semantics to just as great an extent as the converse is true.   I think that the examples which I have presented here give considerable justification for this position and thus feel that it is high time for linguists to grant to semantics the status as an integral part of linguistics which has hitherto been denied it by most.

A Postscript (May, 1967)

Since writing the above paper, I have modified my thinking on certain points treated in it.   First of all, I now feel that the feature [joint] on NP's is merely a makeshift device which will have to be supplanted by several distinct theoretical devices in an adequate account of the phenomena discussed.   One of the devices which will supplant part of the function of this feature appeared implicitly in my discussion of the semantic representation of the different meanings of (87).   The y's which appear in those representations can be considered (following a proposal of Postal's) as indices of the verb:

$$\text{Joint:} \quad \underset{y}{\exists} \underset{x \epsilon M}{\forall} [x \text{ go}_y \text{ to Cleveland}]$$

$$\text{Nonjoint:} \quad \underset{x \epsilon M}{\forall} \underset{y_x}{\exists} [x \text{ go}_{y_x} \text{ to Cleveland}]$$

Ross has called to my attention the fact that the ' joint ' and ' nonjoint ' readings of sentences such as (84) and (87) behave differently with respect to the action nominalization:

(130)   John and Harry's departure for Cleveland (joint)
(131)   John's and Harry's departures for Cleveland (nonjoint)
(132)   The departures of John and of Harry for Cleveland (nonjoint)

The positing of verb indices explains the plurality of the nominalized verb: in the ' joint ' case the verb has the individual index y, whereas in the ' nonjoint ' case it has the set index $\{y_1, y_2\}$, where y_1 is the index corresponding to John's departure and y_2 that corresponding to Harry's departure.   Thus, not only noun phrases but also verbs allow a distinction between set index and individual index.   A set index on a verb is also involved in the adjuncts *twice, many times*, and so forth.   Note the examples

(133)   John denied the accusation five times.
(134)   John's five denials of the accusation
(135)   *John's denials of the accusation five times

Semantically, *five times* is identical to the *five* of *five horses:* it specifies that the cardinal number of a certain set is *five;* these examples suggest that *time* is an 'empty' morpheme which is inserted to support a numerical adjunct to an unnominalized verb.[15]

The plurality of the noun in (131) seems very like that of the noun in:

(141)   John and Harry love their wives.

Note that only in the case of a *ménage à trois* would it be appropriate to use the singular noun *wife*.   Moreover, the word *respective* may appear in (141) without any change of meaning:

(142)   John and Harry love their respective wives.

as well as in (131) and (132):

(143)   John's and Harry's respective departures for Cleveland
(144)   The respective departures of John and Harry for Cleveland

Since *respective* and *respectively* are identical in meaning and are in complementary distribution (*respective* appears only as an adjunct to a noun and *respectively* only as an adjunct to a larger constituent), one is forced to say that the same transformation which produces the sentence

(145)   John and Harry love Mary and Alice respectively.

is involved in the derivation of (142) and that (142) and (145) differ in deep structure only to the extent that where (142) has *John's wife* and *Harry's wife*, (145) has *Mary* and *Alice*.   I conclude from all these considerations that the 'nonjoint' sense of (84) must arise through the *respectively* transformation from

(146)   John go$_{y_1}$ to Cleveland and Harry go$_{y_2}$ to Cleveland.

and that the *respectively* transformation is thus responsible for the set index on *go* in that reading of (84).   However, here a problem arises: corresponding to all the examples discussed so far there are examples which involve not conjoined singular noun phrases but simple plural noun phrases:

(87)   Those men went to Cleveland.
(147)   Those men's respective departures for Cleveland

---

[15] It will be necessary to distinguish between different types of verb indices.   Note that *the many similarities between John and Harry* corresponds not to

(136)   * John and Harry are similar many times.

but to

(137)   John and Harry are similar in many ways.

There will be a different 'empty' morpheme corresponding to each type of verb index. Different index types may contrast with each other:

(138)   John criticized the book many times.
(139)   John criticized the book in many respects.

Both of these examples nominalize to

(140)   John's many criticisms of the book.

(148)   The respective departures of those men for Cleveland
(149)   Those men love their respective wives.

If *respective* is to arise through the *respectively* transformation, which I have hitherto assumed to apply to conjoined structures differing at two places, how is it to arise in examples such as these, which have no conjoined constituent in them? There are two possible solutions to this problem: one is to generalize the *respectively* transformation in some way and the other is to derive all plural noun phrases from underlying conjoined noun phrases. The latter, which has been proposed by Postal, seems attractive in view of the fact that there are already some plural noun phrases (for example, that of (58)) which must be derived from conjoined singular noun phrases. However, there are compelling reasons why this proposal must be rejected. First, for this proposal to yield deep structures which are suitable for correct semantic interpretation, the number of conjuncts underlying a plural noun phrase would have to equal the number of individuals being talked about (for example, ' The 63, 428 persons in Yankee Stadium' could not have merely two conjuncts underlying *persons*), but on the other hand one is not always talking about a definite number of individuals:

(150)   He has written approximately 50 books.
(151)   There were very few persons at the football game.
(152)   There were an enormous number of persons at my party.
(153)   How many times have you failed your French examination?

Moreover, one could not even represent these plural noun phrases as disjunctions of all the conjunctions which have a number of terms in the range specified by *approximately fifty*, and so on, because the range which these expressions denote may vary with what is being talked about (for example, *very few* in (151) may be 5000 and *an enormous number* in (152) may be fifty) and because there are cases in which an indefinite numeral may not be used but a definite numeral within the range denoted by the indefinite numeral may be :[t]

(154)   Those five men are Polish, Irish, Armenian, Italian, and Chinese, respectively.
(155)   *Those several men are Polish, Irish, Armenian, Italian, and Chinese, respectively.

Thus, in order to explain (141)–(149), it will be necessary to change the formulation of the *respectively* transformation so as to make it applicable to cases where there is no conjunction but there are plural noun phrases, or rather, noun phrases with set indices: *pluralia tantum* do not allow *respectively* unless they have a set index, e.g.

(156)   The scissors are respectively sharp and blunt.

can only be interpreted as a reference to two pairs of scissors and not to a single pair of scissors. The correct formulation of the *respectively* transformation must thus involve a set index. That, of course, is natural in view of the fact that the effect of the transformation is to 'distribute' a universal quantifier: the sentences involved can all be represented as involving a universal quantifier, and the result of the *respectively* transformation is something in which a reflex of the set over which the quantifier ranges appears in place of occurrences of the variable which was bound by that quantifier. For example, the semantic representation of (149) is something like $\bigvee_{x \epsilon M}$ [x loves x's wife], where M is the set of men in question, and (142) can be assigned the semantic representation[u] $\bigvee_{x \epsilon \{x_1, x_2\}}$ [x loves x's wife], where x_1 corresponds to *John* and x_2 to *Harry;* the resulting sentence has *those men* or *John and Harry* in place of one occurrence of the bound variable, and the corresponding pronominal form *they* in place of the other occurrence. Moreover, *wife* takes a plural form, since after the *respectively* transformation the noun phrase which it heads has for its index the set of all wives corresponding to any x in the set in question. The difference between (142) and (145) is that the function which appears in the formula that the quantifier in (142) binds is one which is part of the speaker's linguistic competence ($f(x)=x$'s wife), whereas that in (145) is one created ad hoc for the sentence in question ($f(x_1)=$Mary, $f(x_2)=$Alice).[v]

I conclude from these considerations that the class of representations which functions as input to the *respectively* transformation involves not merely set indices but also quantifiers and thus consists of what one would normally be more inclined to call semantic representations than syntactic representations.

We thus arrive at the second major point on which my views have changed since writing the preceding paper, namely, the status of deep structure as a level of linguistic description. In the paper, while quarreling with many of the details of the conception of a grammar presented in Chomsky (1965), I accepted its general outlines and, in particular, the hypothesis that the components of a grammar of a language include a base component, which specifies the membership of a class of potentially well-formed deep structures, a semantic component, which correlates deep structures with their semantic representations, and a transformational component, which correlates deep structures with their surface syntactic representations. Of the three levels of linguistic representation just alluded to, there is no question about the need of positing the existence of semantic and surface syntactic representation, which have indeed figured at least implicitly in virtually every system of linguistic description that has been conceived of. However, it is necessary to provide some justification for the hypothesis of an intermediate level (deep structure) between those two levels: there is no a priori reason why a grammar could not instead consist of, say, a 'formation-rule component', which specifies the membership of a class of well-formed semantic representations, and a 'transformational component', which consists of rules correlating semantic representations with surface syntactic representations in much the same fashion in which Chomsky's 'transformational component' correlates deep structures with surface syntactic representations. Moreover, the burden of proof in choosing between these two conceptions of linguistic competence rests with those who posit the existence of the extra level, just as in phonology the burden of proof rests with those who posit the existence of a ' phonemic ' level intermediate between lexical phonological representation (often called 'systematic phonemic' or 'morphophonemic' representation) and phonetic representation. Transformational grammarians have largely ignored the problem of providing such justification, much in the same way as phonemicists largely ignored the problem of providing justification for a phonemic level, and for similar reasons : just as phonemicists have largely treated phonemics as home ground and morphophonemics as *terra quasi incognita* and have rarely attempted to give a general account of the latter, the attempts being largely programmatic and anecdotal (for example, Chapter 14 of Harris, 1951), so also transformational grammarians have largely stuck to their home ground of syntax and thus have been in no position to take an overall view of the relationship between semantic and surface syntactic representation such as would be necessary to decide whether that relationship is decomposable into two component relationships which could be identified with a system of semantic projection rules and a system of syntactic transformations.

When Halle, Lees, and others took such an overall view of the relationship between lexical phonological representation and phonetic representation, they found unitary phenomena which could not be treated as unitary phenomena within a grammar having separate systems of 'morphophonemic' and 'allophonic' rules which met at a 'phonemic' level (for example, the voicing assimilation in Russian, whose effect is 'allophonic' in the case of [c, č, x] but 'morphophonemic' in the case of all other obstruents, and which thus would have to be treated in a grammar with a phonemic level as two separate rules of limited generality which belonged to separate components of the grammar); accordingly, the question must be asked whether similar phenomena will be found when an overall view of syntax and semantics is taken. I claim to have exhibited just such a phenomenon earlier in this postscript, namely the *respectively* transformation. It has in part the effect of specifying a relationship between a representation involving quantifiers and bound variables and a representation involving ordinary noun phrases, that is, the effect of what in Chomsky (1965) is called a semantic projection rule. However, as pointed out by Paul Postal (personal communication, May 8, 1967), it also subsumes much of what has been regarded as a syntactic transformation of conjunction reduction, for example, the derivation of (84) from a conjoined sentence. Postal points out that if the restriction of conjunction reduction to conjoined structures with only one difference were dropped, all conjunction reduction would be a special case of *respectively;* he observes that the difference between

(157)   That man loves Mary and Alice.
(158)   Those men love Mary and Alice respectively.

is simply whether two underlying occurrences of *that man* have the same index or different indices : both can be said to arise from an underlying structure of the form

(159)   That man loves Mary and that man loves Alice.

by the *respectively* transformation; in either case a conjoined subject *that man and that man* would arise and would be subject to the noun phrase collapsing rule; if the two occurrences of *that man* had the same index, the set-theoretic union of the indices would be simply the original index: $x_1 \cup x_1 = x_1$, and (157) would result. I accordingly conclude that *respectively* cannot be treated as a unitary phenomenon in a grammar with a level of deep structure and that that conception of grammar must thus be rejected in favor of the alternative suggested above, which was proposed in Lakoff and Ross (1967).

If this conclusion is accepted, then the syntactic and semantic components of the earlier theory will have to be replaced by a single system of rules which convert semantic representation through various intermediate stages into surface syntactic representation. An obvious question to raise at this point is whether this component would not in fact consist of two radically different kinds of rules, one defined on semantic representations and one defined on syntactic representations, rather than of a single homogeneous system of rules. To answer this question, it will be necessary to discuss the extent to which semantic representation and syntactic representation are different in their formal nature. At the Texas universals conference, Lakoff pointed out that there is much less difference between these supposedly different kinds of representation than has been hitherto assumed. He observes that there is an almost exact correspondence between the more basic syntactic categories and the primitive terms of symbolic logic and between the rules which he and Ross have proposed as base component universals and the formation rules for symbolic logic which various authors have proposed (for example, the ' relative clause rule ' NP → NP S corresponds to the rule that from a ' term ' x and a ' predicate ' f one may form the term $\{x: f(x)\}$, to be read ' the x's such that $f(x)$'). Moreover, semantic representations involve constituents which are grouped together by parentheses and thus can be represented by trees. Since the categories of the operations and operands which appear in symbolic logic (which I hypothesize to supply the basis for semantic representation) correspond to syntactic categories, semantic representations can be regarded as trees labeled with syntactic category symbols. Furthermore, there is nothing a priori to prevent one from treating semantic representation as involving a linear ordering of constituents. Much confusion in this regard has been created by the mistaken belief that things which are identical in meaning must have identical semantic representations. The notion ' identity of meaning ' can perfectly well be regarded as referring to an equivalence relation defined on semantic representations and two sentences said to be identical in meaning if their semantic representations are equivalent even if not identical. For example, the sentences

(160)   I spent the evening drinking and singing songs.
(161)   I spent the evening singing songs and drinking.

might be assigned semantic representations which differed in the order of two conjoined propositions but which would be equivalent by virtue of a principle[w] $p \wedge q \equiv q \wedge p$. Thus, semantic representations can perfectly well be regarded as ordered trees whose nodes are labeled by syntactic category symbols, so that the only formal difference between semantic and syntactic representations would be the type of constituents which appear as terminal nodes in the trees.   Thus, the system of rules which converts semantic representation into surface structure will be a system of rules which map ordered labeled trees onto ordered labeled trees, and among these rules will be not only the adjunctions, deletions, and permutations which are familiar from the theory of Chomsky (1965) but also ' lexical insertion ' transformations, which insert lexical items in place of portions of labeled trees.   However, ' lexical insertion ' transformations must be part of the machinery of a grammar even within the framework of the theory of Chomsky (1965), since such processes as pronominalization involve the insertion of lexical material under nodes which originally dominated other lexical material.   Moreover, some lexical insertions must take place extremely late in the grammar, as is shown by the following two examples.[x]   (1) The selection of the pronominal noun phrases *the former* and *the latter* cannot be made until after all transformations which move noun phrases have been carried out.   (2) If, after the selection of pronouns, two conjoined pronouns are identical in form, then noun-phrase collapsing must be performed and then a new pronoun selected (this fact was pointed out to me by John Robert Ross) :

(162)   He and she live in Boston and Toledo respectively.
(163)   *He and he live in Boston and Toledo respectively.
(164)   They live in Boston and Toledo respectively.

Chomsky (1965) in effect asserts that all lexical insertion takes place in the base component unless triggered by other transformations, as in the above examples. This view has been challenged in two ways : Gruber (1965) argues that related pairs such as *buy/sell* and *send/receive* arise through transformations which precede lexical insertion, and Lakoff and Ross (1967) argue that the insertion of many idioms takes place after various transformations have applied; in the one case it is argued that some transformations come earlier in the grammar than the theory of *Aspects* would allow, in the other case that some lexical insertion occurs later than it would allow.

One interesting consequence of the conception of grammar which I am advocating here is that it allows lexical items to be inserted in place of constituents which are created by transformations.   A great many transformations proposed in recent years can now be viewed as transformations which combine semantic constituents before lexical insertion, for example, the various nominalization transformations and the transformations forming derived causative and inchoative verbs (Lakoff, 1965).   The distinction between ' transformationally derived ' and ' lexical ', which many linguists have placed great importance on (see especially Chomsky, 1970), thus appears to be a false dichotomy.

[a] In saying that they are different, I was not saying that they have nothing to do with each other. The relation between them would have been clearer if I had paraphrased *sad₂* as 'evoking sad₁-ness', as I did in McCawley (1968e).

[b] It is not clear that this example implies more than just that different people may attach different meanings to *bachelor*: 'unmarried' for some people, but 'has no wife' for others.

[c] At the time I wrote this, I believed that such a rule was different from a transformation that would delete all but the X in 'causes one who wears it to feel X'; I now see no justification for such a belief. My statement that every adjective corresponding to a temperature range can be applied to garments in this way is false: *lukewarm* denotes a temperature range, but one cannot call a garment 'lukewarm'. I should have spoken of temperature sensations, not temperature ranges: water or food can be lukewarm, but a person cannot feel lukewarm (I am grateful to Alan S. Prince for this observation).

[d] Alan S. Prince has called it to my attention that this phenomenon is not restricted to articles of clothing: note

> This blanket isn't warm enough.
> The fire is warm.
> The breeze is cool.,

which refer to sensations that one experiences, not to the temperature of the object (the fire may be 300°C., which is hardly 'warm', and it makes no sense to speak of the temperature of a breeze). Prince also notes that the phenomenon covers a broader range of bodily sensations than just those of temperature:

> This sweater is itchy. (cf. I feel itchy)
> This bed is comfortable. (cf. I feel comfortable)

[e] Some possible counterexamples to this claim are discussed in Yuck (1970) and Kaye (1971). See Perlmutter (1972) for solid objections to my treatment of number here and later in this paper.

[f] This is actually not true. Embedded polite forms are found in e.g. the obsequious style of announcements by train conductors:

> O-wasuremono gozaimasen yoo ni go-tyuui kudasai. 'Please be sure that you don't leave anything behind'

[g] Note that *one* or its antecedent can perfectly well be the antecedent of a reflexive and thus must be supplied with an index:

> A tall Armenian kicked himself, and then a short one slapped himself.

Chomsky (1968: 220) objects to my statements in fn. 6 on the grounds that his conception of index would not force him to have any index on the object NP of *John has a blue hat*; however, the example just cited shows that Chomsky's treatment of indices would require that there be an index in such a NP, since otherwise the reflexives in

> John kicked himself.
> A tall Armenian kicked himself.

could not be derived the same way, which is absurd.

[h] I ignore the incongruity of tense in the two clauses of (48).

[i] See Kuroda (1970) for a valuable critique of the treatment of concord presented here.

[j] Throughout this discussion I have ignored mass nouns. Mass expressions have been incredibly neglected by logicians; there is as yet no satisfying account of quantification of mass expressions. While the treatment of Parsons (1970) has much to recommend it, I feel that his approach of considering all the ways of dividing a mass into discrete parts and applying ordinary quantification to sets of discrete parts of it has things backwards.

I would prefer an approach based on a notion of ' is a part of ' that was equally applicable to masses and to sets, with ordinary quantification being the special case in which the range is individuated.

k In this paper, I took no position as to whether (62) was in fact AMBIGUOUS between (63)–(66). What I showed below is that regardless of whether the NP's in the assumed conjoined source are specified as to their number, the treatment of indices proposed here predicts that the resulting NP will be plural. My position was that (62) is no more and no less ambiguous as to number than *My cousin and my neighbor hurt themselves* is as to gender (*My cousin hurt himself/herself and my neighbor hurt himself/herself*). My feeling is that they are not ambiguous, but I know of no test for ambiguity that is applicable here.

l This proposal is shown untenable in Quang (1969).

m Rather than $\bigvee_{x \in M}$ [x plays tennis well] ' for all x in M, x plays tennis well ', I should have written $\bigvee_{x : x \in M}$ [x plays tennis well] ' for all x such that x is in M, x plays tennis well ', so as to make the notation applicable to cases where there is no reference to a set, $\bigvee_{x : x \text{ is a man}}$ [x is mortal] ' all men are mortal '.

n When I wrote this, I was not very clear as to what I meant by ' equivalent '. Later (1970c), I stated explicitly that logical equivalence (two propositions are ' logically equivalent ' if either can be deduced from the other) is weaker than ' sameness of meaning ' and gave examples of linguistically distinct meanings that were logically equivalent, e.g. $\bigvee_x \bigvee_y f(x, y)$ and $\bigvee_y \bigvee_x f(x,y)$. As Lakoff pointed out at the conference where this paper was read, there is no obvious way to distinguish the ' rule of equivalence ' that I referred to here from the transformation of conjunction reduction that it was supposed to eliminate the need for. One major defect in this whole discussion is that I considered only examples as simple as (70). The proposals that I made in this paper give no clue as to how to derive sentences such as

John burned a Confederate flag and then was arrested by Officer Snopes.
Frank seems to know nothing and is easy to please.,

which contain conjuncts that presumably are created by transformations. A rule of conjunction reduction thus appears to remain necessary.

o When I wrote this, I had not yet come to appreciate how the promiscuous use of ' features ' in syntax impedes progress towards the understanding of anything. Fortunately, I had the good sense to reject this proposal (see the ' Postscript ' to this paper), thereby bringing myself closer to enlightenment.

p This notation is objectionable, since it suggests incorrectly that the formula has a constituent structure X (X (...)), as in the case of the formulas with ∀ above. I should rather have used a notation in which a single ' quantifier ' X binds any number of variables simultaneously.

q See now Ross (1970a), Sadock (1969), and Rutherford (1970).

r Katz and Postal (1964 : 149) in fact briefly considered the performative analysis : ' On the basis of [*Want to go. *Hope to be famous] plus the fact that there are no sentences like *I request that you want to go, *I request that you hope to be famous, a case can be made for deriving imperatives syntactically from sentences of the form *I Verb_{request} you that you will Main Verb* '. Although they point out some significant advantages of this proposal over their treatment with an ' imperative marker ', they drop it, saying merely that ' it certainly deserves further study '. This discrepancy between the arguments presented in Katz and Postal and the analyses adopted there suggests disagreement between its authors.

s I have since learned of non-obscene idioms of this type, e.g. *Keep your shirt on.*

t This fact, as far as I can see, is completely irrelevant.

u While the careful reader will have noted that what I said here constitutes rejection of my prior assumption that (142), etc. were derived from conjoined structures, I would have done well to make clearer that I was rejecting an old analysis for a new one.

ᵛ There are three major objections to this proposal : (i) it is not clear how it could be applied to cases where something other than NP's are conjoined (*Mutt and Jeff are tall and short respectively*), (ii) it is likewise not clear how it could be applied to cases where a conjunct is transformationally derived (see note *n* for examples), and (iii) it does not provide any way to get the conjuncts in the right order, e.g. to insure that (145) will contain *Mary and Alice* rather than *Alice and Mary* (remarkably, only Postal seems to have noticed this ; shame on all other linguists). Showing that *respective* and *respectively* are the same is much easier than all of this suggests : it suffices to consider examples in which there are more than two conjoined/plural constituents and *respective* cooccurs with *respectively* (see 1968b, in press *a*). As should be clear from (in press *a*), a really adequate treatment of *respective*(*ly*) requires a much better understanding of conjoining than I had when I wrote this paper or even than I have now, for that matter.

ʷ My choice of the symbol≡was unfortunate, since it is used for ' if and only if ', which was not what I meant. Cf. fn. *n*.

ˣ These two examples in fact prove nothing, since the phenomena described could perfectly well be accounted for by an output constraint regardless of where the lexical insertions involved take place.

5. Meaning and the Description of Languages*

1 What is Meaning?

A language is a system which correlates meanings with sounds. To describe a language is thus to describe the way in which meanings are correlated with sounds in that language. A quick glance at a sample of the descriptions of languages which are available in print should make it clear to anyone that no one has as yet really succeeded in describing a language. There are many brilliant and insightful descriptions of portions of languages; for example, many languages have been described with great insight from the point of view of phonology (i.e. of the processes whereby the pronunciation of the words and morphemes of the language is adjusted in accordance with the shape of the surrounding words or morphemes and the way in which those processes interact), for a large number of languages linguists have formulated valuable generalizations about the ways in which words may be combined into sentences, and there have been a fair

* This paper was originally published in *Kotoba no Uchū*, vol. 2, nos. 9 (10–18), 10 (38–48), and 11 (51–57). It is to my knowledge the first work published (though not the first one written) in which anyone argued for abolishing the distinction between syntax and semantics in transformational grammar. It is thanks to the speed with which Japanese printers and publishers work that Japan is the first country in which this idea was given wide publicity.

number of interesting studies of the similarities and differences in meaning of selected words in a language.   However, even in the case of a language such as English, which has been the subject of valuable and compendious studies by a large number of outstanding scholars, the published work still does not add up to anything approaching an adequate description of the way in which English correlates meanings with sounds.

One of the chief reasons for this lack of success is the fact that linguists are only beginning to understand how meanings can be described.   While one can describe the sounds of languages by making up a list of the ways in which sounds may resemble or differ from each other and describing each sound by listing the properties on this list which it possesses (this is in essence the principle behind the International Phonetic Alphabet, which was constructed by listing the various ' places of articulation ', ' manners of articulation ', and ' secondary articulations ' which had been observed in various languages and creating an alphabetic symbol for each possible combination of such properties), such an approach is insufficient for the description of meaning, since the meaning of an utterance has a far more complex structure than the sound of an utterance does.   The sound of an utterance can be regarded as simply a sequence of unit sounds and each of those sounds represented by a symbol such as an IPA letter ; while in fact acoustically and articulatorily these ' unit sounds ' are not separate but overlap considerably, a representation as a sequence of symbols is perfectly adequate to represent the sound of an utterance for the purpose of the description of a language.   However, the meaning of an utterance can in no sense be regarded as a sequence of ' unit meanings '.   Many persons naively assume that since a sentence can be regarded as a sequence of words, its meaning is simply a sequence of meanings, namely the meanings of those words.   However, the relation of the meaning of a sentence to its superficial form is in fact much more complicated. For example, to understand the English sentence

(1)   John isn't rich, but he's handsome.

one must not only know the meaning of the element *n't* but must also know that it applies to ' John is rich ': the speaker is denying the proposition ' John is rich ' but is not denying the proposition ' John is rich but he's handsome '.   On the other hand, the sentence

(2)   John doesn't beat his wife because he loves her.

is ambiguous: *n't* may apply either to ' John beats his wife ' (in this case the sentence asserts that John does not beat his wife and states the reason for his not beating her is that he loves her) or it may apply to ' John beats his wife because he loves her ' (in this case the sentence assumes that John beats his wife but states that the reason why he beats her is not that he loves her).   To understand the sentence

(3)   I don't think that John will arrive until Saturday.

one must know that *n't* does not apply to ' *I think that John will arrive until

Saturday ', which is not even a possible sentence of English, but that the sentence has the same meaning as ' I think that John won't arrive until Saturday ' and must know that the combination *n't . . . until Saturday* means ' on Saturday but not before Saturday '.   The sentence

(4)   Harry called Arthur a goddam communist.

is ambiguous : it may mean either that Harry used the term *goddam communist* to refer to Arthur, which implies that Harry strongly dislikes communists, or it may mean that Harry used the term *communist* to refer to Arthur and that the speaker either strongly dislikes communists or is surprised that Harry called Arthur a communist ; in the second meaning the sentence has no implication regarding Harry's feelings towards communists.

These facts imply that to describe a meaning it is necessary not only to list ' unit meanings ' which are involved in it but also to indicate how various ' unit meanings ' are grouped together into more complex meanings, e.g. to show that the meaning of ' John isn't rich ' is a combination of the meaning of *n't* and the meaning of *John is rich*.   Moreover, these facts imply that the meaning of a sentence may involve items which do not appear in the superficial form of the sentence.   For example, the second meaning of (4) has to do with the speaker of the sentence, even though no word such as *I* or *me* appears in the sentence.

2.   Levels of Linguistic Representation

So far I have referred to three ways in which an utterance may be viewed : as meaning, as sound, and as what I referred to as ' superficial form '.   If these three ways of viewing an utterance play a role in linguistic description, then there must be three corresponding ways of representing each utterance : semantic representation, phonetic representation, and ' surface syntactic representation '. Above I spoke as if surface syntactic representation were merely a representation of the utterance as a sequence of morphemes or words.   However, it will prove necessary to regard this mode of representation as also indicating the way in

(5)

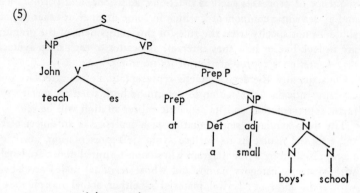

John teaches at a small boys' school.

which these elements are grouped together into larger units and the syntactic categories to which these units belong, since both the grouping of elements and the categories affect how the utterance is pronounced. For example, *small boys' school* is pronounced with a relatively heavy stress on *small* if *boys'* and *school* are grouped together as a unit (with that pronunciation the expression means " small school for boys ") but is pronounced with a relatively weak stress on *small* if *small* and *boys'* are grouped together as a unit (with this pronunciation the expression means " school for small boys "). The surface syntactic representation of a sentence may thus be considered to take the form of a tree diagram such as (5).

The lines in such a diagram represent the way in which smaller units are grouped into larger units; the labels indicate the categories to which the various units belong. Earlier I described phonetic representation in terms which, while highly imprecise, will suffice for the purposes of this paper. The nature of semantic representation is the principal topic of this paper; later in this paper I will make various concrete proposals concerning it, although these proposals will still fall far short of a complete theory of semantic representation.

These three " levels of representation " figure at least implicitly in virtually all descriptions of language which have been published. The version of transformational grammar presented in Chomsky's *Aspects of the Theory of Syntax* (henceforth, *Aspects*) introduces a fourth ' level of representation ', the so-called ' deep syntactic representation ' or ' deep structure '. Chomsky's views, as presented in that work, may be summarized as follows:

1. A description of a language must specify what surface syntactic representations are possible and what semantic representation(s) is (are) correlated with each surface syntactic representation.

2. A language involves mechanisms corresponding to three systems of rules: a ' base component ', which specifies what deep syntactic representations are possible in that language[a], a ' transformational component ', which associates each deep syntactic representation with the corresponding surface syntactic representation(s) by subjecting it to a sequence of processes such as deletions, additions, and permutations, and a ' semantic component ', which in some manner or other (Chomsky does not specify what the rules of this component of the grammar are to look like or how they interact) associates to each deep syntactic representation a representation of its meaning.

3. Consequently, the deep syntactic representation of an utterance must contain sufficient information to determine both what its surface syntactic representation and its semantic representation will be.

4. The deep syntactic representation of a sentence is an object of the same formal nature as its surface syntactic representation, i.e. it can be represented by a tree diagram whose non-terminal nodes are labeled with syntactic category names and whose terminal nodes are labeled with some kind of ' lexical material ': either actual morphemes or abstract complexes of information which play a role in determining

the superficial form of the sentence (e.g. in his discussion of German in *Aspects*, Chomsky proposes deep structures in which there are terminal nodes labeled 'genitive case', 'plural number', 'feminine gender', even though these never occur separately in the superficial form of a sentence but only in items such as a single 'genitive feminine plural' ending). The many intermediate stages involved in the conversion of deep syntactic representation into surface syntactic representation are naturally also of this same formal type.

3. Concerning the Status of 'Deep Structure'

Since the publication of *Aspects*, numerous scholars have been studying the syntax of several languages, especially English, within the framework of the four assumptions listed above. The more that these studies have advanced, the deeper that deep syntactic representations have become: virtually every advance achieved within this framework has required the setting up of deep structures which are further removed from the superficial form of sentences than had previously been thought to be necessary. For example, George Lakoff (1965) has argued that

(6) John opened the door.

is not a simple sentence, as had been previously assumed, but indeed involves two embedded sentences, specifically, that it must be derived from a structure which (neglecting the tense of the verb) has the form

(7)

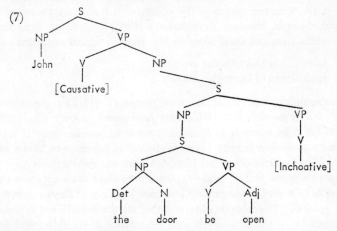

In this structure, [Inchoative] is an abstract element which combines with adjectives to form 'verbs of change' such as are found in

(8) Mary's face reddened. (=Mary's face became red)
(9) The metal hardened. (=The metal became hard)

[Causative] is an abstract element which combines with verbs of change to form

' verbs of causation ', as in

(10)   The physicist hardened the metal.   (=The physicist caused the metal to harden)

(11)   John stopped the car.   (=John caused the car to stop)

Lakoff notes that when a verb of change or causation corresponds to an adjective which has a comparative degree (not all adjectives have a comparative degree; for example, one cannot say *Arthur is more male than Fred), the verb is ambiguous between positive and comparative degree.   Thus, *The metal hardened* may mean either ' The metal became hard ' or ' The metal became harder '; *The physicist hardened the metal* may mean either ' The physicist caused the metal to become hard ' or ' The physicist caused the metal to become harder '.   If these alternative meanings are to correspond to different deep structures (as required by point 3 above), it is necessary to set up a deep structure containing an adjective which may be in the positive degree for the one meaning and the comparative degree for the other meaning.   An especially compelling argument which Lakoff has discovered for this analysis is the possibility of saying

(12)   The physicist finally hardened the metal, but it took him six months to bring it about.

Without an analysis such as Lakoff's it is difficult to see how the second *it* could be explained: neither of the two noun-phrases which occur in the superficial form of ' The physicist hardened the metal ' could possibly be the antecedent of that *it*.   However, Lakoff's analysis provides an antecedent for the *it*: the antecedent is the sentence which is the object of the abstract causative verb. For a second example, consider Rosenbaum's (1965) analysis of verbs such as *seem*.   The verbs *seem* and *want* occur in superficially similar sentences such as

(13)   John seems to know the answer.

(14)   John wants to know the answer.

However, *seem* differs from *want* in many respects: (1) The question *What does John want?* is possible but *What does John seem?* is not; (2) The ' cleft sentence ' *What John wants is to know the answer* is possible but *What John seems is to know the answer* is not; (3) *want* allows the infinitive to have a subject (*John wants Harry to win the prize*) but *seem* does not (one cannot say *John seems Harry to win the prize*); and (4) *seem* allows *there* as its apparent subject (*There seems to be a man in the garden*) but *want* does not (*There wants to be a man in the garden*).   Rosenbaum observed that all these facts are explained if *want* is regarded as a transitive verb with a sentence as its object and *seem* as an intransitive verb with a sentence as its subject in deep structure: see (15) and (16) on the next page.

The superficial form of the first sentence is derived by a transformation which deletes the subject of the embedded sentence if it is identical to the subject of *want;* the superficial form of the second sentence is derived by a transformation which puts the verb-phrase of the embedded sentence after *seem*.

(15)

```
              S
           /     \
        NP         VP
         |        /   \
       John     V      NP
                |        \
              want        S
                        /    \
                      NP      NP
                       |     /   \
                     John   V     NP
                            |    /   \
                          know  Det   N
                                 |    |
                                the  answer
```

(16)

```
                    S
                 /     \
              NP         VP
               |          |
               S          V
            /     \       |
          NP      VP     seem
           |     /   \
         John   V     NP
                |    /   \
              know  Det   N
                     |    |
                    the  answer
```

John wants to know the answer.   *John seems to know the answer.*

In many other cases besides these, scholars working within the framework of *Aspects* have found it necessary to set up deep structures which are much further removed from the superficial form of sentences than are the structures postulated in *Aspects*. These structures not only are further removed from the superficial form of the sentences but are also much more similar to the semantic structures of the sentences in question. For example, *John opened the door* does indeed mean that John caused the door to become open, and *John seems to know the answer* does indeed mean that *John knows the answer* seems to be true.

Since the introduction of the notion 'deep structure' by Chomsky, virtually every 'deep structure' which has been postulated (excluding those which have been demonstrated simply to be wrong) has turned out not really to be a deep structure but to have underlying it a more abstract structure which could more appropriately be called the 'deep structure' of the sentence in question. This fact raises the question of whether there indeed is such a thing as 'deep structure'. As an alternative to Chomsky's conception of linguistic structure, one could propose that in each language there is simply a single system of processes which convert the semantic representation of eacn sentence into its surface syntactic representation and that none of the intermediate stages in the conversion of semantic representation into surface syntactic representation is entitled to any special status such as that which Chomsky ascribes to 'deep structure'. To decide whether Chomsky's conception of language or a conception without a level of deep structure is correct, it is necessary to determine at least in rough outlines what semantic representations must consist of, and on the basis of that knowledge to answer the following two questions, which are crucial for the choice between these two conceptions of language. (1) Are semantic representations objects of a fundamentally different nature than syntactic representations or can syntactic and semantic representations more fruitfully be considered to be basically objects of the same type? (2) Does the relationship between semantic representation and surface syntactic representation involve processes which are of two fundamentally different types and are organized into two separate systems, corresponding to what Chomsky called 'transformations' and 'semantic interpretation rules', or is there in fact no such division of the processes which link the meaning of an utterance with its superficial form?

Later in this paper, I will give reasons for believing that semantic representation and syntactic representation are of essentially the same formal nature and that the meanings of utterances are related to their superficial forms by a single system of transformations of essentially the same type which figure in the syntactic theory of *Aspects*. However, in order to arrive at these conclusions, it will be necessary for me first to say something about a system of representation which I maintain will provide the general framework for the representation of meaning, namely that which appears in certain varieties of symbolic logic.

4. Symbolic Logic and the Representation of Meaning

Symbolic logic developed in the latter half of the 19th century, chiefly through the efforts of mathematicians who were interested in the logical foundations of mathematics and for this purpose wished to have a system for representing the content of propositions and for expressing relations between the content of different propositions. Since these mathematicians were interested almost exclusively in propositions of mathematics and were generally extremely naive in their beliefs about everyday uses of language, publications on symbolic logic have largely ignored ordinary uses of language and have generally given a hopelessly inadequate treatment to the small part of everyday language which they have treated.[1] As a result of this, linguists have generally dismissed symbolic logic as being of little relevance to the study of natural languages. However, rather than simply dismissing symbolic logic outright, linguists would do well to examine the question of whether the notational systems of symbolic logic are inherently incapable of representing meanings adequately or whether the failure of attempts to express meaning in terms of them is due only to the investigators' naiveté and ignorance about natural languages. I will argue below that logicians' formal representations of 'logical structure', if enriched to allow the formal expression of certain linguistic devices which have been ignored in symbolic logic due to the fact that they play no role in propositions of mathematics, form a perfectly adequate general framework for the representation of meaning.

The following types of units have figured in symbolic logic:

(i) the propositional connectives $\wedge$ 'and', $\vee$ 'or', and $\neg$ 'not'. If p and q are two[b] propositions, then $p \wedge q$ is the proposition that p and q are both true, $p \vee q$ is the proposition that at least one of p and q is true, and $\neg p$ is the proposition that p is false.

[1] A notable exception is Reichenbach (1947), which can be recommended highly to linguists interested in symbolic logic, even though its account of meaning is far from satisfactory. I apologize for the profusion of symbolic logic formulas on the next few pages, which have a somewhat formidable appearance; however, I know of no other way of representing the meanings in question.

(ii) individual constant symbols, which denote specific individuals (I will use lower-case letters with subscripts, e.g. x_1, x_9, a_{17} to represent individual constants).

(iii) predicates, which denote properties and relationships (I will use symbols such as $f(x)$, $g(x, y)$, etc. to represent predicates).

(iv) set symbols and the 'quantifiers' $\forall$ ('for all') and $\exists$ ('there exists'); $\underset{x \in M}{\forall} f(x)$ means that the property f is possessed by all members of the set M, e.g. if A is the set of all Americans, then $\underset{x \in A}{\forall}$ (x is rich) is the proposition that all Americans are rich. $\underset{x \in M}{\exists} f(x)$ means that there is at least one member of the set M which has the property f; for example $\underset{x \in A}{\exists}$ (x is rich) is the proposition that at least one American is rich.

(v) descriptions of sets and individuals. $\{x : f(x)\}$ means the set of all things which possess the property f, e.g. $\{x : x$ is an American $\wedge x$ dislikes Lyndon Johnson$\}$ is the set of all Americans who dislike Lyndon Johnson; (ιx) (x murdered Abraham Lincoln) is used to represent 'the individual who murdered Abraham Lincoln'. $\{x : f(x)\}$ and $(\iota x)f(x)$ are really instances of the same thing: (ιx) is appropriate only in the case where exactly one individual possesses the property f, but just like $\{x : f(x)\}$ it indicates 'that which possesses the property f'. In addition, sets can be described by enumerating their members: $\{x_1, x_2, x_3\}$ denotes the set which has the members x_1, x_2, x_3 and no others.

Analogues of all of these devices play an important role in natural languages:

(i) To my knowledge, all languages have ways of expressing the meanings of $\wedge$, $\vee$, and $\neg$, although it is important to note that in many languages the words used are more general than $\wedge$, $\vee$, and $\neg$. For example, the English word *and* may join not only propositions but indeed virtually any kind of items.

(ii) Since processes such as pronominalization and the deletion that takes place in *John wants to know the answer* are contingent not only on two noun phrases containing the same words but on their purporting to refer to the same thing, it is necessary to regard each noun phrase as having a label attached to it corresponding to its 'purported referent'. Such labels, which Chomsky introduced in *Aspects* under the name 'indices', include both individual constants and set constants.

(iii) Predicates are expressed in natural languages by nouns, verbs, and adjectives: *enemy*, *jealous*, and *envy* in

(17) John is Greg's enemy.
(18) John is jealous of Greg.
(19) John envies Greg.

all express relationships between the individuals being referred to as *John* and *Greg*.

(iv)   Words such as *all* and expressions such as *at least one* are two members of a rather large class of expressions which are used to indicate not only the existence of an individual or a set but the absolute or relative number of members in that set, as in

(20)   *A substantial fraction* of my friends are linguists.
(21)   *Most* Americans watch television.

(v)   Set and individual descriptions can be expressed in natural languages by noun phrases involving relative clauses.   Set-description by enumerating the elements of the set is accomplished by the use of conjoined noun phrases, as in

(22)   John, Tom, and Bill are similar.

There are many differences in meaning which appear to be expressible only in terms of these devices.   For example, the sentence

(23)   Those men saw themselves in the mirror.

is ambiguous between the senses (a) each of the men saw himself in the mirror, (b) the entire group of men saw the entire group in the mirror.   It is difficult to imagine how these two meanings could be assigned different deep structures unless those deep structures contained something equivalent to the quantifiers which differ in the two meanings: (a) $\overset{\forall}{x\in M}$ (x saw x), (b) $\overset{\forall}{x\in M}\overset{\forall}{y\in M}$ (x saw y) ; or rather, using subscripts on verbs to represent events describable by those verbs,

(24)   a. $\overset{\forall}{x\in M}\overset{\exists}{y(x)}$ (x see$_{y(x)}$ x in the mirror) (i.e. for each man there was an event in which he saw himself in the mirror),

   b. $\overset{\exists}{y}\overset{\forall}{x\in M}\overset{\forall}{z\in M}$ (x see$_y$ z in the mirror) (i.e. there was a single event in which each of the men saw all of the men in the mirror).

There are several published descriptions of pronominalization within the framework of transformational grammar (Lees and Klima 1963, Ross 1967, Langacker 1969), all of which derive personal and reflexive pronouns from full noun phrases which are identical to other noun phrases (e.g. *John loves himself* is derived from a deep structure having two occurrences of *John*, one as the subject of *love* and one as its object).   However, such an analysis is impossible here, since if *themselves* is derived from an underlying repetition of *those men*, there is no way in which the deep structures of the two meanings of (23) could differ from each other.   The same is also true of the deletion discussed above in connection with the sentence *John wants to know the answer*.

One cannot say that

(25)   Everyone wants to get rich

arises from the deletion of *everyone*, since it is possible to say

(26) Everyone wants everyone to get rich,

which is very different in meaning from (25). The absence of a subject of the embedded sentence is determined not by whether the embedded sentence has as its subject a noun phrase identical to that which is the subject of *want;* it rather depends on a property of the semantic representation of the sentence, namely whether in that representation the index corresponding to the subject of the embedded sentence is the same as the index corresponding to the subject of *want*: the meaning of (25) can be represented roughly as $\bigvee_{x \in A}$ [*x* wants (*x* get rich)] and the meaning of (26)^c as $\bigvee_{x \in A}$ [*x* wants ($\bigvee_{y \in A}$ *y* get rich)], where A is the set of all human beings. These examples make it clear that if things with different meanings are to have different deep structures, the deep structures will have to contain something corresponding to quantifiers and those quantifiers will have to be allowed to occur at a different place in the deep structure from the index which they govern.

In addition, there are syntactic transformations which appear to be stateable only in terms of a symbolic-logic-type representation. Consider, for example, the deletion transformation which gives rise to sentences such as

(27) John knows Mary and so do I.

If this transformation deletes one of two identical constituents, it must be sensitive to not only the words that appear but also their purported reference: (27) says not merely that each of us knows a person named Mary but that we know *the same* Mary. However, the sentence

(28) John loves his wife and so does Bill.

is ambiguous: *so does Bill* may mean either that Bill loves his own wife or that he loves John's wife. Similarly,

(29) John voted for himself and so did Frank.

may mean either that Frank voted for himself or that he voted for John. In these examples, the deletion may take place even though corresponding noun phrases in the two ' identical ' pieces do not have the same purported reference. The only way I know of stating this transformation correctly is to say that it may take place only in a structure whose semantic representation is of the form $f(x_1) \wedge f(x_2)$. The sentences in which the deletion produces an ambiguity are then those in which the first conjunct is a clause that can be divided into ' thing ' and ' property ' in more than one way. For example, *John loves his wife* and *John voted for himself* can be interpreted as a property of x_1 (the index of *John*) in two ways. Let $g(x)$ mean ' *x* loves *x*'s wife ' and Let $h(x)$ mean ' *x* loves x_1's wife '. Then the meaning of *John loves his wife and Bill loves his (own) wife too* can be represented as $g(x_1) \wedge g(x_2)$, where x_2 is the index of *Bill*, and the meaning of *John loves his wife and Bill loves her too* can be represented as $h(x_1) \wedge h(x_2)$. Since both of these meanings meet the condition given above, both are subject to the deletion transformation, and both yield *John loves his wife and so does Bill.* (29) works exactly the same way.

I thus conclude that all of the units and categories of symbolic logic play important roles both in the representation of meaning in natural languages and the formulation of syntactic transformations.   However, are the units and categories of symbolic logic sufficient for these purposes?   To be sufficient for the representation of meaning in natural languages, certain devices will have to be added to the normal repertoire of symbolic logic, specifically,

(1)   It is necessary to admit predicates which assert properties not only of individuals but also of sets and propositions.   Actually, $\wedge$, $\vee$, and $\neg$ are predicates of that type: $\neg$ is the property that the proposition to which it is applied is false, $\wedge$ is the property that the two propositions to which it is applied are both true, and $\vee$ is the property that at least one of the propositions to which it is applied is true.[d]   The discussion of *seem* in §3 indicates that it too is a predicate which asserts property of a proposition, and there will be numerous other such predicates, for example the *may* of *John may have come on the 10:00 train* which asserts that the proposition ' John came on the 10:00 train ' may be true. Quantifiers and the other quantity expressions mentioned above can be regarded as expression a relationship between a set and a predicate.

(2)   It is incorrect to represent the meaning of, say, *The man kissed the woman* by a formula such as $(x_1 \text{ kissed } x_2) \wedge (x_1 \text{ is a man}) \wedge (x_2 \text{ is a woman})$, as is occasionally proposed.   The meaning of such a sentence is not simply a conjunction of three terms but is rather something in which $(x_1$ is a man$)$ and $(x_2$ is a woman$)$ are in some sense subordinate to $(x_1$ kissed $x_2)$.   This is made clear by the fact that the sentence

(30)   John denies that the man kissed the woman.

does not mean that John denied the proposition $(x_1 \text{ kissed } x_2) \wedge (x_1$ is a man$) \wedge (x_2$ is a woman$)$: the denial of that proposition is the proposition $\neg (x_1 \text{ kissed } x_2) \vee \neg (x_1$ is a man$) \vee \neg (x_2$ is a woman$)$.   It rather means that John asserted the proposition $\neg (x_1 \text{ kissed } x_2)$ and identifies x_1 as *the man* and x_2 as *the woman*.

Point (2) relates to an extremely important way in which natural language differs from the propositions involved in mathematics.   In mathematics one enumerates certain objects which he will talk about, defines other objects in terms of these objects, and confines himself to a discussion of objects which he has either postulated or defined and thus has assigned explicit names to; these names are in effect proper nouns.   However, one does not begin a conversation by giving a list of postulates and definitions.   He simply starts talking about whatever topic he feels like talking about and the bulk of the things he talks about will be things for which either there is no proper noun (e.g. there is no proper noun *Glarf* meaning ' the third toe on Lyndon Johnson's left foot ') or the speaker does not know any proper noun (e.g. one can perfectly well use an expression such as *the pretty redhead who you were talking to in the coffee shop* if he

does not know that girl's name).   Moreover, people often talk about things
which either do not exist or which they have identified incorrectly.   Indices
exist in the mind of the speaker rather than in the real world ; they are conceptual
entities which the individual speaker creates in interpreting his experience.
Communication between different persons is possible because (1) different individuals often correctly identify things in the world or make similar incorrect
identifications so that what one speaker says about an item in his mental picture
of the universe, will jibe with something in his hearer's mental picture of the
universe, and (2) the noun phrases which speakers use[e] fulfill a function roughly
comparable to that of postulates and definitions in mathematics : they state
properties which the speaker assumes to be possessed by the conceptual entities
involved in what he is saying and are used chiefly to give the listener sufficient
information to identify the things that the speaker is talking about.   I conclude
that it is necessary for the meaning of an utterance to be divided into a ' proposition ' and a set of ' NP-descriptions ', e.g.[f]

(31)

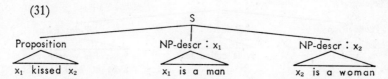

That such representations play a role in syntax is shown by an interesting class of
ambiguities, which appear to have escaped notice until Spring 1967, when Paul
Postal began to investigate them.   In the sentence

(32)   John said that he had seen the woman who lives at 219 Main St.

the woman who lives at 219 Main St. may be interpreted as either part of the
statement being attributed to John or as the speaker's description of the person
to whom John referred (e.g. perhaps John said 'I saw Gloria Goldberg' and
the speaker is describing her as the woman who lives at 219 Main St.).[g]   This
ambiguity is brought out by the fact that the sentence can be continued in two
ways, each of which allows only one of the two interpretations :

(33)   a.   . . . but the woman he saw really lives on Madison Ave.
          b.   . . . but he doesn't know that she lives there.

Similarly, while it is in principle possible that the sentence

(34)   John says that he didn't kiss the girl who he kissed.

is a report of John's having uttered the contradictory sentence I didn't kiss the
girl who I kissed, it is more likely to involve a statement such as I didn't kiss Nancy
reported by a person who is convinced that John really did kiss Nancy.   Similarly
with

(35)   John admits that he kissed the girl who he kissed.

These facts indicate that in certain kinds of embedded sentences the NP-descriptions relating to NP's in the embedded sentence may be either part of the embedded sentence or part of the main sentence. For example, the two meanings of (32) can be represented as

(36)

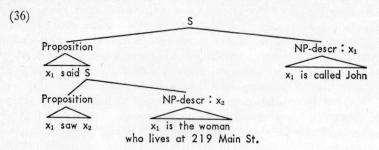

(37)

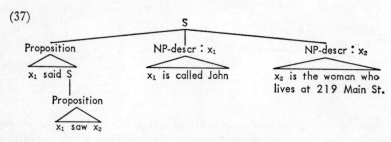

In the one case *the woman who lives at 219 Main St.* is a part of what John said, in the other case it is not. Distinctions relating to what sentence an NP-description is a constituent of are also involved in sentences such as

    (38)   Nancy wants to marry a Norwegian.,

which may mean either that there is a Norwegian who Nancy wants to marry or that Nancy wants her future husband to be Norwegian (although she does not have a specific Norwegian in mind). In the first meaning, the NP-description *x is a Norwegian* is a constituent of the main sentence and in the second meaning it is a constituent of the sentence which is the underlying object of *want*. There is a similar ambiguity in

    (39)   John wants to find the man who killed Harry.

In cases of multiple embeddings, it is possible to get multiple ambiguities corresponding to which of the sentences a given NP-description is a constituent of. For example,

    (40)   John says that Nancy wants to marry a Norwegian

is ambiguous between the three senses (a) there is a person who John says Nancy wants to marry and who the speaker describes as a Norwegian, (b) John says that there is a Norwegian who Nancy wants to marry, and (c) John says that Nancy wants her future husband to be a Norwegian.   It is difficult to see how these three senses could be assigned different deep structures unless those deep structures allowed noun-phrase descriptions to occur separate from the propositions which they are involved in and to be constituents of sentences in which those propositions are embedded.

The postulation of such deep structures would require English to have a transformation which substitutes each NP-description for an occurrence of the corresponding index.   In each of the above diagrams, this transformation would substitute *the woman who lives at 219 Main St.* for the the single occurrence of x_2 and *John* for the first of the two occurrences of x_1.   In this case, only the first occurrence of x_1 is a possible place for substitution of *John*: note that in

(41)   He says that John saw the woman who lives at 219 Main St.

the *he* may not refer to John.   However, in some cases it is possible to substitute an NP-description for any of several occurrences of the index in question, thus giving rise to alternate superficial forms such as

(42)   After John left his apartment, he went to the bank.
(43)   After he left his apartment, John went to the bank.

If deep structures such as the above are postulated, then pronominalization must be regarded in a quite different light than has hitherto been the case: pronominalization consists not of replacing repetitions of a noun phrase by pronouns but rather of determining which occurrence of an index will have the corresponding NP-description substituted for it.   The occurrence of indices for which the substitution is not made are then filled in by pronouns.   As noted above, not all occurrences of an index are possible places for substituting the NP-description: the sentence

(44)   After he left John's apartment, he went to the bank.

is not a variant of the above two (here the first *he* can only refer to someone other than John); in addition, changes in word order affect the possibilities for substituting NP-descriptions: while

(45)   John went to the bank after he left his apartment.

is synonymous with (42),

(46)   He went to the bank after John left his apartment.

is not (here *he* can not refer to John).   An explanation of the possibilities for pronominalization in these sentences is given in Ross (1967) and Langacker (1969). It is tempting to suggest that in the ' deictic ' use of pronouns (e.g. the sentence *Who is he?* in a situation where *he* does not refer to someone mentioned in a previous sentence but rather to someone who the speaker points out by a gesture) the NP-description consists not of lexical material but of the gesture which accompanies such pronouns, that the phonological reflex of a gesture is stress, and that substitution of the NP-description in this case causes the pronoun which arises to be stressed.

The underlying structures proposed in the last paragraph, incidentally, are extremely similar to the superficial form of sentences in many American Indian languages (see, e.g. G. H. Matthews, *Hidatsa Grammar*, Mouton, the Hague, 1965), where a clause consists of a sequence of noun phrases followed by a verb to which is prefixed a sequence of pronouns (the surface analogue to indices), one for each of the noun phrases. These languages have often been described as having a reduplication transformation which adds to the verb pronominal counterparts of all of the noun phrases in the clause. However, these languages could alternatively be described as simply lacking the NP-description substitution which English possesses. Since the indices within the ' proposition ' of each clause are not replaced by NP-descriptions, they are realized as pronouns.

It is necessary to impose a condition that in each semantic representation there be exactly one NP-description for each index in the representation and that that NP-description occur ' higher ' in the representation than all occurrences of the index in question. This condition makes it impossible to use a sentence such as

(47)   Napoleon admired Bonaparte.

to express the proposition than Napoleon Bonaparte admired himself.

5. The Unity of Syntax and Semantics

In the preceding section I have argued that to a very large extent the units and categories which play a role in semantic representation are exactly the units and categories which are involved in the formulation of the syntactic transformations which conditions 1–4 above would make necessary in a description of English. The symbolic logic formulas which I have used to represent meanings make widespread use of parentheses, whose sole function is to indicate the way in which items are grouped together into larger units; since grouping of items into larger units is precisely what is represented by the connections in tree diagrams such as appeared in sections 2 and 3 of this paper, semantic representations may likewise be considered to be trees. Since the rules for combining items into larger units in symbolic logic formulas must be stated in terms of categories such as ' proposition ', ' predicate ', and ' index ', these categories can be regarded as labels on the nodes of these trees. And since, as I noted in the preceding section, these categories all appear to correspond to syntactic categories, the same symbols[h] (S, V, NP, etc.) may be used as node labels in semantic representation as are used in syntactic representations. Accordingly, semantic representations appear to be extremely close in formal nature to syntactic representations, so close in fact that it becomes essential to catalog the conceivable formal differences and determine whether those differences are real or only apparent. The following appear to be the only possible formal differences between semantic and syntactic representations:

(i)   The items in a syntactic representation must be assigned a linear order whereas it is not obvious that linear ordering of items in a semantic representation makes any sense.

Whether this is a real difference between syntactic and semantic representations depends on whether things which have the same meaning must have the same semantic representation. If the synonymous sentences *John and Harry are similar* and *Harry and John are similar* are both to have the same semantic representation, that representation clearly would have to involve no ordering relation between *John* and *Harry*.

However, one could alternatively allow the same meaning to correspond to several different semantic representations and say that sameness of meaning corresponds not to sameness of semantic representation but rather to equivalence of semantic representation. In this view, semantic representations would have a linear ordering and there would be rules such as ' $p \lor q$ is equivalent to $q \lor p$ ' for determining when two different semantic representations are equivalent.[1] This, incidentally, is exactly the approach adopted in mathematics, where all formulas are assumed to have a linear ordering. I am not aware of any evidence which would favor a theory involving unordered semantic representations over a theory involving ordered semantic representations and equivalence relations. Until such evidence is found, the existence of an ordering relation among constituents cannot be accepted as a difference between syntactic and semantic representation.

(ii) Syntactic representations involve lexical items from the language as their terminal nodes, whereas the terminal nodes in a semantic representation are semantic units rather than lexical units. If the intermediate representations between semantic representation and surface syntactic representation split neatly into two groups, those with only lexical items as their terminal nodes and those with only semantic items as their terminal nodes, it would indeed make sense to assert, as Chomsky does, that there is a level of ' deep structure ' which separates a semantic component of a language from a syntactic component; in that case, the insertion of lexical items into a sentence would all take place at a single point in the ' derivational history ' of each sentence, all that precedes that point being semantics and all that follows it being syntax. However, in actual fact, lexical insertion does not all take place at one point. Words such as *former* and *latter* cannot be chosen until after all transformations which change word order have been carried out.[J] For example, in the sentence

(48) It is obvious to John that Bill is a fool, and the former dislikes the latter.,

former refers to John and *latter* to Bill even though the sentence is derived from a structure in which *that Bill is a fool* is the subject of *is obvious to John* and thus *Bill* precedes *John*. Moreover, the insertion of personal pronouns must take place at least two distinct points in a grammar. John R. Ross has pointed out (personal communication) that while one can say

(49) Do you know John and Mary? He and she are a doctor and a

teacher respectively.

one cannot say

(50)   *Do you know John and Bill?   He and he are a doctor and a teacher
       respectively.

but only

(51)   Do you know John and Bill?   They are a doctor and a teacher
       respectively.

English has a rule that if two superficially identical noun phrases are conjoined
they must be collapsed into a single noun phrase.   This rule must apply after
the pronouns *he*, *she*, etc. are inserted; but after the rule has applied it is necessary once more to insert pronouns in. the places where this rule has collapsed
conjoined identical pronouns into a single constituent.

In the case of derived items such as the verbs of change and causation discussed earlier, since the exact morphological process involved varies with the
adjective in question (the causative verb *open* is superficially identical to the
adjective *open*; the causative verb *redden* has the suffix -*en* added to the adjective
red; the causative verb *liquefy* has the suffix -*ify* in place of the suffix of the adjective *liquid;* the causative verb *break* has a different vowel and lacks an ending
which is present in the adjective *broken*)[2] and since not all adjectives have corresponding inchoative and causative verbs (e.g. there is no such verb as **greenen*
or **colden*), the form which results from combining an adjective with the abstract
element [Inchoative] or [Causative] will in effect have to be listed in the dictionary
of the language.   This suggests that the inchoative transformation and causative
transformation referred to earlier may profitably be regarded as processes which
regroup semantic information prior to the insertion of lexical items.   If this
point of view is adopted, then one might well treat the two senses of *persuade*
which occur in

(52)   I persuaded John that the world is flat.
(53)   I persuaded John to help me.

as the causatives of *believe* and *decide* respectively.   On the basis of these various
considerations, it seems plausible to hold that syntactic transformations and the
insertion of lexical items, rather than being accomplished by separate components of a grammar, as Chomsky proposed in *Aspects*, are in fact intermingled
within a single system of rules and that successive stages between the semantic
representation of a sentence and its superficial form involve gradually more
and more lexical material.[k]

(iii)   There are many syntactic categories which appear to play no role in
semantic representation, for example, verb-phrase, preposition, and preposi-

---

[2] This treatment requires the adjective *broken* to be taken as syntactically more basic than
the verb *break*.   The fact that a form which is morphologically basic need not be syntactically basic was noted by Jespersen (*The Philosophy of Grammar*), who observed that
from the point of view of syntax, *goodness* is to *good* as *beauty* is to *beautiful*.

tional phrase.   In addition, grammatical gender and number, while often bearing some relationship to semantic distinctions of sex and number, are usually not identical to those semantic categories.   To go into this question fully here would require far more space than can be spared in an article such as this.   I will simply mention that Lakoff (1965) and Fillmore (1968), both working within the framework of a grammar with a level of deep structure, have given good reason for believing that the categories ' prepositional phrase ' ' preposition ', and ' verb phrase ' are unnecessary in deep structure and must be regarded as created by rules of the syntactic component.[1]   This means that even if there are separate systems of syntactic and semantic rules, the more superficial syntactic representations will contain a wider repertoire of categories than the deeper syntactic representations; consequently, the absence of certain syntactic categories from semantic representation provides no argument for the assertion that syntactic and semantic representations are different in nature.

In summary, I believe that these considerations indicate that syntactic and semantic representations are objects of the same formal nature, namely ordered trees whose non-terminal nodes are labeled by syntactic category symbols, and that in each language there is a single system of transformations which convert semantic representations of sentences into their superficial form;   these transformations include ' lexical transformations ', i.e. transformations which replace a portion of a tree by a lexical item.   One may also draw the conclusion that syntax as a separate branch of linguistics simply does not exist: any generalizations about the way words can be combined in a language is merely the result of constraints on the ways in which semantic material may be combined and of the mechanisms which the language has for the conversion of semantic representations into the superficial forms of sentences.

6. Problems not Discussed Above

I do not wish to give the false impression that this article is an any sense a survey of semantics.   It has been concerned solely with the question of how meanings can be represented and what the relationship of such representations to the description of languages is.   Accordingly, I have failed to treat a great number of extremely interesting and important questions, for example,

(1)   How do the meanings of words change as a language evolves?

(2)   How does a child learn meanings in learning to speak his native language?

(3)   What mechanisms are involved in phenomena such as metaphor, in which a speaker uses familiar words in meanings which they normally do not have,[m] and why is it possible to understand such uses of language?

(4)   To what extent are the units of semantic representation universal?   Are there atomic predicates which play a role in representing meanings in all languages?   If symbolic logic is a valid means of representing meanings in English, is it also a valid means of representing meanings in all other languages?

(5)   To what extent does the lexicon of a language have a structure?   Can

one assert that the existence of certain words in a language implies the existence of certain other words, e.g. can one assert that every adjective has an antonym?

(6) Can all languages express the same ideas? One would be tempted to immediately answer ' no ', due to the obvious fact that languages often lack words for things unknown in the cultures in which they are spoken, e.g. Eskimo probably has no word for ' photon ' and Hottentot probably has no expression for ' third-baseman '. However, if one modifies the question slightly and asks whether all languages could express the same ideas if they were allowed to add words for all the things unknown in the cultures where they are spoken, the answer to the question ceases to be obvious. This question is of course closely related to question 4.

(7) To what extent does one's language affect his thinking? Even if all languages are capable of expressing the same thoughts, the rules of one language might make it difficult to express thought which are easy to express in another language. This conjecture is the celebrated ' Whorf hypothesis' (Whorf 1965). The examples which Whorf gives in favor of his hypothesis are not convincing. However, there has been too little serious study of this topic to allow one to draw any conclusion concerning the correctness of Whorf's hypothesis. One limited respect in which Whorf's hypothesis appears to be correct is that vocabulary may reinforce related beliefs and the terminology which one uses may lead one to retain beliefs which he might otherwise be less ready to retain ; a case of this is discussed in McCawley (1967a).

(8) To what extent is one's ability to learn lexical items conditioned by his knowledge of the world? It is doubtful that one could learn to use the word *banana* correctly unless he acquired a good deal of factual knowledge about bananas.

None of the problems in this small sample of the many crucial questions of linguistics and psychology which revolve about meaning has so far received an adequate solution.

---

[a] I have taken a small liberty with Chomsky's terminology here. Chomsky explicitly allows for the possibility of a structure generated by the base component not corresponding to any surface structure (e.g. his base component generates structures such as [John force Bill [Sam kiss Susan]], which correspond to no surface structure since the conditions for the obligatory application of Equi-NP-Deletion are not met) and reserves the term ' deep structure ' for those structures which are the deep structure *of* something. However, this point is of no consequence, since whether one confers the title of ' deep structure ' on trees that correspond to no surface structure has no empirical consequences.
[b] In (1970c, 1972) I argue that the policy of most logicians to ' reduce ' conjunctions of more than 2 terms to iterated 2-term conjoining is misguided and that conjoining of arbitrarily many propositions at a time must be allowed in semantic structure.
[c] That sentence is actually 3-ways ambiguous. The formula given corresponds to the interpretation in which everyone has the (single) wish that ' everyone get rich '; the other two interpretations correspond to the formulas $\bigvee_{x \in A} \bigvee_{y \in A}$ [x want (y get rich)] ' it is true

of every person that for every person he desires that that (the latter) person get rich ' and $\underset{y \in A}{\text{∀}} \underset{x \in A}{\text{∀}} [x$ want $(y$ get rich$)]$. ' It is true of every person that everyone wants that (the former) person to get rich '.

ᵈ I argue in McCawley (in press *a*) that ∧ and ∨ are one-place predicates predicated of NP's that denote sets of propositions and that they can be identified with ∀ and ∃ respectively. The only difference between ∧ and ∨ is whether the set of propositions is described by enumeration, e.g. {Tom is Irish, Fred is Portuguese}, or by a definite description e.g., {x is mortal : x is a man} (i.e. the set of all propositions ' x is mortal' for which x is a man ; ∨ combined with that set is the content of *All men are mortal*).

ᵉ One gross error of this paper was to assume that this is true of *all* NP's. See Karttunen (1969, 1971a) for excellent demonstrations of the falsehood of this assumption and how it let me into other errors.

ᶠ My proliferation of labels here was unjustified. The things that appear under the nodes labeled ' Proposition ' and ' NP-description ' are of the same type, namely what can reasonably be called ' Sentence '. The indices attached to the ' NP-descr ' nodes serve to indicate which index the sentence below the ' NP-descr ' node corresponds to ; while the sentences below the ' NP-descr ' nodes in this case each contain only one index and thus can only correspond to those indices, it is perfectly possible for such a sentence to contain more than one index, so that some indication is needed of which of them the sentence in question ' characterizes '. The same end could be attained by having something like ' I describe x_1 by S ' in place of the indexed ' NP-descr ' node. The difference between the node-labels ' Proposition ' and ' NP-description ' represents in totally unilluminating fashion the difference in function of the various embedded sentences ; this difference in function can be represented equally unilluminatingly without the use of such node labels :

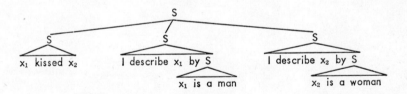

ᵍ This makes it sound as if the difference between the two meanings were simply one of who supplies the words by which some individual is described. However, the same ambiguity exists even when the speaker is referring to something that was said in a foreign language, in which case the person being quoted is not supplying the words. They differ as to what assertion is being attributed to that person, but imply nothing as to his choice of words. When I said ' may mean ', I should have said ' has a meaning which would be appropriate if '.

ʰ The inconsistency between this statement and my employment of the labels ' Proposition ' (distinct from ' Sentence ' !) and ' NP-description ' in the last section should be obvious. In more recent papers, I have concluded that the ' etc.' of this sentence is unnecessary : that no non-terminal node labels other than S, V, NP (= ' sentence ', ' predicate ', ' argument ', to use terminology closer to that of logicians) are called for.

ⁱ In this paper, I did not make clear what kind of equivalence I was talking about and was taken by many as having meant ' logical equivalence ' (two propositions are ' logically equivalent ' if either can be deduced from the other), which was not in fact what I had meant. In later papers (1970c, 1972), I make clear that ' semantic equivalence ' or ' sameness of meaning ' is a much stronger relationship than ' logical equivalence ' and discuss some specific cases where there are linguistic reasons for distinguishing between meanings that are ' logically equivalent '.

[j] I was only able to say this because the theory that I was operating with at the time did not allow for ' output constraints ' (see Ross 1967b, Perlmutter 1970).   The example that I give here is perfectly consistent with *former* and *latter* being inserted very early in derivations but there being an output constraint on where they may occur relative to their antecedents.   For a collection of baffling facts about *former* and *latter* which make clear how little their behavior is understood, see Haiman (1970).

[k] See McCawley (1973) and Lakoff (1971) for arguments that lexical insertions can not all take place at consecutive stages of derivations.

[l] This actually misrepresents Lakoff and Fillmore : they did not propose allowing new categories to arise in the course of the derivation but rather treating the items that had been assigned to such categories by previous linguists as being transformationally derived instances of other categories, e.g. Lakoff treats prepositional phrases as belonging to the category NP but being derived by adjoining a preposition to a NP and treats ' verb phrases ' as residues of embedded sentences which still retain the label S.

[m] I am now convinced that this characterization of metaphor is wrong and that metaphor consists in using words to refer to something to which they ' normally ' could not be used to refer to (although they mean the same thing as they usually do) ; on this point, see Reddy (1969, 1971).

6.   The Annotated Respective,[*]

consisting of the paper 'The respective downfalls of deep structure and autonymous syntax' and admonitions to the young reader concerning how he may profit from it and to what extent he should accept the powerful and compelling argument contained in it for giving up the distinction between syntax and semantics.

PRIMA PARTE The Respective Downfalls of Deep Structure and Autonomous Syntax

Traditionally, linguists have operated, at least implicitly, in terms of three levels of representation: phonetic, surface syntactic, and semantic, i.e. they have discussed utterances in terms of how they are pronounced, in terms of how they divide into morphemes, words, and phrases, and in terms of what meanings the utterances express. In the 20th century, a number of additional 'levels of representation' have been proposed, notably the phonemic level and the level of 'deep structure'. The postulation of these levels is generally accompanied by the postulation of distinct systems of rules which are separated by the level in question: in the one case a system of 'morphophonemic rules' and a system of 'allophonic rules' separated by the 'phonemic level':

$$\ldots \text{—}\underset{\text{repr.}}{\overset{\text{surface}}{\text{—syntactic—}}}\boxed{\underset{\text{rules}}{\overset{\text{morpho-}}{\text{phonemic}}}}\underset{\text{repr.}}{\text{—phonemic—}}\boxed{\underset{\text{rules}}{\text{allophonic}}}\underset{\text{repr.}}{\text{—phonetic}}$$

* 'The respective downfalls . . .' was read at the annual meeting of the Linguistic Society of America, Dec. 30, 1967, in Chicago. It, together with the annotations with which I supplied it for private distribution (in mimeographed form) in 1968, appears here for the first time.

and in the other case a system of ' transformations ' and a system of ' semantic interpretation rules ' separated by the level of ' deep structure ':

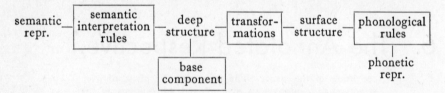

Halle's celebrated argument against the phonemic level was an argument that no such division into separate systems of rules is possible: that the mechanisms relating surface structure to phonetic realization include rules such as the Russian voicing assimilation rule which are neither ' morphophonemic ' rules nor ' allophonic ' rules since the effect of these rules is ' allophonic ' when applied to some segments but ' morphophonemic ' when applied to others. This, of course, does not necessarily mean that the rules relating surface structure and phonetic realization do not divide into two or more separate systems separated by some linguistically significant level; what it means is that if there are two or more such systems of rules, they are not the systems which one would predict from the postulation of a phonemic level.

I am going to argue that much the same thing can be said of the level of ' deep structure ' and the concomitant division of a grammar into ' semantic ' and ' transformational ' components. The argument will be much less conclusive than was the argument against the phonemic level, due to the fact that no one has provided a definition of ' deep structure ' as precise as the definitions of ' phonemic representation ' which the proponents of phonemics were so kind as to provide. The only conditions which Chomsky in *Aspects* imposed on ' deep structure ' are the following

1. Deep structure is the input to the transformations (and thus contains sufficient information to determine superficial form up to ' stylistic variation '),
2. It is the input to the rules of semantic interpretation (and thus contains sufficient information to determine the meaning of the utterance),
3. It is the level at which lexical items are chosen.

While these conditions narrow somewhat the class of ' possible grammars ', they do not bring one much nearer the answer to questions such as: what is the deep structure of the sentence *John and Arthur are tall?* Rather than attempting the staggering task of examining the full range of descriptions allowed by the above conditions and examining the status of the level of ' deep structure ' in each case, I will instead simply examine a certain class of phenomena in English from the point of view of a theory of grammar which does not distinguish ' rules of semantic interpretation ' from ' transformations ':

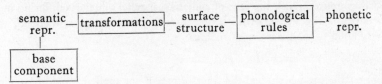

and will then point out that these phenomena are such as to force the proponent of a level of deep structure into the following dilemma: either (a) he will be unable to describe by a single rule something which in fact is a unitary phenomenon and which can be described by a single rule in the deep-structure-less theory, or (b) he will be forced to take as his 'deep structure' a representation either much closer to or much further from semantic representation than which has been hitherto been called 'deep structure' and will be without a principled basis for drawing the line between 'syntax' and 'semantics' there rather than at some different place. Either way, the theory with a level of deep structure will buy one nothing which is not already bought by a theory in which the base component generates the possible semantic representations in the language, in which a dictionary entry is a transformation which replaces a portion of a tree with semantic material at its terminal nodes by a complex of syntactic and phonological information, and in which a single system of transformations (including the 'lexical' transformations just mentioned) converts semantic representations into surface structures.

The phenomenon which I wish to discuss is the use of the words *respective* and *respectively* in English. Transformational grammarians have hitherto always treated sentences such as

(1)   John and Harry love Mary and Alice respectively.

as arising from a conjoined structure, that is, from the deep structure which also underlies the sentence

(2)   John loves Mary and Harry loves Alice.

There is, of course, no need for the resulting number of conjoined structures to be two it can be three or more, as in

(3)   John and Harry gave Mary and Alice a dime and quarter respectively.
(4)   John and Harry gave Mary and Alice a dime and a quarter on Monday and Tuesday respectively.

Since there is in principle no limit to the number of conjoined structures which one could get in this fashion with *respectively*, presumably the transformation in question would apply to conjoined sentences with 'parallel' structure but differing at two or more places and would yield a single sentence with conjoined structures at the places where the source sentences differed. But the restriction to two or more differences is unnecessary, since, as pointed out by Postal (personal communication), the case of conjoined parallel sentences differing at only one place is the well-known phenomenon of ' conjunction reduction ', which is supposed to yield sentences such as

> (5)   John loves Mary and Alice.

from a structure which, had the transformation not applied, would have yielded

> (6)   John loves Mary, and he loves Alice.

Thus *respectively* and conjunction reduction can be considered special cases of a more general phenomenon.   The absence of the word *respectively* in sentences such as (5) need not force (5) to arise differently than (1) does, since the ' dominant ' conjoined expression in a *respectively*-construction may not have *respective* or *respectively* attached to it and consequently, the number of tokens of *respective* and *respectively* in a *respectively*-construction is at most one less than the number of constituents involved :

> (7)   John and Harry gave their respective wives a dime and a quarter respectively.
> (8)   *John and Harry respectively gave their respective wives a dime and a quarter respectively.

Example (7) brings up an interesting fact noted by many scholars, namely that simple plural noun phrases may fill the places of conjoined noun phrases, even in cases where the conjoined noun phrase supposedly arises from a conjoined sentence :

> (9)   Those men gave Mary and Alice respectively a dime and a quarter respectively.
> (10) Those men gave Mary and Alice respectively their respective paychecks.
> (11) Those men gave their respective wives a nickel and a dime respectively.

If these sentences are to be derived in a fashion parallel to (1) then *those men* in (9)–(11) would have to be derived from the conjunction of two non-coreferential tokens of *that man*, which is reasonable in view of the fact that in (9)–(11) *those men* unambiguously refers to two men, one of whom is asserted to have given a dime or his paycheck to the one woman and the other of whom is asserted to have given a quarter or his paycheck to the other woman.   However, what about the occurrence of *those men* in the sentence

> (12) Those men gave their respective wives their respective paychecks.

Here *those men* could as easily refer to 200 men as to 2.   Is (12) then going to be infinitely ambiguous, derivable a different way for each possible number of men involved ?   That proposal has some plausibility in view of the fact that for any number $n \geq 2$ one can find a sentence in which *those men* necessarily refers to a set of n men :

(13) Those men love Mary, Alice, and Elizabeth respectively. (n=3)

(14) Those men love Mary, Alice, Elizabeth, Margaret, and Geraldine respectively. (n=5)

However, the trouble with deriving plural noun phrases from conjunctions of singular noun phrases is that there is no plausible source for sentences involving a plural noun phrase which specifies the number of items vaguely:

(15) The 60 or 70 men that I talked to love their respective wives.

(16) The roughly 700 million inhabitants of China all admire Chairman Mao.

Roughly 700 million is not a number but a description of a number; to describe sentences such as (15) and (16) adequately, it is necessary to have some representation in which a set can be referred to without enumerating its elements and an expression such as *roughly 700 million* or *60 or 70* can be predicated of that set. But if expressions such as *the 60 or 70 men* do not arise through conjunction reduction from conjoined sentences with singular subjects, then the *respective* of (15) can not be derived in the way that I suggested the *respective* of (7) or of

(17) John and Harry love their respective wives.

was derived. Since the occurrences of *respective* in these two sentences fulfill exactly the same function, a description of English cannot be accepted unless it derives them in exactly the same way. But that means that if one accepts the argument that (15) cannot be derived from a conjunction of sentences, he must also give up the notion that (17) and (7) are derived from conjoined sentences. But if, as I argued earlier, *respective*, *respectively*, and conjunction reduction are merely special cases of a single more general phenomenon, this would entail giving up the claim that (5) is derived from the conjunction of two sentences and would force one to say that it has an underlying conjoined object rather than a transformationally derived conjoined object.

This would imply that there is no such transformation as conjunction reduction. It thus becomes necessary here to review the arguments which have been offered in favor of conjunction reduction and evaluate the extent to which they are valid. The evidence which has been offered in favor of conjunction reduction is actually quite skimpy.[a] The first argument to have been offered is Chomsky's observation in *Syntactic Structures* that the conjuncts in a conjoined structure obey the same selectional restrictions as would a single non-conjoined item and consequently, if conjoined constituents are derived by conjunction reduction from conjoined sentences with simple constituents, only the selectional restrictions of the latter need be stated. However, this is no argument, first since Chomsky's observation holds true even in cases where the conjoined constituent cannot plausibly be derived through conjunction reduction, as in

(18) The bus and the truck collided. (*The bus collided.)

(19) His intelligence and his fanatical patriotism are hard to reconcile. (*His intelligence is hard to reconcile).

and second that ' selection ' is not a matter of syntactic features of morphemes but of the semantic properties asserted and presupposed of the entities which the utterance is about and of what follows from these assertions and presuppositions by the rules of logical inference.[1]   Because of the validity of the argument

(20) $f(x)$ for all x in M
      a is in M
      Therefore, $f(a)$

the selectional restrictions imposed in a simple noun-phrase will be imposed on all conjuncts of a conjoined noun-phrase if a conjoined noun phrase can be regarded as the enumeration of the elements of a set.[2]   Thus, facts about selection give no argument for conjunction reduction.   A similar argument applies to the fact that sentences such as (6) are paraphrases of sentences such as (5), which has also been offered as a reason for having a conjunction-reduction transformation.   A third reason which has been given for conjunction reduction is that a conjunction-reduction transformation allows one in a natural way to assign different deep structures to

(21)   John and Harry are erudite.

which has a plausible source as a sentence conjunction, since one can say *John is erudite*, and

(22)   John and Harry are similar.,

which does not because of the deviance of *John is similar*, and also to the two senses of

(23)   John and Harry went to Cleveland.

(in one sense each of them went ; in the other sense they went together).   Lakoff and Peters (1969) thus proposed deriving (21) and the first sense of (23) from underlying conjoined sentences but treating (22) and the second sense of (23) as having underlying conjoined subjects.   However, this treatment does not work since

(24)   The 50 or 60 men who I talked to are erudite.
(25)   The 50 or 60 men who I talked to are similar.

are interpreted exactly the same way as are (21) and (22) and

(26)   The 50 or 60 men who I talked to went to Cleveland.

---

[1] I elaborate on and justify these assertions in McCawley (1968c) and (1968g)
[2] This is correct only for conjunctions of singular noun phrases.   Conjunction in general defines a set as a union of subsets ; instead of (20) I should have given the inference

(20′) $f(x)$ for all x in M
      A is a subset of M
      Therefore, $f(x)$ for all x in A.

has exactly the same ambiguity as (23) does.   Since (24) and (26) cannot be derived through conjunction reduction, neither can (21) and (23).   But if they are
not derived from conjoined sentences, then what *are* they derived from?   I can
think of no way in which a level of deep structure could represent a difference
in structure between (24) and (25) or between the two senses of (26) that did not
in essence simply incorporate the differences in semantic representation between
these sentences into level of deep structure.   *Erudite* expresses a property of an
individual; (21) and (24) assert that each of the individuals in question has that
property.   *Similar* expresses a property of a set[b]; (22) and (25) assert that the
sets designated by *John and Harry* and by *the 50 or 60 men who I talked to* have
that property.   *Go* designates an event in which any number of individuals may
participate; in the first sense of (23) and (26), each individual participates in an
event of going to Cleveland, although not necessarily the same event; in the
second sense there is a single event in which all participate.   The semantic
representations of these sentences can thus be sketched as follows, omitting
many details irrelevant to the question under discussion:

(27)   For all x in {John, Harry}, Erudite (x). $(=(21))$
(28)   Similar ({John, Harry}). $(=(22))$
(29)   For all x in {John, Harry}, $Go_{y_x}(x,$ Cleveland). $(=(23a))$
(30)   For all x in {John, Harry}, $Go_y(x,$ Cleveland). $(=(23b))$

Here {John, Harry} designates a set whose elements are John and Harry, and
the subscript on the verb designates the event being referred to, which may
either be a constant (y) or vary with x (y_x).   The proposal that not only noun
phrases but also verbs have referential indices is due to Postal and is well moti-
vated.   For example, this proposal allows the action nominalization *the invention
of the zilchtron by Arthur* to be described exactly parallel to the agent nominalization *the inventor of the zilchtron* and the result nominalization *John's invention*,
which can all be derived from underlying relative clause constructions if verbs
are indexed.

   In a theory of grammar without a level of deep structure, there would have
to be a transformation which removed the universal quantifier in a structure such
as (27) and replaced the variable by the name of the set which it ranges over,
thus yielding a derived structure like (28).   I will call this transformation ' range
distribution '.   Range distribution can be generalized so as to take in sentences
with *respective* and *respectively*.   Sentence (15), for example, has a semantic representation in which a universal quantifier is applied to a formula containing
multiple occurrences of the variable which it binds:

(31)   For all x in M, Love $(x, y_x(\text{wife}(y_x, x)))$; $M=$' the 50 or 60 . . .'

I propose that range distribution applies here too and replaces all tokens of x
by tokens of M.   Note now that (29) also meets the conditions for range distribution and that there are two occurrences of the bound variable x one as the
subject of *go* and one in the subscript y_x on *go*.   If (29) is used in the action

nominalization transformation, *respective* is possible

(32)   the respective departures of John and Harry for Cleveland.

Moreover, (32) unambiguously corresponds to the first meaning of (23): (32) could not be used to refer to a single event in which John and Harry both participated.   Furthermore, the plural number on *departures* is also explained by range distribution: the underlying verb would receive the derived subscript ' set of all y_x with x in M ', which would in turn be the index of the action nominalization.   Being a set index rather than an individual index, it would cause plural number to be inserted.

But at this point it becomes necessary to return to the sentence which began this discussion, example (1).   Can this sentence be represented in the form required by the above analysis, i.e. as a formula bound by a universal quantifier? There is no obvious candidate for the formula: indeed, the only way to represent the meaning in the form ' for all x in M, x loves $f(x)$ ' would be to define $f(x)$ in a totally ad-hoc basis by listing its values: $f(John)=Mary$, $f(Harry)=Alice$. Must definitions of functions by listing their values become part of the apparatus of linguistic theory?   At the moment I see no alternative to this which would still allow the *respectively* of (1) to arise in the same way as the *respective* of (15) and regard the addition to linguistic theory of ad-hoc definitions of functions by listing their values a much cheaper price to pay than the alternative of treating *respective* and *respectively* as unrelated despite their semantic and morphological identity and their complementary distribution.   Moreover, deriving all sentences with *respective/respectively* from underlying structures such as I suggest explains the fact that only noun phrases which may be the conjuncts of underlying conjunctions can appear in a *respectively* construction: one cannot say

(33)   *The sun and the birds were shining and singing respectively.
(34)   *The score and Yastrzemski are tied and at bat respectively.

even though the putative sources under the conjunction-reduction approach are impeccable:

(35)   The sun was shining and the birds were singing.
(36)   The score is tied and Yastrzemski is at bat.[3],c

I conclude from all of this that to treat *respective, respectively*, and ' distributively interpreted ' plurals as in (21) and (24) as a single phenomenon, a theory with a level of deep structure would have to either draw the line between syntax and semantics much closer to semantics than it has hitherto been done, namely by allowing a deep structure to be a tree with quantifiers and bound variables among its terminal nodes, or to draw the line much closer to surface structure than

[3] These examples were suggested by examples in Wierzbicka (1967b).   Note that if, as I propose here, the first but not the second conjoined NP in (1) is an underlying conjoined NP, the difference in normalness between (36) and *John and Harry were thinking of the score and Yastrzemski respectively* is explained.

has hitherto been done by giving up the idea that sentences with conjoined constituents are transformationally related to conjoined simple sentences and somehow to formulate a single ' rule of semantic interpretation ' which would apply
in all the cases discussed above.   Whether the latter possibility is in fact possible
remains to be seen: only the most tentative approaches to formulating ' rules
of semantic interpretation ' within a theory involving deep structure have been
made, and any generalization regarding what such rules can do is based mainly
on conjecture.   However, whatever the nature of these hypothetical rules, Ockham's razor would militate against their introduction into a theory of language
unless it could be shown that they bought one something which the otherwise
necessary theoretical apparatus did not buy.   In this case the independently
justified notion of transformation already does what the hypothetical ' rule of
semantic interpretation ' was to do, namely to mediate the relevant facet of the
relationship between meaning and superficial form in sentences with plural and
conjoined noun phrases.   Note that the range distribution transformation proposed here is of exactly the same formal nature as certain independently justifiable transformations, notably the transformation which turns indefinite pronouns
into words of the *any* series when they are commanded by a negative.   As
regards the other possibility, that of a deep structure which is extremely abstract
but still distinct from semantic representation, Ockham's razor would again
demand justification for the assertion that the rules relating it to semantic representation proper form a separate sysem from the rules relating it to surface
structure, as well as for the assertion that it is distinct from semantic structure.

FINE DELLA PRIMA PARTE

SECONDA PARTE

Admonition 1:   concerning the chutzpa exhibited in the title of the paper.

I had an ulterior motive in writing and presenting ' The respective downfalls '
at the Dec. 1967 LSA meeting, namely corruption of the young, specifically,
stimulating them to do research based on a model which involved generative
semantics (to the extent that it involves generative anything) and which has a
single system of transformations converting semantic representations into the
corresponding superficial forms, via a sequence of intermediate stages, none of
which deserves to be called a linguistic level.   My description of this as ' corruption of the young ' should not be taken as indicating any disapproval on my
part of the model just sketched, which I in fact consider to be correct.   It rather
indicates that I intended to generate more confidence in that sketch of a model
than is warranted by current knowledge, which I consider a desirable goal in
that it will not be possible to get a sizeable body of conclusions bearing on whether
there is a linguistically significant level between semantics and surface structure
until a sizeable body of research is done in which the researcher tries to do without

such a level.   Indeed, even if an intermediate level such as 'deep structure' is necessary, it will be impossible to substantiate that that is the case until an adequate and comprehensive theory of semantic representation is constructed, and it is doubtful that such a theory will be constructed unless a significant number of scholars adopt a point of view which forces them to do semantics at every stage of the game, as the proposal that I am advocating would.

Admonition 2:   concerning what an adequate semantic representation must involve.

Before the young scholar sets out to explore the largely uncharted terrain which lies between semantic representation and surface structure, he should be aware of certain conditions which must be met by semantic representations if they are to be the input to a single system of rules that is to convert them deterministically (except for matters of 'stylistic variation') into the corresponding surface structure.

(1)   The deplorable practise of calling contradictory sentences 'meaningless' must be avoided, since contradictory sentences are not substitutable for each other *salva veritate*, to say nothing of *salva significatione*: *John thinks that his father had no children* (interpreted in the sense 'John thinks "My father had no children"' rather than in the sense that John thinks that the person who I identify as his father (though John may not) had no children) and *John thinks that he is older than himself* may differ in truth value since a person may subscribe to the one contradiction without subscribing to the other.   The contradictory propositions embedded in these examples thus make different contributions to the meanings of the sentences in question and thus must be regarded as having meanings themselves.

(2)   Similarly, expressions such as *four* and *the square root of sixteen* must be regarded as different in meaning (i.e. making a different contribution to semantic representation) even in cases such as this one where they can be proven to correspond to the same entity.   This follows from the fact that *John believes that four is less than five* and *John believes that the square root of sixteen is less than five* are not logically equivalent: the former can be true and the latter false if John happens not to know that four is the square root of sixteen.   This implies, among other things, that a linguist cannot follow the example of the mathematician who 'defines' 'two' as 'one plus one', 'three' as 'two plus one', etc.   While the mathematician's zeal in reducing his logical primitives to a minimum is admirable, it does not yield results that fit the way that persons learn number words and the corresponding concepts: a 6-year-old learning arithmetic does not learn 'five' as something defined in terms of other numbers but simply learns a bunch of words (which, being gullible, he assumes corresponds to real things because the teacher tells him so) and a bunch of facts, including the facts which the mathematician in his zeal for minimality of foundations takes as the definitions of the terms involved.   For the purposes of natural language, the truth of *Four is the square root of sixteen* must be regarded as follow-

ing from factual knowledge about four and sixteen rather than from their definitions.

(3)   The superficial form (down to morphology) of a direct quotation must be considered part of its meaning.   Thus

    a.   John said, ' Max and Margaret met in Vienna '.
    b.   John said, ' Margaret and Max met in Vienna '.

are not logically equivalent, even though

    c.   John said that Max and Margaret met in Vienna.
    d.   John said that Margaret and Max met in Vienna.

are.   Similarly, if John had said ' I believe Lyndon Johnson to be an imperialist butcher ', then

    e.   John said, ' I believe that Lyndon Johnson is an imperialist butcher '.

would be a misquotation, whereas

    f.   John said that he believed Lyndon Johnson was an imperialist butcher.
    g.   John said that he believed Lyndon Johnson to be an imperialist butcher.

are both correct indirect quotations.

Admonition 3:   concerning lexical insertion.

The conversion of semantic representations into the corresponding superficial forms must involve the insertion of appropriate lexical items in place of various complexes of semantic information.   When I stated in ' The respective downfalls ' that each ' dictionary entry ' is simply a transformation having that effect on some complex (or class of complexes) of semantic information, I avoided the crucial question of where this happens.   It sounds extremely improbable that an ordering of ' lexical ' transformations with respect to other transformations would have to be learned: surely dialects of English could not differ as regards whether the insertion of the lexical item *seem* precedes or follows extraposition.   Moreover, while I argue elsewhere (McCawley 1968c) that lexical insertion cannot all happen at the same place in derivations, the only cases of relatively ' late ' lexical insertion that I have been able to find are cases of items (such as pronouns) which are created through other transformations.   My current guess is that lexical insertion rules are ' anywhere rules ' (this term is introduced in Ross 1970b), i.e., rules which apply at any point in a derivation where the conditions for their application are met.   Anyone operating within the model which I propose will have to decide whether this guess is correct and come up with a counterproposal if he can show it to be incorrect.[d]

Admonition 4:   concerning conjunction reduction.

The case which I presented against conjunction reduction is convincing only because I confined myself to cases of conjoined noun phrases.   It is much harder to propose a plausible underlying structure which did not require conjunction reduction to derive sentences such as

John likes Alice but dislikes Margaret.

In ' The respective downfalls ' I made the tacit assumption that if (1) has an underlying conjoined noun phrase then its derivation does not involve conjunction reduction.   However, that assumption is not completely justified and might turn out to be false on the basis of a deeper analysis of the notion ' topic ', i.e. (1) might have to be analysed as having a topic *John and Harry* attached to a conjoined sentence and the ad-hoc definition of the function f (p. 126) might be a case of conjunction reduction, in which case the universal quantifier would be derived transformationally rather than present as such in semantic representation.   Pending an analysis of topics, conjunction reduction will have to be considered missing in action rather than dead.

FINE DELLA SECONDA PARTE

---

[a] Nonsense.   See note *n* to ' The role of semantics in a grammar ' for a quite solid argument for conjunction reduction that was known in 1967.

[b] This is not quite true as it stands.   *Similar* actually is basically two-place, involving a set and a propositional function, expressing the proposition that the members of the set all have the property expressed by the propositional function.   See McCawley (1970d) for further discussion.

[c] When I wrote footnote 3, I was only beginning to appreciate the problems of determining what can be conjoined.   The question, of course, does not have nearly as simple an answer as footnote 3 suggests.   For more on this question, see McCawley (1972) and R. Lakoff (1971a).

[d] See fn. *n* of ' Lexical insertion in a transformational grammar without deep structure ' for further remarks on this question.

7. Where Do Noun Phrases Come From?[*][1]

1. Background

The contents of this paper is clearly transformational grammar but not so clearly generative grammar. In discussing English, I will be treating the English language not as a class of sentences but as a code which relates messages (semantic representations) to their encoded forms (surface structures). The possibility or impossibility of a given (surface form of a) sentence depends on two quite separate factors, namely the details of the code and the restrictions on possible messages: a surface structure is possible only if there is a message which the code pairs with it. This paper is transformational grammar in that I maintain that the code has roughly the form of the 'transformational component' of a grammar as discussed in Chomsky (1965), i.e. that the 'encoding' of a message can be regarded as involving a series of intermediate stages, each obtained by ap-

[*] This paper first appeared in Roderick Jacobs and Peter S. Rosenbaum (editors), *Readings in English transformational grammar* (Boston: Ginn, 1970), pp. 166–83. A revised version appeared in Danny Steinberg and Leon A. Jakobovits, *Semantics: an interdisciplinary reader* (London and New York: Cambridge University Press), pp. 217–31.
[1] Part of the contents of this paper first appeared |in McCawley (1967b). Conclusions very similar to those presented here were arrived at by Postal independently (Postal, abortion).

plying a transformation to the preceding stage. It is not obviously generative grammar, in that to a large extent I leave open the question of what a ' possible message ' is.

There are several kinds of constraints on ' possible message '. One kind of constraint relates to what might be called the ' logical well-formedness ' of the message. For example, ' or ' is a predicate which may be combined with two or more propositions. However, ' or ' by itself is not a ' possible message ', nor is ' or ' plus a single proposition, nor is ' or ' plus things which are not all propositions; the following loosely represented structures are thus not ' possible messages ':

> or
> or (Max drinks vodka martinis)
> or (China is industrializing rapidly; the Pope).

These constraints on ' possible message ' correspond roughly to what Chomsky (1965) calls ' strict subcategorization '.

In Chomsky (1965), another kind of constraint is discussed, namely ' selectional restrictions ', which are supposed to exclude sentences such as

(1)   *That idea is green with orange stripes.

in which each predicate is combined with the right number of things but the sentence is odd because of ' incompatible ' choices of lexical material. Chomsky treats selectional restrictions as idiosyncrasies of lexical items: each lexical item is assigned ' selectional features ', which express restrictions on what material it may be combined with in ' deep structures ', e.g. the verb *surprise* might have the restriction that it ' requires an animate object ', i.e. that it may only appear in a deep structure in which it is followed by a noun phrase[2] having the property ' animate '. It is not clear that such restrictions, to the extent that they are valid restrictions, have anything to do with deep structures and lexical items rather than with semantic representations and semantic items that appear in them. If it in fact turns out that the ' selectional restrictions ' of all lexical items are predictable from their meanings, then they are not restrictions on how lexical items may be combined but rather restrictions on how semantic material may be combined, i.e. restrictions on ' possible message '.[3] It is worthwhile at this point to consider some examples which are occasionally cited as cases where a selectional restriction is not predictable from the meaning of the

[2] Actually, Chomsky treats the condition as imposed not on the entire noun phrase but only on its head noun. The intenability of that proposal is demonstrated in McCawley (1968c), where I also observe that selectional restrictions cannot be regarded as requiring a noun phrase to possess a property such as ' animate ' but only as excluding those noun phrases having semantic representations incompatible with that property (see also McCawley 1968e).
[3] The position that ' category mistakes ', which may be the only anomalies that can be correctly described as ' selectional violations ', do not correspond to ' possible thoughts ' is ably defended in Drange (1966).

item in question, i.e. cases in which there are two or more words that allegedly have the same meaning but different selectional restrictions. I maintain that in each case the words actually do not have the same meaning. Consider, for example, the Japanese verbs *kaburu, hameru, haku*, etc., which one might gloss as ' put on, said of headwear ', ' put on, said of gloves ', ' put on, said of footwear ', etc., thus suggesting that these verbs have the same meaning but different selectional restrictions. Such a description is incorrect, since the verbs in fact refer to the quite different actions involved in putting on the articles of clothes in question, as is demonstrated by the fact that if one puts on an article of clothing in an unnatural manner (e.g. puts a pair of socks on his hands, uses a necktie to hold up his trousers, etc.), the choice of verb is dictated not by the article of clothing but by the manner in which it is put on, e.g. covering one's head with a pair of gloves would be described by *kaburu* rather than *hameru*. Similarly, one might propose defining the English verbs *kick, slap*, and *punch* as ' strike with the foot ', ' strike with the open hand ', and ' strike with the fist ', suggesting that they have the meaning ' strike ' with different selectional restrictions. However, J. R. Ross (personal communication) has observed that in the bizarre situation in which a person had been subjected to surgery in which his hands and feet were cut off and grafted onto his ankles and wrists respectively, it would be perfectly normal to speak of that person as kicking someone with his fist or slapping someone with his foot. This implies that the verbs refer to the specific motion[4] which the organ in question performs and are thus not simply contextual variants of *strike*.[5] For an excellent compendium of selectional restrictions, some of which are not so obviously predictable from meanings as are those just discussed, I refer the reader to Leisi (1967).

Many so-called selectional restrictions are actually not real restrictions, since ' violations ' of them are quite normal in reports of dreams, reports of other people's beliefs,[6] and science-fiction stories:

(2)   I dreamed that my toothbrush was pregnant.

[4] Dwain Parrack has called to my attention the fact that the meaning of these verbs includes not merely the motion of the organ but the type of surface contact which results. Parrack points out that *slap* requires contact with a more or less flat surface and that one could thus speak of the soles of someone's feet slapping the surface of the water. Similarly, a certain motion of the arm would be a *punch* if the hand were clenched but a *poke* if it were open and only the fingertips were involved in the contact.
[5] It is occasionally suggested (e.g. Bierwisch 1967 : 8) that there is a linguistically significant distinction between interpretations which are possible only by imagining some bizarre situation and interpretations which require no such effort of the imagination. However, it is not clear that this criterion really defines a classification of sentences. How easy one finds it to imagine a situation in which a given sentence would be appropriate depends on such extralinguistic factors as his factual knowledge, the strength of his imagination, and the possible presence of LSD in his bloodstream. I suspect that the sentences which one can interpret without thinking up some story to embed them in are simply those which it is so easy to imagine someone's using that it would require no effort to think up such a story.
[6] Jakobson (1941, §§26–7) points out that many persons, especially children, associate colors with sounds and, for example, will not hesitate to say that the vowel [a] is red.

(3)   I dreamed that I poured my mother into an inkwell.
(4)   I dreamed that I was a proton and fell in love with a shapely green-and-orange-striped electron.
(5)   Max thinks that electrons are green with orange stripes.
(6)   Harry thinks that his toothbrush is trying to kill him.
(7)   Boris believes that ideas are physical objects and claims to have seen several that were green with orange stripes.

While some linguists might suggest that a person who says things like

(8)   My toothbrush is alive and is trying to kill me.

observes different selectional restrictions than normal people do, it is pointless to do so, since the difference in ' selectional restriction ' will correspond exactly to a difference in beliefs about one's relationship with inanimate objects.   A person who utters (8) should be referred to a psychiatric clinic, not to a remedial English course.

Note, however, that dreams, etc. are not completely free as to how semantic material may combine.   For example, the constraint that the complement of the progressive *be* must be headed by an ' activity verb ' may not be violated even in sentences such as

(9)   *I dreamed that Arthur was knowing the answer.
(10)   *Max believes that Arthur is knowing the answer.

Similarly with the restriction that only a quantity of time can elapse :

(11)   *I dreamed that my toothbrush elapsed.

These constraints appear to be real constraints on ' possible message ' ; it is evident that to enumerate these constraints one will have to tackle some of the classical problems of philosophy, namely the question of categories and the question of the distinction between ' essential ' and ' accidental ' properties of things.

2. Semantic Representation

In referring to the ' logical well-formedness ' of a semantic representation, I used the terms ' proposition ' and ' predicate ' as they are used in symbolic logic.   I will in fact argue that symbolic logic, subject to certain modifications, provides an appropriate system for semantic representation within the framework of transformational grammar.   I thus hold that the much-criticised title, *The laws of Thought*, which George Boole gave to the first work on symbolic logic, is actually much more appropriate than has generally been thought the case.

Since the representations of symbolic logic appear at first glance to be of a quite different formal nature from the labeled trees which constitute syntactic representation, one might expect that the mechanisms which link semantic representation and surface syntactic representation would divide into two separate systems, a system of ' semantic rules ', which would operate on repre-

sentations of the one kind, and a system of ' syntactic rules ', which would operate
on representations of the other kind, and that the two kinds of representation
would meet at an intermediate ' level ' corresponding to what Chomsky calls
' deep structure '.   However, as pointed out by Lakoff (remarks at the Texas
Conference on Language Universals, 15 April 1967), the difference in formal
nature between syntactic and logical representation is only apparent.   Lakoff
observes that some of the traditional categories of logic are reducible to others
(e.g. quantifiers can be considered as two-place predicates, one place corresponding to a propositional function and the other to a set)ᵃ and that only
a small inventory of syntactic categories functions in the ' deeper ' stages of
the ' derivational history ' of sentences (Lakoff 1965, Bach 1968).   Many syntactic categories are ' derived ' rather than basic; for example, most prepositions originate as parts of verbs, so that prior to a transformation which adjoins
the ' prepositional ' part of a verb to its object, a verb-plus-PrepP combination
has the form verb-plus-NP.   Likewise, many category differences which had
figured in previous analyses have turned out to hinge merely on whether certain
lexical items do or do not ' trigger ' certain transformations.   For example,
there is no need to set up the categories PredP, Aux, and Modal, which appear
in Chomsky (1965) : one can treat the various auxiliary verbs as simply verbs[7]
which (like the verbs *seem, appear*, etc.) trigger a transformation of ' VP-promotion ', which detaches the VP from the embedded sentence and puts it after the
verb in question :[8]

structure underlying
John is sleeping

result of VP-promotion
transformation

[7] This proposal was first made in Ross (1969b). A slight change which I have made in
Ross's analysis forces me to use the term ' VP-promotion ' for the analogue of the transformation which he and Lakoff call ' *it*-replacement '. I argue in McCawley (1970a)
that English has underlying verb-initial order and that that is still the constituent order
when this transformation applies. This implies that the transformation actually raises
the subject and not the VP into the next higher clause ; indeed, under the newer analysis
there is no such constituent as VP.

and which have the additional peculiarity of being combined with the tense
element by a fairly early transformation (see Hofmann 1966 for details) and
which are thus affected by all subsequent transformations that mention the
'topmost verb' of a clause.   Lakoff and Ross concluded (lectures at Harvard
and M. I. T., Autumn 1966) that the only ' deep' syntactic categories are
Sentence, Noun-Phrase, Verb-Phrase, Conjunction, Noun, and Verb, and that
all other traditionally recognized categories are special cases of these categories that correspond to the 'triggering' of transformations by certain lexical
items.   Bach (1968) then discovered some quite convincing arguments that the
Noun-Verb distinction need not be part of this inventory of categories.   He
argues that all nouns originate in predicate position (e.g. *the anthropologist*
arises from a structure paraphrasable as ' the x such that x is an anthropologist ')
and that the difference between nouns and verbs is that nouns but not verbs
trigger a transformation which replaces a relative clause by its predicate element.
At the Texas Conference on Language Universals, Lakoff observed that the
resulting inventory of categories (Sentence, NP, VP, Conjunction, and ' Contentive '—the term introduced by Bach for the category containing nouns, verbs,
and adjectives) matches in almost one-to-one fashion the categories of symbolic
logic, the only discrepancy being that the category VP has no corresponding
logical category.   However, Lakoff argued, there is in fact virtually no evidence
for a syntactic category of VP ; the various facts that have been cited as evidence
for such a category actually have nothing to do with node labels but only with
the surface immediate constituent structure, and (as argued in Fillmore 1966
and McCawley 1970a), a surface structure having a constituent consisting of
a verb and its objects arises anyway, regardless of whether there is an underlying
constituent VP, just as long as tenses and auxiliary verbs are assumed to originate
outside of the clauses that they appear in.[9]   If one accepts one of the proposals
that would do away with VP as an underlying category (and thus do away with
the phrase structure rule S → NP VP in favor of a rule S → V NP^n or something
such), then not only is the correspondence between ' deep' syntactic categories
and the categories of symbolic logic exact, but the ' phrase structure rules' governing the way in which the ' deep' syntactic categories may be combined correspond exactly to ' formation rules' for symbolic logic, e.g. the ' phrase structure rule' that a Sentence consists of a ' Contentive' plus a sequence of Noun
Phrases corresponds to the ' formation rule' that a proposition consists of an n-
place predicate plus an ' argument' for each of the n places in the predicate.[10]

[8] The analysis of *seem*, etc. as intransitive verbs with a sentence subject is due to Jespersen
(1937 : 57) ; details of this analysis are given by Rosenbaum (1965 : 71–9).   The application of ' VP-promotion' to the first of the two trees causes the topmost two NP nodes
and the two S nodes in the left branch to vanish by virtue of the ' tree-pruning' principles
presented in Ross (1969a).

[9] Fillmore (1966) does not accept Ross's analysis of auxiliaries as verbs but at least agrees
with Ross that auxiliaries originate outside of the clause that they appear in.

[10] The rules will, however, probably differ to the extent that in natural languages n will be
required to be small, say, at most 4.

Since I believe that the correspondence between syntactic and logical categories is slightly different from that proposed by Lakoff (in that I believe that a slightly different kind of symbolic logic is needed for semantic representation), I will not go into the details of the correspondence which Lakoff set up. However, I observe that if such a correspondence is valid, then semantic representations can be considered to be objects of exactly the same formal nature as syntactic representations, namely trees whose non-terminal nodes are labeled by symbols interpretable as syntactic categories. One might object that the trees of syntax are different in formal nature from those which formulas of symbolic logic may be interpreted as, in that the nodes of syntactic trees have a left-to-right ordering relation, whereas it is not clear that there is any left-to-right ordering on the nodes of the trees that I am proposing as semantic representations. Whether this objection is correct depends on whether one holds that things which mean the same must have the same semantic representation or merely that ' equivalence ' of semantic representations can be defined in such a way that things which mean the same have ' equivalent ' representations. The former position would, of course, imply that semantic representations cannot have ordered nodes,[b] since

(12)   John and Harry are similar.
(13)   Harry and John are similar.

would have to have the same semantic representation, and that representation thus could not have the node corresponding to *John* preceding the node corresponding to *Harry* or vice versa.   However, no evidence has as yet been adduced for accepting this position rather than the other one.   Until such evidence is found, the question of the ordering of nodes gives no reason for believing semantic representations to be different in formal nature from syntactic representation. I will thus treat the elements of semantic representations as having a linear order and assume that there are rules such as

(14)   *p or q* is equivalent to *q or p*

which define an equivalence relation[c] on these representations.
    These considerations suggest that there is no natural breaking point between a ' syntactic component ' and ' semantic component ' of a grammar such as the level of ' deep structure ' was envisioned to be in Chomsky (1965)[11] and imply that the burden of proof should be on those who assert that such a breaking point exists.   In McCawley (1968c), I argue that setting up a level of ' deep structure ' makes it impossible to treat as unitary processes certain phenomena which in fact are unitary processes, in particular, that the use of *respective* and *respectively*

---

[11] Since the publication of Chomsky (1965), Chomsky has modified his conception of the role of deep structure considerably.   He no longer regards ' deep structure ' as a ' level ' *intermediate between* semantic representation and surface structure but instead holds (Chomsky 1967 : 407) that ' deep structure completely determines certain highly significant aspects of semantic representation . . . [but] surface structure also contributes in a restricted but important way to semantic interpretation '.[d]

in English involves a phenomenon which can be stated as a single rule if there is no level of 'deep structure', but must be divided into special cases, some of which correspond to 'semantic interpretation rules' and others to 'transformations', if a level of 'deep structure' is accepted.   Since the argument is rather involved, I will not reproduce it here but refer the reader to McCawley (1968c) for details; the general outline of this argument for rejecting a level of 'deep structure' is, of course, identical to that of Halle's celebrated argument (Halle 1959) for rejecting a 'phonemic' level.

3. Noun Phrases and Semantic Representation

The principal respect in which I find existing versions of symbolic logic insufficient for the representation of meaning has to do with noun phrases.   Consider the sentence

(15)   The man killed the woman.

If one accepts the position (expounded and defended in e.g. McCawley 1968c) that each noun phrase occurrence in a syntactic representation must have attached to it an 'index', which corresponds to the 'purported reference' of that noun phrase occurrence, then the structure which underlies (15) will have to have some index x_1 attached to *the man* and some index x_2 attached to *the woman*.   The meaning of (15) will then involve the assertion that x_1 participated as agent and x_2 as patient in a certain event y of killing, the assertion that took place prior to the speech act, and the assertions that x_1 is a man and that x_2 is a woman.   One might propose[e] that the semantic representation of (15) is obtained simply by conjoining all these assertions, with perhaps some additional terms to cover the meaning of *the*, which I have ignored :[12]

(16) $\text{kill}_y(x_1, x_2) \wedge \text{Past}(y) \wedge \text{Man}(x_1) \wedge \text{Woman}(x_2)$.

However, (16) does not correctly represent the meaning of (15).   Note that if one says

(17)   I deny that the man killed the woman.

he is not denying (16).   To deny a conjunction is to assert that at least one of the conjuncts is false.   However, in (17) the speaker is not merely asserting that one of the four terms of (16) is false but is asserting specifically that the first term is false and assuming the other three terms to be true : it would not be correct to say (17) when one means that x_1 did in fact kill x_2 but that x_1 is not a man.   Similarly, when one asks

(18)   Did the man kill the woman?

---

[12] If p and q are propositions, then p $\wedge$ q is the proposition that p and q are both true. One major respect in which (16) fails to be an adequate semantic representation is that it fails to represent the semantic structure underlying *kill*.   Details of the correct representation are given in McCawley (1968b).[f]

he is not asking whether the conjunction (16) is true (i.e. whether all four terms are true) but is assuming the truth of the last three terms and asking whether the first term is true. It thus appears that in some sense the meanings of the expressions *the man* and *the woman* play a subordinate role in the meaning of (15).

To represent meaning correctly, symbolic logic will have to be supplemented by a way of representing this type of 'subordination'. The fact that no such device has been used in symbolic logic so far is a result of the fact that symbolic logic has largely been used as a device for representing the content of propositions of mathematics. This 'subordination' relates to an important way in which the sentences of natural languages differ from mathematical propositions. In mathematics one enumerates certain objects which he will talk about, defines other objects in terms of these objects, and confines himself to a discussion of objects which have been either explicitly postulated or explicitly defined and which thus have been assigned explicit names; these names are in effect proper names. However, one does not begin a conversation by giving a list of postulates and definitions. One simply starts talking about whatever he intends to talk about, and the bulk of the things which he talks about will be things for which either there is no proper name (e.g. there is no proper noun *Glarf* meaning 'the nail on the third toe of Lyndon Johnson's left foot') or the speaker does not know any proper name (e.g. an expression such as *the sexy little redhead that Max was talking to in the coffee shop yesterday* used to refer to someone whose name one does not know). Moreover, people often talk about things which either do not exist or they have identified incorrectly. Indices exist in the mind of the speaker rather than in the real world: they are conceptual entities which the individual creates in interpreting his experience. Communication between different persons is possible because (1) different individuals often correctly identify things or make similar misidentifications, so that what one speaker says about an item in his mental picture of the universe will jibe with something in his hearer's mental picture of the universe, and (2) the noun phrases which speakers use fulfill a function comparable to that of postulates and definitions in mathematics: they state properties which the speaker assumes to be possessed by the conceptual entities involved in what he is saying and are used chiefly to give the listener sufficient information to identify the things that the speaker is talking about.[13] I conclude that it is necessary for semantic representation to separate a clause into a 'proposition' and a set of noun phrases, which provide the material used in identifying the indices of the 'proposition', e.g.[5]

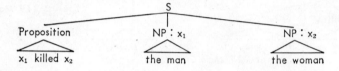

[13] See Donnellan (1966) for some highly insightful observations on this use of NPs.

That representations such as the above play a role in grammar[h] is shown by an interesting class of ambiguities which appears to have escaped the notice of linguists until recently, although it has been discussed by philosophers since the middle ages as the distinction between *de dicto* and *de re* interpretation. The sentence

(19)   Willy said that he had seen the woman who lives at 219 Main St.

is appropriate either to report Willy's having said something such as ' I saw the woman who lives at 219 Main St.' (the *de dicto* interpretation) or to report his having said something such as ' I saw Harriet Rabinowitz ', where the speaker identifies Harriet Rabinowitz as ' the woman who lives at 219 Main St.' (the *de re* interpretation). This ambiguity is brought out by the fact that the sentence can be continued in two ways, each of which allows only one of the two interpretations :

(20)   a. . . . but the woman he had in mind really lives on Pine St. [*de dicto*]
       b. . . . but he doesn't know that she lives there. [*de re*]

Similarly, while

(21)   Boris says that he didn't kiss the girl who he kissed.

might conceivably be a *de dicto* report of Boris's having uttered a contradictory sentence such as ' I didn't kiss the girl who I kissed ', it is more likely to involve a sentence such as ' I didn't kiss Nancy ' reported *de re* by a person who is convinced that Boris really did kiss Nancy. Similarly with

(22)   Harry admits that he kissed the girl who he kissed.
(23)   Joe doesn't know that your sister is your sister.

See Castañeda (1967) for further examples of such ambiguities. These facts indicate that in certain kinds of embedded sentences the lexical material relating to noun phrases in the embedded sentence may be semantically either a part of the embedded sentence or part of a higher sentence. The proposal of the last paragraph makes it possible for representations to show just such a distinction. For example, the two meanings of (19) can be represented as

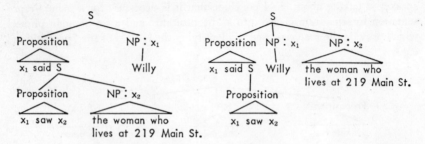

In the first tree *the woman who lives at 219 Main St.* is part of what Willy allegedly said ; in the second tree it is not. Distinctions relating to what sentence a noun

phrase is a constituent of are also involved in ambiguous sentences such as

(24)   Nancy wants to marry a Norwegian.

which may mean either that there is a Norwegian who Nancy wants to marry or that Nancy wants her future husband to be Norwegian (although she may not yet have found a Norwegian that she would want to marry). In the first case *a Norwegian* is a constituent of the main sentence, and in the second case it is a constituent of the sentence which is the underlying object of *want*. There is a similar ambiguity in

(25)   John wants to find the man who killed Harry.

In cases of multiple embeddings, it is possible to get multiple ambiguities. For example, Bach (1968) points out that

(26)   John says that Nancy wants to marry a Norwegian.

is ambiguous between the three senses (i) there is a person who John says Nancy wants to marry and who the speaker identifies as a Norwegian, (ii) John says that Nancy wants to marry a certain person who John identifies as a Norwegian, and (iii) John says that Nancy wants her future husband (whoever he might be) to be Norwegian. It is difficult to see how these three senses could be assigned different 'deep structures' unless those structures allowed noun phrases to occur separate from the propositions that they are involved in and to be constituents in which those propositions are embedded.[14]

Similarly, the ambiguity of[15]

(27)   John thinks he is smarter than he is.

between a sense in which John subscribes to the contradiction 'I am smarter than I am' and the more normal sense which asserts that John is not as smart as he thinks he is, is an ambiguity between an underlying structure in which something such as *the extent to which John is smart* is part of the complement of *think* and one in which it is not. In the one case *the extent to which John is smart* will be John's smartness as identified by John, in the other as identified by the speaker. The sentence

(28)   I wonder why more men don't beat their wives than do.

is ambiguous between (i) I wonder why the number of men who don't beat their wives exceeds the number who do and (ii) I wonder why the number of men who beat their wives is as small as it is. In meaning (ii), the complement of *wonder* is the question 'Why isn't the number of men who beat their wives greater than *n*?' and the lexical material corresponding to *n* (*The number of men who beat their wives* or something such) is an adjunct to the whole sentence rather than part of the complement of *wonder*.

The hypothesis that English sentences are derived from semantic representa-

---

[14] A valiant attempt at a description of these sentences is given in Bach (1968).
[15] I am grateful to Charles J. Fillmore for calling this sentence to my attention.

tions of the form proposed above entails the conclusion that English has a transformation which attaches each noun phrase to an occurrence of the corresponding
index.   In the proposed underlying structure of (19), this transformation would
attach *the woman who lives at 219 Main St.* to the single occurrence of x_2 and
Willy to the first of the two occurrences of x_1.   In this case only the first occurrence of x_1, is a possible place to attach *Willy*: note that in

(29)   He said that Willy had seen the woman who lives at 219 Main St.

the *he* may not refer to Willy.   However, in some cases it is possible to attach
a noun phrase to any of several occurrences of the index in question, so that
there are alternate surface forms such as

(30)   After John left his apartment, he went to the pool hall.
(31)   After he left his apartment, John went to the pool hall.

Since the occurrences of an index to which no full NP is attached are realized as
pronouns, no pronominalization transformation as such is needed.[1]   The important constraint on pronominalization noted by Ross (1967b) and Langacker
(1969) must thus be reformulated as a constraint on the NP-attachment transformation.[j]   Ross and Langacker, working from the assumption that pronouns
are derived by a transformation which replaces one of two identical noun phrases
by a pronoun, concluded that a noun-phrase may trigger the pronominalization
of another noun phrase either if it precedes it or if it follows it and is in a sentence
which the other noun phrase is in a clause subordinate to.   Thus, *he* may refer
to John in

(32)   John went to the pool hall after he left his apartment.

but not in

(33)   He went to the pool hall after John left his apartment.

However, in (31), where *he* is in a clause subordinate to that containing *John*, it
may refer to John.   The effect of this constraint can be imposed on the NP-
attachment transformation by saying that a noun phrase may be attached to any
occurrence of the corresponding index which either precedes or is in a ' higher '
sentence than all other occurrences of that index.
    The treatment of pronominalization which I have just proposed is supported by
sentences of a type first investigated by Emmon Bach and P. S. Peters and also
discovered independently by William Woods and Susumu Kuno:

(34)   A boy who saw her kissed a girl who knew him.

Here *her* is to be interpreted as referring to the girl mentioned in the sentence
and *him* referring to the boy.   Under the conception of pronominalization which
derives a pronoun from a copy of its antecedent, *her* would have to come from
a copy of *a girl who knew a boy who saw her*, which would in turn have to come
from a copy of *a girl who knew a boy who saw a girl who knew him*, etc. and each
of the two noun phrases would have to be derived from an infinitely deep pile

of relative clauses.   However, under the conception of pronominalization which I propose, this anomaly would vanish.   (34) would be derivable from a structure roughly representable as

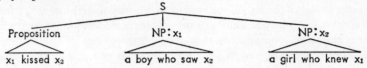

The attachment of noun phrases to index occurrences takes place sequentially. The process may begin with either x_1 or x_2.   What results under the Proposition node will be respectively

(35)   A boy who saw x_2 kissed x_2.

(36) x_1 kissed a girl who knew x_1.

In (35), both occurrences of x_2 are possible places for the attachment of the remaining noun phrase; attaching it to the first occurrence of x_2 yields[k]

(37)   A boy who saw a girl who knew x_1 (=him) kissed x_2 (=her).

and attaching it to the second occurrence of x_2 yields (34).[l]   In (36), only the first occurrence of x_1 meets the constraint formulated above, and attaching the noun phrase there yields (34).   I call the reader's attention to the fact that there are thus two derivations which convert the tree given above into the surface structure of (34), which may or may not be a defect of this account of pronominalization.

4. Implications

The above treatment of noun phrases necessitates some changes in the 'base component' of a grammar: a distinction between 'Sentence' and 'Proposition' must now be drawn,[m] a Proposition is now a 'Contentive' plus a sequence of indices[n] rather than a 'Contentive' plus a sequence of Noun Phrases, and an overall constraint on semantic representations must be imposed to insure that each representation contains neither too few nor too many noun phrases. An obvious first approximation to this constraint is to say that for each index in a semantic representation there must be at most one corresponding noun phrase, and that that noun phrase must be directly dominated by a S node which dominates all occurrences of that index.   Some such constraint is needed anyway to exclude the possibility of saying

(38)   Napoleon loves Bonaparte's wife.

to mean that Napoleon loves his wife (cf. Gruber 1965).   This constraint can be sharpened somewhat.   If a personal pronoun occurs in a sentence which does not contain an antecedent for that pronoun, then either the pronoun has an antecedent in some preceding sentence of the discourse (possibly a sentence spoken by someone other than the speaker of the sentence in question) or the pronoun is used deictically (i.e. is a direct reference to someone or something physically present as the sentence is uttered) and is stressed and accompanied by a gesture. Since the semantic function of the gesture which accompanies a deictic pronoun is the same as that of the lexical material of an ordinary noun phrase, it is tempting to suggest that in these sentences the gesture *is* a noun phrase, that the attachment transformation attaches that noun phrase to one of the occurrences of the index in question, and that the phonetic reflex of a gesture is stress. In support of this proposal, I note that a deictic pronoun may serve as the antecedent of a pronoun under exactly the same conditions under which an ordinary noun phrase may. For example, in

(39)   After he left the office, *he* [gesture] went to the pool hall.

the first *he* may have the second as its antecedent. Such is not the case in

(40)   He went to the pool hall after *he* [gesture] left the office.

This suggests tightening the constraint to make it say that for every index in a semantic representation there is exactly one corresponding noun phrase, except that a noun phrase may be omitted if there is a noun phrase with the same index in an earlier sentence of the discourse.

The proposal that pronouns are derived from index occurrences to which no noun phrase has been attached is further confirmed by the fact that pronouns do not admit ambiguities such as those of sentences (19) and (21)–(23) : in the sentence

(41)   My friends think that he is a woman.

the choice of *he* rather than *she* can only be on the basis of the speaker's knowledge about the person being talked about and cannot be a report of the friends having said ' He is a woman ' of a person who the speaker is convinced really is a woman.

The fact that noun phrases which have a non-restrictive clause are also unambiguously the speaker's contribution :

(42)   John said that his neighbor, who you met at Arthur's party, has just been sent to Devil's Island for possessing pot.

(note that this could not be followed by ' . . . but the chap that John was talking about really isn't his neighbor ') indicates that the formation of non-restrictive clauses takes place before the attachment of noun phrases to their indices.

Another interesting example is provided by the phenomenon of " extraposition " which is manifested in sentences such as

(43)   It surprises me that John beats his wife.

as opposed to

(44)   That John beats his wife surprises me.

Rosenbaum (1965) analyzes (43) and (44) as arising from the same deep structure.

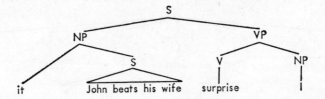

Rosenbaum sets up an optional transformation of extraposition, which moves certain embedded sentences to the end of the clause [thus giving rise to (43)], followed by a transformation which deletes *it* in a noun phrase of the form *it*+S, which will give rise to (44) if extraposition has not applied. While this approach generated the correct sentences and assigned them the correct structural descriptions, there remained a couple of respects in which it was unsatisfactory, namely: 1. it posited deep structures containing an element (the *it*) which contributed nothing to semantic interpretation; and 2. it failed to provide explanation of why *it* and not something else (perhaps *that* or *something*) should appear in extraposed sentences. Since *it* is what results from the pronominalization of a sentence:

(45) That John killed his wife bothers Frank, but it doesn't bother me.

the obvious place to look for an explanation of the *it* is pronominalization. Thus one might propose that extraposition simply reduplicates the embedded clause and that one copy of it is pronominalized.

That proposal is untenable due to the fact that if extraposition reduplicated a sentence, the resulting structure would not meet Ross and Langacker's condition for " backwards " pronominalization, so that only the copy and not the original could be pronominalized, which is the reverse of the actual state of affairs.° However, within the framework proposed above, one can make a closely related proposal which will in fact explain the *it*. Specifically, note that the embedded sentences, being noun phrases, would have to originate in the same positions as items such as *John, your sister*, etc., and then be substituted for the corresponding index. I know of no reason why extraposition would have to follow the noun phrase substitution transformation. If it in fact precedes it, then extraposition can be formulated as a transformation which optionally puts a " propositional " noun phrase at the end of a clause containing the corresponding index. If this option is not carried out, the proposition will be substituted for the index, thus yielding sentences such as (44), whereas if the option is carried out, that index will remain by itself and will thus be realized as a pronoun, giving sentences such as (43). The sentence

(46) It surprises John that it bothers Frank that Harry killed his wife.

thus° arises from the structure

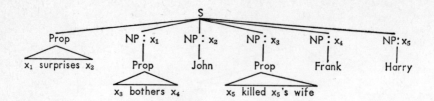

Note that " propositional " NPs can participate in the same ambiguities as can ordinary NPs.

(47)   John admits that Arthur was right.

may be a report of John's having said *I admit that Arthur was right* or his having said *I admit that Muhammed Ali is the greatest living American,* which the speaker describes as an admission that Arthur was right.   Exactly how to represent these two structures is not completely clear to me at the moment; the following represents my current best guess:

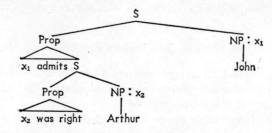

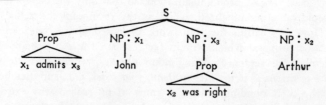

In German and Latin the ambiguity of sentences like (19) is resolved by the mood of the verb in the relative clause: in the *de dicto* meaning, *lives* is put in the subjunctive mood, and in the *de re* meaning it is put in the indicative mood. This indicates that mood is predictable on the basis of the structure prior to the NP-attachment transformation, specifically that a verb is made subjunctive if it is in a noun phrase which is within the complement of certain verbs at that point of the derivation.[16]

Regarding the distinction between ' Sentence ' and ' Proposition ', I observe that verbs differ as to whether they take a ' Sentence ' or a ' Proposition ' as

---

[16] On the syntax of Latin subjunctives, see R. Lakoff (1968)

complement, i.e. whether the complement may contain noun phrases as well as a proposition. The discussion in section 3 implies that *say*, *deny*, and *want* take Sentences rather than Propositions as their complements. On the other hand, *seem* and *begin* take Propositions as complements: note that

(48)   John began beating the man who lives at 219 Main St.

(49)   Max seems to know the woman who lives at 219 Main St.

are unambiguously *de re*. Of course, if these sentences are embedded as the complements of verbs such as *say* or *want*, that verb creates the possibility of a *de dicto* interpretation:

(50)   John wants to begin beating the man who lives at 219 Main St.

(51)   Harry says that Max seems to know the woman who lives at 219 Main St.

The proposal that sentences are derived from structures in which the adjuncts to ' contentives ' are indices rather than full noun phrases renders fairly trivial certain problems which would otherwise present considerable difficulty. For example, it is hard to see how the sentences

(52)   Everyone loves himself.

(53)   Everyone loves everyone.

could be assigned different ' deep structures ' and how the reflexivization transformation could be formulated without ad-hoc restrictions if syntax were to start with ' deep structures ' in which full noun phrases like *everyone* rather than indices were to be the subjects, objects, etc. of verbs and reflexivization were to be contingent on noun phrases being identical. However, if sentences are derived from structures in which the adjuncts of ' Contentives ' are indices, as in the semantic representations that I have proposed, (52) and (53) can be derived from the structures[17],q

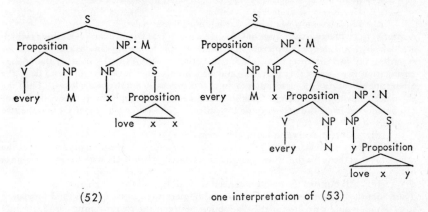

(52)   one interpretation of (53)

[17] $[[x]_{NP} S]_{NP}$ is to be interpreted as ' the set of all x's such that S'; thus, the NP with index M in the second tree represents ' the set of all (people ?) who love everyone '.

Reflexivization is applicable only in the former tree. This proposal also explains why the sequence of words (53), when appropriately stressed, may mean either that everyone has the characteristic of loving everyone or that everyone has the characteristic that everyone loves him.[18] The former corresponds to the tree at the right above and the latter to

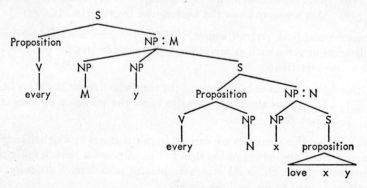

Both structures will yield the same sequence of words since in either case the two indices occurring next to *love* are the only places where the two occurrences of *every* may be attached to their indices by the transformation of quantifier-lowering (Carden 1968).

Finally, I observe that the data which I have discussed here show to be com-

---

[18] These two meanings are ' logically equivalent ', i.e. if either is true, then so necessarily is the other. It is of course reasonable to say that logically equivalent things need not have the same meaning, since any two contradictory propositions are logically equivalent, but one would hardly want to say that the sentences
    (i)   That horse is not a horse.
    (ii) My father had no children.
have the same meaning or that they may be translated into German as
    (i′) Der Kreis ist dreieckig.
    (ii′) Ich küsste ein Mädchen, das ich nie geküsst habe.
respectively. The two meanings of (53) give a much less trivial example of things which are logically equivalent but different in meaning. The following reasons can be cited for regarding the two interpretations of (53) as distinct meanings. (1) To deny the one interpretation is to assert that there is someone who does not love everyone; to deny the other interpretation is to assert that there is someone who not everyone loves. Thus the existence of two quite different things is being *asserted* (although the existence of the one can be *inferred* from the existence of the other). (2) As noted by Peter Geach, the two meanings of
    (iii) Almost everyone loves almost everyone.
are not logically equivalent, since the truth conditions for one meaning may be met at the same time that those for the other meaning are violated. Similarly with the two meanings of
    (iv) All but one of the boys danced with all but one of the girls.
Thus, identical quantifiers cannot in general be permuted *salva veritate*, and formation rules which would provide for the distinction between the two meanings of (53) would provide for the same distinction between meanings involving *every* in place of *almost every* if all quantifiers are treated alike by the formation rules.

pletely untenable the familiar proposal (Chomsky 1957) that each language has a limited repertoire of 'kernel sentences' and that the full range of sentences in the language is obtained by combining and deforming these kernel sentences in various ways.   The sentences discussed require analyses in which structures containing less material than would make up a sentence (i.e. structures which have 'slots' for noun phrases but no corresponding lexical material) are embedded in structures which contain more lexical material than there are slots to put it into.

ᵃ This is one of several proposals that have been made as to what quantifiers are in semantic structure; indeed, another proposal appears later in this paper.   See McCawley (in press *a*) for arguments that a quantifier is a one-place predicate that is predicated of a NP that denotes a set of propositions.
ᵇ In writing this, I gratuitously assumed that there were only two alternatives : totally unordered trees and totally ordered trees.   There are of course other alternatives involving a partial ordering on the nodes, and (12)–(13) only have a bearing on the ordering of the conjuncts of a conjoined NP.
ᶜ See note *n* of ' The role of semantics in a grammar '.
ᵈ See now Chomsky (1970b).
ᵉ (16) is about the most simple-minded thing that one might think of proposing.   I proposed it largely because the most celebrated non-simple-minded proposal that I knew of, namely Russell's treatment of definite descriptions, did not appear to help, since (16) does not imply that there is only one x such that man(x), whereas Russell's formula for *The present king of France is bald* does imply that there is only one individual who is at present king of France :

$$\exists x \ (x \text{ is at present king of France} \wedge x \text{ is bald} \wedge \forall y \ (y \text{ is at present king of France} \supset y{=}x)).$$

One might, however, reconcile himself to a formula like the above on the grounds that (15) would be appropriate only if there is exactly one man and exactly one woman among the individuals under consideration and one could restrict the range of the variables to those individuals.   In that case, one could even propose to represent the content of (15) along the lines of

(16′) $\forall x \forall y \ (\text{man}(x) \wedge \text{woman}(y) \supset \text{kill}_z \ (x,y)).$

Something similar to this was proposed in Quine (1960).   The negation of (16′) is logically equivalent to

(16″) $\exists x \exists y \ (\text{man}(x) \wedge \text{woman}(y) \wedge \sim\!\text{kill}_z \ (x,y)).$

Relative to the assumption which made (16′) possible at all as a representation of (16), namely that there is exactly one man and exactly one woman among the individuals over which the variables range, (16″) is logically equivalent to

(16‴) $\forall x \forall y \ (\text{man}(x) \wedge \text{woman}(y) \supset \sim\!\text{kill}_z \ (x,y)),$

which will correspond to *The man didn't kill the woman* if (16′) corresponds to *The man killed the woman*.   While this proposal, which was called to my attention by both Thomas Gardner and Tae-Yong Pak, does not share the gross defects of (16), I reject it because the presence of a NP *the man* in a sentence does not exclude other men from the range of variables, e.g. one can perfectly well say *The man thinks all men are idiots* or *Many men like the man* in cases where one particular man is under discussion.
ᶠ See now McCawley (in press *b*) for an even more correct analysis.

g See footnote f of ' Meaning and the description of languages ' for a list of the more glaring inadequacies of this tree.

h Or rather, that representations which agree with the above in having the content of NP's outside of the clauses in which the NP's end up play a role in grammar ; the observations below have no bearing on any other characteristics of the above tree.

i This is an oversimplification. While ordinary personal pronouns need not be derived by a pronominalization transformation such as that of Ross (1967b) or Langacker (1969), sentence pronominalizations in examples such as

> Marvin said that there was a unicorn in the garden, and *so* there was.
> Margaret is rumored to have been arrested, but I don't believe *it*.

must in fact be derived through a transformation that replaces one of two identical structures by a pronoun.

j One promising alternative is suggested in Lakoff (abortion *b*) : that the ' antecedent of ' relation is marked in surface structures (in addition to the information usually considered to be present in surface structures) and that the Ross-Langacker constraint is an output constraint (in the sense of Ross 1967a) on the antecedent relation.

The treatment of personal pronouns that I proposed above eliminates one important anomaly that pronominalization appeared to have in earlier treatments : it was the only exception to the principle (Ross 1967a : 340) that ' feature-changing ' rules are ' upper bounded ', i.e. that an element may trigger feature changes only in elements of the same clause or of a ' lower ' clause. However, this anomaly is eliminated only at the expense of introducing a new anomaly, since NP-attachment would violate Ross's ' coordinate structure constraint ', the principle that material may not be moved into or out of a coordinate structure ; NP-attachment has to move material into a coordinate structure in cases such as

> The girl you like and her brother's roommate have just eloped.

k Such a derivation is actually not possible, since material not only may not be moved out of a complex NP (Ross 1967a) but also may not be moved into one (G. Lakoff 1970a). The proposals of this paper thus encounter a major problem : how could (37) be derived at all ?

l Karttunen (1971a) points out some serious flaws in my treatment of the Bach-Peters sentence. Consider analogues to (34) and (37) that have definite NP's, plus a third related sentence :

> (i)   The pilot that shot at it hit the Mig that chased him.
> (ii) The pilot that shot at the Mig that chased him hit it.
> (iii) The Mig that chased the pilot that shot at it was hit by him.

Assuming, for simplicity's sake, that actives and passives have the same semantic structure, my proposals imply that (i), (ii), and (iii) have the same semantic structure. However, as Karttunen notes, (ii) and (iii) differ in meaning (since (ii) presupposes that there is exactly one pilot x such that x shot at the Mig that chased x, (iii) presupposes that there is exactly one Mig y such that y chased the pilot that shot at y, and either of these presuppositions can be true without the other being true), and (i) is ambiguous between the meaning of (ii) and the meaning of (iii). To make my analysis consistent with these facts, it is necessary to correct a really major flaw in it (pointed out in Karttunen 1969), namely that it treats many NP's as ' referential ' (in the sense of Donnellan 1966) whose indices are in fact bound variables (and thus are ' attributive ' NP's, in the sense of Donnellan 1966) and treats the relationship between pronouns and antecedents as being explicated simply by assigning purported referents to the various NP's. For example, my proposal would force me to represent

> (iv) The man who loves his wife kissed her.

as

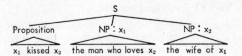

However, under the following circumstances

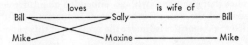

(iv) would be taken as asserting that Bill kissed Sally (since Bill is, within this restricted world, the man who loves his wife), even though Bill cannot be described as *The man who loves Sally* (since Mike also loves Sally).   Karttunen argues that (iv) does not involve ' constant ' indices but rather involves a definite description which is within the scope of another definite description, i.e. (where $[(\iota x)fx]\ gx$ means 'g is true of the x for which fx is true ')

(v) $[(\iota x)(\text{man}(x)\wedge[(\iota y)\ \text{wife}\ (y,x)]\ \text{love}\ (x,y)]\ ([(\iota z)\ \text{wife}\ (z,x)]\ \text{kissed}\ (x,z)).$

It is necessary for ' the wife of x ' to occur twice in this formula in order for each variable to be in the scope of the ' operator ' that binds it.   Thus, if something like (v) is the semantic representation of (iv), the *her* of (iv) will not arise from an index without attached material but will have to be derived by a pronominalization rule that turns a repeated definite description into a pronoun.   If expressions like (v) are used for the semantic representation of (i)-(iii), the derivation of (i)-(iii) from appropriate sources will present no problem.   Specifically, (ii) and (iii) would correspond respectively to

(ii') $[(\iota x)\ (\text{pilot}(x)\wedge[(\iota y)\ (\text{Mig}(y)\wedge\text{chased}\ (y,x)]\ \text{shot-at}\ (x,y)]\ [(\iota z)\ (\text{Mig}(z)\wedge$
       chased $(z,x)]$ hit (x,z).

(iii') $[(\iota y)\ (\text{Mig}\ (y)\wedge[(\iota x)\ (\text{pilot}(x)\wedge\text{shot-at}(x,y)]\ \text{chased}(y,x)]\ [(\iota w)\ (\text{pilot}(w)$
       shot-at$(w,y)]$ hit $(w,y).$,

and the derivation of (i) or (ii) from (ii') or of (i) or (iii) from (iii') would involve pronominalization of one of the underlined definite descriptions under identity with the other.
m I really have not shown that it must be drawn ; indeed, I could have gotten along perfectly well labeling the node S in both cases.
n I was grossly at fault in saying this without having given any consideration to the most interesting class of NP's, ' complements '.   There are in fact compelling reasons for not treating complements as having indices and originating outside their clauses, namely (G. Lakoff, lectures at Linguistic Institute, University of Illinois, summer 1968) (i) complements can not form Bach-Peters sentences :

*That Bill believes it indicates that Tom has denied it.   (with the first *it* referring
       to *Tom deny it* and the second to *Bill believe it*)

(ii) contrary to what I say below about (47), a complement can not be a ' referential NP ', i.e. the speaker's description of a proposition that is assumed to be known.   In (47), *you are right* is not the speaker's description of a proposition that John had called *Mohammed Ali is the greatest living American*.   *Arthur is right* in this case is elliptical for *Arthur is right that Mohammed Ali is the greatest living American*, and (47) is an acceptable report of what John said only because one who assents to S will generally assent to ' x is right that S ' if he knows that x claims that S. (47) would be inappropriate if John has never heard of Arthur or if he doesn't know that Arthur thinks Mohammed Ali is the greatest living American.   An exact analogue to (20b) (which is what I had said (47) in the given situation constituted) would be

*Sam says that he is convinced that $2+2=5$, although he thinks it is (the proposition) that all prime numbers are odd.

^{o} Chapin (1970 : 377) argues that copying of a NP always is accompanied by pronominalization of the original. Thus extraposition can perfectly well be taken to be a copying transformation, with the *it* arising not through ordinary pronominalization but through a universal characteristic of copying transformations.

^{p} I am really ashamed of having used *thus* with reference to considerations as weak as those just enumerated. See note *n* for reasons why the structure proposed here is wrong.

^{q} This proposal implies that a sentence with an embedded quantifier could be ambiguous not only as to the scope of the quantifier but also as to the origin of the NP which describes the set to which the quantifier is (under the proposal of this paper) applied. While a sentence such as

John told me that several of the people planning to kill him are going to review his book.

is ambiguous as to whether *the people planning to kill him* is to be interpreted *de dicto* or *de re*, the ambiguity relates to that NP and not to ' the people planning to kill John who are going to review his book ', which is the NP that *every* would be applied to under the proposal being considered. As far as I can determine, there is no ambiguity with regard to THAT NP. Thus the proposal that a quantifier is predicated of a set of individuals appears to make a false prediction of ambiguity. For arguments that quantifiers are predicated not of set of individuals but sets of propositions, see McCawley (in press *a*).

8. Lexical Insertion in a Transformational Grammar without Deep Structure[*]

By 'deep structure', I mean a linguistically significant level 'between' semantic representation and surface syntactic representation.[a] I have argued elsewhere (McCawley 1967b, 1968b, 1968c, 1970b) that there is no such level, i.e. that there is no principled basis for dividing the rules relating surface structures to the corresponding semantic structures into two systems such as Chomsky (1965) assumed: 'semantic interpretation rules' which relate deep structure to semantic representation, and 'transformations' which relate deep structure to surface structure. In this paper I will assume the following conclusions which I drew in the papers cited above:

1. Syntactic and semantic representations are of the same formal nature, namely labeled trees.

2. There is a single system of rules (henceforth 'transformations') which relates semantic representation to surface structure through intermediate stages.

3. In the 'earlier' stages of the conversion from semantic representation to surface structure, terminal nodes may have for labels 'referential indices' such as were introduced in Chomsky 1965:

* This paper was first published in *Papers from the fourth regional meeting*, *Chicago Linguistic Society* (Chicago: Linguistics Dept. of the University of Chicago), pp. 71–80.

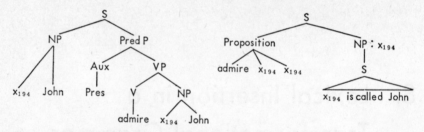

Fig. 1 Deep structure of *John admires* **Fig. 2** An early stage in the derivation
himself, in accordance with unformalized of *John admires himself* according to
proposals of Chomsky 1965.   McCawley 1967b.

In semantic representation, only indices and 'predicates' are terminal node labels. The repertory of predicates will be enormous, although not matching lexical items one-to-one, i.e. some lexical items are semantically complex.

The purpose of this paper is to examine one aspect of how a grammar fitting the above conclusions would have to work, namely, the question of how lexical items get into the representations of sentences. Conclusion 2 implies that the various lexical items get in by transformations. Indeed, each 'dictionary entry' could be regarded as a transformation, namely a transformation which attaches a complex of syntactic and phonological material to a portion of a tree that terminates in semantic material,[b] At what point(s) in a derivation do these transformations apply? I find implausible the suggestion (Lakoff and Ross 1967) that these transformations have an extrinsic ordering with respect to each other and to ordinary transformations, since that would imply that the point where any particular insertion takes place can vary from dialect to dialect, e.g. that two dialects of English might differ as regards whether the morpheme *horse* is inserted before or after extraposition; no such examples have ever been adduced, and it appears highly unlikely that any exist.

I can conceive of four possible ways in which grammars might be constrained so as to prevent the ordering of lexical insertions from being a way in which grammars could differ. The first possibility is that lexical items are not inserted until the very end of the derivation. However, this possibility must be rejected, since the possibility of performing certain transformations depends on the presence of specific morphemes and not just on their meanings, e.g. *for* is deleted when it immediately follows *want* but not (at least for some speakers) when it immediately follows *desire*:

(1) I want you to win the prize.
(2) I desire you to win the prize. (*for some speakers)
(3) *I want for you to win the prize.
(4) I desire for you to win the prize.
(5) a. I want/desire very much for you to win the prize.
    b. What I want/desire is for you to win the prize.

Similarly, particle movement can only affect a verb-particle combination, but a verb-particle combination is often synonymous with a simple verb, e.g.

(6)   He threw Harry out.
(7)   He ejected Harry.

The second possibility is that lexical items are all inserted at the very beginning of a derivation.   The bulk of this paper will be devoted to showing that this possibility must be rejected on the grounds that the complex of semantic material which a lexical item corresponds to need not be a constituent of the semantic representation per se but may be a constituent which arises through a transformation, i.e. I will argue that lexical items can be correlated correctly with their meanings only by recognizing prelexical transformations, which apply to trees that terminate in semantic material rather than in lexical material,[e] and stating the conditions for inserting lexical items in terms of structures derived via these prelexical transformations rather than in terms of the ultimate semantic representation.

What I have just said implies that semantic material is not grouped together in the same way in the semantic representation of a sentence as it is in a lexical item.   For an illustration of this, consider the verb *to kill*.   *Kill* can be resolved into components as *cause to die*[d]; moreover, as least one of those components, namely *die*, is itself semantically complex, meaning ' cease to be alive ', i.e. ' become not alive '.   However, this is not sufficient to describe the semantic representations of sentences involving *kill*, since a sentence involving it refers to two participants, one of whom causes the event in question and the other of whom dies in that event, i.e. the meaning of *x killed y* would require a representation along the lines of

Fig. 3

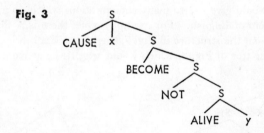

Before *kill* can be inserted into this structure, it is necessary that CAUSE,[1] BECOME, NOT, and ALIVE get grouped into a unit.   An obvious candidate for a transformation that would have that effect is a transformation that adjoins a predicate to the next higher predicate, thus successively converting Fig. 3 into

[1] In the diagrams I capitalize the names of semantic predicates to distinguish them from corresponding lexical items.

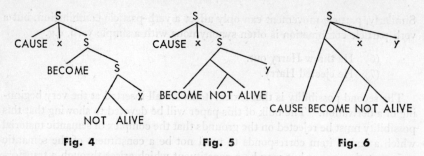

Fig. 4　　　　　　　　**Fig. 5**　　　　　　　　**Fig. 6**

If lexical insertion did not occur until after the application of that transformation, then the ' dictionary entry ' for *kill* could be expressed as a transformation which replaces the subtree at the left in Fig. 6 by *kill*:

I would like now to examine some characteristics which the predicate-raising transformation that I have just posited would have to have. First, it would have to be optional, since there is no need to perform all stages of the last derivation. For example, by failing to perform the last application of predicate-raising, one would obtain sentences such as *John caused Harry to die*. If one did not perform predicate-raising on ALIVE but did perform it on NOT, the configuration

i.e. *y ceased to be alive* would result. Secondly, the transformation as I have described it would give rise to many configurations which do not correspond to any lexical item of English. For example, while there is nothing semantically anomalous about the structure in Fig. 7, there is no English lexical item corresponding to the tree of Fig. 8, which would arise if the above steps were carried out.

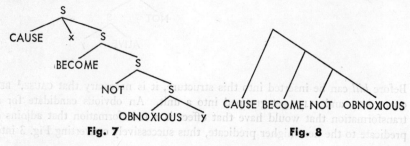

Fig. 7　　　　　　　　　　　　　　**Fig. 8**

Does this mean that the transformation must be restricted so as to preclude the generation of structures like Fig. 8 ? It would hardly be possible to formulate such restrictions, since there is very little that can be said in general about the structures to be excluded : indeed, the structures to be excluded are simply those for which English accidentally has no corresponding lexical items.   Thus, if one were to place such a restriction on the predicate-raising transformation, he would be adding to the grammar something predictable from the rest of the grammar, namely from the existing gaps in the lexicon.   The transformation should thus be unrestricted and the following universal surface structure constraint should be imposed on grammars : a surface structure is well-formed only if all its terminal nodes bear lexical items.   Structures in which Fig. 8 had been generated would thus be excluded, since there would be no material in the lexicon to provide a surface realization of them.   Note, incidentally, that since there is no regular morphological device in English for marking causatives, the different morphemic realizations of CAUSE in stative/causative pairs such as *red/redden*, *able/enable*, and *open/open* would have to be part of the dictionary of English anyway.   The fact that a given stative adjective, e.g. *blue*, has no causative does not require that the morpheme *blue* be marked as an exception to a transformation but only that there be no dictionary entry for such a causative.   The causative of a morpheme can be regarded as the form generated by a composite dictionary entry (along the lines of Gruber 1965) which also generates the morpheme in question, e.g.

(a later suffixation rule would put *en* after *red*).   Note that the predicate-raising transformation includes as special cases the inchoative and causative transformations of Lakoff 1965.[2]

Predicate-raising must thus be a prelexical transformation, i.e. it applies to trees which terminate in semantic matter rather than in lexical matter.   Are there other transformations that have to be treated as prelexical?   One obvious place to look for such a transformation is nominalizations.   Indeed, there is reason to believe that virtually all nominalizations arise through a single prelexical transformation.   Specifically, all nominalizations have semantic representations of the form ' the (an) x such that $f(x)$ ', e.g.

Agent-nom.   The inventor of the wheel.
          (ιx) (x invented the wheel)

[2] Jerry L. Morgan has called it to my attention that the derivation proposed here for sentences with *kill* allows an explanation of the ambiguity of *John almost killed Harry* between ' John almost did something that would have killed Harry ', ' John did something that came close to causing Harry to die' (although it didn't affect Harry), and ' John did something that brought Harry close to death ' ; this would be accounted for if the grammar is provided with a prelexical transformation which moves *almost* into a higher clause.[e]

Action-nom.   The invention of the phonograph by Edison.
          (ιv) (Edison invent$_v$ the phonograph)[3]
Result-nom.   John's invention.
          (ιy) (John invented y)

The head noun of the resulting noun phrase consists of the verb of the embedded sentence plus some element that indicates the relation of the variable to the embedded sentence.   The nominalization transformation lifts the verb from the sentence and adds the appropriate element to it :[4]

This transformation will also sometimes give combinations of material for which no lexical item exists; for example, there is no agent-nominalization *passer corresponding to pass an examination.   In addition, as pointed out by Lakoff (1965), there are lexical gaps of an opposite type, namely items which act like nominalizations but for which no unnominalized verb exists:

(8)   China's aggression against India shocked everyone.
(9)   *China aggressed against India.

Here there will exist dictionary entries for the combinations produced by the

---

[3] ι is Russell's definite-description operator.   A subscript on a verb refers to an event corresponding to that verb.
[4] Since the structures which I hypothesize to underlie nominalizations are of the form that also underlies relative clauses, it may well be that nominalizations share some of the transformations that are involved in relative clauses; for example, the ' relation marker ' may be identifiable with a relative pronoun.   However, I will refrain from taking any position on that question here.

nominalization transformation but not for the ' verb ' which the nominalization transformation affected.   That these nominalizations must have an embedded sentence is shown by the fact that nominalizations show the same behavior[f] as full clauses when used as the object of a verb such as *attempt*.   The complement of *attempt* requires an underlying subject identical to that of *attempt* and loses that subject by the transformation of Equi-NP-deletion:

(10)   John attempted to kill Harry.
(11)   *John attempted for himself to kill Harry.
(12)   *John attempted for Bill to kill Harry.

The same pattern is exhibited when an action nominalization appears instead of an infinitive:

(13)   China attempted aggression against India.
(14)   *China attempted its aggression against India.
(15)   *China attempted Uruguay's aggression against India.

If the nominalization transformation is prelexical, then the following facts (first noted in Warshawsky 1966 and elaborated in Jackendoff 1968) give reason to believe that reflexivization is also prelexical.[g]   The reflexive in

(16)   John showed Harry a picture of himself.

may refer to either John or Harry, whereas that in

(17)   John showed Harry Picasso's picture of himself.

may only refer to Picasso, and

(18)   *John showed Harry Margaret's picture of himself.

is ungrammatical.   These facts appear to conflict with the treatment of reflexives in Lees and Klima (1963), according to which reflexives are derived from noun phrases which repeat a noun phrase that occurs EARLIER IN THE SAME SIMPLE SENTENCE: that condition would appear to be met not only in (16) but also if there were a copy of *John* or *Harry* in place of *himself* in (17) or (18).   Suppose, however, that (following Lakoff 1965) *Bill's picture of John*, etc. are result-nominalizations of a sentence which exists only in nominalized form and whose verb has *picture* as a surface reflex.   In *Bill's picture of John*, this verb would have *Bill* for its underlying subject, but in *a picture of John* it would have an indefinite pronoun for its underlying subject.   Note that (a) this indefinite pronoun must eventually be deleted, (b) deleting it causes the S-node over the embedded sentence to be lost (by the ' tree-pruning' principles of Ross 1969a), (c) the nominalization transformation also causes the loss of the S-node.   If reflexivization follows the deletion of the indefinite pronoun but precedes the nominalization transformation, then at the stage of the derivation where reflexivization applies there will still be an S-node over the embedded sentence in (17–18) but not in (16).   Thus, this rule ordering plus the Lees-Klima constraint on reflexivization would correctly predict the occurrence of reflexives in (16)–(18).

However, this would entail having reflexivization apply before a prelexical rule and thus that it be prelexical itself.

Another transformation which will have to be prelexical is Equi-NP-deletion. This transformation is usually conceived of as deleting the subject of an embedded sentence if it is identical to a certain noun phrase of the next higher sentence:

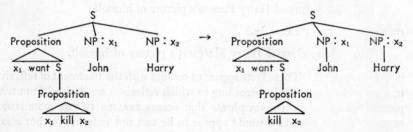

Alternatively, however, it could be regarded as deleting a token of a referential index at a stage of the derivation prior to the rule which attaches noun phrases to indices:

The word *malinger* has a meaning which appears to result from the latter version of Equi-NP-deletion. *Malinger* means 'pretend to be sick'. *Pretend to be sick* is what would arise through Equi-NP-deletion from a semantic representation of the form *x pretends that x is sick*. Thus, treating *malinger* as deriving from a semantic structure corresponding to 'pretend to be sick' entails that Equi-NP-deletion apply prelexically and that *malinger* be inserted in place of a structure which could only arise through Equi-NP-deletion. The proposal that Equi-NP-deletion apply prelexically is implicit in the proposal of Bach (1968) to derive

(19) John is looking for a lion.

from the same structure as underlies

(20) John is trying to find a lion.

Bach points out that having *a lion* originate in the complement of a verb like *try* in (19) allows an explanation of the ambiguity of (19) between a referential sense (in which one is talking about some one lion) and a non-referential sense (in which any lion at all would satisfy the quest). The source which Bach proposes for *look for* thus entails prelexical application of both Equi-NP-deletion and predicate-raising.[5,h]

The existence of prelexical transformations forces one to reject the second possibility suggested above for how lexical insertions could be transformations but their ordering not be a way in which grammars could differ, namely the proposal that all lexical insertion is done at the very beginning of a derivation. I promised four conceivable solutions to that problem and will quickly describe the remaining two, which I will not choose between, since I have no solid evidence for making such a choice. The third possibility is that lexical insertions are ' anywhere rules ', i.e. rules which are not assigned a fixed ordering with respect to other rules but which apply whenever the configuration to which they apply arises. Some evidence for the existence of anywhere rules has been provided in a recent paper by Ross (1970b), who argues that the rule which deletes a repeated verb to yield sentences such as

(21) John ordered kreplach and Harry kishke.

must be an ' anywhere rule '. The fourth possibility relates to a controversial question in the organization of grammars, namely whether there is a cycle in syntax. If the transformations of a language divide into two subsystems, a cycle and a system of postcyclic rules, then requiring all lexical insertions to take place after the cycle but before the postcyclic rules would be another way of constraining lexical insertions so that their ordering would not be a way in which languages could differ.[6,j] This possibility seems especially worth exploring in view of the fact that the transformations which I have found to be prelexical are also transformations which there is reason to believe are in the cycle, and since this possibility would constrain the notion of ' possible lexical item ' so

---

[5] Jerry L. Morgan has pointed out that prelexical Equi-NP-deletion may explain the difference in meaning between

(22) I asked them when to take off my gloves.
  (which has to do with *my* taking off my gloves)

and

(23) I told them when to take off my gloves.
  (which has to do with *their* taking off my gloves).

x asks y Q (with interrogative *ask*) can be paraphrased as *x asks y to tell x Q* (with imperative *ask*). If something of the latter form is in fact the source of interrogative *ask*, then *when to take off my gloves* in (22) would be the complement of a verb with *me* for indirect object, but in (23) it would be the complement of a verb with *them* for indirect object. Thus in (22) Equi-NP-deletion would apply if the subject of *take off* is *I* but would apply in (23) only if the subject of *take off* is *they*.[1]
[6] This idea and those summarized in the remainder of this paragraph are due to George Lakoff.

much more narrowly than would the third possibility.   My mind, at least, bog-
gles at the thought of lexical items whose use would be contingent on the prior
application of such postcyclic transformations as adverb preposing, WH-word
movement, and relative clause extraposition.   Proposal four but not proposal
three would automatically exclude the possibility of any such lexical items.
It should be noted that proposal four would contradict the claim with which
I began this paper, that there is no linguistically significant level between semantic representation and surface structure: the stage of representation directly
before the postcyclic rules start applying would be such a level, in that that
stage would mark a clear break between representations terminating in semantic
items and representations terminating in lexical items.   However, it would be
far from being a breaking point such as Chomsky's ' deep structure ' was supposed to be, since (if Lakoff and Ross's current conclusions about a cycle in
syntax are correct) a great deal of what have always been considered syntactic
rules would apply on the semantic side of that breaking point, e.g. passivization,
Equi-NP-deletion, *there*-insertion, and dative movement.

[a] This is a poor statement of what ' deep structure' means ; see Lakoff (1968a) for a better
one.   I erred in including McCawley (1970b) in the list of papers in which ' I have argued
. . . that there is no such level ' as ' deep structure ' : in that paper, I largely ignored the
question of whether there is such a level and concentrated on exploring the implications
of a set of assumptions which are inconsistent with there being ' deep structure ' in the
' classical ' sense but which leave open the question of whether there is a level of ' deep
structure' in some weaker sense (such as that suggested in the final paragraph of this paper).
Specifically, I assumed that a grammar consists of a system of ' base rules ' that specify
what semantic structures are possible and a system of ' transformations ' which convert
semantic structures step-by-step into surface structures that express them ; this implies
that the closest analogue to a ' base component' generates something other than ' deep
structures' (since the ultimate elements of semantic structures are not lexical items) but
leaves open the question of whether all lexical insertion takes place at the same (later) stage
of a derivation.
[b] This formulation gratuitously excludes the possibility of lexical insertion attaching
phonological material to something containing a piece to which lexical insertion had
already applied.   Binnick (1969) has provided an example showing that possibility to be
necessary; specifically, to explain the parallelism between the pairs *come/bring to, come/
bring about, come/bring around*, etc., *bring* must be attached to a constituent consisting of
CAUSE (a semantic unit) and *come* (an English word) in structures in which the insertion of *come to, come about*, etc. has already taken place.
[c] This repeats the gratuitous assumption noted in fn. *b*.   I should have said ' . . . which
apply to trees, all or some of whose terminal nodes are labeled by semantic rather than
lexical material '.
[d] The English word *cause* is used in a variety of ways.   The ' CAUSE ' that appears in
Fig. 3 corresponds to a relationship between a person and an event, as in *John caused Bill
to die*.   However, *cause* can also be used to express a relationship between an action or
event and an event, as in *John's reckless act caused Bill's death*.   In this paper I bandied
about *cause* and CAUSE with gay abandon and accordingly was grossly inconsistent as
regards what they were supposed to be ; for example, in fn. 2 I use paraphrases that correspond not to Fig. 3 but to something on the order of

```
                    S
          ┌─────┬────┴───┐
          DO    x       NP
                      ┌──┴──┐
                      e     S
                      ┌─────┴─────┐
                 CAUSE'  NP      NP
                         │     ┌──┴──┐
                         e     S
                       ┌───────┴───────┐
                    BECOME             S
                                 ┌─────┴─────┐
                               NOT           S
                                        ┌────┴────┐
                                      ALIVE        y
```

('x does (something) which causes . . .'), in which CAUSE' is a relation between two events, as in the example just cited.   In McCawley (in press b), I present arguments that this last tree rather than Fig. 3 gives the semantic structure of a clause with *kill*.   A work that makes valuable observations about notions of causation and which I unfortunately did not come to fully appreciate until long after I had written this paper is Vendler (1967a).
e Now see Morgan (1969).
f In saying this, I made the mistake of treating nominalizations as if they contained JUST a sentence.   This of course conflicts with my discussion above, in which nominalizations also involve a variable index plus something (in the above case, the definite description operator) which binds that variable.   Actually, it is rather surprising that (13)–(15) appear to behave as if the nominalization contained only a sentence.
g The facts about reflexivization are too mind-blowingly complicated for a solution as simple as that proposed here to work; see Postal (1971), Jackendoff (1968), and Cantrall (1969) for details of reflexivization in English.   The proposal given here incorrectly predicts that the reflexivization of (16) is obligatory (whereas in fact *John showed Harry a picture of him* is fine, with *him* referring to either John or Harry), and it provides no reason for the different behavior of *the* and *a* (*John showed Harry the picture of him/ *himself*).
h One piece of direct evidence that the object of *look for* originates within the complement of something like *try* when it is non-referential is that in languages like French which maintain a distinction between indicative and subjunctive moods, a relative clause is in the indicative mood in a referential NP but in the subjunctive in a non-referential NP:

> Jean cherche un éléphant qui a deux têtes.   'John is looking for an elephant that
>   has two heads' (referential)
> Jean cherche un éléphant qui ait deux têtes.   'John is looking for an elephant that
>   has two heads' (non-referential).

The complements of 'world-creating' verbs are one of the contexts where French demands the subjunctive.   Dougherty (1970 : 556–9) has presented two classes of arguments against the proposal that (19) and (20) be derived from the same source.   His first set of aruguments, which consist of cases where a transformation is applicable to a structure containing *look for* but not to one containing *try to find*, or vice versa, e.g.

> Hitler was being looked for in Argentina.
> *Hitler was being tried to find in Argentina.

merely show that predicate-raising is in the cycle.   The impossibility of the second example follows from the fact that the derived subject of a passive clause is that NP which was second *in that clause* when passive applied.   This means that for the first example to be derivable, *Hitler* must be the second NP in the clause to which passive applies, which it will be if predicate-raising (which as a side-effect causes the constituents of the lower clause to become constituents of the higher clause) is in the cycle and ordered before passivization.   Dougherty's second set of arguments, which are examples of adverbs that may be combined with one of *look for* and *try to find* but not the other are much more interesting and indeed provide evidence that *look for* must have more in it than just *try to find*.   For example, the possibility of a certain class of locatives with *look for* but not *try to find*:

> John looked high and low for a goat.
> *John tried high and low to find a goat.
> Sam looked through the works of Tennyson for a suitable quotation.
> *Sam tried through the works of Tennyson to find a suitable quotation.

gives evidence that *look for* has a semantic structure containing an extra constituent beyond those provided in *try to find*.   I conjecture that these locatives orginate as the object of something as 'examine' and that 'try to find' is really a purpose-clause in sematic structure.

[1] Another example of this type, namely an explanation of why *apologize* has Equi-NP-deletion under identity with its subject rather than its indirect object, is discussed in McCawley (1971b).

[j] Another possibility which I did not consider here is that lexical insertion is in the cycle, but at a fixed point in the cycle, e.g. the last rule in the cycle.   The fact discussed in fn. *b* provides some reason for adopting this alternative over the others considered here. It should be obvious that if lexical insertion is in the cycle, there is no such level as deep structure.

9. Review of *Current Trends in Linguistics*, Vol. 3: Theoretical Foundations[*]

The contents of this volume come from lectures given at the 1964 LSA summer institute at Indiana University. The bulk of the volume is devoted to the lectures given in a series featuring guest lecturers—Noam Chomsky, Joseph Greenberg, Mary Haas, Charles Hockett, Yakov Malkiel, Kenneth Pike, and Uriel Weinreich—who each held forth for one week (four one-hour lectures) on topics relating to current work. Also included are Edward Stankiewiez's Collitz lecture and a lecture by Robert Godel on Saussure. The contributions in this volume correspond fairly closely to the content of the original lectures at Bloomington, except that Hockett's lectures appear in greatly expanded form (so that they now make up about 30% of the entire volume), and Pike chose to replace his lectures by an annotated bibliography of tagmemics. Mouton has also published the contributions by Chomsky, Greenberg, and Hockett as separate volumes in the Janua linguarum, series minor. As far as I can tell, the texts of these three volumes are identical to the corresponding sections of *CTL3*, except for the correction of some minor typographical errors (though not of a couple of major ones) and the addition to Hockett's volume of a preface in which

[*] Edited by Thomas A. Sebeok. Pp. xi, 537. The Hague: Mouton, 1966. $19.50. This review was published in *Language* 44.556–93.

he repudiates much of the content of his lectures. Haas's work has now also been announced for separate publication.[1]

Chomsky's ' Topics in the theory of generative grammar ' (1–60) is one of the first public presentations of the conception of syntax presented in his *Aspects* (1965), which was nearing completion at the time he delivered these lectures. He begins with a survey of his ideas on the goals of linguistic theory which, while it contains little that does not appear in earlier writings of his, nonetheless gives an admirably lucid and concise account of some basic ideas underlying what follows. He then presents a survey of the development of transformational syntactic theory from 1957 to 1964, with attention to the inadequacies of the earlier theory and to the corresponding revisions which were accordingly incorporated into the theory of *Aspects*. At several points there are digressions in which he summarizes and replies to objections raised by various critics. The term ' digression ' is used loosely here, since these replies take up fully half of Chomsky's lecture series. Rumor has it that Chomsky single-handedly made a best-seller out of a certain obscure monograph which his audiences at these and other lectures concluded to be a work of importance because of the amount of time which he devoted to replying to it. There is also a section on phonology; however, it is concerned almost entirely with replies to critics and contains only two brief paragraphs summarizing current work in generative phonology.

After a discussion of the crucial concepts of competence and performance, Chomsky gives the following definition: ' a GENERATIVE GRAMMAR (that is, an explicit grammar that makes no appeal to the reader's " faculté de langage " but rather attempts to incorporate the mechanisms of this faculty) is a system of rules that relate signals to semantic interpretations of these signals'.[2] This definition shows the striking change in Chomsky's attitude to semantics which has taken place since *Syntactic structures*, where he stated that ' the fundamental aim in the linguistic analysis of a language L is to separate the GRAMMATICAL sequences which are the sentences of L from the UNGRAMMATICAL sequences which are not sentences of L and to study the structure of the grammatical sequences. The grammar of L will thus be a device that generates all of the grammatical sequences of L and none of the ungrammatical ones ' (1957: 13). Thus, in 1957 Chomsky had rejected only a portion of the viewpoint labeled by Jakobson as ' cryptanalytic ': while he had rejected the view that linguistic description must be entirely in terms of elements defined in distributional terms, he still retained the view that linguistic data are entirely distributional. In the present work, however, he makes direct reference to semantics in his definition of the term ' deep structure ': ' Let us then introduce the neutral technical

---

[1] Abstracts of the various contributions to this volume, by their respective contributors, can be found in a mammoth review under multiple authorship in *Current Anthropology* 9.125–79 (1968), which also includes replies to the various reviewers.

[2] In light of Chomsky's discussion of competence and performance, it is clear that ' signal ' is here to be interpreted in the sense of ' phonetic representation ', i.e. directions on how to pronounce the utterance, rather than the actual sounds which result from the implementation of these instructions.

notion of " syntactic description ", and take a syntactic description of a sentence to be an (abstract) object of some sort, associated with the sentence, that uniquely determines its semantic interpretation (the latter notion being left unspecified pending further insights into semantic theory) as well as its phonetic form . . . Let us define the " deep structure of a sentence " as that aspect of the S[yntactic] D[escription] that determines its semantic interpretation, and the " surface structure of a sentence " as that aspect of the SD that determines its phonetic form ' (7).   He then presents arguments that the surface structure of a sentence is a labeled tree and that deep structure is not the same as surface structure.

The definition of ' deep structure ' just quoted will undoubtedly cause confusion, since it was constructed to fit a theory of grammar which Chomsky has abandoned since the writing of these lectures and thus does not fit the sense in which he has used the term ' deep structure ' in more recent publications (e.g., 1967, 1970a).   Indeed, unless this definition is supplemented by some heavy constraints on notions like ' rule of semantic interpretation ', it does not define anything : there is a wide range of 'aspects of syntactic description' which could reasonably be proposed as the input to ' rules of semantic interpretation ', and there is indeed nothing a-priori to prevent one from taking ' rule of semantic interpretation ' in so broad a sense as to include the inverses of all transformations and thus take ' deep structure ' to be identical to ' surface structure '.   Chomsky is able to argue that ' deep structure ' differs from ' surface structure ' only on the basis of a number of unstated premises concerning the limits of syntax and semantics.   For example, he writes : ' In the case of [*they don't know how good meat tastes*], for example, a descriptively adequate grammar must not only assign two SD's to the sentence but must also do so in such a way that in one of these the grammatical relations of *good*, *meat*, and *taste* are as in " Meat tastes good ", while in the other they are as in " Meat which is good tastes Adjective " ' (6).   Here Chomsky assumes that the relations he is talking about are grammatical rather than semantic, and accordingly that a grammar must contain two separate systems of rules : ' transformations ', which relate underlying structures, in which these grammatical (by assumption, non-semantic) relations are directly represented, to surface structures, in which they may be neutralized ; and ' rules of semantic interpretation ', applying to the underlying structures. As far as I can tell, Chomsky's ' grammatical relations ' are as much semantic as syntactic : his reason for asserting a particular grammatical relation to hold in an example appears to be simply that there are other items containing tokens of the same LEXICAL ITEMS standing in the same SEMANTIC RELATIONS as in the examples just quoted.[3]   The notion of ' lexical item ' is crucial to Chomsky's no-

---

[3] One major omission in Chomsky's account of ' grammatical relation ' is justification of the assertion that all the things he treats as examples of, e.g., the ' object relation ', belong together.   While it is easy to convince oneself that *John* and *please* are related the same way in *John is easy to please* and *No one can please John*, it is not clear even what would be meant by saying that *John* and *please* are related in those sentences in the same way as are *build* and *seven birdhouses* in *John has built seven birdhouses*, or *imagine* and *a centaur* in *John imagined a centaur*.

tion of ' grammatical relation ' and thus to his distinction between syntax and semantics : both presuppose that all insertion of lexical items takes place at the same point in the derivations of sentences (so that there are for Chomsky only ' syntactic ' representations, which have only ' lexical items ' for their ultimate units, and ' semantic ' representations, which have only semantic units as ultimate ones). Similarly, it is assumed that the rules which affect ' semantic representations ' are wholly separate and of a different nature from those which affect ' syntactic representations '. The crucial role in syntax which ' lexical item ' plays for Chomsky has been made especially clear in a recent paper (1970a), where, although he regards passives and the *easy to please* construction as transformationally derived, he treats adjectives in *-able* as generated by the base component, one of his principal reasons being that some of the *-able* adjectives are based on morphemes which never occur independently, e.g. *malleable* and *legible,* whereas the other two constructions can be derived from underlying structures in which all the verbs and adjectives can be used as independent words. Thus, the absence of verbs such as *malley* and *lege* from the lexicon of English leads him to conclude that the relationship of *that book* to *read* in *That book is easy to read* and in *That book is readable,* even though presumably the same in both cases, is directly represented in the deep structure of only the former, whereas in the latter it is inferred by some rule of semantic interpretation.

The failure to make these assumptions explicit and to provide justification for them is, of course, understandable : the underlying syntactic representations which had been proposed up to 1964 all hugged the ground of surface structure, and the few semantic representations which had been proposed looked so different from those syntactic representations that one could hardly have failed to pronounce them totally different in nature, and to consider the justification for such a pronouncement too obvious to mention. But this is no longer the case. Chomsky's remark (48) that ' the burden of proof is on the linguist who believes . . . that there is . . . a linguistically significant level of representation meeting the conditions of taxonomic phonemics and provided by the phonological rules of the grammar ' applies equally well to the linguist who believes that a level such as ' deep structure ' exists intermediate between semantic and surface syntactic representation.

Chomsky then takes up the question of what minimal requirements must be met if something is to qualify as a theory of language : ' to develop a substantive linguistic theory we must provide : (i) theories of phonetic and semantic representation, (ii) a general account of the notion " syntactic description ", (iii) a specification of the class of potential generative grammars, (iv) a general account of how these grammars function, that is, how they generate SD's and assign to them phonetic and semantic interpretations, thus pairing phonetically represented signals with semantic interpretations ' (8).[4] Requirements (i), (ii), and (iii) are

---

[4] It is interesting to note that this sentence is the first place in these lectures where Chomsky uses the word ' generate ' ; indeed, up to this point he has not even touched on the idea of generating a language, i.e. specifying what are and what are not the grammatical sentences of that language.

clear enough—although I fail to see why (ii) is made a separate heading rather than simply included under (i)—but (iv) is less so. ' How these grammars function ' and ' how they generate SD's' sound as if they refer to a theory of performance; however, a close reading of the remainder of the paragraph reveals that (iv) means something like ' a definition of the expressions " Grammar G generates SD X ", " Grammar G pairs SD X with semantic representation Y ", and " Grammar G pairs SD X with phonetic representation Z ", valid for all grammars of the class specified under (iii) '. Chomsky then takes up a fifth requirement which he wishes to impose on theories of language, namely that the theory provide an ' evaluation measure ' for grammars, i.e. a definition of a relation of ' more highly valued than ' among the grammars permitted by the theory. He asserts that these five requirements can be interpreted as the specification of

a hypothetical language-acquisition device AD that can provide as ' output ' a descriptively adequate grammar G for the language L on the basis of certain primary linguistic data from L as input; that is, a device represented schematically as:

primary linguistic data → | AD | → G

We want the device AD to be language-independent—that is, capable of learning any human language and only these. We want it, in other words, to provide an implicit definition of the notion ' human language ' Were we able to develop the specifications for a language-acquisition device of this sort, we could realistically claim to be able to provide an explanation for the linguistic intuition—the tacit competence—of the speaker of the language. This explanation would be based on the assumption that the specifications of the device AD provide the basis for language acquisition, primary linguistic data from some language providing the empirical conditions under which the development of a generative grammar takes place (10).

The flaw in this account of the relationship between language acquisition and linguistic theory is this last point, which in effect likens the child to a linguist who elicits ten notebooks full of data from his informants in New Guinea and doesn't start writing his grammar until he is on the boat back to the United States. Language acquisition involves the child's being continually in the process of constructing and revising his grammar, the appropriate diagram for the process not being that given by Chomsky but one involving feedback.[5]

data → | AD | → G

Since language acquisition takes place via some such trial-and-error process

[5] I have intentionally omitted the words ' primary linguistic ' from before ' data ' : any data which give the child any information about the meaning of a sentence or a morpheme may play a role in language acquisition, even data which are neither ' primary ' nor ' linguistic '. ' Data ' here must include not only things that the ' informants ' say, but also the circumstances under which they have said them, and things that the learner himself says and his observations of the results which follow upon his saying them.

rather than by the accumulation of a large body of unanalysed data, it is not evident that any notion of 'evaluation measure' is needed to explicate learning. It might well be that each time the child revises his grammar he simply selects at random one of a set of possible modifications in his grammar; if the modification brings his language into closer accord with that of his 'informants', he keeps the modification, and if it does not, he will certainly encounter data that would trigger further modification. Explication of language acquisition would require not the setting up of an evaluation measure but rather a characterization of the possible revisions which a learner may make in his grammars, given the grammar and a datum which is inconsistent with that grammar.[6] It should also be noted that no explicit proposal has ever been made for an evaluation measure of the type which Chomsky envisions (a numerical measure of 'cost', in which the various rules and dictionary entries make a specifiable contribution to the 'cost' of the grammar and the grammar with the lowest 'cost' is 'most highly valued'). While proposals have been made for evaluation measures defined on various parts of a grammar, notably phonology, no proposal has ever been made which would allow the costs of phonological rules, transformations, phrase structure rules, dictionary entries, and semantic interpretation rules to be measured in the same units and a total cost assigned to the entire grammar; indeed, even in phonology, where most of the concrete proposals for evaluation measures lie, no one has made any satisfactory proposal for the contribution to cost made by such non-phonological items as syntactic categories and morphemic features like inflectional type. The actual practice of transformational grammarians recently has been to rely very little on evaluation measures but rather to choose between grammars on the basis either of 'crucial experiments' (i.e. eliciting data for which the two grammars have different implications), or of data from other languages, which permit tighter universal constraints to be imposed on the class of possible grammars.

Chomsky's Section II is devoted to replies to criticisms by Reichling, Uhlenbeck, Dixon, and Harman of the ideas sketched in section I; also included are lengthy footnotes in which criticisms by Hill, Longacre, and Gleason are dealt with. Chomsky argues in most cases that the criticisms are the result of either terminological equivocation (for example, Dixon asserts that preliterate cultures have no conception of 'grammaticality' but later says that members of these cultures 'have firm ideas concerning what is in their language', which is precisely what Chomsky meant by 'grammaticality'), or arbitrary restrictions on the subject matter of linguistics and its parts (for example, Uhlenbeck's restriction of 'syntax' to the study of relationships which are overtly expressed in the surface structure of sentences). Much of Chomsky's criticism of Harman's (1963) 'defense of phrase structure' revolves about the point that this is a defense of something other than phrase structure, since the term 'phrase structure' refers to something which does not allow for the discontinuous constituents, 'complex symbols', and deletions which Harman's 'extended phrase structure'

---

[6] Further remarks along these lines are contained in McCawley (1968f).

involves. Here there is some quite pointless name-calling—for example, Chomsky's parenthetical remark that ' extended phrase structure grammar has no more connection with phrase structure grammar than antelopes have with ants ' (24). Actually, Harman's use of the term ' phrase structure ' here is about as objectionable as Chomsky's use of the term ' transformational grammar ' to designate the system of syntactic description of *Aspects*: the difference between that and the ' transformational grammar ' of *Syntactic structures* is comparable in magnitude to that between ' extended phrase structure grammar ' and the ' phrase structure grammar ' described in Chomsky and Miller (1963). Chomsky's concern with terminology here obscures two important issues which Harman's paper raises : (1) can the inadequacies of ' phrase structure ' summarized in such works as Postal (1964) be met by more general systems of syntactic description which operate entirely in terms of surface structure? and (2) is Chomsky's definition of ' phrase structure ' the most correct formalization possible of the kind of syntactic description which it purports to formalize, namely the immediate constituent analysis of such linguists as Bloch and Wells? Since Harman appears to have advanced his extension of ' phrase structure ' as a positive answer to the first question, it is in that framework that it must be judged, and had Chomsky concentrated on that question, he could have made a far more devastating criticism of it than he presented. Harman is able to dispense with agreement transformations only at the cost of having separate rules, e.g. to select the number of the subject NP (which must be attached as a feature of the S-node which dominates it, so as to allow that feature to be ' inherited ' by the VP through Harman's ' feature inheritance ' mechanisms), and to select the number of all other NP's.[7] Since the inheritance of features from a common dominating node in the surface structure is Harman's only means of incorporating selectional restrictions into a grammar, and since there are infinitely many types of verb-NP selectional restrictions which can hold in surface structure,[8] Harman's treatment would require an infinite number of selectional features and infinitely many rules to attach them to the relevant S-nodes.

Chomsky then turns to a summary of the development of transformational syntactic theory from 1955 to 1964. He devotes particular attention to characteristics of the theory presented in *Syntactic structures* which he has found deficient or inadequate, and to the changes which he proposes to remedy these defects. The chief defects which he notes in the earlier theory are as follows : (a) It allowed a much wider range of ways of combining sentences via ' gener-

[7] Because Harman neglected to include the latter type of rule in his restatement of the rules of Chomsky (1957), his rules generate only sentences in which all NP's have the same number.

[8] This follows from the fact that the subject of an embedded clause may be deleted if identical to a certain NP in the containing clause ; the occurrence of the latter NP in the surface structure then will meet both the selectional restriction imposed by the verb of which it was originally subject or object, and the selectional restriction imposed by the verb of which the deleted NP was subject. But the latter NP may in addition have to meet selectional restrictions imposed by the deletion of the subject of a still ' lower ' embedded clause, etc.

alized transformations' than was actually utilized in language. (Specifically, as first noted by Fillmore, the possibility of applying 'singulary transformations' to a 'matrix sentence' before embedding another sentence in it by a 'generalized transformation' was never utilized.) (b) It allowed alternative analyses in which an element (e.g., English *not*) was either inserted by an optional transformation or was selected by a phrase-structure rule and assigned its correct position by an obligatory transformation; but the latter type of analysis always turned out to be correct whenever syntactic grounds could be found for preferring one of these analyses. (c) It provided for no 'componential' representation of lexical categories, thus allowing no non-ad-hoc way of referring to the classes defined by intersecting categorizations such as common/proper, animate/inanimate, count/mass, etc. The proposed revisions of the theory are: (a) 'Generalized transformations' are eliminated from the theory; the phrase structure rules generate structures that may involve sentences within sentences; the transformational component contains only 'singulary' transformations and applies in cyclic fashion: the transformations first apply in order to the innermost sentence, then they apply to the next 'higher' sentence in that structure, etc.[9] (b) Optional transformations are restricted to the realm of 'stylistic variation' (e.g., the 'particle separation' transformation, which yields variants such as *He looked up the information, He looked the information up*). (c) Lexical items are represented as complexes of (generally binary) feature specifications, and the rewriting rules of the base component of the earlier theory are supplemented by rules which create feature complexes that specify the classes of lexical items which may occupy the positions in question.[10] Because of the constraint on optional transformations, Chomsky is able to say that the structures generated by the base component contain all the information which is relevant to semantic interpretation, and thus that the base component generates 'deep structures'. In the earlier theory, supplemented by Katz and Fodor's semantics (1963), 'deep structure' as defined above would be a 'T-marker'—a tree whose terminal nodes correspond to 'kernel phrase-markers' and whose non-terminal nodes are labeled by generalized and optional transformations.[11] Katz and Fodor's programmatic

[9] Since the appearance of Chomsky (1965), it has been discovered that this conception of the organization of the transformational component is an over-simplification. The transformational component splits up into at least two sub-systems, the CYCLE and the POST-CYCLIC transformations, and perhaps three: a PRE-CYCLIC transformation seems needed for the 'sentence pronominalization' exhibited in *John is believed to have murdered his wife, but Harry doubts it*. As Lakoff observes, this must be pre-cyclic, since the cyclic transformations of subject-raising and passivization break apart the sentence *John has murdered his wife*, which is the antecedent of *it;* this implies that if the transformation were cyclic or post-cyclic, the antecedent would no longer be available when the transformation applies. See Ross (1967a, 1967b), for some discussion of the question of which transformations are cyclic and which post-cyclic.
[10] For a detailed critique of the conception of 'base component' presented in Chomsky (1965), see McCawley (1968g).
[11] It is misleading for Chomsky to include items such as Chomsky (1956, 1957), and Lees (1957) in a list of publications in which 'the validation . . . has been attempted' of the assertion that 'the deep structure of a sentence is in general not identical to its surface structure, but is a much more abstract representation of grammatical relations and syntactic organization' (21-2), since none of these works concerned itself particularly with the question of what 'aspect of the SD . . . determines its semantic interpretation'.

description of semantic interpretation involves two types of 'projection rules' (= 'semantic interpretation rules') : 'type 1' rules, which attach 'semantic readings' to the nodes in 'kernel phrase-markers' on the basis of the semantic readings of the nodes which they dominate, and 'type 2' rules, which attach semantic readings to 'derived structures' on the basis of the transformation which yields the structure and the semantic reading of the input(s) to that transformation. Type 1 projection rules are an application to underlying representations of an idea which many authors have suggested in connection with surface structure (e.g. Pike 1943; Wells 1947, §35), but none to my knowledge have applied systematically. Chomsky, following Katz and Postal (1964), argues that no type 2 projection rules are needed : that the transformations of *Syntactic structures* which changed the meaning of what they applied to (e.g. the negation and question transformations) were incorrect, and that there were syntactic grounds for deriving the sentences in question from structures containing elements of interrogation, negation, etc. Subsequently, Chomsky has retracted the claim that no transformations have semantic effects and now holds a position substantially the same as that of Jackendoff (1968), where it is argued that the structures generated by the base component[12] determine only certain aspects of meaning, and that the surface structure of a sentence and possibly also some of the intermediate stages in its derivation are needed to deduce the full meaning of the sentence—i.e., the input to the system of 'semantic interpretation rules' is not a single P-marker but the entire derivation of the sentence.   I will withhold criticism of this approach until an account of its details appears (only a brief hint of Chomsky's present position has been published, 1967 : 407).[a]

One significant innovation in the syntactic theory which Chomsky expounds in these lectures is that of allowing the base component to generate structures, not all of which underlie sentences; the transformations then act as a 'filter', rejecting certain structures when they cannot undergo some transformation which is necessary if a sentence is to result.   For example, Chomsky analyzes

(1)   I expected the man who quit work to be fired

as having an underlying structure containing the embedded sentence *the man quit work*, to which a transformation would apply turning *the man* into *who*.   He points out (41) that had the embedded sentence been *the boy quit work*, that transformation would have been inapplicable, since it is contingent on a noun phrase in the embedded sentence being identical to the noun phrase to which it is adjoined,[13] and no sentence would result.   But one important gap in Chomsky's

---

[12] Chomsky (1967) and Jackendoff use the term 'deep structure' for this level of representation, rather than in the sense of Chomsky's definition quoted above.

[13] The analysis of relative clauses as underlying adjuncts to full noun phrases is probably wrong.   Michael Brame (personal communication) has pointed out that noun phrases such as *the headway which I've made on my dissertation, the umbrage which John took at my proposal, the aspersions which John cast on Max's character*, and *the axe that you have to grind* have as 'head' a portion of an idiom contained in the relative clause, and thus argues that the head noun in all relative clause constructions originates within the relative clause.[b]   A language in which such an analysis is inescapable is treated in Bird (1968).

theory is a correct account of the conditions under which this ' filtering ' would
have to take place.   Chomsky's proposal that every embedded sentence must
undergo some transformation, ' combining ' it with the sentence in which it is
embedded, is inadequate, since it ignores the role of the verb in determining
whether it is necessary for a transformation to apply.   Given the kind of underlying structures proposed in *Aspects*, *try* would require that the transformation of
Equi-NP-deletion apply: i.e., the structure roughly sketched as (*John tried
(John open the door*)) would underlie *John tried to open the door*, but (*John tried
(Arthur open the door*)) would not underlie anything.   But *want* would not require it: i.e., (*John wanted (John open the door*)) and (*John wanted (Arthur open
the door*)) would both underlie sentences, namely *John wanted to open the door* and
John wanted Arthur to open the door respectively.   This gap is filled by the extension of Chomsky's theory proposed in Lakoff (1965).   Postal (1967) has recently
pointed out that the Chomsky-Lakoff conception of ' filtering ' blurs an important distinction among the structures which it rejects—namely, that some of the
structures rejected are semantically incoherent, e.g. (*John tried (Arthur open the
door*)) and *the man (the boy quit work*), and would have to be excluded regardless
of what transformations English has; but others are perfectly intelligible and
may in some dialects yield a grammatical sentence.   For example, for some
speakers *hope to* requires Equi-NP-deletion, but for others it does not: for both
groups of speakers

>   (2)   I hope to win the prize

is grammatical, but only for the second group is

>   (3)   I hope for you to win the prize

grammatical.   Postal argues that two separate types of mechanisms are required
to exclude the two types of inadmissible structures: constraints on semantic
well-formedness, which exclude structures like (*John tried (Arthur open the door*))
and are completely independent of the transformational component of the grammar; and a theory of exceptions like Lakoff's, which, however, would be confined to true transformational idiosyncrasies of lexical items, as in the case of
hope.   Evidence confirming Postal's position is presented by Perlmutter (1968a),
who shows the inadequacy of the formulation of various restrictions as requirements that a certain transformation apply (or not apply).   For example, Lakoff's
assertion that verbs such as *scream* do not allow Equi-NP-deletion, as in

>   (4)   I screamed for John to open the door
>   (5)   *I screamed to open the door,

is false, as witness sentences such as

>   (6)   I screamed to be allowed to leave.

The proper generalization can be stated only in terms of the semantic structure
of the sentences, not in terms of the transformational derivation: the complement of *scream* must have an agent, which must be different from the agent of

scream.

The final section of Chomsky's lectures is devoted to phonology.   It begins with a brief description (overly brief, in my opinion) of his conception of the phonological component of a grammar and the representations which the rules of the phonological component operate on.   It is unfortunate that Chomsky devotes so little space to discussing the notion of CYCLE, which at the time was known largely through an oral tradition and about which gross misunderstanding was rampant :   a discussion of how phonological rules must be organized, and why, would have been far more valuable than the repetition of Halle's celebrated argument against a phonemic level and the answers to criticisms by Marckwardt and Lamb which form the bulk of this section.   One rather trivial point mentioned by Chomsky in his sketch of generative phonology has been responsible for a good deal of confusion, as manifested by rather weird rules reported to have turned up in term papers by students who had attended these lectures.   Chomsky states that ' each lexical entry is simply a SET of specified features ' (44, emphasis added) and mentions that the features include phonological features such as ' $[\pm \text{Voiced}_n]$, where n is an integer indicating position '.   This passage seems to imply the absurd proposal that phonology operates not in terms of features like [Voiced], [Nasal], and [Syllabic] but rather in terms of features like [Voiced$_3$], [Nasal$_{12}$], and [Syllabic$_9$]—i.e., as if it allowed phonological rules like ' the 3rd segment becomes nasal if the 8th segment is voiceless ', but excluded rules which were not contingent on absolute position, e.g., a rule which voices any consonant that is followed by a voiced consonant.   It is clear from all of Chomsky's prior and subsequent writings that he intended no such thing :   all of the phonological rules that he writes are based on the positions of segments relative to each other and not on their absolute positions.

I will pass over Chomsky's reply to Marckwardt's 1957 criticism of the 1956 Chomsky-Halle-Lukoff paper on English stress, since the points covered were not particularly live issues even in 1964, let alone at the time I write this review. One amusing sequence of misunderstandings appears in this section :   Chomsky-Halle-Lukoff treated the example *excess profits tax* as having the constituents *excess profits* and *tax ;*   Marckwardt accused Chomsky-Halle-Lukoff of analyzing it as *excess* plus *profits tax ;*   and Chomsky accuses Marckwardt of objecting to the analysis as *excess profits* plus *tax.*

Chomsky's reply to Lamb's then unpublished criticism of Halle's argument against a phonemic level (see now Lamb 1966b) is that Lamb's proposals have no bearing on Halle's argument :   what Lamb suggests as a ' phonemic representation ' is not phonemic in either the American or the Praguean sense, since it distinguishes between Russian [č] and [j] (Lamb's /jh/ and /j/) even though they are predictable variants of one another, and marks the voicelessness of the [č] of such words as *čest'*, even though it is non-distinctive.   While Chomsky's criticism is correct, there is one further aspect of Lamb's proposal which deserves comment, namely that his ' phonemic representations ' appear to revolve crucially about the notion of ' markedness ', and to involve the constraint that the marked term of an opposition must be indicated in a phonemic representation even if it is non-distinctive.   The latter principle, plus Lamb's questionable interpretation of ' voiceless ' as the marked member of the voicing opposition, would presumably be his justification for calling his representation ' phonemic '. However, the basis for his notion of markedness is unclear, since he obviously rejects the principle that the possibility of the marked member of an opposition implies the possibility of the unmarked member.

Greenberg's ' Language universals ' (61–112) deals with the closely related topics of implicational universals (i.e. assertions of the form ' all languages which have the property f also have the property g ') and markedness.   The only real fault in this extremely lucid and informative study is some equivocation on the meaning of ' marked ' and ' unmarked '.   Greenberg sometimes uses ' marked ' to mean possessing some positive characteristic (e.g. participation of some articulatory organ, or presence of some affix) which is lacking in the ' unmarked ' member; but also sometimes uses ' marked ' to mean ' less normal ', as in his discussion of Klamath phoneme frequencies (66), where he identifies voiceless sonorants and voiced obstruents as ' marked ' and voiced sonorants and voiceless obstruents as ' unmarked '.   This latter conception of markedness involves not simply interpreting certain feature specifications as ' marked ' wherever they occur, but either (a) speaking of various feature specifications as being marked relative to specific environments (e.g., saying that [+voiced] is marked when it appears in the same segment as [+obstruent], or when it appears in a segment that is [+consonantal] and is followed by a segment that is [+consonantal, −voiced]); or (b) speaking not of marked feature specifications, but only of marked combinations of feature specifications (e.g., speaking of the combination [+obstruent, +voiced] or the combination [+consonantal, +voiced] [+consonantal, −voiced] as being marked), without attaching the markedness to any specific feature specification in the combination;   (a) is explored in the last chapter of Chomsky and Halle (1968);   (b) is as yet virgin territory.   A notion of markedness relative to an environment is implicit in one Praguean notion, namely that of ' externally determined neutralization ' (i.e. neutralization by assimilation or dissimilation).   The fact that in many languages consonants become voiced before a voiced consonant is not taken as a counter-example to Trubetzkoy's principle that the unmarked member of an opposition appears when the opposition is neutralized.   Treating consonants in that position as unmarked for voicing (as Jakobson does) implies that in that position ' voiceless ' is the MARKED member of the opposition, even though it is the unmarked member elsewhere. It is not clear that the ' internally determined neutralization ' to which Trubetzkoy's principle refers actually exists: the examples which are usually cited of it, such as the devoicing and deaspiration of Sanskrit stops in sentence-final position, can be viewed as assimilation to the features of the pause which is potentially present at the end of the sentence.   If there is no ' internally determined neutralization ', can any sense be attached to statements that one segment type is less marked than another, irrespective of environment?   Greenberg touches briefly (71) on a notion that may justify an affirmative answer to this question, namely Sapir's notion of a phoneme as an 'ideal articulation', i.e. a segment which is 'fully specified' for all features, non-distinctive as well as distinctive, and which is converted into 'inorganic' variants in various environments.[14]   Greenberg illustrates this notion by quoting Daniel Jones (1962 : 20) on Dutch : 'The sound *g* exists but only before voiced consonants, e.g. before *d* in [zagduk] (*zakdoek*, handkerchief) . . . *g* is therefore a member of the *k* phoneme in that language'.   Greenberg comments, 'It is psychologically interesting that Jones here identifies the phoneme with its basic allophone, the unvoiced *k* as against the marked and assimilative voiced allophone *g*.   I believe that in general where phonemicists are forced to a choice of symbols for a phoneme with a number of differing allophones, they choose one which phonetically represents the unmarked feature'.   The interpretation that I would put on the choice of *k* for the underlying segment here is that if one were to set up underlying *k*'s in the morphemes in question, all of the [g]'s could be derived by a 'natural' phonological rule, namely a rule which regressively assimilates voicing in consonant sequences, whereas if underlying *g*'s had been set up, there would be no 'natural' phonological rule to derive the [k]'s—i.e., intervocalic stops do not naturally devoice, as would be necessary to derive *maken* from an underlying form with a *g*.   The intuition which Greenberg expresses in the last quotation appears equivalent to the intuition that there are languages in which all [k]'s and [g]'s can be derived by natural rules from [k]'s but not from [g]'s, but that there are no languages in which all [k]'s and [g]'s can be derived by natural rules from [g]'s but not from [k]'s.   I tend to believe in the validity of the notion of 'absolute markedness' involved in Greenberg's comment on Jones, but I note two points.   First, the validity of the notion can only be established by making use of the notion of 'markedness relative to environment', since the 'natural' phonological rules are what determines markedness relative to their environments ; i.e., the unmarked value of a feature relative to an environment is simply the value produced by a 'natural' phonological rule having that environment.[15] Second, the statistical tables which Greenberg gives only provide a first approximation to the frequencies of 'absolutely marked' and 'absolutely unmarked' members of oppositions, since the statistics are based on phonemic representations which may contain tokens of the 'marked' segment (e.g., a voiced stop) which got that way through an assimilation.

Greenberg convincingly illustrates the thesis that tokens of the marked member of an opposition are less frequent than tokens of the unmarked member by presenting phoneme counts for voicing, aspiration, and glottalization of consonants in Hausa, Klamath, Coos, Yurok, Chiricahua, and Maidu ; for vowel length in Icelandic, Sanskrit, Czech, Hungarian, Finnish, Karok, and Chiricahua ; and for palatalization in Russian.   The only quarrel which I have with these statistics, beyond the caveat at the end of my preceding paragraph, is that

---

[14] See McCawley (1967a) for justification of this interpretation of Sapir's conception of 'phoneme'.
[15] I am indebted to David L. Stampe for this observation.

the figure of 91.7% short vowels and 8.3% long vowels for Finnish is misleading, in that Finnish has long vowels only in the stressed (first) syllable (except for some long vowels in recent loan words and some long vowels which arise from the loss of intervocalic [h] or [t]), and the diphthongs *ie, üö, uo*, which Greenberg counts as two tokens of a short vowel, arise historically from the breaking of long mid vowels and still function in the language as the long counterparts of short mid vowels.   Statistics on the first syllable which lumped *ie, üö, uo* with the long vowels would yield figures quite different from Greenberg's.

From phonology Greenberg turns to morphological categories.   He presents statistics on the frequencies of the number, person, tense, voice, and mood categories of Sanskrit, Latin, Russian, French, Spanish, and English, and a sizeable body of facts about neutralizations, zero expression of unmarked categories, and the use of the unmarked form for things unspecified or mixed as regards the opposition in question, e.g. the use of the masculine form in referring to a person whose sex is not known to the speaker, or in agreement with a conjunction of both masculine and feminine nouns.   I am not fully convinced by Greenberg's argument that the category ' singular ' is unmarked relative to ' plural '.   The statistical predominance of singular over plural may be merely a reflection of what people have occasion to talk about rather than of the system which they use in talking.   Compare, for example, the fact (84) that the Spanish, French, and German number words decrease in frequency as the number they refer to increases, except that ' round ' numbers like 10 are more frequent than the immediately preceding numbers ; this fact undoubtedly reflects the fact that one more often has occasion to talk about three objects than about four, and implies no preference for the word *tres* over the word *cuatro* on the part of Spanish speakers.   There are a number of facts which I can cite in support of the thesis that ' plural ' is less marked than ' singular ': (a) plural is normal when it is not known whether one or more than one individual is being referred to (e.g., application forms give headings like *schools attended* and *children ;* many English speakers use *they* when the antecedent is *who, nobody,* or *anybody*); (b) in languages which have an indefinite article, the singular indefinite article is always historically and usually synchronically related to the word for ' one ', whereas the plural indefinite article more often than not is zero; and (c) plural count nouns pattern like singular mass nouns in all significant respects—they both take a zero indefinite article, they both participate in a partitive construction, and in English they both take a zero generic article rather than the generic *the* of singular count nouns—

(7)   Gold is valuable.
(8)   Women are fickle.
(9)   The automobile is an invention of the devil.

Greenberg's discussion of number would have been much more valuable if he had extended his coverage to include systems other than the singular/plural and singular/dual/plural systems which figure in his examples.   For example, I would have welcomed some observations and statistics on Kiowa (E. Trager

1960 : 67), in which the principal number opposition is between ' natural number ' (which may be unit, pair, or herd, depending on what is being talked about) and deviation from ' natural number ', or in Hopi (Voegelin and Voegelin 1967), whose number categories are singular, paucal, and plural, ' paucal ' meaning the minimum number beyond one that makes sense semantically.   If features are assigned to the three Hopi number categories as follows—

	Singular	Paucal	Plural
unit	+	−	−
minimum	+	+	−

—then the Hopi verb, which takes one form if the subject is singular or paucal and a different form if the subject is plural, can be said to be inflected for the feature of ' minimum ' and to exhibit simple agreement on that feature, rather than (as the Voegelins, following tradition, describe it) inflected for plurality and taking singular agreement with a paucal subject.

Another category discussed by Greenberg, for which different criteria for markedness give conflicting results, is person.   The criteria of statistical predominance and zero expression both indicate that 3rd person is less marked than 1st or 2nd.   However, the criterion of the unmarked category representing mixed category membership would make 3rd person the most marked of the three categories, since *you and I* and *he and I* are 1st person, while *you and he* is 2nd person.   Person in this respect is reminiscent of the ' male ' and ' female ' speech forms of Yana, where ' female ' forms must be used if the speaker or any of the addressees is a woman.   I have no idea why this neutralization works differently from the gender neutralization of Spanish, where conjoining masculine with feminine nouns yields an item that takes masculine agreement.   Another mystery within the sphere of ' mixed membership ' is why many languages do not allow the present tense (or any other tense, for that matter) to be used for an action which extends from the past into the future, e.g. **John rests (is resting, rested, will rest) from an hour ago to an hour from now.*

Greenberg illustrates markedness in semantic oppositions by citing statistics showing that the ' positive ' member of pairs like *good/bad, long/short, mucho/ poco, largo/corto* occurs much more frequently than the ' negative ' member, and he points out that the opposition is neutralized in favor of the ' positive ' member in expressions which refer to the scale as a whole rather than to one of its poles : *How wide is it?   *How narrow is it?   Its length is two feet ;   *Its shortness is two feet.*   He notes that if a language lacks a word for one member of such a pair, it is always the ' negative ' term which is lacking, and which is expressed only by combining a negative element like ' not ' or ' without ' with the word for the ' positive ' pole.

One problem involving markedness of semantic categories which Greenberg does not touch on is how to speak of markedness in cases (common in semantics but impossible in phonology) where there is a three-way contrast between two members of an opposition and something unspecified with respect to that opposition—e.g., *brother/sister/sibling* or *father/mother/parent*.   In both of these exam-

ples, the ' unspecified ' word is much less frequent than either of the two ' specified ' words.   It would be interesting to determine whether the notion of markedness can be extended in some way which would provide a principled basis
for calling *sibling* more marked than *brother* or *sister*, or whether it is just fortuitous that it is less frequent.

The bulk of the section on semantic universals is devoted to kinship terminology and contains abundant illustrations of neutralizations reflecting markedness
relations ; e.g., ' The Bavenda example also involves neutralization of the distinction between lineal and collateral in the marked second ascending generation
as against the unmarked first ascending ' (101).   In this section Greenberg
suggests a number of implicational universals, the most striking of which is the
proposal that ' ascending generations are unmarked as against descending generations of equal genealogical distance from ego ' (103), and that consequently the
existence of a distinction in the terminology for the *n*th descending generation
implies the existence of that distinction in the terminology for the *n*th ascending
generation (e.g. there are languages which have separate terms for ' grandfather '
and ' grandmother ' and only a single term for ' grandchild,' but no languages
which have separate terms for ' grandson ' and ' granddaughter ' but only a single
term for ' grandparent ').   It is tempting to conjecture that this universal is
part of a more general universal which contains as special cases a corresponding
universal cited by Greenberg about relative age (there are languages such as
Malay which distinguish ' elder brother ' and ' elder sister ' but have only a
single term for ' younger sibling ', but no languages which distinguish ' younger
brother ' and ' younger sister ' and have only a single term for ' elder sibling '),
and a universal which I conjecture to hold for tense, namely that a distinction
among future tenses presupposes a corresponding distinction among past tenses.
It is easy to find examples of languages whose tense systems divide the past more
finely than the future ; for example, while English distinguishes simple past
(event simultaneous with past reference point, cf. Reichenbach 1947 : 287–98)
from past perfect (event prior to past reference point), the future with *will* is
used to cover the mirror images of both (event simultaneous with future reference
point, event later than future reference point).   Bemba (a Bantu language of
Zambia, Sharman 1956) distinguishes a remote past from a recent past up to
yesterday, but has a single tense for future starting from tomorrow.   Do past
time, age seniority, and generational seniority involve a single feature of ' priori-
ty ' in terms of which a single universal covering all the above cases can be
framed ?

Greenberg's study closes with a brief appendix on the results of word-associa-
tion experiments by Palermo and Jenkins, which show strikingly that unmarked
stimuli almost invariably elicit unmarked responses, whereas a sizeable proportion of stimuli in a marked morphological category elicit responses in the unmarked category.

Haas's ' Historical linguistics and the genetic relationship of languages ' (113–
53), unlike most of the contributions to this volume, lays no claim to theoretical

novelty; it is rather an elementary (and quite readable) introduction to a well-established line of inquiry, namely historical reconstruction in the Brugmann-Bloomfield tradition, copiously illustrated with examples from Haas's own work on the Muskogean and Algonkian languages.   It is a shame that Mouton has taken so long to issue this study as a separate volume, since it is very well suited for use as a reading in an introductory course in historical linguistics.   The reasoning which went into the various reconstructions is generally made admirably clear; only in a couple of cases is the reader left wondering why various symbols start appearing in reconstructed forms, as on p. 129, where it is not made clear why $*x^w$ is set up as the antecedent of an f-p-zero correspondence in the Muskogean languages.   A particularly beautiful example discussed is the reconstruction of the Muskogean conjugational paradigm, which is shown to have the same peculiar asymmetry as does Tunica (the 1sg. affix is a suffix, *Musk. -*li*, Tun. -*ni*, whereas the other person-number affixes are prefixes).   The only point on which I would chide the author is her failure to emphasize that a reconstructed proto-language should purport to be a language, and that considerations of what is a possible language bear directly on the question of what may be admitted as a reconstruction.   If one reconstructs ' proto-forms ' involving non-phonetic symbols in cases where the phonetic nature of the proto-segment is unclear (as in some of Haas's reconstructions, 126), the reconstructed system does not really purport to be a language.   A fair amount of space is devoted to comments on dead controversies such as Kroeber's notions on comparison and typology; the value of this study would have been enhanced if less space had been devoted to such matters and more to Muskogean and Algonkian.

Hockett's ' Language, mathematics, and linguistics ' (155–304) does not do justice to any of the three topics mentioned in its title.   The mathematics is amateurish; the linguistics is a procession of straw men, whom Hockett does not even bother to knock down but leaves tottering on their straw legs ; and language is largely ignored.

Chapter 1, a survey of set theory, is reasonably competent but is marred by a number of boners—e.g., the ' proof' on p. 172 that every symmetric transitive relation is reflexive is a classical fallacy; many textbooks, e.g. Birkhoff and MacLane (1953 : 32), give as an exercise finding the fallacy in that ' proof '.   The treatment of the topic of recursive and recursively enumerable sets is a mess. The ' proof ' on pp. 178–9 that a certain recursively enumerable set is not recursive in fact proves nothing about that set : one does not prove the non-existence of methods for testing membership in a set merely by trying a method out and showing that it does not work—that can be done for any set, recursive or not. The uncertainty expressed (179) as to whether there are sets which are not recursively enumerable is difficult to understand, since there is an obvious proof that there are such sets : the set of all sets of integers is non-denumerable ; the set of all Turing machines is denumerable ; each recursively enumerable set corresponds to a Turing machine ; therefore there are sets of integers which are not recursively enumerable.   Hockett's remarks here suggest that he does not fully appreciate how broad a range the term ' set ' covers.

Chapter 2 deals with certain systems invented by Hockett for generating sets of strings of symbols (since I cannot bring myself to use the term ' harp ', which Hockett uses for ' set of strings ', I will henceforth substitute the term STRING LANGUAGE, as opposed to TREE LANGUAGE.)   His ' linear generative grammar ' has the distinction of being the only system of set enumeration ever proposed that is more general than a Turing machine : the postulates are the same as those for a ' rewriting system ' (Chomsky and Miller 1963 : 292), except that Hockett allows the rules to be any functions that map strings onto strings ; i.e., he does not even require that the functions be computable, let alone of the very special nature that corresponds to the rules of a rewriting system.   However, it is not clear that he really intends this mind-boggling generality, since two pages later he starts writing down rules in the format usual for rewriting rules, and he makes clear that he intends them to apply in the way that rewriting rules apply.   One amazing abuse of accepted terminology is the definition of ' context-free phrase structure rule ' as a rule of the form ' $a \rightarrow b$, where a and b are non-null strings over A and $a \neq b$; it may also be required that b not be shorter than a nor a permutation of a. A string s is acceptable as instring for the rule just if it can be decomposed into xay, where x and y are any strings . . . ; the corresponding outstring is then xby' (190–1).   What Hockett has defined here is not ' context-free phrase structure rule ' but ' rewriting rule '.

Within the framework of his ' linear generative grammar ', Hockett proposes two types of rules which can be viewed as analogs of phrase structure rules and transformations respectively.   The remainder of the chapter is devoted to discussion of grammars consisting of rules of these two types.   Hockett treats the two types of rules as comprising a single system but only gives examples in which the phrase-structure-type rules apply before any of the transformation type rules ; he does not make clear whether such is always supposed to be the case. He considers the sequence of rules which apply in a derivation in such a system, and observes that if all ' locally obligatory rules ' are deleted from the full sequence (he calls a rule ' locally obligatory ' at a certain point of a derivation if, within the restricted class of derivations which he considers, only that rule may be applied to the string thus far generated), the resulting ' effective rule chain ' lists those steps in the derivation which could make any difference in the eventual result.   He accordingly contrasts the string language H(G) generated by a grammar G with the set E(G) of effective rule chains corresponding to derivations in G, and points out that an effective rule chain C can be regarded as a set of directions for using G to generate the corresponding sentence g(C).   He then comes out with the following quite baffling statement : ' We are thus led to discover, between generative grammar and certain older views, a much closer kinship than has been discerned heretofore.   Let us not modify our definition of linear grammars in any way, but, for a moment, let us replace two technical terms.   Instead of " terminal character ", let us say " phoneme ", and instead of " rule ", let us say " morpheme ".   We have then, in effect, the two-stratum model for a natural spoken language, incorporating the design feature of duality of patterning, as proposed variously by Saussure, Hjelmslev, and many others, including me. H(G) becomes the set of all strings of phonemes; E(G) becomes the set of all strings of morphemes ' (201). It is one thing to identify the morpheme *horse* with a phrase structure rule N → *horse*, but quite another thing to speak of morphemes of particle separation, subject raising, and relative pronoun deletion, corresponding to optional transformations that figure in the sentences *He ate the cookies up, I believe John to be a genius*, and *The girl I kissed slapped me* respectively. Moreover, transformations may rearrange or delete items, so that the eventual string of morphemes generated may differ radically in both order and composition from the sequence of phrase structure rules which introduced the morphemes, even if the phrase structure rules were constrained (as demanded by Hockett) to introduce morphemes in their UNDERLYING left-to-right order.[16]

Chapter 3 discusses some alternatives for a system of rules to convert the output of a ' linear grammar ' into some kind of phonological form (Hockett does not make clear what conditions are to be imposed on the representations eventually arrived at—e.g., whether they are to be ' phonemic ' in any sense). He assumes throughout that the input to this system of rules must be a string of alphabetic symbols and the output a ' stepmatrix ', which he defines as a sequence of segments, each represented as a set of ' components ' chosen from a vocabulary containing such items as Af[frication], Al[veolarity], and Ap[icality].

The first alternative which Hockett considers for the phonological component of his grammar is ' the rewrite format ',[17] where rules apply in ordered fashion (i.e. the rules are numbered from 1 to n, and the output from rule i is the input to rule $i+1$ for $1 \leq i < n$), in a format that mixes ' components ', names of ' morphophonemes ', and names of classes of morphophonemes. Since his symbolism distinguishes nasal from non-nasal segments, e.g., by the presence of the component Na vs. its absence, rather than by different specifications [+nas] vs. [−nas], it can express a rule that applies to all nasal segments, but not a rule that applies to all non-nasal segments. Due to his assumption that the input to his phonological component must be a string of morphophonemes, Hockett is forced in his Potawatomi example to include 29 superfluous rules at the beginning of the phonological component, to turn the morphophonemes into sets of components before the real phonology begins. These rules could have been dispensed with if he had simply taken the underlying forms of his morphemes to be ' stepmatrices ' rather than strings of morphophonemes. The phonological

---

[16] It is not clear that this constraint can be met. While a context-free grammar can be restricted to left-to-right derivations without affecting the language generated, a context-sensitive grammar cannot be (Matthews 1963). I argue elsewhere (McCawley 1968g) that the question of the sequence in which phrase structure rules apply is meaningless, and that the base component of a grammar is most profitably regarded as a set of conditions on the well-formedness of trees, rather than as a set of rules for constructing a string or tree from scratch.

[17] It is misleading for Hockett to speak of three ' formats ', since the major distinction between the alternatives he treats is not the way in which an individual rule is expressed, but the way in which the rules of a system interact.

rules proper in this example are rather questionable: the second part of the environment of R8 is superfluous; a small change in underlying forms (namely having an underlying ' U ' at the end of certain prefixes) would make R6 unnecessary; and Hockett has to use two two-part rules to describe the process whereby a semivowel followed by a homorganic segment becomes [ʔ]—

> R13 w → ʔ in env __o
>   or __w
> R14 y → ʔ in env __i
>   or __y

—because his symbolism makes no provision for expressing feature agreement between segments.

Hockett contrasts this proposal with the ' realizational format ', modeled after Lamb (1964). In this mode of rule application, rules apply ' simultaneously ': each rule consists of a list of environments where a morphophoneme might occur IN THE INPUT TO THE PHONOLOGICAL RULES, and the realization of the morphophoneme in each environment. There are no intermediate stages between input and output, as there are with ordered rules or with the ' unordered sequential ' rules of the mathematical systems discussed in Chomsky and Miller. The principal reason why many linguists have described phonology in terms of ordered rules is that a large fraction of generalizations about phonological processes can be captured only when the processes are stated in terms of the effects of other processes; there is a striking example of this in the Potawatomi rule that semivowels become [ʔ] before a homorganic segment, since that generalization has to do not with the underlying environment of the semivowel but with its environment after rules of vowel truncation and syncope have applied. Accordingly, Hockett's ' realizational format ' not only must make $w \to$ ʔ and $y \to$ ʔ two separate rules, but must state the environments of these rules so as to allow the w and the following w or o, or the y and the following y or i, to be separated by any vowel or vowel sequence which the truncation and syncope rules would delete—i.e., the environments of the truncation and syncope rules must in effect be made part of the environment of the $w \to$ ʔ and $y \to$ ʔ.[18] Indeed, a good fraction of the environments of the rules involve bits and pieces of the environments of several other rules.

After a brief consideration of a third alternative (the ' stepmatricial format ', which I will ignore, since Hockett does nothing with it beyond defining it), Hockett makes the following admission: ' I began with a prejudice in favor of Lamb's realizational approach, and after hitting on the cute notion of letting terminal strings from one partial grammar be rule chains for the other, I began

---

[18] Hockett makes these environments look less complicated than they are by using a cover symbol to lump single vowels together with vowel sequences to which truncaton would apply, and by subscripting consonants to mark whether syncope will apply to the following vowel. The algorithm for subscripting takes him nearly a page to state; and the subscripts, which are involved in over half of the realizational rules, are merely an ad-hoc abbreviation for this highly complicated algorithm.

to hope that the stepmatricial format would best.   Things did not work out that way.   Working with Potawatomi, I found the rewrite format surprisingly easy to set up.   The realizational format was rather more difficult.   The stepmatricial format was so hard that I gave up.   Thinking that all this might stem from the nature of Potawatomi, or from my long-standing habits of handling that language, I turned to the Yawelmani dialect of Yokuts.   Here, again, the rewrite format was fairly straightforward, but my patience gave out before I could cast the data into either of the other formats ' (229).

Chapter 4, ' From phonons to the speech signal ' presents in a straightforward fashion a general scheme for associating to the discrete output of the phonological component of a grammar a representation in terms of continuous physical parameters.   Here Hockett again displays his exasperating tendency to use well established terms in peculiar ways, in this case by using the term ' distinctive feature ' to denote a local maximum of the probability distribution of a physical parameter involved in the speech signal.   The concept which Hockett has defined has no discernible relation to distinctiveness, since there will be local maxima of the probability distribution for all physical parameters that are involved in a given variety of speech, not just the ones that function distinctively in it.   Moreover, Hockett's definition does not define, but rather logically presupposes the other sense in which ' distinctive feature ' has been used, namely a universal set of acoustic or articulatory parameters, differences on which may function distinctively in languages.

Chapter 5, ' Binary tree grammars ', deals with proposals for extending the version of transformational grammar given in chapter 2 to cover embedding and conjoining (which Hockett does not distinguish clearly).   Two alternatives are considered here, one in which embedding and conjoining transformations are functions of two variables, much as in Chomsky 1957 ; and one in which transformations are functions of a single variable, phrase structure rules generate complex structures that may contain several sentences as well as special symbols which ' trigger ' transformations, all transformations are obligatory and delete the corresponding special symbol when they apply, and any output structure containing any of those symbols is rejected as ill-formed.   This latter alternative has a superficial similarity to the theory of Chomsky (1965),[19] but turns out on closer examination to be a notational variant of the first alternative, since Hockett's phrase structure rules do not generate sentences embedded within sentences, but rather ' kernel sentences ' grouped together with transformation-triggering symbols (' time bombs ', as Hockett calls them), as in Fig. 1a, which Hockett proposes as the structure underlying *I heard Bill say you were coming* (Hockett uses *I* in place of Chomsky's *S*).   If the triggering symbols were made the labels on the nodes which here directly dominate them, the result would be precisely the ' T-markers ' which function in the first of Hockett's two alternatives (Fig. 1b).

[19] Hockett mentions (252) that when he wrote this section he did not have access to Chomsky 1965, but only to second-hand reports of the ideas presented in that work.

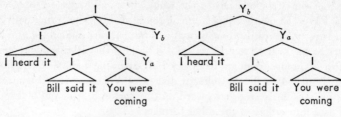

Fig. 1a   **Fig. 1b**

Chapter 6, ' Conversion grammars ', begins with a discussion of graph theory and then turns to its main topic, an elaboration of the syntactic theory that was hinted at in Lamb (1964).   Indeed, this section is the fullest exposition available of that theory, which differs in a number of significant respects from that of Lamb (1966a).   In this theory, henceforth 1964-SG, several ' strata ' or ' levels of representation ' intervene between meaning and sound, among them the ' sememic ', ' lexemic ', and ' morphemic ' strata ; and for each pair of consecutive strata there is a set of simultaneously applying ' realizational rules ' relating corresponding representations on the two strata.   Sememic representations are assumed to be labeled unordered graphs (' networks '), and lexemic representations to be labeled ordered trees.[20]   Hockett divides the ' semons ' (the labels on the nodes in the sememic networks) into three classes, called ' links ', ' kernels ', and ' modifiers '.   ' Kernels ', of which Hockett cites only two, appear to be merely names of parts of speech : ' being '=noun, ' do '=verb ; indeed, he states (273) : ' we may say that " man " consists of two components, one of which is *noun* (or, as Lamb has it in his networks, *being*) '.   This terminology is a continuation of the deplorable practice (traceable back to Bloomfield) of saying ' actor ' and ' action ' in place of ' subject ' and ' predicate ', and thus indulging in the absurdity of calling *Pike's peak* an ' actor ' and *is high* an ' action ' in *Pike's peak is high* (Bloch and Trager 1942 : 75).   The two ' links ' which Hockett cites, *agt* (agent) and *gl* (goal), also belong to this infelicitous terminological tradition.   Fillmore (1966, 1968) has rightly pointed out that the semantic relationship of the subject to the verb in *John fell into a manhole* is the same as that of the object to the verb, in *Sam kicked Harry*, rather than that of the subject to the verb, and that these semantic relationships have syntactic significance :

(10)   What Sam did was kick Harry.
(11)   *What John did was fall into a manhole.
(12)   What happened to John was that he fell into a manhole.
(13)   *What happened to Sam was that he kicked Harry.
(14)   What happened to Harry was that Sam kicked him.

---

[20] This is one of the major respects in which Lamb's more recent theories differ from 1964-SG.   In Lamb (1966a), the systems of ' tactic rules ' for the various strata are all of the same nature and thus generate representations that are all of the same formal nature, namely strings of items, each item being at most a finite set of components—i.e., all representations are ' stepmatrices ', and networks and trees are no longer part of the representations of utterances.

The only role which the Lamb-Hockett *agt* and *gl* appear to play is that of distinguishing which noun phrase is to precede the verb when nothing such as passivization occurs, which hardly qualifies them for the name ' sememes '.

Hockett illustrates sememic networks by diagramming 22 sentences, most of which deal with men shooting tigers. He distinguishes between actives and passives by connecting the sememe *decl*[*arative*] or *inter*[*rogative*] to the *agt* sememe in active sentences and to the *gl* sememe in passive sentences. There is no apparent way of extending this device in a consistent way to the active-passive distinction in subordinate clauses. The subordinate clauses in Hockett's examples contain nothing to mark an active-passive distinction ;[21] and if one puts *decl* in the subordinate clauses of his diagrams, there is no longer any way to tell whether the diagram is supposed to represent, e.g., *The man who I saw shot the tiger*, or *I saw the man who shot the tiger*. Moreover, a proposal such as he presents is inconsistent with the fact that the superficial subject of a passive clause need not correspond to a coherent portion of semantic structure, as witness *My leg has been pulled* and *No headway has been made ;* in the latter example the surface subject is put together out of a piece of the idiom *make headway*, an indefinite adverb of quantity, and a negative which has the whole sentence as scope. Hockett attaches the number morphemes *sg* and *pl*, not to *being* sememe of the noun phrase in question, but to the corresponding *agt* or *gl* sememe, giving as justification ' *sg* and *pl*—and various others—must be concorders, dominating a link, and, therefore, dominating both of the nodes that are dominated by the link, because—in simple traditional terms—if a subject is singular then so is its verb, and similarly for plural ' (283). He appears unaware of the fact that an item may end up as the subject of a verb that originates several sentences away from it, as illustrated by Lakoff's example *The bagel is believed by Myron to be thought by Irving to have been eaten by Seymour*, in which the superficial subject of the outermost clause originated as the underlying object of the innermost clause. Since a verb may thus have to agree with a noun phrase to which it has no underlying grammatical relation, the agreement features must be regarded as belonging to noun phrases and not to underlying relations. However, the fact that agreement features must come off of the noun phrase was obvious to begin with, since features which play no role in the meaning of the sentence may be involved in agreement, e.g. grammatical gender.

Loops occur in Hockett's diagrams only in the case of coreferential noun phrases, as in *The man shot himself*, which Hockett diagrams as in Fig. 2. This structure has one advantage over that proposed as the deep structure of such sentences in Chomsky's *Aspects*, namely avoidance of redundantly repeating the lexical material of *the man* or the corresponding semantic material. A major defect which it shares with the proposals of *Aspects* is that it makes no provision for the fact that the purported reference of a constituent has to be separated from the corresponding lexical material to account adequately for the meaning of such

---

[21] This section has the distinction of being the first published work in stratificational grammar to give examples containing subordinate clauses.

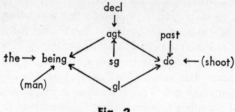

Fig. 2

sentences as *John denies that he kissed the girl who he kissed*.   This sentence is ambiguous, between a sense which asserts that John uttered a contradiction such as ' I deny that I kissed the girl who I kissed ', and a sense which asserts that John denies having kissed a certain person, whom the speaker describes as ' the girl who John kissed '.   Both senses involve some proposition *X kissed Y* in the complement of *deny ;* they differ as to whether the identification of *Y* as *the girl who X kissed* is also part of the complement of *deny*.   The only way I can see of adequately representing this difference is in terms of structures such as those of Fig. 3, in which the lexical material of noun phrases is separate from the corresponding ' referential indices. '[c]   A similar analysis is needed for Peter Geach's sentence *Sir John Carstairs seduced his widow's sister two weeks before he married his widow*, which is bizarre if *his widow* is taken as semantically within the scope

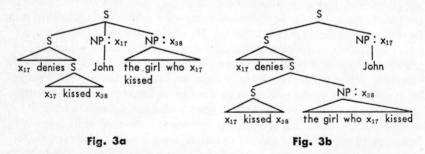

Fig. 3a   **Fig. 3b**

of the past tense morpheme, but not if it is taken as outside its scope (i.e., as referring to the woman who is NOW his widow).   If Hockett's diagrams were modified in this direction, the only reason ever advanced for having ' networks ' rather than trees for ' sememic ' representations would vanish : diagrams such as those of Fig. 3 already indicate coreferentiality without redundant duplication of lexical or semantic material.   Moreover, multiple tokens of referential indices would make unnecessary the rule which Hockett would otherwise need, which would disconnect all his multiple connections and attach pronouns at the loose ends.   It is highly unlikely that such a rule could be stated, since whether a pronoun can refer to a given noun phrase depends not on the semantic structure of the sentence, but on the structure which results after applying a large number of transformations (Ross 1967b).   In addition, there is no obvious way in which a network could represent the ' scope ' of an item such as negation, which is represented quite naturally in a tree where negation is a predicate whose ' scope ' is a sentence that is the underlying grammatical subject of the negation element.

The last four pages of chapter 6 are devoted to a discussion of ' semolexemic rules ', which map sememic networks onto lexemic trees.   Hockett's discussion revolves mainly about the question of how to isolate the portions of the network which will correspond to various lexemes; he has little to say about how the semolexemic rules would impose a linear order on the resulting lexemes, or how the rules to sever multiple connections and insert pronouns would work.   He avoids entirely the question of whether all these rules can apply simultaneously, as 1964–SG would require them to.   Since some of the semolexemic rules create items that would have to be fitted into the ordering by other rules, it is hard to see how they could apply simultaneously without the same facts about word order being repeated in two different sets of rules.

Hockett's contribution to this volume concludes with a highly programmatic chapter ' Ensembles of grammars ', which deals with the relationships between grammars for related varieties of language (styles, idiolects, historical stages in a language, stages in the acquisition of a language).

Malkiel's ' Genetic analysis of word formation ' (305–64) revolves about two questions that have recently become major issues in theoretical linguistics: the role of derivational morphology in a synchronic description, and the mechanisms of linguistic change.   This study of the spread of derivational affixes and the meanings of derived forms (mainly confined to the Romance languages) is of value more as a compendium of fascinating problems than as a source of an-swers to them; indeed, Malkiel poses two or three problems for every one that he attempts a solution to.   The following are a sample of the topics discussed: (a) derived forms in Spanish having a chain of suffixes in which the first suffix either does not occur without the second (e.g. *humo* ' smoke ', *humareda* ' cloud of smoke ', but no **humar*), or occurs only in a form unrelated in meaning (e.g. *carne* ' meat ', *carnicero* ' butcher ', but *carniza* ' remains, leftovers', originally ' slice of meat ') ; (b) the development in Spanish of a large class of adjectives in *-ido* whose meanings have to do with ' inadequacy' (e.g. *desanguido* ' anemic'), some of which are historically participles of verbs in *-ir* but most of which are not (note pairs such as *colorado* ' colored, red ' but *descolorido* ' colorless ', *sabroso* ' tasty ' but *desabrido* ' insipid ') ; (c) the split of Latin *-ālis* into the contrasting French suffixes *-al* and *-el*.   The explanations which Malkiel offers for the phe-nomena discussed include somewhat dubious ' hole in the pattern ' arguments— e.g., his suggestion that ' the extraordinary commonness and efficacy of triadic arrangements in Spanish morphology ' was a factor in the development of adjec-tives in *-uno* (337);   however, he is careful to warn against making ' a kind of fetish or deus ex machina out of the triadic vowel gamut in Spanish or out of any comparable arrangement or ideal architectural design in some other lan-guage '.   There are cogent observations about the role of ' suffixoids ' such as the *-er* of *hammer* as selectional factors favoring the development of homopho-nous derivational affixes, as in the case of Spanish *-iego*.   Malkiel's felicitous

terminological innovations ' suffixoid ' and ' prefixoid ' (by analogy with such
biological terms as ' hominoid ') are more than enough to atone for the somewhat grating figures of speech (e.g. ' semantic orchestration ') which he occasionally indulges in.

Pike's ' Guide to publications related to tagmemic theory ' (265–94) is an annotated bibliography that appears in place of his Bloomington lectures, which
he chose to withdraw on the grounds that their content largely overlaps other
works already in press.   While Pike has done linguistics a real service by com-
piling this list of publications, most of which appeared in rather obscure places,
he could have done an even greater service by combining it with a concise and
coherent account of his theory, illustrated with abundant examples from a language such as English or Spanish which his readers can be expected to know.
This would have rendered the exposition more readily intelligible than are works
dealing with highly exotic languages, as virtually all the items in the bibliography
do.[22]

Weinreich describes his ' Explorations in semantic theory ' (295–77) as follows :
' It is the purpose of the present paper to explore a semantic theory which might
fit into a comprehensive and highly explicit theory of linguistic structure.   A
recent attempt to achieve this goal was made by Katz and Fodor (1963).   The
immediate impact of their work testifies to its importance . . . In a number of
ways, however, the proposals of Katz and Fodor (hereinafter KF) are unsatisfactory.   Since an analysis of these inadequacies is a prerequisite to the development of alternative proposals, the first portion of this paper is devoted to a critical
discussion of KF.   The next part develops, in outline, a semantic theory which
would contribute to a more satisfying conception of linguistics as a whole.   The
concluding remarks compare the two approaches ' (396–7).

Weinreich's criticisms of KF, almost all of which are valid, include a number
concerning the sharp division between syntax and semantics which KF maintain but which Weinreich rejects.   KF require syntax to be entirely seman-
tics-free, in keeping with their slogan, ' Linguistic description minus grammar
equals semantics '.   This has an interesting consequence for their conception of
' dictionary ': phonologically and syntactically identical items must be regarded
as the same element in syntax, and thus must correspond to a single ' dictionary
entry ', which lists the various senses of the item as sub-entries.[23]   It is for this
reason that the KF projection rules took the form of a procedure for disambig-

---

[22] See now, however, Brend (1968).
[23] Chomsky (1965) and Chomsky's contribution to this volume, even though written at
roughly the same time, take opposite positions on this question : in the former work,
Chomsky adopts the KF conception of lexical item ; in the latter (p. 5), he adopts Weinreich's.   I have pointed out (McCawley 1968c) that these two positions have different
empirical consequences, since they imply different predictions about what will count as
identical for the purposes of deletion transformations, and that only Weinreich's position
would prevent the derivation of anomalous sentences such as * *John is as sad that as book*
through an illicit deletion, in which the basic sense sad_1 was treated as identical to the
derived sense $sad_2 =$ ' evoking sad_1-ness '.

uating utterances that contain polysemous ' lexical items '.   Weinreich sees no reason (nor do I) for recognizing a unit *bank* which contains *bank* ' financial institution ' and *bank* ' land next to a river ' as pieces ; he accordingly treats *I went to the bank* as the surface manifestation of two separate sentences rather than (as in KF) a single sentence containing an ambiguous ' lexical item ' :

A scientific approach which distinguishes between competence (knowledge of a language) and performance (use of a language) ought to regard the automatic disambiguation of potential ambiguities as a matter of hearer performance . . . The grammar of a language, too, produces ambiguous expressions (e.g. *Boiling champagne is interesting, He studied the whole year, Please make her dress fast*).   But each sentence, ambiguous at its surface, corresponds to two distinct, unambiguous deep structures.   Its ambiguity arises from the existence of transformational rules which produce identical surface results from different deep sources, and from the simultaneous existence of words which can function in dual syntactic capacities (e.g. *boil* as both a transitive and an intransitive verb).   But grammatical theory is NOT required to explain how a hearer of such ambiguous expressions guesses which of two deep structures is represented by a given occurrence of a surface structure . . . Semantic theories can and should be so formulated as to guarantee that deep structures (including their lexical components) are specified as unambiguous in the first place and proceed from there to account for the interpretation of a complex expression from the known meanings of its components. (398–9).

Two important questions raised by Weinreich are (a) what is the structure of the lexicon ? and (b) what kind of unit appears at the terminal nodes of syntactic trees ? Weinreich's answer to (b) is that the unit in question is an item consisting of a specification of syntactic behavior, a specification of phonological behavior, and a specification of a single meaning ; I will henceforth refer to such a complex of information as a LEXICAL UNIT.   While Weinreich is less clear about the answer to (a) than to (b), he leaves no doubt that he does not intend the lexicon to be merely a list of lexical units, and indeed criticizes KF for adopting a notation which ' does not discriminate between fortuitous homonymy and lexicologically interesting polysemy ', the former illustrated by *rock* ' stone ' and *rock* ' move undulatingly ', the latter by *cook* ' prepare food' and *cook* ' one who prepares food '.   Katz (1967 : 148–9) has replied that this is no criticism at all, that there are only degrees of similarity between lexical units, and no valid distinction can be drawn between ' fortuitous homonymy ' and ' true polysemy '.   In this case I would criticize both Weinreich and Katz for formulating the question incorrectly as a result of having placed too great importance (as in KF and in Uhlenbeck 1967) on mere phonological identity ; the proper question to raise is whether a distinction between related and unrelated lexical units can be justified.   In the case of the two *cook*'s, an obvious question to raise is whether the two lexical units both have to be in the lexicon—i.e., whether the noun *cook* is not transformationally derived from the verb *cook*, thus requiring only the latter to appear in the lexicon.   The derivation of the noun *cook* is not quite as simple as that, however : the surface realization of stative agent nominalizations (*-er, -ist*, zero, etc.) is largely unpredictable,[24] since we cannot predict which verbs have stative agent nominali-

---

[24] It is necessary to distinguish between a stative agent nominalization (*John is a composer*) and an active agent nominalization (*John is the composer of that song*).

zations, and since there are nouns which have the meaning of a stative agent nominalization (e.g., *surgeon*) but for which no corresponding verb exists.   Since the surface form (and indeed possibility) of these nominalizations is idiosyncratic to the words in question, it is by definition to be included in the lexicon.[25] These facts can be represented by a composite dictionary entry in which, e.g., it is indicated that ' prepare (food) by heating ' is represented as *cook*, and that ' one who by habit/profession____ ' adjoined to it is represented as zero.   In such a dictionary entry the two lexical units *cook* are not merely similar : the dictionary entry for the one is contained in the other.   I have no clear feeling as to whether *fool* ' stupid person ' and *fool* ' succeed in deceiving ' should be regarded as synchronically related ; here, as in the clearer case of the two *rock*'s, neither would be contained in the other,[26] nor would any third lexical unit be contained in both.   Perhaps the notion of total inclusion of one lexical unit within another will provide the answer to the question of when words are to be related within the lexicon ; I see no hope of the KF representations or Katz's later revisions of them casting any light on that question.

Weinreich also criticizes KF on the grounds that their semantic representations are too unstructured to be adequate to represent meanings.   KF's representations of the meanings of words and larger constituents are merely strings of symbols (' markers ' and ' distinguishers ') with no indication of constituent structure,[27] and accordingly, no indication of the scope of negation, quantifiers, etc., as would be needed to represent the difference between the two meanings of *John doesn't beat his wife because he loves her*.   Weinreich states,

For KF, the meaning of a complex expression (such as a phrase or sentence) is an unstructured heap of features . . . The projection rules as formulated in KF destroy the SEMANTIC STRUCTURE and reduce the words of a sentence to a heap . . . What is particularly ironic is that an enterprise in semantics inspired by the most sophisticated syntactic research ever undertaken should end up with a fundamentally asyntactic theory of meaning . . . To avoid similar defects in an alternative theory, it may be useful to consider how KF maneuvered itself into a position of bankruptcy on the most essential issue.   Apparently this happened when the authors modeled a theory of linguistic meaning on the concept of the multiplication of classes.   As logicians have long known, to express the fact that a *colorful ball* is something which is both colorful and a ball, we may say that *colorful ball* contains the semantic features of both *ball* and *colorful*.   The process involved in deriving a compound meaning is expressible as a Boolean class conjunction.   One would have thought that with the development of the calculus of many-place predicates, the logic of Boolean (one-place) predicates would be permanently dropped as a model for natural language; yet KF persists in the belief, widespread among 19th century logicians, that Boolean operations are an adequate model for combinatorial semantics (410–1).

[25] An argument that nominalizations are derived by ' prelexical transformations ' is given in McCawley (1968d).   The notion of ' prelexical transformation ' is introduced in Gruber (1965) and further elaborated in Gruber (1967).
[26] These remarks presuppose that semantic representation is in the form of a labeled tree, rather than in the less highly structured forms of representation that appear in KF and Weinreich.
[27] In Katz (1964) and subsequent works, more highly structured representations are used ; in particular, ' markers ' are no longer regarded as atomic but come with slots into which other markers may be inserted.

As will be seen below, Weinreich's counterproposal is itself open to much of the above criticism.   However, he at least recognized, as KF did not, that ' the most essential issue ' in semantic theory is the question of finding a mode of semantic representation which distinguishes exactly those differences in meaning which can be observed in the sentences of a natural language.

Weinreich also criticizes KF's separation of the semantic representation into ' markers ', ' distinguishers ', and ' selectional restrictions '.   The unfeasibility of the distinction between ' markers ' (semantic features which may play a role in selectional restrictions) and ' distinguishers ' (the semantic residue after extraction of the ' markers ') has been demonstrated adequately by Bolinger (1965), who shows that there would be no residue if the type of argument employed in KF for the extraction of ' markers ' were applied systematically to their examples. (See also McCawley 1968c, g, where it is argued that selectional restrictions can involve any property which appears in semantic representations—e.g., *diagonalize* requires an object denoting a matrix ; *benign* in the sense of ' non-cancerous ' requires a subject which denotes a tumor).   Katz (1966) dispenses with the marker/distinguisher dichotomy, but in 1967 he resurrects it and defends it against Weinreich's objections, on the grounds that color properties do not figure in selectional restrictions but are involved in semantic representations, and play a role in determining the contradictoriness of sentences such as *Red pencils are green*.   However, Katz's claim that color properties do not figure in selectional restrictions cannot be maintained, in view of the anomaly of using *blacken* with an object that denotes something already black.[28]   Weinreich's rejection of the marker/selectional-restriction dichotomy involves treating selectional restrictions as embedded contradictions.   Specifically, he regards a selectional restriction not (like Katz) as a condition which a constituent must meet in order to be compatible with the item that imposes the restriction, but rather as semantic material which that item causes to be added to the constituent in question—e.g., *hit* does not require that its direct object contain the semantic marker ' physical object ', but rather causes ' physical object ' to be added to the semantic representation of the direct object.   His proposal is an extension of an idea in Katz and Postal (1964), where it was argued that the above transfer of features takes place when a selectional restriction is imposed on a pronoun, so as to insure that, e.g., the *it* of *He hit it* receives the semantic marker ' physical object '.   Weinreich argues that what Katz and Postal had taken to be an idiosyncrasy of pronouns is indeed a general characteristic of selectional restrictions.   This proposal is attractive in that it explains a peculiar gap in Katz (1966) : while Katz allows selectional restrictions in the form of either a positive condition (a configuration of markers which the semantic representation of the constituent in question must contain if there is to be no anomaly) or a negative condition (a configuration of

[28] This restriction follows from the meaning of *blacken* (' cause to become black ') and from the fact that something cannot become what it already is.   The selectional restriction is thus not a restriction on the word *blacken*, but on a semantic unit involved in its meaning.   This may not be a real counterexample to Katz's claim, although the restriction appears to be inexpressible in Katz's symbolism.

markers which the semantic representation of the constituent in question must not contain if there is to be no anomaly), no valid instances of a positive condition have ever been cited.[29]   For example, it is incorrect to say that *hit* requires its direct object to contain the marker ' physical object ', since there is nothing anomalous about *He hit several things*, whose direct object is unspecified as to physical-object-hood.   Even stating the restriction as a negative condition is not particularly easy : what would be required is a negative condition excluding any semantic representation that was inconsistent with ' physical object '.   While Weinreich's proposal obviously avoids this difficulty, it is still not sufficient as an account of selectional restrictions, since it would incorrectly predict that

> (15)   *Things are difficult to diagonalize

would be synonymous to and as well-formed as

> (16)   Matrices are difficult to diagonalize,

since the selectional restriction imposed by *diagonalize* would cause the semantic markers corresponding to matrixhood to be added to its object (=the surface subject of *difficult*).   An adequate treatment of these examples would require semantic representation to be modified in the direction of symbolic logic, specifically by recognizing that (15) and (16) both involve a universal or ' near universal ' quantifier applied to the propositional function *x is difficult to diagonalize*, and differ as regards whether the range of the variable *x* is defined by *thing* or by *matrix*.   In such a semantic representation, the ' object ' of *diagonalize* is not *matrices* but the variable *x*.[30]   Needless to say, neither Katz's nor Weinreich's account of selectional restrictions would yield any result if applied to representations of the form just suggested ; however, in a revision of Weinreich's proposal suggested by Fillmore (personal communication),[d] a distinction is drawn between the meaning of a predicate and presuppositions about the item(s) of which it is predicated ; it is asserted that selectional restrictions fall into the latter category, and that a selectional violation occurs when a sentence involves mutually contradictory presuppositions, or a contradiction between what is presupposed of something and what is asserted of it.   Fillmore observes that his notion of ' selectional restriction ' avoids the constraint, inherent in Katz's system, that an item can only impose a selectional restriction on ANOTHER constituent ; it is thus possible to say that ' unmarried ' is the meaning of *bachelor*, and that ' human ', ' male ' and ' adult ' are only selectional restrictions.   Fillmore argues that this is necessary since one can apply the term *bachelor* to a person he knows to be human, male, and adult, to assert that he is unmarried, but one cannot apply

---

[29] If all selectional restrictions are negative conditions, then Katz and Postal's restricted proposal for transferring semantic matter from a selectional restriction to the restricted constituent would make no sense, since it presupposes a positively formulated restriction.

[30] I do not mean to imply by my choice of words that notions ' subject ', ' object ', etc., are of relevance to semantic representation.   For a cogent argument that ' subject ', object ', etc., play a role only in relatively superficial syntactic representations and result from the neutralization of a wide range of semantic relations, see Fillmore (1968).

the term *bachelor* to a person he knows to be human, unmarried, and male, to assert that he is adult (see McCawley 1968g for further discussion of Fillmore's proposal)

One criticism of KF by Weinreich which does not stand up relates to ' infinite polysemy '.   Weinreich suggests (411–2) that KF's notion of dictionary entry might be such that no finite number of ' readings ' for a lexical item would suffice to characterize the ways in which it can be used.   However, the one example which Weinreich cites provides no support for this.   He considers the verb *eat* and, on the basis of the observation that one does not do the same thing in eating bread as in eating soup, concludes that ' *eat* has a slightly different meaning in *eat bread* and *eat soup* ', and gives a KF-like dictionary entry describing these two ' meanings ' in terms of units like (Chew), (Swallow), and (Spoon).   He gives no reason for his conclusion that a KF dictionary entry would have to distinguish separate meanings for all of the various actions that are subsumed under *eat*.   Indeed, just the action alone does not determine whether ' eating ' is going on :   it would not be correct to say that a person was eating Pepsi-Cola if he were consuming Pepsi-Cola with a spoon in the way that one eats soup.   I conjecture that the appropriateness of *eat* depends on whether the substance being consumed counts as ' food '.   While there is no reason for any worries about ' infinite polysemy ', the question still remains whether *eat* can be assigned a single sense.   Note that my conjecture that *eat* requires an object which is ' food ' only applies to the consumption of liquids :   one can perfectly well talk about eating coal or dirt or one's hat.   Assigning *eat* a single sense would require an extremely peculiar selectional restriction :   that the object be either food or solid.   However, assigning two different senses to *eat* would conflict with the fact noted by Weinreich (411) that sentences like *I'd like to eat something* do not feel ambiguous.

Weinreich's proposals for an alternative semantic theory are much less satisfactory than are his criticisms of KF.   For semantic representations, he proposes formulas which are equivalent to dependency trees whose nodes are labeled by sets of semantic markers.[31]   One major difficulty which this proposal shares with that of KF is the absence of ' indices ' corresponding to the things that the sentence purports to refer to, or variables such as are involved in examples like (15).   This deficiency is largely responsible for the totally ad-hoc formulas which appear in Weinreich's brief discussion of tenses and determiners (426–8), where he introduces the symbols δ and ξ for the ' subject delimitation ' and ' predicate delimitation ' which he finds in the *some* and ' Past ' of

(17)   Some boys were hungry.

Since there are infinitely many possible relationships between the noun phrase to which a quantifier is attached and the clause which is the scope of that quan-

---

[31] The infelicitous notation which Weinreich uses would prevent any node from having more than one dependent.   It is not clear whether he intended such a restriction.   (On dependency trees, see Hays 1964.)

tifier, quantifiers cannot be adequately represented by symbols tied to a specific relation like ' subject ', as Weinreich's δ is.   Moreover, it is incorrect for Weinreich to attach δ to the meaning of *boy* and ξ to the meaning of *be hungry* in his discussion of (17), since ' Past ' does not describe *be hungry* but rather the time which the clause has reference to, and *some* does not describe *boys* but rather the set of boys who are asserted to have been hungry at that time.   The meaning of (17) cannot be represented adequately without three indices: one for the point in time being referred to, one for the set whose existence is asserted, and one a variable over that set, needed since *hungry* is predicated not of the set but of each of its members.

The first two examples which Weinreich gives of his semantic representation illustrate two further major deficiencies of it.   Weinreich represents *daughter* by a one-noded tree with the markers ' female ' and ' offspring ' as labels on that node, thus missing the fact that *daughter* is a ' transitive ' noun: one cannot be just a daughter but only someone's daughter.   However, only the component ' offspring ' bears any relation to the ' direct object ' of *daughter*, which means that if Weinreich were to represent the ' object ' by a dependent node (as he does elsewhere), he would be forced either to violate the meaning relationships by making that node dependent as much on ' female ' as on ' offspring ', or to broaden his representations so as to allow a marker to be a ' simultaneous component ' not only with another marker but with an entire tree.   No such problem arises in a representation based on symbolic logic, where a formula like Female(x) $\wedge$ Offspring (x, y) would be available.   Weinreich's second example is *chair*, which he represents as a two-noded tree in which a node labeled ' furniture ' has a dependent node labeled ' sitting '.   Aside from the obvious omissions (namely the characteristics which distinguish chairs from benches and stools, which Weinreich clearly was aware of), this representation has the gross defect of lacking any indication of what relationship ' sit ' has to ' furniture ': agent, object, instrument, etc.   The relationship of *chair* to sitting is different from that of *crutch* to walking or that of *victim* to misfortune, and an adequate semantic representation must somehow express that relationship.

Fortunately, Weinreich does not always keep his discussion of semantic representation within the bounds of his hopelessly inadequate symbolism, and thus allows himself to say some quite cogent things.   For example, he points out that a single word may have the same meaning as an expression of arbitrary syntactic complexity, and he gives examples of single words whose meanings are matched by syntactically complex items, e.g. *dentist*=' (one who by profession) fixes teeth ' *munch*=' chew with a crunching sound '.   He eventually concludes that ' every relation that may hold between components of a sentence also occurs among the components of meaning of a dictionary entry.   This is as much as to say that the semantic part of a dictionary is a sentence—more specifically, a deep-structure sentence, i.e. a Generalized Phrase-Marker ' (446).   These observations contain the germ of the idea (subsequently adopted by Lakoff, Ross, Bach, Gruber, and myself, among others) that there is no real distinction between syntax and semantics, that the rules for combining material into sentences are really rules for combining semantic material, and that the dictionary is part of a single system of rules (' transformations ') for associating semantic representations with surface structures.   However, syntax was not far enough advanced in 1964 to make it reasonable for Weinreich to push his ideas to such conclusions.

Weinreich in addition proposes modifying the theory of the base component in Chomsky (1965) to allow for the generation and construal of metaphors.   Observing that morphemes functioning as nouns, verbs, or adjectives may have a metaphoric interpretation, but morphemes functioning as articles, modals, etc. may not, Weinreich (434) generalizes Chomsky's ' lexical insertion rule ' so as to allow any lexical item whatever to be inserted under a node labeled N, V, or Adj (e.g. *if* to be inserted under a node labeled N) ;   he then (455ff.) sketches a procedure which would alter the meaning of a lexical item inserted in an incongruous environment so as to generate an appropriate metaphoric reading.   This ' construal rule ', however, is inconsistent with his conception of semantic representation, since it assumes that the meaning of a lexical item is expressed as a set of feature specifications.   Weinreich illustrates the rule, whose effect is to change into their opposites those feature specifications which are incompatible with the environment in which the lexical item is used, by discussing sentences such as

(18)   Scientists study the if.

This, he suggests, could be interpreted as something like ' scientists study what is hypothetical ' on the basis of features like [+Condition], which he supposes would appear in the semantic representations of both *if* and nouns like *condition*. Some of his examples, e.g.

(19)   He trues the rumor,

interpreted as ' He causes the rumor to become true ', are not really metaphor but rather the extension of unproductive and semi-productive derivational processes, in this case the formation of causatives by zero affixation.   There are a number of reasons why an approach such as this cannot give an adequate account of metaphor.   First of all, it is not necessary that a sentence containing a metaphoric expression be anomalous if interpreted literally ;   for example, there is nothing anomalous about the literal reading of the expression *pregnant oyster*, the German equivalent of which is used by many Berliners as a name for the Kongresshalle.   Secondly, the interpretation of a metaphor may require more than merely linguistic knowledge.   For example, to interpret Dylan Thomas's *our eunuch dreams*, one needs to know not only that a eunuch is a man who has been castrated, but also that castration destroys sexual potency, and one must somehow also know that sexual potency is to be taken as a symbol for efficacy in general.

With all its flaws, Weinreich's ' Explorations ' contains a great deal of original and thought-provoking material.   The excellence of its best parts makes clear that Weinreich would have made many major contributions to semantic theory if it had not been for his tragically premature death.

The first appendix to this volume is ' F. de Saussure's theory of language ' by Robert Godel (479–93), a fascinating study of the development of the ideas of one of the most enigmatic figures in the history of linguistics.   Of the book which forms most linguists' only contact with Saussure, the *Cours de linguistique générale*, Godel writes, ' I would remind you that de Saussure never published a book or monograph on general linguistics . . . The book published in 1916 by his disciples and friends, Ch. Bally and A. Sechehaye, is a mixture of the various contents of the three courses, as they had been preserved in a few students' notebooks . . . Bally and Sechehaye deserve unqualified approval for their ac-curacy and insight : one can only admire their skill in assembling a variety of material into a clear and consistent exposition.   Yet, they may have been too careful in " weeding out " every discrepancy and unevenness, and setting out the absolute coherence of the theory, its—so to speak—monolithic unity ' (482). The *Cours* gives the reader no hint that Saussure was acutely aware of the exist-ence of basic problems in linguistic theory for which he had no satisfactory answer.   Godel mentions in particular Saussure's growing concern in his last years about the problem of extending his notion of ' sign ' to units larger than morphemes : ' The " principle of arbitrariness " had been previously presented without qualification ; in 1911 de Saussure explained that it actually applies to linguistic signs which cannot be analyzed into smaller constituents ; in compound signs, arbitrariness is balanced by " motivation ".   Death prevented him from developing these new ideas ' (482).   Along the same line, Godel says, concerning the much-quoted statement in the *Cours* that the sentence belongs to parole and not to langue,

Paradigmatic connections surely belong in the system, since the system, as de Saussure pointed out in a previous chapter, is stored in the memory of each individual.   As to the syntagmatic connections, they require a creative act on the speaker's part—an actual combination of two or more members.   This can hardly be true of such syntagms as compound words, derivates, or usual phrases : de Saussure meant sentences.   This reasoning leads to amazing conclusions.   First, syntagmatics turns out not to be an homogeneous object : only one part of it is included in the system, namely such syntagms as consist of morphemes or ' sub-units '.   Furthermore, sentences are no longer auto-matically brought forth by the rules of the language ; they are produced by individual creative acts and consequently belong in ' speaking ' (la parole), not in ' language ' (la langue).   Here, and only here, I cannot help feeling a positive contradiction in the theory. De Saussure, too, must have felt it, for he expresses himself with such caution, in his third course, that I do not venture to record his conclusion as a well-considered and definitive opinion (490).

Saussure could of course hardly be expected to observe that while the creative process to which he refers is not a part of langue, the results of that process are. Such a realization would have necessitated a large-scale revision of his concep-tion of ' sign ', so as to include sentence-sized signifié and signifiant, and Saussure was in no position to get that deeply into semantic theory, since he can scarcely be said to have had any clear conception of signifié at all.   Godel rightly chides the editors of the *Cours* for ' adding to the genuine diagram a second one with the design of a tree for the signifié of Lat. *arbor*, thus suggesting to the readers the very erroneous conception against which de Saussure warned his students, that is, the idea of the signifié being the image of an object ' (486) ; but it is anybody's guess just what kind of arrangement of what kind of units would correspond to ' concept " arbre " ', which Saussure gives as the upper half of the diagram in question.   Saussure thus managed to conceive of a language as a code (he actually used the word *code* in his last course) without having any clear conception of the nature of the ' messages ' which that code encodes.

Godel also makes noteworthy observations about Saussure's conception of parole, which does not appear until the 1907 lectures (compare the synchrony/diachrony distinction, which was utilized in even his earliest works.)   As Godel observes, this term translates very well as ' performance ', in view of Saussure's use of the word ' exécution '.   Godel comments further about the extent to which Saussure's concerns were philosophical :

Like Descartes, he started from a radical doubt.   In human speech, he perceived, there is no given definite object which lends itself to observation and analysis.   There is only a most complex phenomenon, involving physical and psychological processes, individual freedom and social constraint, change and stability.   Such a phenomenon is not liable to classification or description.   The first scientific approach, therefore, is to make distinctions : what is essential in human speech ? What is primary ? What is real ? These questions can be answered, and the distinctions made, only on the basis of valid criteria. Thus, before applying any experimental method, one must formulate a theory of human speech.   Reason must act and work out the principles : it would be useless to try to study and explain facts as long as the very nature of the facts is at issue (481).

The second appendix to this volume, Stankiewicz's ' Slavic morphophonemics in its typological and diachronic aspects ', consists of a large body of facts and observations about Slavic consonantal and accentual alternations, preceded by a sizeable theoretical introduction and followed by a brief epilogue which summarizes the generalizations about Slavic which were arrived at in the body of the lecture and relates them to some of the ideas of the introduction.   My lack of training in Slavic linguistics forces me to concentrate my attention here on the outer sections of the lecture.

I normally interpret ' typology ' as having to do with clusters of characteristics that ' go together ' because of implicational universals of language, as abundantly illustrated in Greenberg's contribution to this volume.   Stankiewicz sometimes uses ' typology ' in that sense—' The aim of typology is the formulation and verification of generalizations about language, arrived at on the basis of empirical investigations of the languages of the world ' (497)—but more often uses it in two other senses.   First, it may refer to comparison of structural characteristics ; the first paragraph of the lecture, for example, begins with a contrast between ' two complementary approaches to the comparison of languages, known respectively as the " genetic " or " reconstructive " and the " typological " or " general linguistic " approach ', but is otherwise devoted to an attack on the atomism of the historical reconstructions of the Neogrammarians and Meillet : ' The method depends neither on a full description of synchronic states, nor on an analysis of phonological or grammatical relations.   Its focus of interest lies in the material aspect of linguistic forms, irrespective of their functions within the system '.   Second, it may refer to the study of what Stankiewicz calls (498) ' stability of the system ', i.e., characteristics which are relatively impervious to change.   Stankiewicz rightly observes that typology (presumably in all three senses) is not opposed to the genetic study of language but ought to be an integral part of it.   The one major gap in his presentation is that he does not specify the different roles of these three kinds of typology in historical reconstruction—e.g., the fact that implicational universals show certain directions of language change to be natural and others abnormal or impossible, and accordingly provide grounds for choosing between alternative reconstructions (Jakobson 1958).   A consideration of the different relations of the various ' typologies ' to historical reconstruction would necessarily involve one in the question of distinguishing between those structural features which happen fortuitously not to change and those which remain unchanged as a result of some universal principles.   It is not clear which of these two categories are appropriate for many of Stankiewicz's correlations of morphophonemic alternation with morphological category oppositions.   For example, it is hard to see how any universal principles could be involved in preserving the following situation : ' Thus inanimate masculine (dialectally also neuter) substantives of the I declension (non-feminine) and feminine substantives of the III declension utilize the accentual alternation to oppose the marked case of the locative to the other cases, whereas inanimate feminine substantives of the II declension oppose accentually the unmarked case of the acc. (dialectally also dat.) to the other cases.   The plural, on the other hand, may oppose the stem-accented non-oblique (nom. and acc.) to the desinence-accented oblique cases of masculine and feminine substantives ' (519).

Much of this lecture is concerned with the role of morphological categories in grammar.   While there is no doubt that, in many of the cases cited by Stankiewicz, the conditions for an alternation can only be stated satisfactorily in terms of a morphological category (for example, the stress alternation in Slovenian discussed on pp. 509–10), the argument that he gives for a morphological rather than phonological environment for the Russian transitive softening[32] rule is unconvincing.   Halle (1963) is rightly criticized for adhocness in setting up an otherwise unnecessary vowel in the underlying form of the comparatives of certain adjectives, to make them fit the environment (__ unrounded vowel+ rounded vowel) which he had proposed as the condition for transitive softening —e.g., $bogat+A+o \rightarrow bog\acute{a}\check{c}e$.   Not only does the 'A' otherwise never occur, but (as Stankiewicz observes) positing it complicates the syntax, since adjectives otherwise do not exhibit any morpheme separating the stem from the comparative morpheme or the agreement marker.   However, it is not necessary to reject Halle's phonological environment in favor of the list of morphological categories which Stankiewicz proposes, which would have to make reference to some pho-

---

[32] In this alternation, underlying velars and apicals become alveo-palatals, and labials acquire a following palatalized *l*.

nological characteristics anyway, namely whether the verbalizing suffix is *i* or *a* and whether the comparative morpheme is stressed. A small change in Halle's rules, proposed by T. M. Lightner and S.-Y. Kuroda, makes unnecessary Halle's ad-hoc proposal. They propose that transitive softening occurs in a number of stages: first an unrounded vowel before a rounded vowel is turned into [j], and then various assimilatory changes affect *Cj* sequences. Since there is transitive softening before an unstressed comparative ending (pronounced [i], which could come from underlying/i e a o/), but not before a stressed comparative ending, pronounced [éji], a rule which deletes the first vowel of the comparative ending when it is unstressed would create a *Cj* sequence, and this would then be subject to the assimilations alluded to above. Moreover, Lightner (1965) observes that this treatment allows one in a natural fashion to account for the difference in the effect of transitive softening on *kovat'/kuju* ' hammer ' (inf. and 1sg. pres.) and *lovit'/lovl'u* ' hunt '. Given underlying forms $((kou+a+o)+u)$ and $((lou+i+i)+u)$, conditions for transitive softening are met within the inner constituent of the one form but only within the outer constituent of the other. If the rule turning an unrounded vowel into [j] before a rounded vowel is part of a cycle, and applies before the rules which turn prevocalic [u] into [v] and simplify *Vu* clusters, then the application of the cycle to the inner constituents will yield $(ku+j+o)$ and $(lov+i)$, and the further application of the cycle to the outer constituents will yield $(ku+j+u)$ and $(lov+j+u)$, whence [*kuju*] and [*lovl'u*].

One important point which Stankiewicz makes is that Halle's rules are not valid for those Russian dialects which have *bros'ut* rather than standard Russian *bros'at* for ' they throw ': Halle's rules would yield **brošut* if *ut* were taken for the 3pl. ending. Two questions are raised here. First, is it necessary that dialects of the same language differ only superficially? While there are innumerable cases of dialects whose apparent diversity can correctly be ascribed to slightly different rules applying to exactly the same underlying forms, there are also obvious cases of differences in underlying representation of morphemes; for example, many speakers of English distinguish phonetically between *horse* and *hoarse*, whereas others (such as myself) not only do not make such a distinction but do not even perceive it in the speech of others unless making a conscious attempt to do so. Clearly these two classes of speakers differ not merely in the presence vs. absence of some low-level rule but also in the underlying phonological form which they have learned for the relevant morphemes. Cases of rule difference involving relatively ' deep ' phonological rules can be found by considering language acquisition: rules such as the reflexes of the English great vowel shift (governing the alternations in *sane/sanity*, *profound/profundity*, etc.) probably are not learned until relatively late in the child's development, but must nonetheless come ' early ' in the ordering of rules; the idiolect of a child who has not yet learned this rule and the idiolect of his parents, while ' closely related ' by anyone's standards, nonetheless differ not only as regards the presence of a very ' early ' rule but also as regards the underlying representations of all of the morphemes to which the rule applies.[33]   I thus endorse Hermann Paul's remark, ' Wir müssen eigentlich so viele Sprachen unterscheiden, als es Individuen gibt '.[34]   The linguist should not feel obliged to reduce all varieties of a language to a single pattern : his task is rather to separate the differences from the shared characteristics.   This brings up the second question raised by Stankiewicz's comment on the dialects that have *bros'ut* : does Halle's treatment of standard Russian make it look more different from these dialects than it actually is ?   Not having studied those dialects, I am unable to answer this question ; however, I note that an affirmative answer to it, if justified, would be a devastating argument against Halle's rules.   Among the types of facts that might be marshalled in support of that conclusion, the most important may be facts of language acquisition in both the *bros'ut* dialects and the standard language.   I argued above that Chomsky's notion of evaluation measure cannot be considered an explication of language acquisition, since a child never has the full corpus of its experiences to look at at one time, and so may choose among possible modifications of its grammar not on the basis of any global properties of the new grammar but on the basis of its closeness to the child's current grammar.   That is, the optimal way of learning a certain variety of speech may have as its result a grammar which no proposed evaluation measure would pick as ' optimal '.   By the same token, a consideration of language acquisition would be of crucial importance for evaluating many of the facts which Stankiewicz cites : the elimination of the *k-č* palatalization from nominal paradigms but its preservation in verbal paradigms, for example, might have its explanation in the order in which the various forms of the paradigm are learned.   Such an explanation is certainly at the bottom of many cases of ' analogical leveling '.   Thus an ' optimal ' grammar of Old Russian would have had a rule whereby a consonant becomes pala-

---

[33] This observation is the basis of the only plausible argument that I have heard (due to David Johns) for believing that a speaker's internal representation of underlying forms is in terms of atomic segment units, rather than complexes of features : when a child learns a rule which, generative phonological theory would predict, causes him to change the underlying forms of all the relevant morphemes (e.g. replace all underlying *i*'s by *ē*'s), the child never starts producing the anomalous forms which would result if he had to search through his entire vocabulary, making the appropriate changes in a hundred or so morphemes, and had missed a couple of items in the search.   This fact would be explained if the underlying forms were made up of segment-sized units and the learning process had merely changed rules of the type for which I castigated Hockett above, which associated sets of feature specifications to segment names.   An alternative explanation of this fact has been suggested by Stampe (abortion), who proposes that (contrary to the assumption of all generative phonologists so far) lexical representations of morphemes are not all at the same ' depth ', and a morpheme is not subject to rules earlier than the first one that figures in alternations involving that morpheme.[e]
[34] Stankiewicz cites this remark and describes it as ' in the same vein ' as Joos's ' Languages could differ from each other unpredictably and without limit '.   While Joos's remark entails ' rejection of general principles and linguistic universals ' (495), Paul's does not (although I grant that Paul would probably have endorsed Joos's remark) ; indeed, it is only by having extensive recourse to language universals that one can come to grips with the full range of variation of human language, and pinpoint the actual differences between varieties of speech.

talized before a front vowel, and a rule whereby *e* becomes *o* before a non-palatalized consonant.   However, since these rules yield noun paradigms having [e] only in the locative singular and [o] everywhere else, a child who had not yet learned the *e* → *o* rule could only internalize the word for ' honey ' as /m′od/ rather than /med/ ; then, when he added the locative to his repertory of cases, he would have internalized a grammar that would generate the modern Russian form *m′od′e* rather than the old Russian form *m′ed′e*.[f]

[a] The most explicitly formulated analyses within this framework which I have seen are in Jackendoff (1971) and Jackendoff (1972).

[b] See now Chiba (1972) for an exposition and defense of Brame's proposal,   Examples such as *Parky pulled the strings that got me my job*, in which a relative clause is attached to part of an idiom (*pull strings*) that is entirely within the main clause, indicate that the head noun can not always originate inside the relative clause.

[c] See note *l* of ' Where do NP's come from ? ' for discussion of a major defect in trees such as those of Fig. 3.   I was right about the material of NP's originating outside of their clauses, but wrong about their just hanging in the air as they do in Fig. 3.

[d] See now Fillmore (1967 : 5–6).

[e] This proposal is also made in Chafe (1968).

[f] See Darden (1971) for an excellent argument that Russian in fact did develop underlying forms with palatal consonants shortly after the loss of ' jers ' caused there to be a surface contrast between plain and palatalized consonants.

10. A Note on Multiple Negations
or Why You Don't Not Say No Sentences Like This One*

This note is concerned with sentences in which something containing a negation is negated, as in

   (1)   Not many of the boys didn't talk to John.

not with the use of multiple negative words to express a single negation, as in substandard English

   (2)   Nobody didn't do nothing. (=standard *Nobody did anything*.)

Different varieties of standard English differ as to which sentences with multiple negations are grammatical.   For example, many speakers reject (1), which many other speakers find impeccable, whereas apparently all speakers reject

   (3)   *John didn't talk to not many of the boys.[a]

* This paper was written in summer 1968 and is published here for the first time.   My reason for withholding it from publication was the desire to add something cogent to it on the matter of the great individual variation in acceptability of the examples discussed, which has been impressed on me by reactions from audiences before whom I have given oral versions of this paper.   As will be clear from what follows, I have not progressed materially towards that goal since writing the paper.   Guy Carden has collected some interesting data on idiolect variation with respect to multiple negations, which he summarizes and interprets in Carden (1972).

Hitherto, transformational treatments of negation in English (e.g. Klima 1964) have attempted to exclude the non-occurring multiple negations by contraining the rules of the base component so as not to generate those deep structures which would yield the ungrammatical sentences in question.   Such attempts, however, are doomed to failure, since there are cases of sentences which should presumably have the same deep structure but only one of which contains an admissible combination of negatives.

(4) a.   Not many of the boys didn't consult John.
    b.   *John wasn't consulted by not many of the boys.
(5) a.   *The doctor didn't examine not many of the students.
    b.   Not many of the students weren't examined by the doctor.
(6) a.   Max doesn't believe that no one loves him.
    b.   *Max doesn't believe no one to love him.

It thus appears necessary that the base component generate structures which could potentially underlie ungrammatical combinations of negatives and that at least some of the ungrammatical sentences in question be excluded either through constraints on the relevant transformations or through OUTPUT CONSTRAINTS in the sense of Ross (1967a) and Perlmutter (1968).   As Jackendoff (1969) pointed out in the case of a similar class of sentences, any attempt to formulate restrictions on specific transformations so as to exclude (4a, 5b, 6a), etc. would yield extraordinarily complicated constraints which fail to capture a crucial generalization.   For example, the passive transformation would presumably have to be constrained so as to be inapplicable if the subject has a negated quantifier and the verb is negated but obligatory if the verb is negated and the object contains a negated quantifier.   Moreover, because of the examples

(7) a.   Not many of the beggars weren't given handouts.
    b.   *Handouts weren't given to not many of the beggars.
    c.   *They didn't give not many of the beggars handouts.
(8) a.   Not many of the prizes weren't given to people who deserved them.
    b.   *People who deserved them weren't given not many of the prizes.
    c.   *They didn't give not many of the prizes to people who deserved
         them.

the dative movement transformation, which applies in the derivation of those passive sentences in which the indirect object becomes the subject, would have to be inapplicable if the indirect object has a negated quantifier and the verb is negated but obligatory if the direct object has a negated quantifier and the verb is negated.   Such involved restrictions as these are simply circuitous ways of expressing a generalization about the permitted outputs of the entire system of transformation, namely that (in the variety of English for which (1) is grammatical) no derivation is allowed which terminates with a structure which has two negative words in the same VP.[1]   Accordingly, it appears that an output cons-

[1] In view of mounting evidence that no such label as VP is justifiable, this provisional formulation of the constraint will have to be revised.   I do not attempt that revision here

traint rather than constraints on specific transformations is needed to exclude sentences such as (4b, 5a, 6b). Moreover, such an output constraint also correctly excludes certain sentences which no constraint on transformations could exclude.

(9)   *Not many of the boys didn't kiss not many of the girls.

Further confirmation that an output constraint is needed to exclude English sentences with multiple negations is given by the following examples:

(10)   John doesn't like Brahms, and neither does Harry; but not Max—
        Max loves Brahms.
(11)   Q: Who didn't say anything?   (a) Nobody.
                                         (b) Not Max.
(12)   Q: How many of the boys did Sam not talk to?
        A: Not many of them.

The A's in these examples arise from the deletion of *doesn't like Brahms*, *didn't say anything*, and *Sam didn't talk to*. If this (normally optional) deletion did not take place, the sentences

(13)   *Max doesn't not like Brahms.
(14)   Nobody didn't say anything.
(15)   *Sam didn't talk to not many of them.

would arise. (13) and (15) are presumably ungrammatical in all varieties of English. (14) is ungrammatical in the variety which rejects (1). However, (10)–(12) are acceptable in both varieties of English.[2] Thus, as in Perlmutter's (1968) example of the order of Spanish enclitic pronouns, combinations which are inadmissible in surface structure must be allowed to appear in intermediate stages of derivations, but only those derivations are permitted in which the offending material is eventually eliminated. This state of affairs is typical of output constraints.

It should be noted that if multiple negations are excluded by an output constraint, there is no need for the base component to impose any restrictions whatever on multiple negation: *not* can be regarded as an intransitive verb with a sentential subject, the surface structure of negative sentences arises through the same transformations of VP-promotion[3] as operates in the case of sentences with *seem*:[4]

since I wish to avoid lengthy discussion of matters not of direct relevance to this argument. Presumably the variety of English which rejects (1) has a more general output constraint, namely one which excludes sentences having negative elements as ' clause mates ' in the sense of Postal (1971).
[2] Other cases are known of questions which allow an abbreviated answer but not a full answer. For example, *Is that book any good?* allows the answer *Yes, it is*, but does not allow any unabbreviated affirmative answer.
[3] If (as I argue in McCawley 1970a) English has underlying verb-initial word order, then the transformation in question will move not the VP but the first NP from the lower to the higher sentence. With verb-initial order, there is of course no such thing as a VP.
[4] The analysis of *seem* as an intransitive verb with sentence subject is due to Jespersen (1937: 57).

and structures in which e.g. 17 consecutive *not*'s had been generated would yield surface structures violating the output constraint proposed above unless some transformation (such as the deletion involved in (10–12) had applied in such a way as to eliminate all violations of the constraint.

The conclusion that the base component of a grammar need not impose any constraint on multiple negations is exactly what one would expect, given the conclusion (for which I argue in McCawley 1968 c,d) that there is no level of deep structure as distinct from semantic representation and that the base component of a grammar consists of conditions on the well-formedness of semantic representations. Since there is nothing semantically odd about the negation of a negative sentence, the base component of a grammar without a separate level of deep structure would generate semantic representations involving arbitrarily complicated multiple negations, and only output constraints and constraints on transformations would be available as means of excluding sentences which are ungrammatical because of multiple negations.

A similar conclusion can be drawn about double comparatives. There is nothing semantically odd about the comparative of a comparative, since such a thing can be expressed by a paraphrase:

(16) My German is better than my French to a greater extent than it has ever been.

Moreover, it is possible to form a comparative construction with the verb *prefer*, which includes a comparison in its meaning and indeed allows a *than*-phrase if its object is in the infinitive form.[5]

(17) I prefer to read pornography than to watch television.
(18) I prefer to read pornography than to watch television more than I ever have before.

Similarly, *X's senior*, which means ' older than X ' allows measure expressions and comparatives:

(19) Lionel is my senior by 2 years.

[5] This point is made by Jespersen (1924 : 248–9). Jespersen uses the term ' latent comparisons ' for such sentences as (17)–(20).

(20) My new wife is more my senior than my old wife was.

That the absence of double comparatives like

(21) *My German is $\begin{Bmatrix} \text{more better} \\ \text{betterer} \end{Bmatrix}$ than my French than it was before.

is due to an output constraint is shown by the existence of sentences such as

(22) When I was in college, my German was better than my French, and
      now it's even more so.,

which require a double comparative as an intermediate stage in their derivation; the double comparative is eliminated by the pronominalization transformation which creates the *so*.

[a] (3) and some later examples possess a characteristic which is itself sufficient to make the sentence ungrammatical. Specifically, *not many* in surface structure can only appear either earlier than the verb or in certain kinds of adverbial expressions:

Not many boys stayed.
*John talked to not many boys.
Bill interviewed 100 boys, not many of whom John had talked to.
He dropped the bombs with not many regrets.
*He dropped bombs on not many Fridays.

While (3) is thus ungrammatical independently of multiple negation, the argument that I give here can be salvaged by replacing *not many* by *no one* or *no students*. My statement of where *not many* may occur in surface structure is only a first approximation. The following examples, due to Robert Fox, make clear that things are more complicated:

*That virtue was exhibited by not many people.
Courage is a virtue that was exhibited by not many people.

11. English as a VSO Language[*]

Evidence is presented that the superficial Subject-Verb-
Object word order of English arises by a transformation from
an underlying constituent order in which clauses begin with
verbs—or more correctly, predicates: the representation in
question here is a semantic one in which noun, verb, adjective,
conjunction, etc. are undifferentiated.

1. A Prerequisite

To increase the likelihood of this paper's being intelligible, I will preface it
with a brief summary (largely a restatement of results in unpublished papers by
Ross and George Lakoff) of an important notion that recurs in it, namely that
of the CYCLE.

I will assume in what follows that the transformational component of a
grammar divides up into three sub-systems of rules: pre-cyclic transformations,
the cycle, and post-cyclic transformations.   I will ignore pre-cyclic transformations, since the one known pre-cyclic transformation (namely the sentence
pronominalization which gives rise to the *it* of such sentences as *Margaret is
believed by many to be pregnant, but she denies it*) is irrelevant to my argument.
The rules of the cycle are ordered, as are the post-cyclic transformations.   All
the rules of the cycle apply in sequence first to the innermost sentence, then
all the rules of the cycle apply to the next higher sentence, etc.   Thus, an
application of a rule of the cycle to an embedded sentence precedes all applications of that or any other cyclic transformation to the sentence in which it is
embedded.

[*] This paper originally appeared in *Language* 46. 286–99.

The following illustrates the kind of grounds on which one can conclude that certain transformations have to be in the cycle. There is a transformation, called EQUI-NP-DELETION, which deletes the first noun phrase of an embedded clause if it matches a certain *NP* of the clause containing it, as in *Max wants to drink a daiquiri*, where the subject of *drink* has been deleted under identity with the subject of *want* (Fig. 1).[1] There is another transformation (known under a variety of names) which I will refer to as SUBJECT-RAISING; it applies to certain sentences containing an embedded clause, moving both the subject and the remainder of the embedded clause into the higher clause,[a] as in *Arthur seems to admire Spiro*, which arises from an underlying structure in which *seem* is an intransitive verb whose subject is the sentence *Arthur admires Spiro* (Fig. 2).

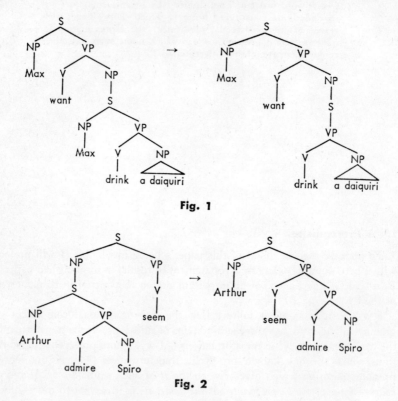

Fig. 1

Fig. 2

The interaction of these two transformations is seen in the sentences

    (1)   Boris wants to seem to understand physics.
    (2)   Boris seems to want to understand physics.

In (1), Equi-NP-deletion must apply to S_0 (Fig. 3a); however, it cannot apply

[1] In this and subsequent diagrams, I will ignore tense. See McCawley (1971) for some details of what is omitted here.

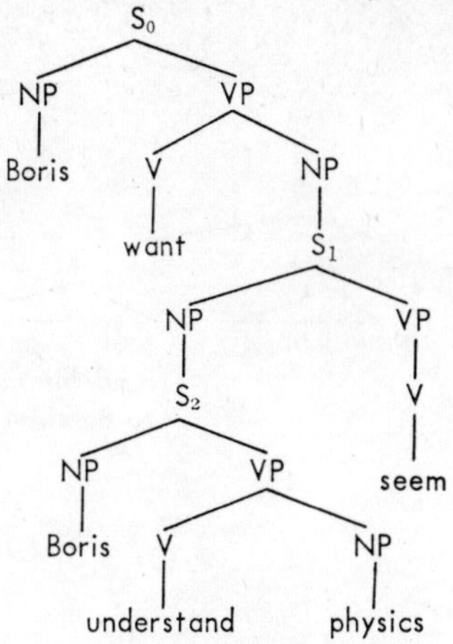

Fig. 3a

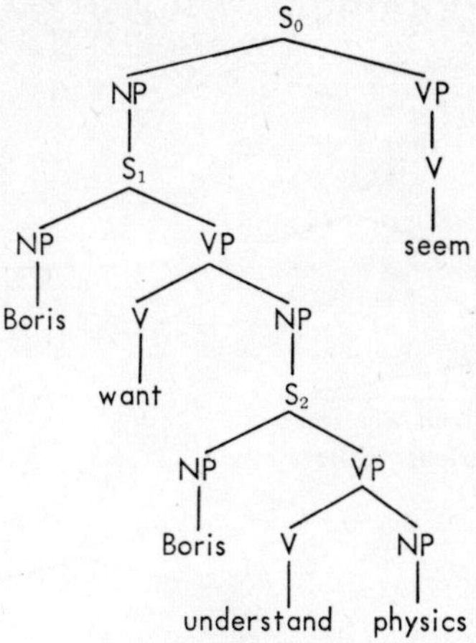

Fig. 3b

to S_0 unless S_1 has a subject which matches that of S_0. *Boris* does not become the subject of S_1 until Subject-raising applies to S_1. Therefore, Subject-raising must apply to S_1 before Equi-NP-deletion applies to S_0. In (2), Equi-NP-deletion must apply to S_1 so as to delete the subject of S_2 (Fig. 3b); but for Equi-NP-deletion to apply to S_1, the subject of S_1 must be the same as the subject of S_2, which implies that Equi-NP-deletion must apply to S_1 before Subject-raising applies to S_0 and causes *Boris* to cease to be the subject of S_1 and to become the subject of S_0. Thus, Subject-raising on a lower sentence must apply before Equi-NP-deletion on a higher sentence, and Equi-NP-deletion on a lower sentence must apply before Subject-raising on a higher sentence. Both Subject-raising and Equi-NP-deletion must be in the cycle: if either or both were pre-cyclic or post-cyclic, then all the applications of one would precede all the applications of the other, and at least one of the above derivations would be impossible. There are indeed cases where an application of Equi-NP-deletion must intervene between two applications of Subject-raising, as in

(3)   Boris seems to want to appear to understand physics

where, using the same arguments as above and the same subscripting scheme, Subject-raising on S_2 must precede Equi-NP-deletion on S_1, which must in turn precede Subject-raising on S_0. I emphasize that I mean MUST precede and not just MAY precede: given the assumed formulations of the transformations, these are the only sequences of rule applications which would generate these sentences. It should also be noted that one can argue that a transformation is in the cycle only on the basis of its interaction with other transformations, not just on the basis of its specific effect.[b]

In the case of post-cyclic rules, all applications of one transformation precede all applications of the next transformation. As an example of the kind of grounds on which one can conclude that a transformation must be post-cyclic, consider

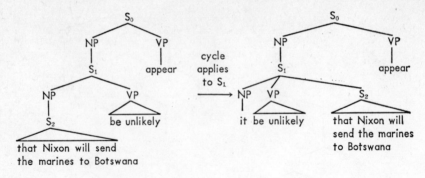

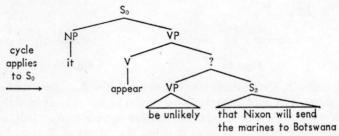

Fig. 4

the transformation of EXTRAPOSITION, which moves (usually optionally) certain embedded clauses to the end of the clause in which they are embedded, thus giving as optional variants such pairs as

(4) a. That Nixon will send the marines to Botswana is unlikely.
     b. It is unlikely that Nixon will send the marines to Botswana.

If Extraposition were in the cycle, certain sentences would be assigned the wrong surface constituent structure; for example, in the sentence

(5) It appears to be unlikely that Nixon will send the marines to Botswana

the words *to be unlikely that Nixon will send the marines to Botswana* would be a constituent in surface structure (Fig. 4). That constituent structure would imply that (5) could be divided into the phonological phrases *it appears* and *to be unlikely that Nixon will send the marines to Botswana*,[2] as in cases which clearly have the surface constituent structure that appears in Fig. 4, e.g. *He desires to be assured that Nixon will send the marines to Botswana*. However, it is actually highly unnatural to make an intonation break after *appears* in (5). The only place where it is natural to divide (5) into phonological phrases is after *unlikely*. But the hypothesis that Extraposition is post-cylcic yields a surface

---

[2] The highest constituent boundary (after *it*) is not a possible intonation break, since the constituent it follows is unstressed.

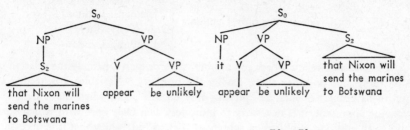

Fig. 5a   **Fig. 5b**

structure which implies that exactly that intonation break should be possible:
the cycle would not affect S_1, and its application to S_0 would yield Fig. 5a,
which post-cyclic Extraposition would convert into Fig. 5b, in which *appears
to be unlikely* is a surface constituent and the highest constituent boundary not
preceded or followed only by unstressed material is thus between *unlikely* and
that.

2. On the Formulation of the Cyclic Transformations

The notions ' cycle ' and ' post-cyclic transformation ' were proposed at
a time when everyone believed in a distinction between syntax and semantics.
They were proposed as part of a theory of syntax; that is, they were supposed
to relate deep structures to surface structures, where deep structures were by
assumption syntactic, not semantic, objects.   More recently, some linguists,
including me, have rejected the distinction between syntax and semantics and
have treated transformations as mechanisms for associating semantic representations with the corresponding surface structures, without recourse to any level of
' deep structure ' as distinct from semantic representation.   The rejection of a
dividing line between syntax and semantics appears not to require any modification of earlier conclusions as regards what transformations are and how they
interact.   In particular, the notions of ' cycle ' and ' post-cyclic transformation ' carry over unchanged to the newer concept of grammar.

Semantic representation in my current concept of grammar is something not
far removed from the representations that appear in most varieties of symbolic
logic.[3]   In particular, it is necessary that semantic representations contain
VARIABLES if they are to express the difference in meaning between sentences
such as

(6)   a.   Only Lyndon pities himself. $\text{Only}_x(\text{Pity}(x, x), \text{Lyndon})$
      b.   Only Lyndon pities Lyndon. $\text{Only}_x(\text{Pity}(x, \text{Lyndon}), \text{Lyndon})$
      c.   Only Lyndon pities only himself. $\text{Only}_x(\text{Only}_y(\text{Pity}(x, y), x),$
                                          $\text{Lyndon})$

---

[3] See McCawley (1970c), for a fairly detailed account of semantic representation.

d.   Only Lyndon pities only Lyndon.
$$\begin{cases} \text{Only}_x(\text{Only}_y(\text{Pity}(x, y), \\ \quad \text{Lyndon}), \text{Lyndon}) \\ \text{Only}_y(\text{Only}_x(\text{Pity}(x, y), \\ \quad \text{Lyndon}), \text{Lyndon}) \end{cases}$$

Only expresses a relation between a thing and a property, namely the relation of that thing and no other thing having the property. Variables are needed to represent properties such as ' pitying only oneself ', and when more than one variable is present, it is necessary to indicate which *Only* goes with which variable. In addition, ambiguous sentences such as (6d)[4] show that it is necessary for semantic representation to indicate the immediate constituent structure of the semantic elements, since the only difference in meaning between the two readings of (6d) lies in which of the two *Only*'s applies to a property containing the other one. One reading of (6d) is paraphrasable as ' Lyndon is the only person who pities only Lyndon ', the other as ' Lyndon is the only person who only Lyndon pities '.

I should emphasize that the ultimate elements of semantic representations need not correspond to the words of surface structure (as they appear to in the highly oversimplified case just discussed), but will rather be the various semantic elements involved in the meanings of the words (plus, generally, semantic elements that are not given overt expression). Some of the tranformations will be PRE-LEXICAL, i.e. they will apply before the point or points in the derivation at which lexical items are chosen (Gruber 1965, McCawley 1968). One of the effects of pre-lexical transformations is to group semantic elements together into word-sized units; an example of a pre-lexical transformation will be discussed later.

In the above examples, I have followed the usual practise of modern logicians and written the predicates *Pity* and *Only* before the items that they apply to. Thus, my semantic representations correspond to a word order in which verbs precede their subjects. It is, of course, natural that logicians should have used such a mode of representation: first and last are positions that are in some sense ' special ', and the logicians in question have put the predicates in a speical position because of their special role in the proposition. My main concern here is the question of whether such semantic representations are syntactically justified, i.e. the question of whether a dividing line can be found between ' early ' transformations, which give evidence of operating on inputs that have predicates at the beginning of clauses, and ' later ' transformations, which give evidence of applying to structures with predicates second in the clause.

Ignoring the one known pre-cyclic transformation, which turns out to be irrelevant to this question, the earliest transformations in the grammar are those of the cycle. It has been observed by John Kimball that the transformations that

---

[4] For many speakers, (6d) allows only the former of the two readings given above. See G. Lakoff (1971, in prep.) for a presentation of the formal devices needed to exclude the second reading of (6d) in the grammar of a dialect that does not admit that reading. There is much more to *only* than I have suggested here; see Horn (1969) for details.

have thus far been shown to be in the cycle all give outputs of the same general shape as the structures generated by the base component. If this observation of Kimball's (which, it should be emphasized, has not been very widely tested as yet) turns out to be a universal property of cyclic transformations, then a language with underlying predicate-first order would retain predicate-first order throughout the cycle and could become a surface verb-second language only through a POST-CYCLIC transformation of *V-NP* inversion. An obvious question to ask, then, is what effect the assumption of underlying predicate-first order would have on the cycle in English. To answer that question, it is necessary first to determine whether the same transformations would be cyclic for predicate-first order as would be cyclic for predicate-second order. With one exception, all the cyclicity arguments I know of are valid regardless of whether the transformations apply to inputs with predicate-first or predicate-second order. The one exception has to do with the transformation of DATIVE-MOVEMENT, which yields *I gave $10 to Max* as an optional variant of *I gave Max $10*. The argument that Dative-movement must be in the cycle is based on an argument that Dative-movement must apply before Passive, which is known on other grounds to be in the cycle. However, the latter argument depends crucially on the assumption of predicate-second order: in the version of Passive which would be required by predicate-first order, Passive and Dative-movement could apply in either order. Thus, except possibly for Dative-movement, the same transformations are in the cycle regardless of whether the basic constituent order is predicate first or predicate second.

Of the 15 transformations of English that I can argue must be in the cycle, there are ten[e] for which it makes no significant difference whether they apply to structures with predicate first or predicate second. For example, the cyclic transformation of quantifier lowering, which attaches quantifiers to the noun phrases that they go with, would require only a trivial difference in formulation if it is to apply to a structure with predicate first instead of predicate second; specifically, the transformation would be formulated with the quantifier to the left rather than to the right of the clause into which it is inserted.[5] For the remaining five cyclic transformations, the underlying constituent order makes a significant difference in the complexity of the conditions under which the transformation applies, or in its effect. In each case, the version of the transformation that assumes predicate-first order is significantly simpler in the sense of either involving fewer elementary operations or applying under conditions which can be stated without the use of the more exotic notational devices that have figured in transformational rules.

The first of these transformations is the passive transformation. I should begin by pointing out that no existing formulation of a passive transformation even

---

[5] Arguments that quantifiers originate as predicates of structures containing embedded clauses into which the quantifiers are eventually inserted are given in Carden (1967) and Lakoff (1969a).

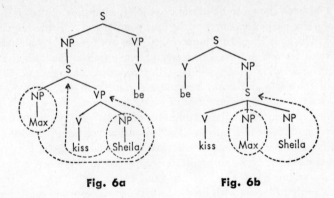

Fig. 6a   Fig. 6b

comes close to explaining the various mysteries connected with passives,[6,d] e.g.
the question of why *Hubert loves God* is not funny in the same way that *God is
loved by Hubert* is.   While I have no concrete proposal for how passives work, I
think that investigations of passives so far have at least established that passives
arise from some structure containing an active clause and that the surface *by-*
phrase arises from the subject of the underlying active through a movement
transformation.   Given that assumption, then if the passive transformation, whatever it is, applies to a structure with verb second, it has to move two noun
phrases: it has to move the underlying subject to the end of the clause, and the
underlying object into subject position (Fig. 6a).   However, if Passive applies to
structures with verb first, then only one noun phrase need be moved: if the subject is moved to the end of the clause, the object will then automatically be in
' subject position ', i.e. it will directly follow the verb and thus will become surface
subject by *V-NP* inversion[7] (Fig. 6b).

[6] The most attractive proposal in print is that in Hasegawa (1968), namely that the passive
be is an underlying transitive verb; e.g. *Boris was denounced by Vassily* would be derived
from something like *Boris be [Vassily denounce Boris]*ₛ.   Chomsky (1970a: 212) criticizes
this analysis on the grounds that some passives have surface subjects which otherwise do
not occur in subject position, e.g. *Advantage was taken of Bill;* he argues that the appropriate surface subjects of passives can be generated only by having the surface subject
of the passive originate within an underlying active, rather than outside the active, as in
Hasegawa's proposal.   The proposal of an intransitive passive *be* which figures in Fig. 6
is due to Lakoff and Ross.   I suspect that, Chomsky's examples notwithstanding, some
variant of Hasegawa's proposal will be needed to explain the difference in grammaticality
of passives of various idioms, e.g. *My leg has been pulled* vs. **The bucket has been kicked.*
A variant of Hasegawa's proposal in which an element of the complement of *be* could be
substituted for a ' related ' but not necessarily identical subject of *be* would incorporate
the intuition that those fragments of idioms which can be derived subjects of passives ' go
proxy for ' what the sentence is really about.   However, I have not yet succeeded in turning this highly speculative suggestion into an explicit analysis, and I am aware of such
difficult cases as *The hatchet has been buried between them* and the example cited above.
[7] One of the many gross oversimplifications in this account of passives is my failure to
take prepositions into account.   I subscribe to the proposal (Fillmore 1968: 32–3) that at
some stage of every derivation, every *NP* will have a preposition.   The obvious supple-

Similarly, the transformation of THERE-INSERTION which creates the *there* of
existential sentences such as

 (7) There is a unicorn in the garden

has to both create the *there* and move the underlying subject of *be* if it applies
to an input with verb-second order.[e] However, if it applies to an input with verb-
first order, it is only necessary that it insert *there* after the *be;* the *NP* which
would have become the surface subject had *there* not been inserted need not be
moved, since it is no longer in the environment where *V-NP* inversion would affect it (Fig. 7). Here I must interject two remarks about *There*-insertion. First,

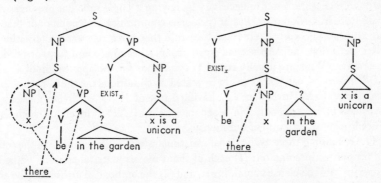

Fig. 7a   **Fig. 7b**

the formulations occasionally given in which *there* is inserted when the subject
is ' indefinite ' are inadequate, since *There*-insertion only applies to a clause which
is in the immediate scope of an existential quantifier. Note that

 (8) John thinks that someone is in the garden

is ambiguous (one reading: ' John thinks that there is someone who is in the garden '; the other reading: ' There is someone such that John thinks that that
person is in the garden '), whereas

 (9) John thinks that there is someone in the garden

allows ony the former reading. Hence, of the two semantic representations that
are realizable as (8), only one is subject to *There*-insertion; and since the crucial
difference between those semantic representations is the location of the existential quantifier, the transformation creating *there* must mention that the next
predicate up from the affected clause must be an existential quantifier. Second,

mentary proposal that the dictionary entry of each verb contain a specification of which
preposition goes with which *NP* would imply that the prepositions must be inserted before Passive changes the orientations of the *NP*'s relative to the verb, and thus that lexical
insertion of the verb must take place during the application of the cycle to the lower *S* in
tree such as that of Fig. 6b, and that *V-NP* inversion actually interchanges the verb and
the following prepositional phrase (whose preposition is later deleted).

this formulation of *There*-insertion implies that, for the argument I am giving for underlying predicate-first order to be valid, *V-NP* inversion will have to be post-cyclic (as, of course, would be predicted from Kimball's conjecture): if it were in the cycle, then when *There*-insertion applied, the clause in which *there* was to be inserted would have already undergone *V-NP* inversion. Thus *V-NP* inversion must be post-cyclic if underlying predicate-first order is to have the advantage over underlying predicate-second order that I propose it has.

I thus maintain that the ' standard ' formulations of Passive and *There*-insertion are really composed of two things: the essential transformation and whatever juggling of *NP*'s is necessary to yield verb-second order. The predicate-first proposal makes the latter unnecessary by having a single rule that produces verb-second order. Moreover, Postal (personal communication) points out that this rule comes at no cost: there must be a rule that gives rise to an alternation between verb-first and verb-second word orders so as to account for word order in questions. What are usually stated as conditions for the application of a rule of *NP-V* inversion can just as easily be stated as conditions for the non-application of a rule of *V-NP* inversion; i.e., having a rule of *V-NP* inversion makes it unnecessary to have in addition a separate rule of *NP-V* inversion such as has figured in most accounts of questions.

The remaining three cyclic transformations which are relevant have the following properties in common: (1) each of them moves material from an embedded clause up into the clause containing it, and (2) the embedded clause may be either the underlying subject or the underlying object of the clause containing it. One of these transformations is Subject-raising. I have already given cases where Subject-rasing lifts material out of the underlying subject of intransitive verbs such as *seem* and *appear*. It also lifts material out of the objects of transitive verbs such as *believe* (in this case, optionally), thus giving as optional variants

> (10)   a.   Sam believes that his brother is a necrophiliac.
>   b.   Sam believes his brother to be a necrophiliac.

The next of these transformations is that of NEGATIVE-RAISING, which optionally moves a negative from an embedded clause to the next higher clause. It applies both to the object complements of certain transitive verbs, giving optional variants such as[f]

> (11)   a.   I think that Harry won't be here until Friday
>   b.   I don't think that Harry will be here until Friday

and to the subject complements of certain intransitive verbs (or adjectives), giving optional variants such as

> (12)   a.   It's likely that Nixon won't send the marines to Botswana until 1972.
>   b.   It's not likely that Nixon will send the marines to Botswana until 1972.

The third transformation is the pre-lexical transformation of PREDICATE-RAISING,

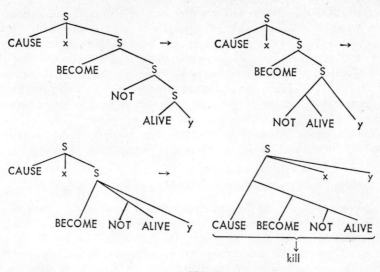

Fig. 8

which optionally adjoins the predicate of an embedded sentence to the predicate of the next higher sentence.   For example, the word *kill* is insertable only in a structure derived through three pre-lexical applications of Predicate-raising to a structure of roughly the form ' *x* causes *y* to become not alive ' (Fig. 8).[g] Note that in the first two applications the clause whose predicate is raised is the subject of the next higher clause, but in the third application it is the object. If these three transformations apply to inputs that have prdicate-first word order, it is extremely simple to state what they do: each applies to a sentence of the form *Predicate* + optional *NP* + *Sentence;* Subject-raising takes the subject of the embedded sentence and puts it outside and to the left of that sentence; Negative-raising takes a negative marker, if that is the predicate of the embedded sentence, and puts it in front of the upper sentence; Predicate-raising adjoins the predicate of the lower sentence to the right of the predicate of the upper sentence.   To formulate any of these three transformations if they applied to structures that had predicate-second order would require great ingenuity in the manipulation of symbols, since either the thing being extracted from the embedded sentence would have to move to the right when extracted from a subject complement and to the left when extracted from an object complement (this is the case with Negative-raising and Predicate-raising), or it would be moved over different things depending on whether it is extracted from a subject complement or an object complement.

The simplifications which underlying predicate-first order brings about are important in connection with placing limits on the class of possible transformations.   In particular, it may be possible to impose the constraint (first proposed, I believe, by Hasegawa, p. 242) that each transformation may perform only one elementary operation: Passive and *There*-insertion were the two best examples of

transformations that had to perform two or more elementary operations, and
under my analysis they are no longer examples of that. It may also be possible
to banish from linguistics the ubiquitous curly brackets: the number of supposed
rules in both phonology and syntax that have been formulated using curly
brackets and which have turned out to be wrong is rather large—large enough
to lead me to conjecture that in fact all formulations involving curly brackets
are wrong. Three examples that a defender of curly brackets might have cited
in their defense have just bitten the dust.

I can give two additional pieces of evidence for underlying predicate-first order.
First, when items such as *only* and *even* apply semantically to an entire clause,
as in

(13)   The judge only sent you to prison; your wife didn't leave you too

they precede the verb. If the underlying order is predicate-first, then no extra
rule is needed to put these *only*'s and *even*'s in the right place: they would originate directly before the clause containing the verb in question, and *V-NP* inversion would move the *NP* not only across the verb but also across the *only* or *even*.[h]
Second, having underlying predicate-first order in English provides a partial
explanation of why English conjunctions precede the conjuncts that they go
with, while in verb-final languages such as Japanese, conjunctions follow the
conjuncts that they go with. Here I accept Ross's conclusion that the surface
structure of an English expression such as *John and Harry and Bill* has an im-
mediate-constituent structure with pre-posed conjunctions and its Japanese
counterpart *Taroo to Ziroo to Saburoo to* post-posed conjunctions, and that these
structures arise from an underlying structure containing a sinle conjunction
through a rule of Conjunction distribution (Fig. 9). Ross conjectures that
there is a universal relation between verb position and conjunction position in
languages with fixed word order: that languages with verb first or verb second
have preposed conjunctions, but languages with verb last have post-posed conjunctions.[8,i] The assumption that all verb-second languages are underlying verb-
first languages would explain the portion of this conjecture which relates to conjoined structures that are derived by conjunction reduction from conjoined sen-

[8] Most modern Indic and Iranian languages have all the typological characteristics of
verb-first and verb-second languages except for the characteristic of having the verb first
or second: they normally have the verb at the end of the clause. Like English, they have
pre-posed conjunctions and transformations that move material to the end of the clause,
and allow ' gapping to the right ', i.e. deletion of later copies of a repeated verb, as in *John
ordered spinach, Harry potatoes, and Sam turnips*. A true verb-final language such as
Japanese has only post-posed conjunctions, does not have Extraposition, and allows only
gapping to the left, i.e. deletions giving surface structures of the form *John spinach, Harry
potatoes, and Sam turnips ordered*. These facts lead Ross (1970b) to conclude that Hindi
is an underlying verb-second language whose surface verb-final order arises by a transformation.

Some cases which do not fit neatly into this typology have been called to my attention by
Charles A. Ferguson and Robert Underhill. Bengali has developed some post-posed
conjunctions alongside of the original pre-posed conjunctions, and Turkish has both post-
posed (native) and pre-posed (Arabic loan) conjunctions.

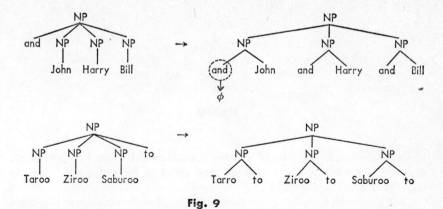

Fig. 9

tences. My analyses so far have implicitly rejected the traditional distinction between 'predicate' and 'logical operator': I have written such 'logical operators' as negation and quantifiers as if they were simply predicates predicated of sentences. A natural extension of this policy (which is defended in McCawley, 1970c, in press *a*) would be to treat sentential conjunctions such as *and* and *or* as predicates that are predicated of sets of sentences.[9] But under that analysis, in a language with predicate-first order, *and* and *or* would precede the descriptions of the sets of sentences of which they are predicated.

One aspect of the analysis being presented which the reader will have undoubtedly noticed is the absence of any constituents labeled *VP*. The absence of such a label is, of course, implicit in the proposal of predicate-first word order: if the subject of a verb originates between that verb and its object, there could hardly be an underlying constituent consisting of verb and object. The absence of the label *VP*, I maintain, is no great loss. The few existing arguments that purport to provide evidence for a syntactic category of *VP* in English actually only provide evidence that surface structure has a constituent consisting of the verb and its objects but not the subject. Lakoff and Ross have observed that this constituent structure arises automatically, given the transformations referred to above; they have argued that the supposed *VP*'s are merely remnants of embedded sentences, and that what little evidence can be found bearing on their category membership indicates that they retain the label *S* rather than requiring a new label *VP*.[j] For example, 'VP-deletion' gives evidence for a surface constituent consisting of a verb and its objects, since the deleted matter in

(14) Zorn's lemma implies the axiom of choice, and the hypo-turtle axiom does too.

is clearly *imply the axiom of choice*. However, *imply the axiom of choice* will be a

---

[9] Indeed, I maintain that *and* and *or* are really positional variants of quantifiers. The difference between *and* and *all* is simply whether the set of sentences to which it applies is defined by enumeration or by a definite description.

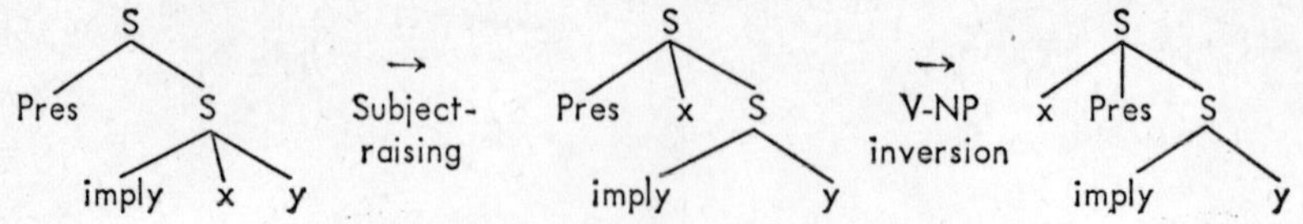

Fig. 10

surface constituent regardless of whether there is an underlying *VP* constituent, provided one assumes the transformations given so far and treats tenses as underlying predicates (Fig. 10).

I will close with a remark on typology. The familiar classification of languages with fixed word order into *VSO* languages, *SVO* languages, etc. has the defect of ignoring what happens when a clause contains more than a verb, its subject, and one object. For example, one can easily imagine several radically different word-order types which would all give subject-verb-object word order when only those three constituents were present: one language might have the verb second in all clauses, another might have the verb next-to-last in all clauses, and a third might require that the verb always be followed by the same number of constituents that it is preceded by. It is of importance to ask whether all these different kinds of *SVO* language actually exist. As far as I know, they do not: the ' *SVO* languages ' that I have heard of all have the verb second, regardless of how many constituents the clause contains. I conjecture that the absence of other types can be explained as follows: there are basically only two word-order types, verb-initial and verb-final; other surface word-order types arise from one or the other of these through transformations; however, different transformations are possible in verb-initial languages than in verb-final languages. Ross (1970b) has observed that underlying verb-final languages do not have transformations which would cause anything to follow the verb. If Ross is correct in his conjecture that no transformation may change verb-final order[10], then there would be no possibility of an underlying verb-final language having an obligatory *NP-V* inversion which would turn it into a verb-penultimate language; however, there is nothing to prevent a verb-initial language from having a *V-NP* inversion that turns it into a surface verb-second language.[k]

---

[10] The one possible counterexample to this claim that I know of is the variety of Japanese-influenced Hawaiian English treated in Susumu Nagara's dissertation (Univ. of Wisconsin, 1969). This dialect has verbs second in the clause but otherwise agrees with Japanese in word order. It may well turn out that it must be analyzed as having underlying SOV order which is converted by a transformation into SVO.

[a] Depending on whether it applies to an input with verb-first or verb-second order, it is respectively the subject or the VP that strictly speaking is MOVED into the main clause. However, in either case, both end up as constituents of the main clause: in the case of verb-second order, the 'tree-pruning principles' of Ross (1969a) eliminate both the lower S node and the NP node which had dominated it, leaving *Arthur* as the derived subject of the main clause, and in the case of verb-first order, the raising of the subject is what creates the ' VP ' to begin with, since under the verb-first proposal there is no node label ' VP ' and the constituents which had been labeled ' VP ' in earlier work are embedded sentences which have lost their subjects.

[b] The conception of ' cycle ' presented here should not be confused with that which figures in recent work by Chomsky, Emonds, Bresnan, and others, in which there are no postcyclic transformations but certain transformations of the cycle are marked as being ' last-cyclic ', that is, only applying to non-subordinate clauses.   Care should be taken to avoid confusing ' last-cyclic ' with ' postcyclic '.   An instance where ' post-cyclic ' has evidently been used with the meaning of ' last-cyclic ' is the argument at the beginning of appendix II of Bresnan (1971), which appears to contain a prima facie contradiction but becomes consistent if Bresnan is taken to mean ' last-cyclic ' where she says ' post-cyclic '.

[c] As best as I can determine, the ten rules that I had in mind when I wrote this are: quantifier lowering, conjunction reduction, the rule that yields clauses with *respectively*, *too-either* suppletion, tough-movement (as in *John is tough to deal with*), quantifier separation (as in *The men all left*), Equi-NP-deletion, reflexivization, conjunct movement, and psych-movement (as in the stative sense of *John annoys me*).   I have no idea why I included psych-movement in this list, since the position of the verb does seem to make a difference in its formulation: as in the case of passive, two NP's must be moved if it applies to structures with verb second, but only one if it applies to structures with verb first.   I no longer believe in the conjunct movement transformation (Lakoff and Peters 1969), according to which *Tom is similar to Dick* arose from an underlying structure with a conjoined subject (as in *Tom and Dick are similar*) by one of the conjuncts being moved to the end.   Conjunction reduction and the rule that forms *respectively* constructions are undoubtedly the same rule.   Jackendoff (1972: 370) observes that Dative-movement must be in the cycle, regardless of underlying word order, due to the possibility of *A book seems to have been given to John.*

[d] See now R. Lakoff (1971b).

[e] See now Kuno (1971) for a critique of this analysis of existential clauses.   Under the analysis proposed by Kuno, in which *there* arises through the copying of a locative expression plus concommitant pronominalization of the original (in accordance with proposal of Chapin 1970 that copying of a NP is always accompanied by pronominalization of the original), the rule determining the occurrence of *there* no longer gives any evidence for underlying word order.

[f] Emonds (unpublished work) argues that since

    (i)   *That Nixon will invade Botswana until 1972 isn't likely.

is ungrammatical, negative transportation has to apply later than extraposition and only moves the negative to the left, and is hence irrelevant to my claim.   Since the ordering which Emonds proposes is not consistent with both extraposition being postcyclic (as argued above) and negative transportation being in the cycle (as argued in R. Lakoff 1969), to accept it one must be prepared to refute one of the latter two arguments.   The only way I can see of retaining the conclusions that extraposition and negative-transportation are respectively postcyclic and cyclic is to attribute the ungrammaticality of (i) to an output constraint requiring the negative *until* to be not merely commanded by its ' trigger ' (as all ' negative polarity items' must be) but also preceded by it.   While such a proposal may seem terribly ad hoc, it is supported by some differences between negative *until* and other negative polarity items:

    (ii)   That Bill would give you a red cent isn't likely.
   (iii)   That Bill would give you a red cent is hard to believe.
   (iv)   *That Nixon would invade Botswana until 1972 is hard to believe.
    (v)   It's hard to believe that Nixon would invade Botswana until 1972.

ᵍ See McCawley (in press *b*) for discussion of some major inadequacies in this representation. I argue there for a semantic structure which matches the informal paraphrase of '*x* killed *y*' as '*x* did something which caused it to come about that *y* is not alive', i.e. the notion of ' causation ' involved is not a relation between a person and an event (as in Fig. 8) but between two events (or between an action and an event; I regard actions as a special class of events), and the subject of *kill* is not the underlying subject of ' cause ' but of ' do ', which expresses a relation between a person and an action.

ʰ Baker (1971: 174) argues that regardless of whether the basic word order in English is verb-first or verb-second, a NP-V inversion rule is needed (over and above any V-NP inversion rule), since as my proposals stand they would leave *only* in initial position in a question corresponding to my (13), and thus a rule moving the auxiliary to the beginning would be needed so that (i) and not (ii) or (iii) would arise:

    (i)   Did the judge only sentence you to prison (or did your wife leave you too)?
   (ii)   *Only did the judge sentence you to prison?
   (iii)   *Only the judge sentenced you to prison?

To see whether such a rule is really necessary, let us first take up the other respect in which (ii)-(iii) differ from (i), namely that *only* is at the beginning and not before the verb *sentence*. Note that if there is an auxiliary verb other than just the tense, an *only* which has the whole sentence for its scope comes after the first auxiliary verb:

   (iv)   The judge will only sentence you to prison; your wife won't leave you too.
    (v)   Your son is only smoking pot; your daughter isn't engaging in prostitution too.
   (vi)   Your daughter has only gotten pregnant; your son hasn't become a linguist too.
   (vii)   Your son has only been smoking pot; your daughter hasn't been engaging in prostitution too.
   (viii)   *Your son has been only smoking pot; your daughter hasn't been engaging in prostitution too.

There must thus be some rule which, if an auxiliary verb is the next verb down from *only*, puts the *only* immediately before the complement of that verb (and of course even if one subscribes to the *Syntactic Structures* analysis of auxiliary verbs he must have a movement rule involving *only* and auxiliary verbs, since *only* follows *be* in (v) but precedes it in (vii)). Since the following is ungrammatical:

   (ix)   *The judge did only sentence you to prison; your wife didn't leave you too.,

either the *only*-movement rule is inapplicable when there is a tense without a following auxiliary, or it is applicable even in that case and the affix attachment rule ignores the intervening *only* in converting the intermediate stage [. . . *Past only sentence* . . .] into [. . . *only sentence Past* . . .]. In the latter case, the rule would move *only* over the familiar Tense+{*have, be,* Modal} combination and would thus follow the rule (Hofmann 1966, restated in McCawley 1971a: fn. 1) that combines a tense with an immediately lower auxiliary verb. If the *only*-movement rule applies before V-NP inversion, then in (13) and (i) the input to V-NP inversion will have Past rather than *only* as its main verb, and inversion of *Past the judge* will occur if it does not have the interrogative performative for the next verb up (and is not in one of the other environments that inhibits V-NP inversion). Having the affix attachment rule ignore an intervening *only* is not a particularly attractive proposal, but evidently, regardless of whether there is underlying verb-first or verb-second order, one of the relevant rules (e.g. the NP-V inversion rule if the basic order is verb-second) will have to ignore an *only* that intervenes between the elements that the rule otherwise requires to be adjacent. While my proposal thus does not require a NP-V inversion rule, it should be clear that the possibility of sentence like (13) does not yield any argument for underlying verb-first order.

Newmeyer (1971) also contends that under the verb-first analysis a second inversion rule would be necessary. Specifically, he says that when my V-NP inversion rule applies, tenses would still have to be independent verbs (i.e. not yet adjoined to the next lower verb), but then in a declarative clause (thus, a clause in which V-NP is not inhibited), V-NP inversion would apply to both verbs:

```
        S                                       S
      /   \                                    /  \
     V     NP           →                     NP    VP
     |      |                                  |    / \
   Pres     S                                  S  Pres
          / | \                              / | \
         V  NP NP                           NP V  NP
         |   |   |                          |  |   |
        see John Bill                      John see Bill
```

and the non-sentence

    *John see Bills.

would result. However, that conclusion does not follow: there must in any case be a rule which adjoins tenses to the appropriate verbs, and that rule could just as well be formulated as applying to a tree in which the tense follows the clause as to one in which it precedes it, as in the second of the above trees. Whether such a structure occurs in the derivation of *John sees Bill* will depend on whether tenses trigger Subject-raising, as I assumed (albeit without real justification) in my discussion of (14). In that case, the result of applying V-NP inversion to the upper S would give an intermediate stage in which the tense precedes the verb to which it is to be attached.

ⁱ See Ferguson (1971) for reasons why what I said in the first sentence of footnote 8 is a gross exageration.
ʲ One obvious question to ask at this point is why these constituents, if still labeled S (as in Fig. 10), do not undergo V-NP inversion, thus yielding

    (i)   *Arthur seemed to Spiro admire.
    (ii)   *The robber forced Schwartz to him give his money.

or perhaps

    (iii)   *Arthur seems Spiro to admire.
    (iv)   *The robber forced Schwartz him to give his money.

It is possible to formulate V-NP inversion so as to avoid such sentences by making it a global rule in the sense of G. Lakoff (1970b), i.e. a rule which refers to non-consecutive stages of a derivation. Specifically, it could be formulated as applying only if the NP is the ' cyclic subject ' of the V, i.e. was the first NP in the clause headed by that V when the cycle finished applying to that clause. There are two aspects of this formulation about which I have worries that I am at present unable to resolve. (a) According to what I said in footnote *h*, some of the verbs to which V-NP inversion applies will be composite verbs derived by a postcyclic rule. Can one justify treating the derived verb as having the cyclic subject of one of its components as ' its cyclic subject '? This problem would not arise if, as George Lakoff conjectures (personal communication), the rule combining tenses with auxiliary verbs is in fact predicate raising (and thus in the cycle) and its obligatory non-application in sentences like *Did he leave?* must be incorporated into the grammar in the form of a global or even transderivational condition. However, it has not yet been shown that that approach is feasible. (b) If, as I conjecture, no language has a non-global postcyclic V-NP inversion rule (i.e. there is no language in which word-order works exactly like English except that sentences like (iii-iv) are good and sentences like *Arthur seems to admire Spiro* are bad), is there any way to constrain the class of grammars defined by a theory of global rules so as to allow a grammar of English but disallow grammars of the imaginary languages just sketched?

The following seems at first glance to be an alternative approach to V-NP inversion which does without global rules; however, on closer examination it turns out to incorporate global rules plus a putative language universal.   Suppose that, in view of what I said about the VP's of earlier grammatical descriptions being S's that have lost their subjects, one supplements a theory of grammar by the principle that when a S loses its subject its node label is automatically changed from S to VP (thus, VP would not exist in semantic representation but would arise in the course of a derivation).   Then V-NP inversion could be formulated as applying to the first V of an S (NB: not of a VP).   This apparently non-global rule would in fact be a notational variant of a global rule, since the only way for a VP to arise would be for the cyclic subject of the V in question to be deleted or raised when the cycle applied to a higher clause; the proposed relabeling would amount to a constraint on grammars that all rules referring to a S must exempt S's that have lost their cyclic subjects.

ᵏ Since preparing this annotated edition of ' English as a *VSO* language ', I have received a copy of a valuable critique by Arlene Berman (1974) of the original paper.   Berman's discussion brings out an important inconsistency in my position.   While I took it as an advantage of the VSO proposal that it allows Subject-raising, Negative-raising and Predicate-raising to be given a formulation in which it is immaterial whether the embedded clause is in subject or object position, I ignored the fact that there are other rules of the cycle (notably, *Tough*-movement) for which it matters whether a particular NP is subject or not and which, under the VSO hypothesis, must be stated as global rules in order to insure that the correct NP is moved, e.g. to distinguish *Max is impossible for Bill to describe* from **Max is impossible to sleep*, both of which would be of the form [impossible X [V Max Y]ₛ]ₛ when *Tough*-movement applies, under the VSO hypothesis.

I am by now reasonably convinced that neither global rules nor SVO order is an appropriate means of distinguishing subject from non-subjects and lean towards the position taken in unpublished work by Postal and Perlmutter, according to which the rules of the cycle operate in terms of ' grammatical relations ' rather than constituent order.   Berman observes that an important factual area missing from both her treatment and mine is the details of analogues in surface VSO languages to the English rules that she and I discuss. If English is a deep SVO language but Breton, Masai, and Yucatec Mayan are deep VSO languages, then very different transformational SD's ought to be possible in the two kinds of languages.   An adherent of deep SVO order for English could make a good case for his position by showing that English and Masai have significantly different SD's for their cyclic transformations.

I remain convinced that ' standard ' formulations of passive and *There*-insertion conflate two processes, one of which is a general rule imposing SVO order on English clauses. However, I strongly suspect that the latter rule should be stated as imposing order on an unordered structure containing specifications of grammatical relations rather than as an order change on VSO structures.

12.   Review of Otto Jespersen, Analytic Syntax[*]

When I first read Jespersen's *Analytic syntax*, it immediately assumed first place on my list of out-of-print books that I wished someone would reprint. Holt and Samuel Levin deserve the thanks of the linguistic profession for making this fascinating masterpiece again generally available.

Analytic syntax (henceforth, *AS*) is a relatively late work of Jespersen's. He was 77 when it was first published, 13 years after the appearance of *The philosophy of grammar* and 6 years before his death; the principal works following it are the fifth, sixth, and unfinished seventh volumes of the *Modern English grammar on historical principles*. *AS* consists of two parts of roughly equal length, the first a collection of well over 1000 analyzed examples (mainly from English, but with occasional examples from most of the other languages of Europe), the second part a commentary on the system of analysis used in the first part and a comparison of it with systems of analysis proposed by Brøndal, Hammerich, and others. The examples are grouped according to syntactic

* (Transatlantic series in linguistics, ed. by Samuel R. Levin.) New York: Holt, Rinehart and Winston, 1969. Pp. xv, 160. (Photographic reproduction of 1937 edition, originally published by Allen and Unwin, London). $2.95.

This review first appeared in *Language* 46. 442–9 (1970).

phenomena which they illustrate, and many near-minimal pairs for crucial contrasts are cited: *the advance of science*, in which *science* is subject, and *the advancement of science*, in which it is object (58); *He promised her to go*, in which the 'latent' subject of *go* is coreferential with *he*, and *He allowed her to go*, in which it is coreferential with *her* (49).

The analyses are best described as annotated surface structures. An analysis takes the form of a string of symbols and brackets which indicate (subject to some qualifications) surface immediate constituent structure, both superficial and underlying grammatical relations, 'latent' (='understood') elements, and coreferentiality relations. For example, Jespersen analyzes *John is easy to deceive* (p. 52) as S(O*) V P(2 pI*), which can be interpreted as follows: *John* is the subject of the main clause and consists of an object which (as indicated by the asterisks) is the object of the infinitive; then comes the verb of the main clause, *is;* then the 'predicative' of the main clause, *easy to deceive*, which consists of a 'secondary' (which for the moment can be taken to mean 'adjective') *easy* followed by a constituent (note the significant use of spaces) consisting of the preposition *to* and the infinitve *deceive*, which the asterisks connect to its object, *John*. As an example of coreferentiality and 'latency', consider *He is dressing*, which Jespersen analyses (153) as S V O°(S). The degree sign indicates latency; the S in parentheses after the O indicates that the (understood) object consists of something coreferential with the subject. Repeated relation letters such as S and O are used to indicate coreferentiality; if two clauses have non-coreferential subjects, objects, or the like, subscripts are used to indicate non-coreferentiality, as in *We heard him shout* (43), which is S V O(S$_2$I). Coreferentiality can also be indicated by Jespersen's ubiquitous paired asterisks, as in *Zionism—what is that to me?* (35), which is [1*] P? V S* p1. An especially interesting example of core-ferentiality is *Come here at once, Mary!*, which is analysed as {S*V} 3 3 [1*]!. Braces indicate multiple functions incorporated into the same word; Jespersen is thus analyzing an imperative verb as incorporating the functions of both sub-ject and verb. The asterisks indicate coreferentiality between the incorporated subject and the vocative. Jespersen always uses asterisks to indicate coreferen-tiality involving the symbol 1 'primary', which is never subscripted; in other cases he vacillates between asterisks and repeated symbols. On p. 26 he gives formulas for six readings of *John told Robert's son that he must help him*, making considerable use of both devices in representing the various coreferentiality relations.

Discontinuous constituents are also indicated by a variety of notations. Sometimes paired asterisks are used, as in *What are you talking of?* 1?* v S V p* (p. 33) and *He gave the boys a shilling each* S V O* O [1*] (37). In other cases he does not treat one of the parts of a discontinuous constituent as S, O etc. (as he does in the last example, where he treats *boys* as the indirect object), but writes $\frac{1}{2}$S, etc. before the two parts, as in *She seems to notice it* $\frac{1}{2}$S V $\frac{1}{2}$S(IO) (p. 47); Jespersen thus treats *seem* (also *fail, happen, be sure*) as an intransitive verb with a discontinuous sentential subject. This device also appears in such examples as *She was made to cry* $\frac{1}{2}$S^r V^b $\frac{1}{2}$S^r(I) (p. 46) and *The door was* *painted red* $\frac{1}{2}$S^r V^b $\frac{1}{2}$S^r(P).[1]

The analyses generally show wonderful insights into subtle distinctions which are obscured in surface structure. For example, Jespersen analyzes *Too many cooks spoil the broth* (p. 42) as S(3PS$_2$) V O, thus treating the sentence as having a sentential subject and paraphrasable with a semi-sentence such as **Cooks being too many spoils the broth;*[2] he contrasts this with *Too many cooks are dirty*, which for him is a simple sentence, analysed as S(32^{q}1) V P. Another example analyzed like *Too many cooks spoil the broth* is *No news is good news* S(PS$_2$) V P(21), in which *no* is treated as a predicate; similarly with *You must put up with no hot dinner.* He analyzes the surface adjectives in *an utter fool, a perfect stranger, an awful smell,* and *a comparative rarity* as consisting of a tertiary (=adverb) which modifies ' some adjectival or verbal idea contained in the primary' (11), and remarks further that ' *We were great friends; F. Nous étions de grands amis* may be symbolized in the same way, though there is no corresponding adverb '. And if I am interpreting his sometimes inconsistent symbolism correctly,[3] he analyzes *He helped her to cook the food* (53) as involving an understood conjoined subject of the infinitive, referring jointly to the subject and object of the main clause.

In the quotations given above, Jespersen has used the terms ' notional subject ' etc. to refer to what I have called ' underlying grammatical relations.'[4] Jespersen

---

[1] Raised *b* means ' passive ', raised *r* ' result '. O^r is thus ' object of result ', as in *He made her cry* S V O^r(S$_2$I), which appears earlier on the same page. Jespersen's comments on these examples are worth quoting: ' It is easy enough, of course, to transcribe *She was seen to run (heard to cry)* S V^b I, but this simple formulation does not cut deep enough, as it says nothing of the role of the infinitive and thus does not really cover the grammatical facts. Note that in the active the object is not simply *her* but *her run, her cry* O(S$_2$I). The correct notional subject of the passive is therefore *she (to) run, she (to) cry,* though these words are not pronounced in immediate sequence. This analysis is even more patent when we have in the active an O^r, as in *He made her cry* S V O^r(S$_2$ I)— passive *She was made to cry* S V^b I. What is made is not *she* but *she . . . to cry.* In other words, *she* is not the complete notional subject, though it is the " grammatical subject " that determines the form of the verb (*I am made to cry, they are made to cry,* etc.) The infinitive, too, forms part of the subject, and this has to be symbolized.'

[2] In my dialect, the facts of number agreement provide additional support for such an analysis: for me the sentence would have to be *Too many cooks spoils the broth,* with a singular verb. See Ross (1969d: 256) for another case where a plural noun phrase which is the remnant of an entire clause takes singular number agreement.

[3] His formula S V O pl(S$^0_{1\&2}$ I O$_2$) is the only instance in the book where a subscript consists of more than a single symbol; & is used elsewhere to symbolize a conjunction. My suggested interpretation of the term in question could have been symbolized in his system as S$^0_2$ (S & O).

[4] I do not mean to imply by my choice of words that I regard the notion ' grammatical relation ' as coherent, viable, or even useful. I am amazed at the extent to which the amount of space devoted by some transformational grammarians to defining that notion exceeds the amount of space that they devote to using it, the difference often being by a factor of infinity. See Fillmore (1968) for arguments that ' deep subject ', ' deep object' etc. cover a wide variety of totally unrelated things, and McCawley (1968e: 558) for some remarks suggesting that the supposed ' intuitions about grammatical relations ' that Chomsky often refers to are really intuitions about meaning.

states his policy especially clearly on p. 141: '... it is one of the most important principles of our symbolization to take into consideration solely notional relations without regard to the actual forms in which these happen to be clothed in each language'; he says this in justification for his use of O for items which appear in cases other than the accusative, e.g. the genitive object of German *Ich erinnere mich des Tages* 'I remember the day'. Jespersen is exaggerating when he says that he takes into account solely notional relations, since his formulas assign roles to all surface constituents, regardless of whether they contribute anything semantically to the sentence (e.g., he represents *Ich erinnere mich des Tages* as having two objects, but *I remember the day* as having only one), and since his use of relation symbols is restricted by the lexicon of the language: '... the symbols O and *O* are used ... for what is governed by a preposition (thus pO and p*O*), if the notional relation is the same that would (with other verbs) be expressed by a simple O or *O*' (143). However, he pushes his system of analysis remarkably far within (and occasionally beyond) these self-imposed restrictions. Note in particular the occasional instances where Jespersen analyzes a word in terms of a structure such as would correspond to a phrasal expression of the same idea: he calls the *pre* of *pre-war* a preposition (10); he sets up a deleted preposition before the first *house* of *house-to-house calls* (18), and a deleted conjunction between *Franco* and *Prussian* in *Franco-Prussian war* (17). Occasionally he analyzes a word as a derived form, even when the supposed source for it does not exist in the language: note his use (61) of the symbols Y (participle) and O in his formula for *un homme avide de sang* 12(YpO), and the remark quoted above in which he sets up an adverbial source for the *great* of *We were great friends*.

One thing of which readers of *AS* should be forewarned is that Jespersen's formulas are often abbreviated versions of more detailed formulas which he writes only when he particularly wants to emphasize some structural characteristic that he usually takes for granted. Consider, for example, his treatment of auxiliary verbs. In most of his formulas, Jespersen ignores an auxiliary verb whenever it is adjacent to the verb with which it is connected, and otherwise represents it with a *v*. However, on occasion he represents auxiliaries as 'main verbs' (i.e. writes V instead of *v*), e.g. S V O°(I) for (*Can he sing? Yes,*) *he can* (55). Jespersen makes clear (92) that in general he regards auxiliary verbs as true verbs (which, among other things, have their own subjects and objects), but he generally omits their true relationships from his formulas for reasons of convenience:

It is best, for the sake of convenience, to take forms like *will drink, would drink*, ... as wholes to be symbolized V. A more explicit but inconvenient way of symbolizing is the following:
    He will drink whisky; he should drink whisky; he can drink whisky S V O (IO₂)—
      with the infinitive as (part of) the object ...
    He has been drinking whisky S V O(YP(Y₂O₂)).
So, instead, we write simply S V O for all of these.[5]

[5] Y is defined as 'Agent-substantive or participle, e.g. *admirer, admiring, admired*'; P means 'predicative'.

Compare also Jespersen's statement (144) that writing S V^b rather than S V P(Y^b) for *He was loved* is ' a practical but harmless simplification, similar in character to that which makes us write *has killed, will kill*, etc. simply as V '.   His analysis of auxiliary verbs is thus very close to that of Ross (1969b), despite the fact that the abbreviated notations cause many of his formulas to give the appearance of involving an analysis like that of Chomsky (1957), in which ' auxiliary' is a separate category from verb.

There are a number of other places in *AS* where Jespersen indicates that certain details of structure are to be understood even though not directly represented in the formulas: ' The regimen[6] of a preposition is everywhere supposed to be a primary except where special relations are to be taken into account; but 1 need not be specially written when the regimen is a simple S, O, *O*, I, G, X, or Y without any additions ' (117).   ' It is not, however, necessary to indicate expressly that [the combination of preposition and regimen] is a tertiary ' (32). An especially interesting example of understood details is the following (123–4):

An infinitive always denotes a nexus between a subject and the verbal idea, though the subject need not be expressly stated . . . Therefore, when we say that an infinitive is a primary (subject, or object), what we really mean is that the infinitival nexus, not the infinitive as such, is subject or object.   Now we understand why it is possible to have a tertiary in *to sing merrily is a pleasure* and *I want to sing merrily*, for those sentences, if fully symbolized, are S(S° I 3) V P and S V O(S° I 3): within each of the parentheses we have the three ranks 123, and the verbal element here as in *I sing merrily* is secondary.

Thus, if the details were filled in in Jespersen's formulas, there would be a much greater number of ' understood subjects ' than he actually writes.

A great many details of constituent structure appear to have been left out of the formulas, although most of the evidence for this assertion must come from a comparison with other works from Jespersen's later years.   For example, Jespersen writes S$_1$ & S$_2$ V for *John and Mary came* (112), which contains no indication that *John and Mary* is even a constituent, let alone the subject of *come;* but in 1933: 97 he states that ' In *The cat and the dog do not agree very well*, there are not two grammatical subjects, but *the cat and the dog* together is the subject of the sentence, as will be seen from a comparison with the synonymous expression *They do not agree very well.*'   Since Jespersen states emphatically in his 1933 work that a verb has only one subject, and since *AS* is full of comments about points on which he has changed his mind, it is safe to assume that he has not changed his mind here, and that he considers *John and Mary* not only a constituent but indeed the subject of *come*, though he does not represent that directly in his formula.   It should be noted that Jespersen gave surface constituent structure less than its rightful due.   For example, the formula cited above for *We heard him shout* represents *him shout* as a (deep and surface?) constituent, even though *him* can be shown to be a constituent of the main clause in surface structure, since it reflexivizes under identity with the subject of that

---

[6] Jesepersen does not use the term ' object of a preposition ', substituting instead ' regimen '.   Where he uses an O or *O* after a preposition, it indicates a relationship to the verb, not to the preposition.

clause: *He heard himself shout.*[7]   Likewise, his formula for *She seems to notice it* does not indicate the status of *seems to notice it* as a surface constituent and *she* as surface subject.   In both 1933: 107–8 and *AS* 47, Jespersen speaks, e.g., of the *he* of *He is believed to be rich* as the 'grammatical subject', but as only part of the 'notional subject' *he-to-be-rich;* however, only the latter of these two statements is represented in the formulas of *AS*.   I have no doubt that one of the principal causes of Jespersen's relative neglect of surface constituent structure is his relative neglect of an important matter that would have forced a serious consideration of surface structure on him, namely the formulation of precise and general rules for relating meaning to superficial form.   Note the skimpiness and gross inadequacy of the statements in Jespersen (1933) of the conditions under which reflexives occur: 'When the subject and object are identical, we use for the latter a so-called reflexive pronoun ... The reflexive pronouns are also used after prepositions ... But if the preposition has a purely local meaning, the simple forms without *self* are used' (1933: 111–2).   This suggests that he never tried seriously to formulate a necessary and sufficient condition for the use of reflexives, and thus never realized that the antecedent of a reflexive need not be the subject of the clause (*I talked to Schwartz about himself*), and normally must be in the same clause as the reflexive.[8]   To formulate an adequate rule of reflexivization and make it consistent with Jespersen's observations about grammatical relations, it would be necessary to assign a sentence multiple syntactic representations in which the relations of constituency, subjecthood etc. can differ; i.e., Jespersen's system of representing sentences in terms of surface structures containing annotations of underlying syntactic and semantic relationships is in principle incapable of providing an adequate basis for the formulation of the rules needed to account for sentences whose immediate constituent structure and grammatical relations change in the course of a derivation.

I should say a word about some peculiarly Jespersenian concepts which appear throughout the book and which have occurred a number of times in the above discussion: nexus, junction, and rank.   Nexus and junction are two ways in which elements of a sentence can be related to each other; they appear to differ principally in that the elements of a nexus have grammatical relations such as 'subject' to one another, whereas the elements of a junction have only 'dependency' relations to one another.   In a passage quoted above, Jespersen states that every verb, infinitive, gerund, participle, or 'nexus-substantive' (=nominalization) implies a nexus, i.e. involves an explicit or implicit subject and possibly

[7] It is interesting to note that Whitney (1888: 179) described certain elements as being logically constituents of an embedded clause but grammatically constituents of the main clause, which he says 'is shown by the circumstance that that object, when designating the same person or thing with the subject of the verb, is expressed by the reflexive instead of the personal pronoun: thus, *er wollte SICH nicht halten lassen*'.   Whitney thus based his judgment of constituent structure on something quite similar to the statement of the conditions for reflexivization given in Lees & Klima (1963).
[8] Jackendoff (1968) has discovered cases of optional reflexivization into subordinate clauses, e.g. *The fact that there is a picture of him/himself hanging in the post office bothers Harry.*

also object, etc. 'Junctions' appear to be those combinations not involving any such nexus-forming element, except as some kind of subordinate element. Jespersen's 'ranks' (symbolized by 1, 2, 3, 4, . . . in the formulas, but in many cases not represented directly) refer to depth in a hierarchy of subordination: a secondary 'specifies' a primary, a tertiary specifies a secondary, etc. Jespersen takes the unusual position that nouns and noun phrases in either a nexus or a junction are primaries, and that a verb 'specifies' its subject, object etc.; he is thus able to say (123) that the same (dependency) relations prevail in *the furiously barking dog* as in *The dog barked furiously;* 'Dog in both cases is the fixed, supreme point, to which the others are subordinated in a descending scale'. There is a hint on p. 135 that he takes grammatical concord as evidence that the determined element of the concord relationship specifies the determining element (which would fit this assignment of ranks well); but he never says so in as many words. It should be noted that 'secondary' is thus the only level in the rank hierarchy for which an element can simultaneously 'specify' more than one element of the next higher (=numerically lower) rank. The formulas do not indicate directly which element(s) are 'specified' by a given secondary, tertiary, etc., but it is generally the 'nearest' element of the next higher rank, except when paired asterisks indicate otherwise.

Jespersen's explanations of rank, nexus, and junction, which can be found in works of his dating at least as far back as 1913, are far from satisfactory. In *AS*, his characterizations of nexus and junction rest heavily on analogies which I find unenlightening (120–1):

The difference between junction and nexus can, perhaps, be appreciated by means of my old comparison: a junction is like a picture, a nexus like a drama. Junction is agglutination, nexus is fusion. A junction describes, a nexus puts something in action, sets something going. Junction is static, nexus dynamic. Or we may say that in a junction we add one dead piece to another, as bricks are placed on top of and by the side of one another to build a house. But in a nexus we get life and movement. With a junction we are in the realm of mechanics, while a nexus belongs to biology. Junction is dead, nexus living; something happens in a nexus.

One matter which I doubt can be given a consistent interpretation in terms of what Jespersen says about rank, nexus, and junctions is that of predicate adjectives. Jespersen states (135) that predicate nouns are primaries, and predicate adjectives secondaries; however, the former claim seems inconsistent with his characterization of primaries as 'what is talked about' (122), and the latter seems hard to reconcile with his treatment of the copula as a verb and thus a secondary. Indeed, the only way I can think of to reconcile the assignment of both copula and predicate adjective to the rank of secondary would be to adopt an analysis of a type which Jespersen explicitly rejects (132–5): Hammerich's proposal that the copula is an intransitive verb predicated of a sentence of the form NP+Adjective (e.g., the immediate constituents of *Das Pferd ist krank* would be *Das Pferd krank* and *ist*) or the closely related proposal of Ross (1969a).

In a couple of instances, I find Jespersen's analyses unintelligible or unmotivated.   For example, his formula for *This is a hard nut to crack* (52) is accurately described by that sentence itself: S V P(21) (O* pI*).   I would have taken the last term as a misprint for P(21(O* pI*)) were it not that it is directly followed by four more examples involving the same manner of combining the symbols. Jespersen's comment that ' In most of these (21) should perhaps stand after the starred form ' does not particularly help, since it would seem to imply that his examples *This is a hard nut to crack* and *He is an easy man to make fun of* had their elements related as in ' . . . to crack a hard nut ' and ' . . . to make fun of an easy man ', which is absurd.   I am also puzzled as to Jespersen's intentions where he uses braces to indicate multiple functions combined in one word. In many cases the word is a completely transparent combination of stem and affix, but the order of the elements within the braces is the opposite of the order of the corresponding parts of the word, as in Finnish *purteni* ' my boat ' $\{1^2 1\}$, Finnish *emme tuo* ' we do not bring ' $\{S\ v^n\}V$, and Portuguese *É triste combateres* ' It is a pity that you fight ' V P S($\{S_2 I\}$).   These examples suggest that the order of symbols corresponds to the word order which would be used if the content of the affix were expressed by an independent word.   However, since there are cases where Jespersen writes ' latent ' elements in positions other than those where the language would allow them to be realized, e.g. his analysis of *To see is to believe* as S(IS°∞) V P(IS°∞), with the latent indefinite subject after the infinitive, Jespersen's policy on the underlying order of elements can only be said to be unclear and his practice inconsistent.   I am also at a total loss to see why Jespersen did not extend his ' split subject ' analysis to sentences like *She seems angry*, which he asserts, without giving any reason, not to be parallel to *She seems to be angry* (47).

However, whatever faults *AS* may have, it is a sheer joy to read and an incomparable source of insight into the workings of the English language.   It is a work which every linguist should read with great care, and which it should be unthinkable to omit from the training of any linguistics student.

13. On the Applicability of Vice Versa*

In the simplest cases, *vice versa* stands for a clause obtained by interchanging two elements of another clause, as in *Max loves Susan and vice versa* (= . . . and *Susan loves Max*). The sentences given below are of relevance to the as yet unsolved problem of what elements of a clause may be interchanged in this construction. Certain morphological differences are ignored in deciding whether one clause counts as " obtained from the other by interchange ", e.g. the difference between *-er* and *-ist* in (1) and between *Engl(ish)* and *Anglo-* in (7), although not quite everything goes, e.g. *woman* and *gynec-* do not count as the same in (26). It appears to be bad to interchange something inside a definite description with something outside of it (10). This fact may be related to the impossibility of interchanging something in a nonrestrictive clause with something outside it ((12), cf. (11)).

The *'s and ?'s represent my own reactions to these sentences, assuming the interpretations given in parentheses. I have found great variation in the reactions of informants to these sentences. Sources are noted in square brackets after sentences which I did not concoct myself.

(1) Few philosophers take biology courses, and vice versa. (=and

* This note first appeared in *Linguistic Inquiry* 1. 278–80 (1970).

few biologists take philosophy courses).

(2) New Yorkers like Chicago, and vice versa. (=and Chicagoans like New York).

(3) Westerners are fascinated by the Orient, and vice versa. (=and Orientals are fascinated by the West).

(4) Glaswegians like Cambridge, and vice versa. (=and Cantabrigians like Glasgow).

(5) Murderers are likely to commit rape, and vice versa. (=and rapists are likely to commit murder).

(6) Virgins abhor prostitution, and vice versa. (=and prostitutes abhor virginity).

(7) Many Frenchmen are Anglophobes, and vice versa. (=and many Englishmen are Francophobes). [Susan Houston]

(8) Many Frenchmen have learned Italian, and vice versa. (=and many Italians have learned French). [George Lakoff]

(9) *Many Frenchmen have learned Sanskrit, and vice versa. (=and many Sanskrit speakers have learned French). [Harold Koch, reported by George Lakoff]

(10) *The Frenchman next door has learned Italian, and vice versa. (=and the Italian next door has learned French).

(11) Frenchmen who can speak Italian are common, and vice versa. (=and Italians who can speak French are common).

(12) *Frenchmen, who can speak Italian, are common, and vice versa. (=and Italians, who can speak French, are common).

(13) *Air Canada has flights to India, and vice versa. (=and Air India has flights to Canada).

(14) On most harpsichords the white keys are black, and vice versa. (=and the black keys are white).

(15) Many Baltimore fans live in Los Angeles, and vice versa. (=and many Los Angeles fans live in Baltimore).

(16) *Many Oriole fans live in Los Angeles, and vice versa. (=and many Dodger fans live in Baltimore).

(17) ?Many Catholics are anti-Semitic, and vice versa. (=and many Jews are anti-Catholic).

(18) In many languages, all nouns are deverbal, but in Gwamba-mamba it's vice versa. (=all verbs are denominal).

(19) ?My big brother is little, and vice versa. (=and my little brother is big).

(20) It's common for a person's big brother to be littler than him, and vice versa. (=and for his little brother to be bigger than him).

(21) ?Children who don't have fathers require fraternal love, and vice versa. (=and children who don't have brothers require paternal love).

(22) ?When my glass is empty, I fill it, and vice versa. (=and when my glass is full, I empty it). [François Truffaut]

(23) (?) When the door is open, I close it, and vice versa.   (=and when the door is closed, I open it).

(24) Bus-drivers rarely travel in airplanes, and vice versa. (=and airplane pilots rarely travel in buses).

(25) ?Bus-drivers rarely travel in submarines, and vice versa. (=and those who steer submarines [whatever they are called] rarely travel in buses). [Is (25) any better for a person whose vocabulary includes a word for someone who steers a submarine?]

(26) *Many women are gerontologists, and vice versa.   (=and many old people are gynecologists).

14. Semantic Representation^{*, 1}

This paper will deal with the representation of the meanings of both sentences and lexical items.   Actually, the question of how to represent the meanings of sentences and the question of how to represent the meanings of lexical items have closely related answers, since (as observed by Weinreich 1966: 446) elements of meaning combine in the same way within a single lexical item as they do in a sentence containing several lexical items, e.g. the meaning of the word *dentist*, roughly paraphraseable as ' physician who treats teeth ', not only involves the meanings of *treat* and of *teeth* but involves exactly the same semantic relation between them as in the paraphrase.   Weinreich concluded that semantic representations must be ' syntactic ' in form (by which he evidently meant that semantic representation must at least indicate the immediate constituent structure of the seman-

* This paper first appeared in Paul M. Garvin (editor), *Cognition: a multiple view* (New York: Spartan Books, 1970), pp. 227–47.
¹ I was originally asked to contribute to this symposium a paper on ' semantic features '. What I have to say about semantic representation will be relevant to the topic of ' semantic features ' only to the extent that virtually everything that I say can be used as the basis of an argument that meanings can not be represented adequately by a feature representation.   I will not give any such arguments here, since I have more important things to devote this space to and since I tire easily of flogging dead horses; anyone interested in such arguments can easily construct them out of what follows.

tic elements and show subordination and coordination between them) and that
the same 'syntax' governs the combinations of elements of meaning in individual lexical items as in entire sentences.

Examples showing that semantic representation must indicate the immediate
constituent structure of the elements involved in it (i.e. examples showing that
different meanings can consist of the same semantic elements combined in different ways) are easy to come by. For example, the two meanings of the ambiguous sentence

(1) John doesn't beat his wife because he loves her.

(*a:* the reason that John doesn't beat his wife is that he loves her; *b:* the reason
that John beats his wife is not that he loves her) differ as regards whether the
element of negation applies to the meaning of *John beats his wife* or to the meaning of *John beats his wife because he loves her.*

A second thing that semantic representations must include is some indication
of presupposed coreference.[2] For example, semantic representation must distinguish between three meanings of

(2) John told Harry that his wife was pretty.

(*a: his* refers to John; *b: his* refers to Harry; *c: his* refers to some third person).
Note that the device of repeating the antecedent that I have just used in explaining the three senses cannot in general be used to indicate coreference, since
the same expression may be used in referring to different things, as when one says

(3) John admires John.

in talking about two different people named John (see also Castañeda 1966).
Thus, the semantic representation of a sentence must involve 'referential indices'
for each of the things being talked about, and the referential index must be kept
distinct from the linguistic material used to describe that individual. Thus, the
semantic representation of (3) must involve two referential indices (say, x and y),
as opposed to the sentence

(4) John admires himself.

which will involve a single referential index (say, x) which appears twice. In (3),
'x admires y' is asserted of two individuals both described by the name *John:*

[2] It is necessary to distinguish between presupposition, assertion, and inference. The
coreferentiality of *I* and *my father's brother's only nephew* is a matter of inference rather
than of presupposition. *My father's brother's only nephew* has a denotation only when
used by a person whose father has a brother who has only one nephew (it thus differs in
meaning from *I*, whose applicability is independent of what relatives one has). In cases
where it has a denotation, one can conclude that that denotation is the same as the denotation of *I* only by applying rules of logical inference to the meaning of *father's brother's
only nephew* and to the presupposition that the speaker has a father who has a brother
who has only one nephew. Inferred coreferentiality is irrelevant to grammar, as is wit-
nessed by the fact that *My father's brother's only nephew* is treated as third person, not
first person, by rules of agreement and pronoun choice.

in (4), ' x admires x ' is asserted of a single individual who is described by the name *John*.

A more interesting example of the need for separating referential indices from the expressions used to describe the individuals that they are supposed to refer to is given by sentences such as

    (5)   Max denies that he kissed the girl who he kissed.

While (5) could be used to report a self-contradictory utterance by Max such as ' I didn't kiss the girl who I kissed ', one would be more likely to interpret *the girl that he kissed* not as part of Max's alleged statement but as the speaker's description of someone who figured in Max's statement.   These two interpretations of (5) both involve an expression such as ' x kissed y ' in the complement of *deny* but differ as regards whether the description of y as *the girl that x kissed* is or is not within the complement of *deny*, i.e. roughly[a]

    (6)   a. x deny (x kissed y; y: the girl who x kissed); x: Max.
             b. x deny (x kissed y); y: the girl who x kissed; x: Max.

Note also the distinction between a pronoun referring to an individual and a pronoun referring to that individual's name.   In Quine's example (1961: 139)

    (7)   Giorgione is so-called because of his size.,

the *so* of *so-called* refers not to the person Giorgione but to the name *Giorgione*. The fact that from (7) and the fact that *Giorgione* is another name for Barbarelli one cannot conclude

    (8)   Barbarelli is so-called because of his size.

does not indicate any failure of Leibniz's principle of the substitutability of identicals (restated by Quine as ' Given a true statement of identity, one of its two terms may be substituted for the other in any true statement and the result will be true ') but merely shows that that principle relates to semantic representations and not to the surface form of sentences. (7) is a statement not just about the person Giorgione but about both him and the name *Giorgione*.   The result of changing the description of the person referred to in (7) from *Giorgione* to *Barbarelli* in the semantic representation of (7) would not be (8) but rather

    (9)   Barbarelli is called Giorgione because of his size.

Thus, two different kinds of antecedent relation must be distinguished: that illustrated by (5), in which the antecedent of *he* is the referential index of *Max*, and that illustrated in (7), in which the antecedent of *so* is the name *Giorgione* and not the referential index which that name happens to be attached to.

Semantic representations will have to indicate not only presupposed coreference (which is indicated by multiple occurrences of the same index) but also presupposed set membership and set inclusion.   Note, for example, the difference in meaning between

(10) Max is more intelligent than móst Americans.
(11) Max is more intelligent than most Américans.

(' denotes primary stress). In (10), Max is presupposed to be an American; in (11), he is presupposed not to be an American. The same is true of the sentences

(12) CIA agents are more stupid than móst Americans.
(13) Smersh agents are more stupid than most Américans.

Semantic representations may contain not only the ' constant ' referential indices discussed so far,[b] but also ' variable ' indices, which range over the members of some set under discussion. For example, in the sentence

(14) Every person who works for the CIA hates himself.,

the semantic immediate constituents are not *every person who works for the CIA* and *hates himself* but rather *every*, *x works for the CIA*, and *x hates x*, i.e. the property *x hates x* is being ascribed to every individual *x* that meets the condition *x works for the CIA*. As evidence for this assertion, consider the example (Partee 1970: 153)

(15) Few rules are both explicit and easy to read.

As noted in Jespersen (1937: 52), the grammatical subject of

(16) John is easy to please.

is semantically the object of *please;* (16) may indeed be paraphrased as 'for one to please John is easy ', which is closer to the semantic structure of (16). Thus, in (15) the property which it is asserted that few rules have is the property ' *x* is explicit, and for one to read *x* is easy'. It is clear that the semantic representation of this property, when resolved into ultimate semantic units, will have a form involving several tokens of *x* and will not be of the form ' *x* is *p* ' (where *p* is an expression not containing *x*) which means that what *few* and *rules* are combined with semantically in (15) is not a ' predicate ' but something having the form of an entire sentence.

As an example both of the need for variables in semantic representation and of the need for semantic representations to show an immediate constituent structure of the elements involved in them, consider the sentence

(17) One of you is clearly lying.

(17) has two readings (*a:* it is clear that there is one of you who is lying; *b:* there is one of you such that it is clear that he is lying) which involve the propositional function *x is lying* combined in different ways with ' one ' and ' clear ':

(18) a. Clear (One$_x$ (*x* is lying; *x* among ' you ')).
      b. One$_x$ (Clear (*x* is lying); *x* among ' you ').

The meanings of sentences with more than one quantifier justify one important aspect of the representations (18), namely that there be an indication of which variables each quantifier ' binds '.   For example,

(19)   You can fool some of the people all of the time.

has two interpretations (*a:* there are some people who you can fool all the time; *b:* at any time there are some people that you can fool) which would have to be represented as something on the lines of

(20)   a. $Some_x$ (All_t (you can fool x at t; t a time); x a person).
      b. All_t ($Some_x$ (you can fool x at t; x a person); t a time).

If the quantifiers were associated with different variables than those indicated, the resulting meanings would not be expressible by (19); for example, if ' Some ' were associated with t and 'All' with x in (20a), the result would mean ' there are times at which you can fool all the people ', which is not a possible paraphrase of (19).[c]

It should be evident by now that I am proposing a system of semantic representation that is along the lines of the notational systems used in symbolic logic.   I would like at this point to catalog the most significant respects in which my proposals differ from the more usual variants of symbolic logic.

(i)   I regard immediate constituent structure rather than parentheses as basic. Thus I consider the representations that I have sketched above as being more correctly given graphic form as tree diagrams than as strings of symbols, e.g.

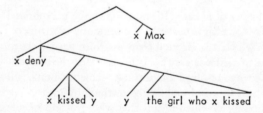

($\triangle$ indicates an omission of details of internal structure).

My principal reason for this policy is that semantic representations are to form the input to a system of transformations that relate meaning to superficial form, and to the extent that these transformations have been formulated and justified, they appear to be stateable only in terms of constituent structure and constituent type, rather than in terms of configurations of parentheses and terminal symbols.[3] If, in addition, it turns out to be necessary to operate in terms of semantic representations in which symbols have no left-to-right ordering, as may well be the

---

[3] Proposals for semantic representation require justification not only on purely semantic grounds but also with regard to their relationship to a total linguistic description.   An example will shortly be given in which one proposal for semantic representation is preferred over another because the former but not the latter gives rise to representations that fit otherwise valid generalizations regarding what may be the antecedent of a pronoun.

case, it would be impossible to use parentheses to represent such constituent structure differences as difference in the scope of quantifier or a negation.[d]

(ii) The repertoire of quantifiers will have to be much broader than that generally found in symbolic logic. For example, not only *all* and *some* but also *most*, *almost all*, *hardly any*, and *many* must be available.

(iii) *And* and exclusive and inclusive *or* ('exclusive *or*'='either but not both'=Latin *aut;* 'inclusive *or*'='either or both'=Latin *vel*) cannot be regarded as just binary operators but must be allowed to take an arbitrary number of operands.[e] The frequently encountered 'definition' of e.g.[4] $p \vee q \vee r$ as $(p \vee q) \vee r$, supposedly justified by the fact that $(p \vee q) \vee r$ is 'logically equivalent to' $p \vee (q \vee r)$, i.e. an expression built up with binary inclusive *or*'s has the same truth value regardless of how the operands are grouped together, is in fact not an admissible definition in a system of semantic representation, since the three formulas in question are semantically distinct, even if logically equivalent. Consider the following sentences, assuming *or* to be interpreted in the inclusive sense:

(21) Either John likes Sally, or John likes Margaret, or Arthur likes Margaret.

(22) Either John likes either Sally or Margaret, or Arthur likes Margaret.

(23) Either John likes Sally, or either John or Arthur likes Margaret.

Here at least visceral reaction dictates that (21) be represented in the form $p \vee q \vee r$, (22) in the form $(p \vee q) \vee r$ and (23) in the form $p \vee (q \vee r)$. In the case of *and*, this grouping may correspond to asserted similarities, as in Wundt's (1900: 310) example

(24) Alexander, Cäsar und Napoleon waren grosse Feldherren und ausgezeichnete Staatsmänner.

which Wundt points out 'can be decomposed logically into the six simple assertions "Alexander war Feldherr", "Alexander war Staatsmann", etc.; however, the real sense of [the example], which consists in these three men being both things, generals and statesmen together, is thereby lost' (my translation).[5] A case where more than visceral feeling demands that one distinguish between a multi-place operation and an iterated binary operation is exclusive *or*. While exclusive *or* has the property that $p \vee_e (q \vee_e r)$ is logically equivalent to $(p \vee_e q) \vee_e r$, the exclusive sense of English *or* does not correspond to $p \vee_e (q \vee_e r)$, since the latter is true when either one or three of p, q, r are true (and false when none or two of them are true), whereas an English sentence that involves the exclusive sense of *or*, e.g.

(25) Did Max study physics, biology, or music?

(‾‾‾ denotes falling intonation) presupposes that Max studied exactly one of

[4] In the ensuing formulas I will symbolize inclusive *or* by $\vee$, exclusive *or* by $\vee_e$, and logical *and* (which is to be distinguished from the 'and then' sense of *and*, as in *Susan got married and had a baby*) by $\wedge$.
[5] I am grateful to W. K. Percival for bringing this quotation to my attention.

physics, biology, and music, not that he studied one or three but not two of them. Iterated binary $\vee_e$ is true if an odd number of the conjuncts are true and false if an even number are true; not only does the exclusive sense of English *or* not match that truth table, but I am certain that no conjunction in any language does. Thus, a system of semantic representation for English must involve an exclusive *or* which allows arbitrarily many operands, is true if exactly one of the operands is true and false otherwise, and is thus neither semantically nor logically equivalent to iterated binary exclusive *or*.

(iv) The quantifiers must be ' restricted quantifiers ' (e.g. ' for all x such that x is a dog, x likes to bite postmen ') rather than the ' unrestricted quantifiers ' (e.g. ' for all x, if x is a dog, then x likes to bite postmen ') that usually appear in works on symbolic logic. Some quantifier words make existential presuppositions about their ranges (e.g. *All dogs like to bite postmen* involves a presupposition that there are dogs); however, no existential presupposition is involved in the formulas with unrestricted quantifiers which logicians often use to symbolize the content of English sentences with *all*. Note in particular that ' for all x, if x is a dog, then x likes to bite postmen ' is logically equivalent to ' for all x, if x does not like to bite postmen, then x is not a dog ', which would be the putative representation of *All things that do not like to bite postmen are non-dogs* in a system of representation that had only unrestricted quantifiers. However, the latter sentence presupposes the existence of things that do not like to bite postmen but makes no presupposition that there are dogs, whereas the original sentence makes a presupposition that there are dogs but makes no presupposition about whether there are things that do not like to bite postmen.

(v) Adequate semantic representation of sentences involving ' shifters ' (Jakobson 1957) such as *I, you, here, now*, . . . , gestures and deictic words like *this* and *that*, and tenses, will have to include reference to the speech act. The most promising approach to this aspect of semantic representation (and to the syntactic properties of the above items and the category of person) is Ross's (1970a) elaboration of Austin's (1962) notion of ' performative verb '. Specifically, Ross argues that the semantic representation of each sentence (actually, in the framework of Ross's paper, the ' deep structure ' of every sentence; everything that Ross says about performatives in ' deep structure ' carries over to semantic representation) is of a form paraphraseable as ' I declare to you that . . . ', ' I request of you that . . . ', ' I promise to you that . . . ', i.e. a structure whose topmost verb expresses the ' illocutionary act ' which the speaker is performing in saying the sentence (Austin called such verbs ' performative verbs '); thus, a simple declarative sentence like

(26) Lyndon Johnson is an imperialist butcher.

will have a semantic representation paraphraseable as ' I declare to you that Lyndon Johnson is an imperialist butcher '. Activity verbs in general have to be supplied with referential indices, which correspond to the events that the speaker applies the verb to; all that was said above about indices applies to these indices, e.g. they too can be either constants or variables; a variable event index is needed to represent the meaning of the sentence

(27)   I have often eaten pizza and had a stomach ache an hour later.,

which asserts that there have been many events x such that x was an event of my eating a pizza and x was followed an hour later by my having a stomach ache. Since performative verbs are activity verbs, they too will have to be supplied with event indices.   The event index on the performative and the indices that appear as its 'subject' and 'indirect object' will be involved in assigning the categories of tense and person: person is assigned to noun phrases on the basis of whether the index of the noun phrase is presupposed to be identical to or include the speaker index (first person) or the addressee index but not the speaker index (second person) or neither (third person); tenses are assigned on the basis of presupposed time relations of 'prior', 'simultaneous', or 'posterior' to the speech event (cf. McCawley 1971a).

(vi)   The range of indices will have to be enormous.   In particular, it will have to include not only indices that purport to refer to physical objects but also indices corresponding to mythical or literary objects, so that one can represent the meaning of sentences such as

(28)   The Trobriand Islanders believe in Santa Claus, but they call him Ubu Ubu.

There will also have to be indices corresponding to 'intensional objects', so that one can represent the ambiguity of

(29)   The morning star is beautiful.

(which may be either a description of how the sky looks from Earth or a description of the landscapes on the planet Venus) and grapple with problem of why a person who answers 'Yes' to the question 'Is Mount Fuji beautiful?' and shows you the marvelous photographs of it that he took from Misaka Pass is not disagreeing with a person who answers 'No' and tells you about all the garbage that he found littering its slopes when he climbed it; they are not talking about the same thing, although the same physical object is involved in their assertions.

(vii)   I reject the traditional distinction between 'predicate' and 'logical operator' and treat 'logical operators' such as quantifiers, conjunctions, and negation as predicates which are predicated of pairs of propositional functions (in the case of quantifiers), sets of propositions or propositional functions (in the case of conjunctions), and single proposition or propositional functions (in the case of negation).   I know of no valid criterion which would distinguish 'logical operators' from other predicates.   For example, the fact that quantifiers 'bind variables' does not distinguish them from everything else, since (as shown by Baker 1970) verbs such as *ask* and *inquire* also bind variables.   For example,

(30)   Who asked which person had said what?

is ambiguous as to which interrogative words are associated with the verb *ask* and which are associated with the understood performative verb of asking (cf.

(iv) above).   On one interpretation, (30) would call for answers like ' John asked which person had said what '; on another interpretation it would call for answers like ' John asked which person had said " Burn, baby, burn." '   On the first interpretation, *who* is associated with the understood performative and *which* and *what* with *ask;* on the second interpertation, *who* and *what* are associated with the performative and *which* with *ask*[6].   It is doubtful that the binding of variables found with verbs of inquiring can be attributed to quantifiers that one might hypothesize to appear in the semantic representation of these verbs: it is generally agreed that the relationship of *Who did Max kill?* to *Max killed someone* is one of presupposition rather than of semantic inclusion.

So far I have been talking about how semantic representation may differ. I will now turn for a moment to the question of sameness of semantic representation: under what conditions must one say that two sentences (or words or what have you) have the same meaning?   One obvious proposal that might be made is that two sentences should be said to have the same meaning if they are true under the same conditions (this is roughly the proposal of Lewis 1946).   This proposal fails for at least three reasons.   First, many types of sentences have no truth value: for example,

(31)   Leave me alone!
(32)   Where is the men's room?
(33)   I hereby promise never to call you a revisionist again.

can never be true or false; but they still have meanings.   Second, all self-contradictory sentences have the same truth conditons (namely, that they are always false[7]) but may differ in meaning.   For example,

(34)   Any girl who has five brothers is an only child.
(35)   All triangles have 2 edges and 5 vertices.

clearly do not have the same meaning, as is evidenced by the fact that they could not be translated into German the same way and by the fact that if they are embedded in a context like *Max believes that . . .*, sentences of different truth value may result (i.e. it is perfectly possible for a person to subscribe to some

---

[6] If *what* were associated with *ask* and *which* with the performative, a different sentence would result: *Who asked what which person had said?*.   This shows that the question-word preposing rule must be stated in terms of ' binding ': it applies to an interrogative word that is ' bound ' by a verb of inquiring *in the next higher clause.*   This of course implies that there must BE a higher clause in an ' independent question '.   It is thus necessary to accept the ' performative analysis ' of Ross (1970a) in order to be able to state a single uniform rule for preposing question words.
[7] This is an oversimplification.   The self-contradictory sentence

The present king of France both is bald and has a full head of hair.

makes the presupposition that there is currently a king of France. If uttered at a time when there is a king of France, it is false, but if uttered at any other time, it is neither true nor false.   Sentences that presuppose the existence of a ' topic ' have a truth value only when that presupposition is true (see Strawson 1951, 1964 for further discussion of this point).

contradictions while rejecting others; indeed, it is rather common). Third, even in the case of meanings that must be either true or false, there are cases in which there are reasons for considering two meanings as distinct even though they are true under exactly the same conditions. For example, the sentence

(36) Everyone loves everyone.

has the two interpretations: (a) everyone has the property of loving everyone; (b) eveyone has the property of everyone loving him, i.e. roughly

(37) a. Every_x $(\text{Every}_y$ $(x \text{ loves } y))$
      b. Every_y $(\text{Every}_x$ $(x \text{ loves } y))$.

The truth conditions for (37a) and (37b) are the same: either is true if *x loves y* is true for all pairs of persons (x, y) and is false if there is a pair of persons (x, y) such that *x loves y* is false. However, the following arguments can be given for saying that (37a) and (37b) are two distinct meanings. (i) A counterexample to (37a) would be a person that does not love everyone; a counterexample to (37b) would be a person that not everyone loves. Thus disproving (37a) or (37b) by a counterexample would involve discovering two quite different persons, although the existence of the one person of course entails the existence of the other. (ii) The difference in position of the two *every*'s in (37a) and (37b) could make a difference in truth value if the quantifier were something other than *every*; indeed it is only in the case of ' extreme ' quantifiers such as *all* and *some* that consecutive occurrences of the quantifier may be permuted without changing truth value (I am grateful to Peter Geach for this observation). For example, the sentence

(38) Most of the boys danced with most of the girls.

has three interpretations: (a) ' *x* danced with most of the girls ' is true of most of the boys; (b) ' Most of the boys danced with *x* ' is true of most of the girls; (c) the dancing involved most of the boys and most of the girls. Assuming that *most* means more than half, the following diagram of who danced with whom illustrates a case in which (a) is true and (b) is false:

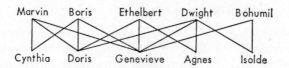

In this case there were four boys who danced with most of the girls, so that (a) is true, but there were only two girls who most of the boys danced with, so that (b) is false. Thus, the ' formation rules ' that govern how quantifiers may combine with other semantic material in semantic representation must for at least some quantifiers allow differences in position of multiple tokens of the quantifier such as are found in (37). For these formation rules to generate two distinct representations in the case of *most, almost all, all but one*, etc. but not in the case of *all*,

every, some, the rules would have to treat *every*, etc. as combining with propositional functions in a different way than *most*, etc. do, a conclusion that I find
counter-intuitive.   (iii) The results which one obtains by embedding (37a) and
(37b) in larger contexts may differ in truth value.   For example, one could
realize that (37a) was true without realizing that (37b) was true.   (iv) A sentence
such as

> (39)   Everyone loves everyone; that is true even of Max.

is ambiguous as to whether the second clause means ' . . . even Max loves everyone ' or ' . . . even Max is loved by everyone '; only (37a) contains an antecedent
for the first interpretation of *that*, and only (37b) contains an antecedent for
the second interpretation of *that*.

Another example of logically equivalent but semantically distinct sentences
is given by the pair *There are parents* and *There are children*.   Katz and Martin
(1967) cite these sentences (which are taken from Abelard) as an example of
' synonymous ' sentences.   However, they can be seen not to be synonymous
since the result of conjoining them, *There are parents and there are children* does
not violate the constraint against redundant conjoining, whereas the result of
conjoining two really synonymous sentences does: **There are bachelors and
there are unmarried men.*

Some of the above arguments against the proposition that sameness of meaning should be equated with guaranteed sameness of truth value suggest an alternative proposal: that two supposedly different meanings be considered really the
same if substituting one for the other in a larger semantic representation can
never change the truth value of the entire structure.   I emphasize two important
aspects of this proposal: (1) The proposal has to do with substitution on the semantic level and not with substitution on surface syntactic level.   Thus the fact that

> (40)   a.   Max said, ' Santa Claus gave Johnny a toy guillotine '.
>   b.   Max said, ' Santa Claus gave a toy guillotine to Johnny '.

may differ in truth value has no bearing on whether

> (41)   a.   Santa Claus gave Johnny a toy guillotine.
>   b.   Santa Claus gave a toy guillotine to Johnny.

have the same meaning.   (2) The substitution may take place even in so-called
' opaque ' contexts (Quine 1960, 1961) such as ' Harry believes that ____ ' or
' It is obvious that ____ ' (or rather, the semantic frames corresponding to those
surface contexts).

While this proposal is clearly open to attack,[8] I find it the only non-vacuous
proposal that stands a fighting chance of being right.   One interesting consequence of this proposal is that if semantic representations are to match meanings

---

[8] Attacks on closely related proposals (which have to do with substitutability *salva
veritate* in the surface form of sentences) can be found in Mates (1949) and Putnam
(1953).   I find Sellars' (1954) refutation of the main conclusion of these papers convincing.

one-to-one, then the symbols in semantic representations will have to be at least in part unordered.   Since

(42)   a.   John and Margaret have eloped.
       b.   Margaret and John have eloped.

are substitutable *salva veritate* even in opaque contexts such as ' Max knows that _____ ' (e.g. one would be contradicting himself if he said *Max knows that John and Margaret have eloped, but he doesn't know that Margaret and John have eloped*), (42a) and (42b) have the same meaning.   If the symbols in semantic representations have a full left-to-right order, then the part of the semantic representation of (42a) that corresponds to *John* would either precede or follow the part that corresponds to *Margaret*, and interchanging them would yield a different structure, which would be the semantic representation of (42b) (since the role of *John* in (42a) is the same as that of *Margaret* in (42b) and vice versa), so that (42a) and (42b) would have different semantic representations.   Consequently, either the symbols in semantic representations are not completely ordered or several semantic representations may correspond to the same meaning.   I have no clear feeling as to which of these alternatives is correct.   If the former is correct, then grammars will have to be supplemented by rules that impose a linear order on unordered structures: if the latter is correct, then grammars will have to be supplemented by rules of semantic equivalence between semantic representations.[9]

This paper so far has dealt with the semantic representations of entire sentences.   I will turn now to the question of the semantic representations of lexical items, or to put it more correctly, the question of the relation of lexical items to semantic representation—I should emphasize here that lexical items may be related in a sufficiently indirect way to semantic representations of sentences in which they appear that they will not directly match portions of those semantic representations.   Indeed, it is quite easy to find cases in which the semantic elements that are involved in a lexical item are separated from each other in the semantic representations of sentences involving that lexical item.   For example, consider the verb *kill*.   I have argued (McCawley 1968d) that the meaning of a clause containing *kill* involves elements that I will write Cause (a two-place relation, predicated of a person and an event), Become (a one-place predicate, predicated of a sentence, which describes a state of affairs), Not (a one-place predicate, predicated of a sentence), and Alive (a one-place predicate, predicated of an individual).[f]   The semantic representation of something of the form ' x kill y ' would be:[10]

[9] It should be noted that such rules of semantic equivalence are of a totally different nature from the ' rules of semantic interpretation ' of Katz and Fodor (1963) and Jackendoff (1968).   ' Rules of semantic interpretation ' relate two distinct ' levels of representation ', whereas ' rules of semantic equivalence ' relate things on the same level, i.e. the same class of representations appear in the ' inputs ' to rules of equivalence such as ' $p \lor q$ is equivalent to $q \lor p$ ' as appear in the ' outputs ' of these rules.
[10] The practise of writing predicates before the things that they apply to has ample syntactic justification; in McCawley (1970a) I argue that English has underlying verb-first word order, which is changed into the surface verb-second order by a post-cyclic transformation.

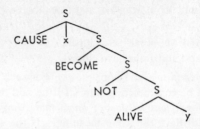

I proposed that English has a system of mechanisms for regrouping semantic elements, one of these being a transformation of 'Predicate raising', which optionally adjoins a predicate to the predicate of the next higher sentence. If Predicate raising is applied in turn to each of the predicates in the above structure, what results is

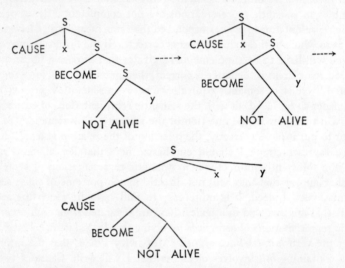

Thus, eventually a structure is obtained in which Cause, Become, Not, and Alive are joined together, and it is that stage of the derivation[11] rather than semantic representation per se at which it is determined what lexical items may be used in a sentence with a given semantic representation. If different options are exercised in applying these mechanisms of regrouping semantic items, different choices of lexical items will be required.[12] For example, if only the option of

[11] I say 'stage of the derivation' rather than 'level of representation' since it is highly doubtful that all lexical insertion takes place at the same stage of derivations. See McCawley (1968d), McCawley (in press b), and Lakoff (in preparation) for discussion.

[12] It is of course possible for these operations to yield combinations of semantic material for which the language has no lexical item. Thus, it is fortuitous that there is no English verb that means 'cause to cease to be bald' or 'become rectangular'. Similarly, in idiolects of English which lack the word *sibling*, it will undoubtedly still be necessary to represent the meanings of *brother* and *sister* in terms of a predicate Sibling; semantic

raising Not were exercised in the above example, the resulting sentence would presumably be

(43)   John caused Harry to cease to be alive.

An interesting piece of evidence for the indirect relation of lexical items to semantic representation has been found by J. L. Morgan (1969), who observes that adverbs like *almost* and *again* sometimes modify not an entire lexical item but only a piece of its semantic representation[13].   For example, Morgan notes that

(44)   I almost killed Louie.

is ambiguous between (a) I almost did something such that, had I done it, Louie would have died from it, (b) I did something which came close to causing Louie to die (although it might not have affected him at all), (c) I did something that caused Louie to become almost dead.   Morgan also observes that these three senses fit in different ways into ' pseudo-cleft ' sentences:

(45)   What I almost did was kill Louie.

can only involve (a), whereas

(46)   What I did was almost kill Louie.

can only be either (b) or (c) and

(47)   What I did to Louie was almost kill him.

can only be (c).

The conception of grammar within which I am investigating 'prelexical transformations' such as Predicate raising is a version of transformational grammar in which there is no such level as Chomsky's ' deep structure ', the base component of a grammar generates semantic representations, and the ' dictionary entries ' for the various lexical items are in effect transformations which insert those lexical items in place of various complexes of semantic material that may arise through prelexical transformations.   The conception of ' transformation' and of the way in which transformations interact (e.g. the conclusion that there is a ' cycle ' of transformations which is followed[14] by a system of ' post-cyclic' transformations, the transformations of each of these two systems being ordered) is the same as in recent versions of transformational grammar with a level of ' deep

representations involving Sibling in these idiolects will not give rise to sentences unless Sibling is combined with other semantic material (e.g. Male or Female) by some prelexical transformation or other.

[13] Keyser (1968: 365–6) makes similar observations about the word *back*.

[14] ' Follow ' refers here to logical rather than temporal precedence.   The temporal sequence of psychological events involved in producing a given sentence can vary wildly from occasion to occasion (depending e.g. on the extent to which the speaker has already decided what idea he wants to express).   The common misconception that acceptance of transformational grammar commits one to the position that the various stages of a transformational derivation exist as a temporal sequence of events in the speaker's mind can only be attributed to widespread lack of imagination in conceiving of ways that a real-time production model could utilize a system of ordered rules.

structure'. Indeed, there is some reason for believing that all cyclic transformations are prelexical (McCawley 1968d); part of the evidence for that conclusion
is the existence of lexical items whose meanings appear to be paraphraseable only
in terms of the outputs of these transformations, e.g. reflexivization (*suicide*=
' killing oneself '), passivization (*under surveilance*=' being watched '), and Equi-
NP-Deletion (*malinger*=' pretend to be sick ')

Another prelexical transformation that is involved in lexical items of English
is discussed in Rice (1968).   This transformation, which I will call ' generalized
conjunction reduction ', is involved in such lexical items as *daughter*. *Daughter*
is a ' transitive noun ': it expresses a binary relation.   Of the two components
that it is usually broken down into, Offspring and Female, the former expresses
a binary relation but the latter is a one-place predicate.   If semantic representation is to represent Daughter (x, y) in terms of these two predicates, the representation would presumably have to be Offspring (x, y) $\wedge$ Female (x), or in tree
representation,

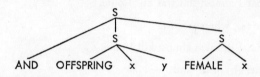

To convert such a representation into one in which Offspring and Female are
combined into a single constituent, a transformation appears to be needed which
will combine corresponding pieces of (at least some types of) conjoined structure,
e.g. convert the above into

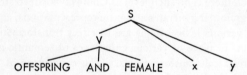

and will have to be applicable even in cases such as the above, where the two (or
more) conjuncts are not of exactly parallel form.   Rice illustrated this transformation by the word *fetch*, which can be paraphrased as ' go, acquire, and then
return with '.   Note that in this case the conjunction is the asymmetric *and then*
rather than the symmetric *and* which was involved in *daughter*.   Kenneth Hale
(personal communication) points out that generalized conjunction reduction is
manifested in some Australian languages, where ' fetch ' is expressed by a compound verb that is literally go-take-come.   Hale notes that the object of this verb
must be the underlying object of its middle part, since the other two parts of the
compound are intransitive.

One novel aspect of this approach to lexical insertion is that it allows sharp
limits to be put on what is a ' possible lexical item ' in each language.   Specifically, this approach predicts that a language will only permit lexical items which

correspond to syntactic constituents that would arise from well-formed semantic representations through existing prelexical transformations. This would explain why English has no verb *glarf meaning ' give one's brother and ', as in a sentence *John glarfed Harry a dime that was supposed to mean ' John gave his brother and Harry a dime'. Since no existing prelexical transformation of English (or any other language, I would imagine) would combine a verb with a conjunction and one conjunct taken from its indirect object, the configuration of semantic elements for which the putative verb *glarf would be inserted would never arise.[15] The only earlier work that I know of which concerns itself with the question of ' possible lexical item ' is the work by Lounsbury and others on kinship terminology in which systems of kinship terms are described via rules that are of the general form ' if term A covers the relative linked to ego in manner x, then it also covers the relative linked to ego in manner $f(x)$ '. Such rules obviously exclude the possibility of many non-occurring terms. The type of restriction embodied in Lounsbury's rules probably can not be made to follow from prelexical transformations; for example, English kinship terms ignore the sex of the ego and of linking relatives (e.g. there are no separate words for ' paternal grandfather ' and ' maternal grandfather '), but there is nothing to prevent structures specifying sex for ego or linking relatives from being converted into lexical-item-sized constituents by prelexical transformations. Inded, there is no obvious restriction that could be placed on ' generalized conjunction reduction ' which would prevent it from applying to Offspring $(x, y) \land$ Female (y), the result of which should be a possible lexical item meaning ' child whose mother is ',[16] which would violate the constraint that English kinship terms ignore the sex of the ego. Thus, the proposal of prelexical transformations will give only a partial answer to the question of what is a possible lexical item in a given language.[g]

[a] The only detail of this proposal which should be taken seriously is that the content of the NP's originates outside of the clauses in which they appear. See note l of ' Where do noun phrases come from? ' for discussion of some serious defects in my analysis.
[b] It is not true that only constants have appeared so far. Had I treated (6a) correctly (see note l of ' Where do noun phrases come from ? '), it would have been clear that y has to be a variable. I am inclined to believe that (6b) corresponds to two different meanings (thus that (5) is 3-ways and not 2-ways ambiguous), one in which y is a constant and one in which it is a variable bound by a ' definite description operator ', but it is not completely clear that that is the case.
[c] This is actually false. If ' Some ' were associated with t and 'All' with x, the result

[15] The impossibility of such a verb follows from the view of grammar presented here plus Ross's (1967a) ' coordinate structure constraint ', according to which no transformation can move material into or out of a coordinate structure; this constraint is needed to account for the ungrammaticality of sentences such as *What did you buy a hammer and? (in which what is moved out of a conjoined object) and *John and even Harry are similar (in which even is moved into a conjoined subject).
[16] There is such a word in Western Apache.

would be incoherent, since 'x a person ' would not be within the scope of the quantifier which binds x.   If only ' restricted quantification ' (see point (iv) below) is allowed, the locations of the various variables are sufficient to allow one to determine which quantifier binds which variable.

[d] See now McCawley (1972) for a demonstration that considerations of logic also demand a tree representation.

[e] I now maintain that conjunctions are quantifiers and that a quantifier is a one-place predicate that is predicated of a set of propositions.   The set of propositions may be defined either by enumeration (in which case the quantifier is expressed as a conjunction) or by a definite description (e.g. in *All men are mortal*, 'All ' is predicated of the set of all propositions x *is mortal* for which x is a man).   See McCawley (1972).

[f] See note *d* of ' Lexical insertion in a transformational grammar without deep structure '.

[g] For further discussion of kinship terminology within this framework, see McCawley (1973 : lecture 4).

15. Tense and Time Reference in English*

Ross (1969b) has contested the celebrated analysis of English auxiliaries presented in Chomsky (1957, 1965) on the grounds that while Chomsky's analysis makes it necessary to treat auxiliaries as not within the category ' Verb ' (and indeed, not all belonging to any one category), in fact most transformations treat auxiliaries in exactly the same way that they treat ' main ' verbs,[1] i.e. the one known source of evidence for category membership argues that auxiliaries are really verbs and that the traditional term ' auxiliary verb ' is syntactically justified. Ross proposes that the deep structure of a sentence such as

* This paper was read at the First Annual Ohio State Semantics Festival, April 15, 1969 (the Second Annual Ohio State Semantics Festival has been tentatively scheduled for November 1982). It first appeared in Charles J. Fillmore and D. T. Langendoen (editors), *Studies in linguistic semantics* (New York: Holt, Rinehart and Winston, 1971), pp. 96–113.

Some of the conclusions in this paper were arrived at independently by Huddleston (1969). See now also Robin Lakoff (1971c) and Dahl (1971).
[1] Auxiliaries are exceptional by virtue of undergoing a transformation of ' tense attraction ' which combines them with an immediately preceding tense morpheme. All other transformations that might appear to treat auxiliaries in a special way (e.g. Subject-verb inversion) are simply transformations that follow ' tense attraction ' and have a structural description calling for the first verb.

(1) John had been smoking pot.

is not

(2)

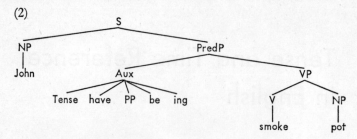

as Chomsky's proposals would have it, but rather

(3)

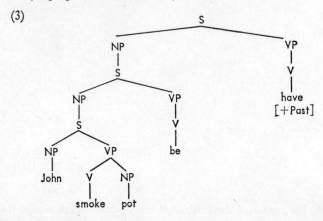

Successive applications of the cyclic transformation known variously as 'subject raising', 'it-replacement', or 'VP raising' plus application of 'complementizer placement' to add PP and -ing to the complements of *have* and *be* respectively convert (3) into

(4)

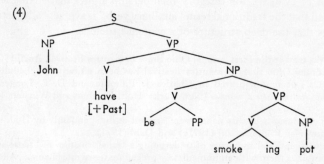

Ross notes that the resulting surface structure gives additional support for his proposal, namely that the parts of a sentence such as (1) which can be pronominalized are syntactic constituents in Ross's analysis but not in Chomsky's; for example,

(5) They say that John had been smoking pot, which he had.

involves pronominalization of *been smoking pot*, thus providing evidence that *been smoking pot* is a constituent at the point of the derivation where this pronominalization takes place; *been smoking pot* is a constituent in (4) but not in the surface structure that would result from Chomsky's analysis.

This paper will be devoted to refining Ross's analysis and relating it to semantics. The refinements that I will propose in Ross's analysis relate to tense. Specifically, I will propose that tenses are not features but are themselves underlying verbs[2] and that all occurrences of the auxiliary *have* are underlying past tenses, so that (1) will be derived not from (3) but rather from

(6)

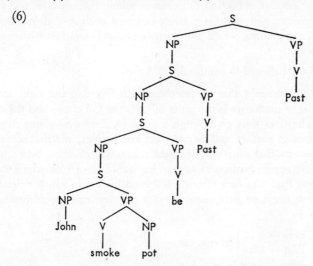

These refinements will add several items to the already huge list of advantages which Ross's analysis buys over Chomsky's; in particular, they will make it possible to show that the various restrictions on the co-occurrence of auxiliaries which Chomsky summarized in the celebrated formula

(7) Aux → Tense (Modal) (*have* PP) (*be ing*)

are consequences of other more general syntactic facts, i.e. Ross's analysis allows one to explain why those combinations of auxiliaries occur rather than any other set of combinations that one could summarize with a formula along the lines of (7).

The argument that *have* is an underlying past tense is based on Hofmann's (1966) observation that in certain environments the distinction between simple past, present perfect, and past perfect is neutralized in favor of *have*. For ex-

---

[2] I had already assumed this conclusion in footnote 1.

ample, the sentences

> (8)   John is believed to have arrived at 2: 00 yesterday.
> (9)   John is believed to have drunk a gallon of beer by now.
> (10) John is believed to have already met Sue when he married Cynthia.

involved embedded clauses which would have to be in the simple past, present perfect, and past perfect if used as independent clauses:

> (11) John arrived at 2: 00 yesterday.   (*has arrived, *had arrived)
> (12) John has drunk a gallon of beer by now.   (*drank, *had drunk)
> (13) John had already met Sue when he married Cynthia.   (*met, *has met)

A grammar will have to provide some mechanism for matching time adverbs with appropriate auxiliaries both in full clauses, where there is a four-way contrast between present, past, present perfect, and past perfect, and in infinitives and certain other structures, which allow only a two-way contrast between *have* and nothing, as in

> (14) John is believed to admire Spiro Agnew.

Hofmann rightly concludes that the mechanism for getting the right adverbs to go with the right auxiliaries is the same in both the full clause and the infinitive and that infinitives thus go through a stage in their derivations in which present, past, present perfect, and past perfect are distinct, and that some later rule or rules converts that four-way distinction into a distinction between zero and *have*. A first approximation to such rules would be a rule which deletes Present and turns Past into *have* after *to*, followed by a rule which deletes one of the *have*'s from the *have have* sequence that the first rule would produce in past perfect cases:

> (15)   a. $\left.\begin{array}{l}\text{Pres} \rightarrow \emptyset \\ \text{Past} \rightarrow have\end{array}\right\}$ in env. *to*___
>
>   b.   *have*$_{\text{AUX}}$ → ∅ in env. *have* ___

Hofmann notes that the same neutralization takes place in other environments, for example, with the *-ing* complementizer:

> (16) John's having arrived at 2: 00 yesterday surprises me.
> (17) John's having drunk a gallon of beer by now surprises me.
> (18) John's having already met Sue when he married Cynthia surprises me.

and most importantly, after modals:

> (19) John may have arrived at 2: 00 yesterday.
> (20) John may have drunk a gallon of beer by now.
> (21) John may have already met Sue when he married Cynthia.

This last fact implies that there must be more underlying combinations of auxiliaries than Chomsky's formula allows: since the same rules govern which time adverbs go with *have* and which ones exclude *have* as in the cases discussed already, there must be a stage of the derivation at which modals can be followed by present, past, present perfect, and past perfect. The correct rule, of course, will not simply give a list of environments such as *to*, *-ing*, and Modal as the environments where tense replacement takes place. There is a generalization which unites all these cases, namely that these are the environments in which the tense morpheme would not undergo subject-verb agreement. Thus, tense replacement can be made applicable simply to those tense markers to which subject-verb agreement has not applied:

(22) (replaces (15a)) $\left. \begin{array}{l} \text{Pres} \rightarrow \emptyset \\ \text{Past} \rightarrow have \end{array} \right\}$ if agreement has not applied.

But since all occurrences of the auxiliary *have* are in environments in which subject-verb agreement would not be applicable, the generalized version of tense replacement that I have just proposed would permit one to take all underlying *have*'s as underlying past tenses.

I am now in a position to fulfill my promise to show that a refinement of Ross's analysis provides an explanation of why only the combinations of auxiliaries tabulated in Chomsky's formula occur. (a) Tense can only occur first, since tense in any other position is either deleted or turned into *have*. (b) Modals can be preceded only by tense because of their defective morphology: if modals appeared anywhere else they would have to be in an infinitive or participial form, and English modals do not have such forms.[3,a] (c) Progressive *be* can only occur last, because of the constraint that the topmost verb of its complement must be non-stative:

(23) John is acting like Harry.
(24) *John is resembling Harry.

If the auxiliaries under discussion are verbs, they are surely stative verbs; thus the same constraint which excludes (24) would also exclude

(25) *John is having drunk bourbon.

(d) There could not be more than one *have* since any *have*'s in a structure not already excluded by (b) or (c) would have to be contiguous and since all but one of a string of contiguous *have*'s would be deleted.[4]

---

[3] The attractive proposal that modals are suppletive, e.g. that *can* is obligatorily replaced by *be able to* in infinitive and participial forms, probably is not feasible since the modals and their corresponding periphrastic forms are not always semantically equivalent. Note, for example, the sentences (brought to my attention by Louanna Furbee)

How can I tell you?
How am I able to tell you?

[4] One important item that I have failed to discuss is the passive *be*. I suspect that grounds will eventually be found for saying that *Max has been caught by the police* is not the passive of *The police have caught Max* but rather the present perfect of tenseless *Max be caught by the police* and that things such as *The police have caught Max* strictly speaking have no passive. However, confirmation or refutation of this conclusion will have to await an adequate account of what passive is applicable to. This conjecture, if true, would imply that no special rule was needed to get passive *be* in the right place relative to other auxiliaries.

This analysis would appear to allow infinitely many sources for either a present perfect or a past perfect: if something with a sense for its main verb can be embedded as the subject of a tense, as in (6), there should be no limit as to how far this could be continued, and all of the infinitely many conceivable combinations of Past and Present ought to be generated, e.g. 37 consecutive Pasts. Those combinations in which there were two or more embedded pasts would yield a past perfect by tense replacement and *have*-deletion, and those combinations having only one embedded past would yield a present perfect. For example, if 37 consecutive Pasts were generated, 36 of them would become *have* and 35 of those *have*'s would be deleted, thus leaving a Past Perfect.

How ambiguous are present perfect and past perfect in fact? The past perfects found in the sentences

(26)   When John married Sue, he had met Cynthia 5 years before.

(27)   When John married Sue, he had read *Principia Mathematica* 5 times.

are reasonable candidates for analysis as the past of a past and the past of a present perfect respectively, since the content of the main clause, if expressed at the time when John married Sue, would require past tense and present perfect respectively:

(28)   John met Cynthia 5 years ago.

(29)   John has read *Principia Mathematica* 5 times.

Moreover, analyzing them as a past with an embedded past or present perfect allows one to explain why a past perfect allows two time adverbs; at a more underlying level of structure, there is only one time adverb per clause, and the past perfect would arise from an embedding structure, whose main clause and embedded clause could each supply one time adverb.

This gives reasons for setting up two sources for a past perfect, but that is far short of the infinitely many sources that I suggested. What about a third source, the past of a past perfect? I know of no good examples of a past perfect with three time adverbs, but there are examples of past perfects with two time adverbs and an implicit reference to a third point in past time, as in a discourse containing the sentence

(30)   When John had married Sue, he had known Cynthia for 5 years.,

which is possible only if the discourse has already mentioned some past time which is taken as the 'reference point' of 'John had married Sue'; (30) could then be analyzed as the past (the unmentioned reference point) of the past (John's marrying Sue) of a present perfect (John has known Cynthia for 5 years).[5] Thus, if a 'reference point' is taken to be a tense, with or without time adverb,

---

[5] Fischer (1967) points out that French distinguishes a 'doubly past' past perfect from a 'triply past' past perfect:

Après que Pierre *a eu fini* ses devoirs, il est allé jouer.   'After Pierre finished his homework, he went out to play'

Après que Pierre *avait eu fini* ses devoirs, il était allé jouer.   'After Pierre had finished his homework, he had gone out to play'.

whose subject is an embedded sentence corresponding to the event or state that is being described relative to that reference point, there is some reason for allowing the potentially limitless freedom of combination of underlying tenses which my revision of Ross's analysis appears to demand, except that the occasion would hardly ever arise for one to use so many subsidiary ' reference points ' as to require tenses piled more than three deep.

I turn now to the present perfect. The present perfect obviously is not merely the present of a past in the same sense that the past perfect can be the past of a past: the obvious parallel to using the past perfect for something which at a designated reference point in the past would have been reported in the past tense ought to be using the present perfect for something which at a designated reference point in the present would be reported in the past; but since the present is the only point in the present, that characterization would amount to the absurdity that the present perfect is used for what the past is used for. I am not going to argue that the present perfect is ultimately the present of a past but rather that through deletions it acquires a derived constituent structure having a Present as its highest verb and Past as its next highest verb, that is, what I had suggested as a deep structure in the revision of Ross's analysis proposed above is really just an intermediate stage in a derivation.

The present perfect in English has the following uses:
(a) to indicate that a state of affairs prevailed throughout some interval stretching from the past into the present (' Universal '):

(31)   I've known Max since 1960.

(b) to indicate the existence of past events (' Existential '):

(32)   I have read *Principia Mathematica* 5 times.

(c) to indicate that the direct effect of a past event still continues (' Stative'):

(33)   I can't come to your party tonight—I've caught the flu.

(d) to report hot news (' Hot News '):

(34)   Malcolm X has just been assassinated.

While some doubt might be raised as to whether (b, c, d) are distinct senses, it can easily be shown that they are. For example

(35)   Max has been fired.

is ambiguous and not vague between the three senses ' There are occasions on which Max was fired ', ' Max is currently out of work, having been fired ', and ' Max has been fired, which I presume is news to you ', as can be seen by considering the sentence

(36)   Max has been fired, and so has Fred.,

which can cover the case of both Max and Fred on occasion having been fired, the case of both of them being out of work as a result of being fired, or the case of two pieces of hot news dealing respectively with the firing of Max and the firing of Fred, but it could not be used to assert that Max is out of work and that Fred, who we may assume to have a job currently, has at sometime been fired. I will argue that all four of the senses of the present perfect correspond to semantic representations in which something that provides the source of a past tense is embedded in something that provides the source of a present tense, and that accordingly, deletions can give rise to a structure of the type proposed above.

The universal and existential present perfects appear both to involve a quantifier that ranges over an interval stretching from the past into the present and differ as regards whether that quantifier is universal or existential.   I have argued elsewhere (McCawley, 1970c) that the semantics of natural languages involves not the 'unrestricted quantification' found in most logic textbooks, where 'All men are mortal' is transcribed '(All_x (Man (x)$\supset$Mortal (x)))', but 're-stricted quantification' such as would be found in a transcription '$All_{x:\;Man(x)}$ Mortal (x)', i.e. that a quantifier is combined not with one but with two propositional functions, one giving the 'range' of the variable, and one giving the property that is being asserted of things in that range.[b] I propose that these two propositional functions provide the sources of the two tenses that I wish these present perfects to be derived from: the range provides the present tense, since it must be an interval containing the present, and the propositional function being asserted provides the past tense, since it is being asserted of events or times that are in the past.   I assume that the tense morpheme corresponding to the range would be put in the clause corresponding to the quantifier.   At some later point in the derivation, these quantifiers are deleted, leaving as traces only their tenses and such words as *ever*, *already*, and *sometimes*, and a time adverb describing the range, e.g. *since Tuesday*, *during the last 5 years*.   In many languages the universal and existential cases are not treated alike; for example, in German and Japanese translations of a universal present perfect, the tense of the scope is lost, and a simple present appears:

(37)   Sie warten seit 5 Uhr.   ' They have been waiting since 5:00.'
(38)   Gozi kara mat-te   i-ru.
       5: 00 from wait-participle be-present

In Japanese, the existential case is treated exactly like any other existential sentence:

(39)   Tanaka-san -wa hon -o   kai-ta   koto -ga   ar-u
       Mr. Tanaka topic book object write-past fact subject exist-pres.
       'Mr. Tanaka has written books.'

One major advantage to treating present perfects as derived from a semantic representation such as I have sketched is that much of the cooccurrence restrictions between auxiliaries and time adverbs is thereby explained.   For example, this treatment explains, at least for these two uses of the present perfect, why adverbs designating points in time cannot be used with the present perfect: since the time adverb of the scope of the quantifier is a bound variable which the quantifier binds, *I have written a letter yesterday* would be excluded for exactly the same reason as * *I talked to someone the butcher:* in both cases a constant and a variable would be filling the same position.

The condition that the range of the quantifier include the present is closely connected with the question of the presuppositions of present perfects. Chomsky (1970b) discusses the oddity of[6]

(40) [*] Einstein has visited Princeton.

as compared with

(41) Princeton has been visited by Einstein.

and states that it illustrates a principle whereby the surface subject of certain types of present perfect is presupposed to refer to someone who is alive. I contend, however, that the false proposition that Einstein is alive is not, strictly speaking, presupposed by (40) but is merely inferrable from the presupposition of (40) plus factual knowledge such as the knowledge that one must be alive to visit Princeton, and moreover, that the presupposition has nothing to do with the question of what is the surface subject. Note first that whether a sentence in the present perfect commits the speaker to the belief that the subject refers to someone who is alive depends on the rest of the sentence:

(42) Frege has contributed a lot to my thinking.
(43) Frege has been denounced by many people.
(44) [*] Frege has been frightened by many people.

and also depends on stress. Presumably Chomsky intended (40) and (41) to be read with primary stress on *Princeton* and *Einstein* respectively; however,

(45) Eínstein has visited Prînceton.

does not commit one to the belief that Einstein is alive, whereas

(46) [*] Prínceton has been visited by Eînstein.

does. This last fact suggests that topic rather than subject is directly related to presuppositions. In (45) one is talking about events of visiting Princeton, not just events of Einstein visiting Princeton, but in (46) about events of Einstein visiting. The former kind of events can still happen since Princeton still exists, but the latter cannot, since Einstein is no longer alive. Frege has to be alive for people to frighten him, but he doesn't have to be alive for people to denounce him. Actually, the property of being alive is not directly involved in the oddity of (40), since a person who believes that the dead return to haunt the living could perfectly well say (40) without contradicting his knowledge that Einstein is dead. Likewise, a person who holds both that belief and the belief that Frege is as neurotic a ghost as he was a living person could perfectly well say (44).

The presupposition in an existential present perfect thus appears to be that

[6] I will use [*] to indicate oddity caused by the absurdity of the presuppositions that a sentence involves.

the range of the variable which the existential quantifier binds is a period during which the event or state designated by the propositional function in the scope of the quantifier can happen or be the case.   Since the present perfect can only be used if the range includes the present, the presupposition is that the present is included in the period in which the designatum of the propositional function in question can happen or be the case.[7]

I will now give a number of illustrations of this principle.

(47)   My mother has changed my diaper many times.

would be appropriate if said by a linguistically precocious 2-year-old who still wore diapers but not if said by a man who stopped wearing diapers 30 years ago. Leech (1969) points out that

(48)   Have you seen the Monet exhibition?

would be appropriate only in referring to an exhibition which the speaker believes still to be running, whereas one would have to say

(49)   Did you see the Monet exhibition?

if referring to an exhibition which one believes to have already closed.   However, a presupposition that the exhibition is still running is not sufficient to make (48) appropriate; for example, one would have to use (49) and not (48) if speaking to a person who one knows to have recently suffered an injury which will keep him in the hospital until long after the exhibition closes.   The sentence

(50)   Many people have died in automobile accidents.

does not commit one to the belief that those designated by the subject are alive, nor should it, since (50) is about events of a person dying in an auto accident, which can still happen, as compared with

(51)   [*] Dennis Brain has died in an auto accident. [ignore the ' hot news ' sense],

which is about events of Dennis Brain dying in an auto accident, of which there can be only one.   The sentence

(52)   Dennis Brain and other famous musicians have died in auto accidents.

is again about the propositional function ' x dies in an event t of the type "auto accident." ' It is non-anomalous since *Dennis Brain* does not appear in this propositional function but only in the expression giving the range of the variable x[8], similarly with Chomsky's example

[7] This must be interpreted in such a way that gaps in a discontinuous interval are ignored. The present can perfectly well fall into a gap in a discontinuous period in which something can happen, as in

Max has often gotten up at 8 AM.   (said at 10 PM)

[8] Note that this implies that (52) cannot be derived by conjunction reduction from a conjoined sentence having *Dennis Brain* in one conjunct and *many other famous musicians* in the other.

(53) Marco Polo and many others have climbed Everest.

One extension of this construction which I can get at least marginally is illustrated by

(54) Many people have climbed Everest; for example, Marco Polo has climbed it.

The present perfect here is repeated in a clause which provides an example of the kind of event which a preceding existential present perfect asserts to have occurred. I do not understand the details of the derivation of a sentence such as (54) nor can I characterize the range of cases in which this phenomenon can occur. I suspect that it is the same phenomenon which Chomsky (1970b) observes when he writes 'it seems to me that if Hilary had just announced that he had succeeded in climbing Everest, it would have been appropriate, without the presupposition that Marco Polo is alive, to have said " But Marco Polo has done it too." '

The stative present perfects would presumably correspond to a semantic representation in which a description of the event is embedded in a context like ' the direct result of ____ continues ', which would again involve a source for a past tense embedded in a source for a present tense, so that again a deletion could give rise to the desired Present+Past configuration. However, in this case I am at a total loss to find a detailed analysis which would correctly explain what effect the sentence refers to, e.g. why it is that

(55) John has gone to the office.

refers to the effect of John's not being here (not, as is often erroneously supposed, the effect of John's being at the office),

(56) The police have arrested my wife, so we can't come to your party.

to the effect of my wife's being in jail,

(57) I've caught the flu.

to the effect of my being sick with the flu, and

(58) Have you seen my slippers?

to the effect of your being in a position to inform me regarding the whereabouts of my slippers. The oddity (noted by Leech) of ' Yes, six months ago ' as an answer to (58) comes from the answer assuming an existential interpretation of a present perfect that would normally be intended as a stative. Note, incidentally, that the commonly encountered description of this use of the present perfect as ascribing a state to the subject of the clause is incorrect, since in (56) it is the speaker's wife and not the police that is being asserted to be in the state in question.

In the hot news present perfect, it is clear that the status as news of the thing being reported is essential to the acceptability of the sentence. Since a person reporting hot news presupposes that his addressee does not yet know the news that he is reporting, the following possibility presents itself for relating this use of the present perfect to the existential use: one might say that the ' hot news ' present perfect is an existential present perfect in which the speaker bases the range of the quantifier not on his own presuppositions as to when the event in question might happen but on his estimate of his addressee's presuppositions: if the addressee does not know that Malcolm X has been killed, then for him the period in which Malcolm X might be killed extends indefinitely far into the future and thus includes the present. This analysis is supported by the fact that it would be normal to say things like *Kennedy has been assassinated* or *Krushchev has been deposed* to a person who has just been rescued from a remote island where he had been marooned since 1960. However, note that this type of present perfect also occurs in questions:

(59)   Has there been an accident?

and in a past setting:

(60)   When I arrived in New York, Malcolm X had just been assassinated.

This last example makes me a little suspicious of the cute idea that I suggested above of basing the choice of tense on the speaker's estimate of his hearer's presuppositions. Perhaps the only hope for an analysis of this use of the present perfect is to introduce a quite ad-hoc principle that the period in which something is supposed ' available for happening ' is always extended forwards so as to include the time that it would take for news of its happening to get around and that in the case of a sentence actually being used to convey the news, ' get around ' is taken to mean ' get to the person to whom the sentence is addressed '.

It is possible for two of these senses of the present perfect to be combined, as in a hot news report of an existential present perfect:

(61)   Have you heard the news? Sinatra has been sleeping with Ladybird.

Such combinations of these senses present no new problems: if the (admittedly programmatic) analysis of the different present perfects sketched above works for the simple cases, then it will automatically handle things like (61) also. The structure underlying an existential present perfect would be embedded in the structure underlying a hot news present perfect, and the resulting Present-Past-Present-Past combination would become Present-*have* by tense replacement and *have*-deletion.

I have so far thrown around the word ' tense ' with rather gay abandon, an abandon whose gaiety was especially unjustified when I was talking about semantic representations. The embedded pasts that I talked about were not absolute pasts but rather pasts relative to the context in which they were embedded, i.e. they expressed ' prior to ' rather than ' past '. Of course, if one adopts Ross's (1970a) proposal that all sentences arise from a structure whose topmost verb is a (often unexpressed) ' performative verb ', which indicates the illocutionary force (question, command, promise, warning, etc.) which the sentence is intended to have, then absolute pasts also mean ' prior to ' relative to the context in which they are embedded, since they are embedded in a context which refers to the time of the speech act, i.e. the present. However, the tense morpheme does not just express the time relationship between the clause it is in and the next higher clause—it also refers to the time of the clause that it is in, and indeed, refers to it in a way that is rather like the way in which personal pronouns refer to what they stand for. For example, a past tense normally requires an antecedent: the sentence

(62) *The farmer killed the duckling.[9]

is odd unless the prior context provides a time for the past tense to refer to; the oddity of (62) without such an antecedent for the past tense is exactly the oddity that is felt in

(63) *He resembles Mike.

when uttered in a context which has not provided any prior mention of a person for the *he* to refer to. Moreover, the relation between a past tense and its antecedent satisfies Langacker's (1969) pronomialization constraint—that a pronoun must be preceded or commanded[10] by its antecedent:

(64) Although Max was tired last night, he couldn't sleep.
(65) Although Max was tired, he couldn't sleep last night.
(66) Max couldn't sleep last night, although he was tired.
(67) *Max couldn't sleep, although he was tired last night.

In addition, treating tenses as some kind of pronoun allows one to avoid having to set up two different *and*'s, one symmetric and the other asymmetric (=*and then*). Note that especially in narratives one may get several consecutive sentences or clauses which all contain past tenses but which refer not to simultaneous events but to consecutive events, each past tense referring to a time shortly after that which the preceding past tense referred to. For example, in

(68) The Lone Ranger broke$_{t1}$ the window with the barrel of his gun, took$_{t2}$ aim, and pulled$_{t3}$ the trigger.,

t_2 contains an implicit reference to t_1 ('shortly after t_1') and t_3 contains an implicit reference to t_2 ('shortly after t_2'). If we in fact say that t_1 is the antecedent of t_2 and that t_2 is the antecedent of t_3, then Langacker's constraint explains why (68) is not equivalent to

(69) The Lone Ranger pulled the trigger, took aim, and broke the window with the barrel of his gun.

[9] I am grateful to Sydney M. Lamb for bringing this interesting example to my attention.
[10] A node in a labeled tree is said to command all the nodes in the portion of the tree dominated by the lowest node labeled S which dominates the node in question, i.e. a node commands all the nodes which are in the same ' simplex sentence ' as it is in and all the nodes that are in clauses subordinate to that ' simplex sentence '.

In a coordinate structure, pronouns cannot be commanded by their antecedents and therefore must be preceded by them; hence, t_1 must precede t_2 if it is to be its antecedent.   Thus there is no need to say that the *and* of (68) is different from the ' symmetric ' *and* of

> (70)   John is tall and handsome.

I have argued that the past tense morpheme is an intransitive verb, that it is a two-place predicate meaning ' prior to ', and that it is a pronoun.   Can I have it all three ways?   I can if I take the point of view that ' Past ' is a predicate meaning ' prior to ' in the same sense in which *she* is a predicate meaning ' female ', i.e. that pronouns both stand for things and express presuppositions about the things they stand for.   In my above examples, I treated *last night* as the antecedent of a past tense, that is, I treated the tense as being the pronominal form of a time adverb.   Since a sentence like *Max was tired last night* involves both a time adverb and a matching tense morpheme but semantically only makes one reference to the time involved, my suggestion that tenses are pronominal in nature would entail having a reduplication rule which added a pronominal copy of every time adverb.   There is nothing to prevent this pronominal copy from being added in predicate position, i.e. the time adverb reduplication transformation could be so formulated as to create derived structures in which tenses appear in main-verb position and those constituents which will give rise to explicit time adverbs will appear in other positions than main-verb position.   This proposal for English, incidentally, matches exactly Kiparsky's (1969) proposal for the history of tense in Indo-European.   Kiparsky argues that in proto-Indo-European, tense morphemes were in complementary distribution with overt time adverbs and thus could be considered as belonging to the same grammatical category as them and that the development of the modern Indo-European languages from this stage involved the copying of features of the referents of time adverbs onto the verb, first optionally and later obligatorily.

I will close by commenting briefly on some important matters which I have not yet touched on.   The future tense appears to present no major difficulties for the above analysis.   The future tense in English differs mainly morphologically from the present and past:[c] its marker is morphologically a modal verb rather than an affix.   The future marker is deleted or replaced by the present tense morpheme in a number of environments.   For example, it is deleted after *may*, as in

> (71)   John may beat his wife.,

which may be either an embedded habitual present (=It may be that John beats his wife) or an embedded future (=It may be that John will beat his wife), as contrasted with

> (72)   John must beat his wife.,

which can be interpreted as an embedded habitual present but not as an embedded future.[11]   The future marker is replaced by a present tense in conditional clauses and certain time adverbial clauses:[12]

(73)   If he comes tomorrow, I'll give him some money.

There is no ' mirror image ' of the past perfect, i.e. a combination of auxiliaries to indicate something that follows a future reference point; the simple future is used in this case:

(74)   When I get the money, I'll pay you within a week.

It thus appears that future is deleted when it directly follows future.   There is likewise no special future analogue to the present perfect: a simple future is used to express the existence of future events or to express that something is the case through an interval starting at the present and running into the future:

(75)   Max will die before he's 30.
(76)   I'll work here until I find a better job.

One interesting restriction on the future (called to my attention by Michael Stewart) is that a past embedded in a future may not refer to something that the speaker knows to have already happened; thus

(77)   When you see Max, he'll have received his Ph. D. a week earlier.

is normal if the awarding of the degree is to take place between now and your seeing Max or even if it is due to take place today and the speaker does not know whether it has already taken place, but it is odd if the speaker knows that Max received the degree three days ago and you are to see him in four days.

While the analysis given above allowed in principle for presents and pasts to be embedded in one another to one's heart's content, examples of embedded pasts were much easier to come by than were examples of embedded presents; indeed, the only examples of embedded presents to be found above are the presents of embedded present perfects.   Another peculiarity of the analysis given suggests that even these examples of embedded presents are spurious and that there are in fact no embedded presents.   Specifically, consider the present tense that was introduced by the ' range ' of a present perfect.   In the case where the range of something asserting the existence of past events does not contain the present, the ' range ' does not contribute its own tense: a past tense is used rather than a past perfect, as in

[11] This deletion of the future marker is one of several transformations which are triggered by some but not all modals.   If one takes uniform syntactic behavior as the criterion for setting up a syntactic category, then modals fail in a spectacular way to form a syntactic category: no two of them have exactly the same syntactic properties.
   I have ignored additional readings which (71) and (72) allow. (71) is at least seven ways ambiguous.
[12] Note that this rule applies only to the future marker and not to the other senses of *will* such as ' consent ', as is shown by Palmer's example (1965: 110) *If he'll come tomorrow, I'll give him some money.*

(78)   Henry VIII got married six times.

This suggest that the rule creating the outer tense of present perfects applies only in present contexts.   This in turn implies that present tense differs from past tense in more ways than it has generally been held to: it marks an absolute rather than a relative time relation.[13]

Another problem which I have not touched on and which this treatment provides no clue on is the problem of why tense is an obligatory category in English. Note that the obligatoriness of tense is the only aspect of Chomsky's auxiliary formula (7) which does not follow from the refinement of Ross's analysis which I presented.   I suspect that the obligatoriness of tense must be described by an output condition, but I must leave the proof or refutation of that conjecture to another time and perhaps another linguist.

[a] See also Larkin (1969).
[b] See McCawley (1972) for arguments that a quantifier is actually a one-place predicate that is predicated of a set of propositions, in this case, the set of all propositions ' x is mortal ' for which x is a man.
[c] See Dahl (1971) for a number of reasons why this statement is an exaggeration.

---

[13] It is actually an overstatement to refer to the present tense as ' absolute ', since certain ' word-creating ' contexts (see Lakoff 1968 for more on this concept) have their own present time, e.g.

I've just seen a movie in which someone steals the crown jewels.

Note that this is one of the few contexts in which a non-habitual present tense is possible in English.

16. *Similar in that S**

Similar can be used either intransitively with a plural subject or transitively (with no restriction on the number of the subject), and can be used either with or without a constituent of the form *in that S:*

(1) Max and Fred are similar.
(2) Max is similar to Fred.
(3) Max and Fred are similar in that they both admire Lawrence Welk.
(4) Max is similar to Fred in that they both admire Lawrence Welk.

There are several restrictions on *in that S*. First, the S must express a property which counts as a " similarity ":

(5) ??Max and Fred are similar in that they both have a prime number of uncles.
(6) ??Max and Fred are similar in that they both had lunch at the Tai Sam Yon today.
(7) ??Max and Fred are similar in that they both live next door to someone who has an aunt that was once arrested in Syracuse for shoplifting.

* This note first appeared in *Linguistic Inquiry* 1. 556–9 (1970).

I conjecture that a " similarity " is a shared property which the speaker assumes will generally be accompanied by shared properties beyond the ones that trivially follow from the given one, e.g. one might expect people who admire Lawrence Welk to enjoy accordion-playing and possibly even to have voted for Eisenhower, but one would hardly expect such characteristics to be shared by persons who have a prime number of uncles.

Secondly, transitive *similar* and intransitive *similar* do not allow the same S's after *in that:*

> (8)   John is similar to Susan in that he has red hair.
> (9)   *John and Susan are similar in that he has red hair.

Subject to one exception to be noted below, the *S of X are similar in that S* must explicitly attribute the property in question to all the individuals included in the reference of the subject, either by means of a conjoined or quantified NP (e.g. (3)) or by being a conjunction of clauses each of which attributes the property to one of the individuals:

> (10)   John and Susan are similar in that
>   hé has red hair and shé has red hair tóo.
>   he has red hair and so does she.
>   he has red hair and she also has that color of hair.
>   he has red hair and her hair is also red.
>   · his hair is red and so is hers.
>   he is a redhead and her hair is red too.

Transitive *similar* allows all of the above possibilities for *in that S*, and in addition, it allows S's which mention only the individual referred to by the subject:

> (11)   John is similar to Susan in that he has red hair. (cf. (9))

With one interesting exception, transitive *similar* does not allow an *in that S* which does not mention the subject of *similar:*

> (12)   *John is similar to Susan in that she has red hair.
> (13)   John is similar to Susan in that shé has red hair tóo.

Since the embedded S of (13) presupposes that John has red hair, it appears that the attribution of the property to the subject of *similar* must be present in the embedded S either explicitly or as a presupposition associated with one of the words of the embedded S. Interestingly enough, embedded S's like that of (13) are possible even with intransitive *similar:*

> (14)   John and Susan are similar in that $\left\{ {shé \atop hé} \right\}$ has red hair tóo.

With intransitive *similar*, it does not matter which of the conjuncts in the embedded S attributes the shared property to which of the individuals denoted by the subject, whereas with transitive *similar*, the conjunct attributing the property to the subject normally precedes the conjunct attributing it to the object:

(15) John and Susan are similar in that he has red hair and she has red hair too.

(16) John and Susan are similar in that she has red hair and he has red hair too.

(17) John is similar to Susan in that he has red hair and she has red hair too.

(18) ?John is similar to Susan in that she has red hair and he has red hair too.

A fact which may have serious implications for the status of conjunction reduction is that there is no parallel difference in acceptability between the embedded S's that would presumably be derived by conjunction reduction from the same structures as underlie (17)–(18):

(19) John is similar to Susan in that he and she both have red hair.

(20) John is similar to Susan in that she and he both have red hair.

The above facts provide further support for certain details of Postal's (1970) analysis of *remind*, namely that one sense of *remind* arises from a structure containing an embedded sentence of the form " *x* is similar to *y* ", where *x* is the " subject " of *remind* and *y* the " second object " (e.g. *John reminds me of Harry* is derived from a structure which underlies *John is similar to Harry*). Specifically, *remind* allows *in that S*, and the S follows exactly the same paradigm as with transitive *similar*:

(21) John reminds me of Susan in that
        he has red hair.
        they both have red hair.
        they have the same color of hair.
        hé has red hair and shé has red hair tóo.
        *she has red hair.
        shé has red hair tóo.

In an *in that S* containing a conjoined or quantified NP referring to the individuals to whom the similarity is being attributed, the quantifier must be universal and must have as its scope the entire embedded S:

(22) Max and Fred are similar in that
        *one of them likes Lawrence Welk.
        they both don't like Lawrence Welk.
        *they don't both like Lawrence Welk.
        Sam thinks that both of them like Lawrence Welk.

Note that the last sentence allows the interpretation " for each$_i$ of them, Sam thinks that he$_i$ likes Lawrence Welk ", but not the interpretation " Sam thinks that for each$_i$ of them, he$_i$ likes Lawrence Welk", although *Sam thinks that both of them like Lawrence Welk* allows either interpretation. This fact provides support for the proposal that *no* and *none* are derived from structures of the form

" all_x (not $(f(x))$) ", since otherwise it would not be possible to reconcile the grammaticality of the sentence

(23) Those guys are similar in that none of them can stand Lawrence Welk.

with the generalization made above regarding what the S of *in that S* may be.

17.   On the Deep Structure of Negative Clauses[*]

Katz and Postal (1964) proposed the following deep structure for negative clauses:

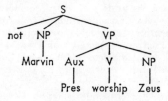

underlying *Marvin does't worship Zeus.*

Their arguments had to do with the question of whether negative clauses have the same underlying structure as positive clauses (as proposed in *Syntactic Structures;* according to that proposal, a clause *becomes* negative through a transformation which inserts a negative element into a hitherto positive clause) or whether the difference between positive and negative clauses is present at every

[*] This paper is an elaboration of a handout for a seminar which I gave at the Research Institute of Logopedics and Phoniatrics, University of Tokyo in May 1970. It was published in *Eigo Kyōiku* vol. 19, no. 6, pp. 72–5. (1970).

stage of the derivation.   Their arguments thus have to do with the presence of *not* in the deep structure, not with the specific place where they put it; and indeed, they could just as easily have put it at the end of the clause or between the NP and the VP as at the beginning or could have had it hanging from the VP node or from the Aux node or from an extra S node (above the original S node) as from the S node: on the basis of what they say, their choice of where to put *not* is completely arbitrary.

A non-arbitrary choice among these alternatives can be made by bringing in facts about pronominalization.   The most usual interpretation[1] of the following sentences (whose significance was first noted by George Lakoff):

(1)   Fred won't marry Cynthia, even though the fortune-teller predicted it.

(2)   Bert doesn't comb his hair unless you insist on it.

can be paraphrased as.

(1)   a.   Fred won't marry Cynthia, even though the fortune-teller predicted that he will marry her.

(2)   a.   Bert doesn't comb his hair unless you insist that he comb it.,

i.e. *it* refers to the positive counterpart of the negative clause.   Under the following assumptions

(i)   anaphoric pronouns arise through a transformation which turns one of two identical items into a pronoun,[2]

(ii)   the operands of a transformation are *constituents* (i.e. what is deleted or is moved or is copied or is compared with another item is a constituent, i.e. consists of a single node plus all which that node dominates),

---

[1] (1) is actually ambiguous: *it* could refer either to the positive clause (*Fred will marry Cynthia*) or to the negative clause (*Fred won't marry Cynthia*).   The reason why the first interpretation is more easy to see has to do with the presupposition involved in *even though*.   'X even though Y' involves a presupposition of (roughly) 'Y would lead one not to expect X'.   The second interpretation would thus involve the presupposition ' The fortune-teller's predicting that Fred won't marry Cynthia would lead one not to expect that Fred won't marry Cynthia ', and that presupposition would be true only under peculiar circumstances, e.g. that Fred does everything in his power to make the fortune-teller's predictions come out false.

[2] Actually, this assumption is far too strong.   In fact, only sentence-pronouns are derived from copies of their antecedents.[a]   The reason why sentence pronominalization must be treated differently from ' ordinary ' pronominalization is that only ' ordinary ' pronouns may be involved in sentences of the type discovered by Bach (1970) in which each of two pronouns refers to a noun phrase containing the other:

The boy who wanted *IT* got THE PRIZE THAT *HE* DESERVED.
*That Fred believes *IT* implies THAT MAX DENIES *IT*.

(One pronoun-antecedent pair is indicated by italicization, the other by capitalization).   This difference, which along with some other differences was first noted by George Lakoff, is explained by an analysis in which sentence-pronouns are derived from copies of their antecedents but ordinary pronouns are not, since under that analysis the starred sentence would require an infinitely deep deep structure (and hence could not be derived) whereas the other sentence would not.

(iii) the deep structure of a sentence is sufficient to determine the meaning
       of the sentence,
the only one of the above possibilities which is consistent with the observation
about (1) and (2) is that in which *not* hangs from a S-node which is higher than
the S-node which dominates the positive clause:

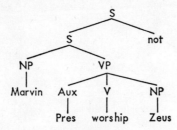

NB: later this tree will be revised further

Assumptions (i)—(iii) make it necessary that at the point in the derivation of (1)
at which the pronominalization transformation applies, the structure underlying
(1) contain two copies of a constituent having the meaning of *Fred will marry
Cynthia* (the second copy becomes *it* and the first copy causes the pronominalization of the second copy).   Of the various alternatives available, only one in which
negative clauses are derived from structures in which the negative element is
outside of the structure that would underlie a positive clause meet this last condition:

The above argument establishes one detail of the underlying structure of
negative clauses, namely their *immediate constituent structure*.   However, it says
nothing about the *labeling* nor about whether the negative element originates to
the left or to the right of the sentence with which it is combined.   I will argue
that in fact *not* is an intransitive verb and thus that its orientation relative to the
sentence that it is combined with is the same as the orientation of verbs with

respect to their subjects in general.   Under the popular assumption that English
has underlying subject-verb-object word order, this would mean that the underlying structure would be[3]

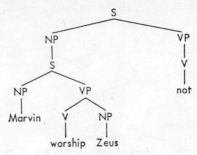

Under the alternative position that English has underlying verb-first word order,[4]
the underlying structure would be

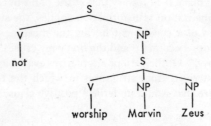

Either way, the orientation of *not* with respect to the rest of the sentence will be
non-arbitrary.

The argument that *not* is a verb depends crucially on general assumptions about
what node labels are.   *Not* is obviously not a verb morphologically, and if one
took the position that items which behave at all differently in syntax or morphology
have to have different node labels, *not* could not be given the same label as *want*
or *desire*.   It should be noted, however, that under that position *want* and *desire*
could not be given the same node label either, since they differ in the use of *for*
in their complement:

(3)   I desire for him to leave.
(4)   *I want for him to leave.
(5)   I desire him to leave. (*for many speakers, OK for others)
(6)   I want him to leave. (OK for everyone)

---

[3] I have omitted 'Aux' from this and subsequent trees.   An argument similar to that
given above can be constructed to show that tenses also originate outside of the clauses in
which they appear in surface structure; the full deep structure of the example would
involve at least one more S-node and one more verb (the tense).   Arguments that tenses
and auxiliary verbs are verbs (and hence that no such constituent as 'Aux' need be assumed) are given in Ross (1969b) and McCawley (1971a).
[4] I argue for this position in McCawley (1970a)

When the complement does not directly follow the verb, *want* and *desire* behave identically:

(7)   What I want/desire is for him to leave.
(8)   *What I want/desire is him to leave.
(9)   I want/desire very much for him to leave.
(10) *I want/desire very much him to leave.

Evidently, *want* and *desire* combine with other elements in deep structure in exactly the same way and differ only with respect to the applicability of a transformation which deletes *for* when it immediately follows the verb: if the verb is *want*, this transformation is obligatory, but if the verb is *desire*, the transformation is optional for some speakers and inapplicable for others.

The position that items which behave at all differently in syntax or morphology must have different node labels appears to be assumed in *Syntactic Structures* and Lees (1960). In particular, Lees has different node labels for items that differ only in the applicability of a transformation; for example, he has different labels for those transitive verbs which undergo deletion of an indefinite object (as in *He is eating*) and those which do not. An alternative position is to distinguish node labels from ' rule features ': things which combine into deep structures in the same way are given the same node labels, though they may have different rule features, corresponding to differences in which transformations they make obligatory or inapplicable.[5] The differences that may be expressed by rule features are not all as minor as that between *want* and *desire:* as Lakoff (1965) has pointed out, verbs and adjectives appear in the same kinds of deep structures and can be said to differ principally in the applicability of a transformation which inserts the copula *be*, which adjectives but not verbs require.[6]

If the latter position is adopted, *not* can be argued to be a verb on the grounds that it appears in the same deep structure configurations as other things which are labeled as verbs, e.g. *seem*: both *not* and *seem* combine with a sentence to yield a sentence.[7] Apparent differences between the ways in which *not* and *seem* combine with other items can be shown not to require that they be labeled dif-

---

[5] Sameness of deep combinability is a *sufficient* condition for sameness of node labeling but not a *necessary* condition: transitive and intransitive verbs will both be labeled V even though they do not combine with the same things in deep structure.

[6] This transformation exists solely because of the morphological difference between verbs and adjectives: adjectives do not allow verbal inflections, and *be* is inserted whenever verbal inflections are required and something is needed to carry them. The difference in the use of the copula in English and Japanese appears to exactly match the differences in the inflectability of adjectives: in Japanese, the copula is used with uninflected adjectives (*zyoozu da*) or when an inflected adjective requires an inflection which adjectives do not allow (in particular, politeness: *takai desu*).[b] It is especially noteworthy that only those inflections which the adjective cannot take go on the copula: *takakatta desu*, not **takai desita*. The arguments that verbs and adjectives belong to the same category are also applicable to nouns; See Bach (1968).

[7] The analysis of *seem* as an intransitive verb with sentential subject (e.g. the subject of *Edgar seems to admire Adolph* is *Edgar admires Adolph*) is due to Jespersen; it is discussed at length in *Analytic Syntax;* see also my review of *Analytic Syntax*.

ferently.   For example, both *seem* and its complement have a tense:

(11)   Arthur seems to have inherited some money last year.

contains both the present tense of *seem* and an element (*have*) which manifests
the past tense of *inherit* (note that the embedded sentence must be in the past
and not in the present perfect: *Arthur inherited some money last year* is grammatical but **Arthur has inherited some money last year* is not); but in a negative
clause, only one tense appears.   However, *not* in this respect behaves like
manage, remember to, and *get to*, whose complements have the same time reference
as does the main clause and which exhibit only one tense:[8]

(12)   Harry has finally managed to finish his thesis.
(13)   I didn't remember to take out the garbage.
(14)   Yesterday Sam got to fly in the same plane as the Under-secretary
       of Commerce.

There are many languages (e.g. Finnish) in which the negative element is
morphologically a verb: it is inflected for tense and for agreement with its surface
subject.   English differs from Finnish in having rules which insert a semantically empty verb (the *do* of *I don't have any money*) or puts *not* after a verb which
at earlier stages of the derivation it precedes (*I haven't bombed the White House
yet*), thus avoiding structures in which *not* would have to be inflected.   The
analysis proposed here identifies the difference between Finnish and English as
a difference in morphology plus the transformations needed to avoid combinations
which the morphology of the language does not allow.   Under an alternative in
which *not* is not treated as a verb, there would be no stage of a derivation at
which English sentences would exactly parallel the corresponding Finnish
sentences.

Treatments of negation as in Katz-Postal require a phrase-structure rule such
as

(15)   S → (not) NP VP

which explicitly mentions *not*. (15) allows only one negative element per clause,
whereas the treatment advocated above places no limit on the number of negative
elements: there is nothing to prevent *not* from having as subject a sentence whose
verb is *not* and whose subject is a sentence whose verb is *not*, etc. At first glance,
this seems to argue in favor of the Katz-Postal treatment, since sentences with
multiple negatives are ungrammatical in most cases:

(16)   *I didn't not not not talk to him.

However, not all sentences with multiple negatives are not grammatical, as is
illustrated by the last clause and by the following example:

(17)   No one didn't say anything.,

and neither proposal is by itself sufficient to distinguish the grammatical instances

[8] These verbs are discussed in Karttunen (1971b).

of multiple negation from the ungrammatical ones.   Actually, no proposal for deep structures can be sufficient to distinguish between grammatical and ungrammatical multiple negation, since the grammaticality of the sentence depends not on the way that negatives are combined in deep structure but on the way in which they are combined in surface struture:

(18)   Nobody wasn't given anything. (*nobody=not+anybody*)
(19)   ?They didn't give anybody nothing.
(20)   *They didn't give nothing to anybody.

Evidently, the negations in (18)—(20) are combined in exactly the same way in deep structure and the difference in grammaticality between them corresponds to differences which arise in later stages of the derivation.   Thus, an output constraint[9] is apparently necessary to describe the differences in grammaticality between various sentences with multiple negatives.   Since this constraint will be sufficient to exclude sentences such as (16), there is no need for a restriction on the number of negatives per clause to be built into a phrase structure rule as in (15).   A rule such as (15), which only allows negatives in a specific position in deep structure, is inadequate not only on the grounds of not allowing enough negatives but also on the grounds of not allowing enough ways of combining a negative with other elements.   There are sentences such as the following, which differ semantically as regards whether a negation is ' inside or outside the scope ' of another element and which thus make it necessary for deep structures to differ as to whether the negative or the other element (adverb or auxiliary verb: both will be verbs in deep structure) is ' higher ':

(21)   a.   I often don't answer my mail.
       b.   I don't often answer my mail.
(22)   a.   Have you never kissed a girl?
       b.   Have you ever not kissed a girl?

---

[a] In correcting one error, I have erred in the opposite direction.   Karttunen (1969, 1971a) has presented excellent arguments that there is a pronominalization transformation which applies to ' definite descriptions ', e.g. that *her* in

The man who loves his wife kissed her.

must be derived from a copy of *his wife* (see note *l* of ' Where do noun phrases come from? '). Further evidence for Karttunen's conclusion comes from a consideration of the sentence.

In 1963, Walter Winchell predicted that the winner of the 1964 election would be arrested for drunk driving, and Jimmy the Greek predicted that he would open a barbershop in Scranton, Pa.

The first conjunct may be interpreted either *de dicto* (i.e. *the winner of the 1964 election* is part of what is ascribed to Winchell, and the ascription is correct if Winchell said some-

---

[9] Extensive discussion of the notion of ' output constraint ' is given in Perlmutter (1970). The details of the constraint on multiple negatives are not yet clear.   There is considerable variation among speakers as to which combinations of negatives are grammatical.

thing like ' Whoever gets elected next year will get busted for driving while enebriated ')
or *de re* (i.e. *the winner of the 1964 election* is the speaker's description of a specific person
who figured in Winchell's alleged prediction, and Winchell is being quoted correctly if his
actual statement was e.g. ' The fuzz will pinch Lyndon Johnson for driving his car completely plastered ').   Since the *he* of the second clause may also be interpreted either *de
dicto* or *de re* (depending on which the first clause was), then the proposals of ' Where do
noun phrases come from? ' imply that whatever underlies *the winner of the 1964 election*
may originate either inside the complement of both tokens of *predict* or outside the complement of both tokens of *predict*.   But if that material originates inside the complement
of both tokens of *predict*, then that material must occur twice in the semantic structure of
the *de dicto* interpretation.   But that means that one of those two tokens of whatever
underlies *the winner of the 1964 election* must be eliminated by a transformation, i.e. the
de dicto interpretation of the above example involves a pronominalization transformation.
b The significance of what I am saying here is significantly weakened by the fact that it
took an act of the Ministry of Education to impose the form *takai desu* on millions of
Japanese who didn't grow up speaking that way.

18. A Program for Logic[*]

1. Constituent Structure in Linguistics and Logic

Chomsky's *Aspects* (1965) described and presented justification for a model of linguistic structure according to which the relation between sentences (or better, the surface structures of sentences) and their semantic structures was mediated by a level of DEEP STRUCTURE: a grammar consisted of a BASE COMPONENT, which was a set of rules that specified what deep structures were possible in the language in question, a TRANSFORMATIONAL COMPONENT, which was a system of rules that specified how deep structures corresponded to surface structures,[1] and a SEMANT-

* A preliminary version of this paper was given at a conference on logic and natural language at the Center for Advanced Studies in the Behavioral Sciences, Palo Alto, Calif., August 1969.   My chief reason for calling it 'A program for logic' is that Peter Geach's contribution to the same conference was entitled 'A program for syntax'.   It appeared first in Donald Davidson and Gilbert H. Harman (editors), *The semantics of natural language* (Dordrecht: Reidel), 1972.
[1] Things are somewhat more complicated than this makes them sound, in that it is possible for a deep structure to be perfectly well-formed but for there to be no way in which the transformations could associate a surface structure with it, as in the case of a deep structure for a question that would ask for the x such that ' You were talking to Susan and x'.   The sentence that one might expect to correspond to that deep structure, namely *Who(m) were you talking to Susan and?*, is not grammatical, its ungrammaticality following

IC COMPONENT, which was a system of rules that associated a set of semantic representations to each deep structure. Since the appearance of *Aspects*, there have been two opposing lines of development in transformational grammar, the principal differences between which relate to the syntax/semantics dichotomy which the theory of *Aspects* presupposes. In the remainder of this paper, I will ignore the line of development represented by the recent works of Chomsky and Jackendoff (see e.g. Chomsky 1970), which upholds the dichotomy between syntax and semantics, and will concentrate on the other line of development, represented by the recent works of Ross, Lakoff, Postal, and myself, which rejects any dividing line between syntax and semantics (such as the level of ' deep structure ' had constituted) or any distinction between ' transformations ' and ' rules of semantic interpretation '.

My chief reason for pursuing a conception of grammar in which there is no dividing line between syntax and semantics is that in all significant respects in which putative deep structures proposed within the framework of *Aspects* have differed from semantic structure, they have been shown to be wrong. I will illustrate this sweeping conclusion with an example that I consider fairly typical. Katz and Postal (1964) proposed that negative clauses have a deep structure as in Fig. 1, in which the negative clause is composed of three constituents: the negative element and the two elements (a noun-phrase and a verb-phrase) of which the corresponding positive clause would be composed. I will argue below that negative clauses have a different constituent structure, namely that of the negative element plus a sentence (rather than plus the pieces of a sentence), as in Fig. 2. The deep structure given in Fig. 1 can be shown wrong and that in

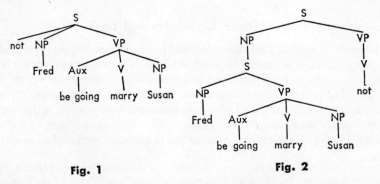

Fig. 1   **Fig. 2**

Fig. 2 right (at least, right in the respect in which it differs from Fig. 1) by the following argument. It is possible for the pronoun *it* to have a clause for its antecedent, as in

from the general principle (Ross 1967a) that transformations may not move material out of a coordinate structure. In the example in question, the transformation which moves interrogative elements to the beginning of the clause would have to move the *who(m)* of the coordinate structure *Susan and who(m)* to the beginning of the clause (since it is an obligatory transformation) but is not allowed to do so (since otherwise Ross's constraint would be violated), and hence no surface structure at all results.

(1) Max told me that Eleanor had eloped with Schwartz, but I refused to believe it.

Lakoff in unpublished work has demonstrated that this type of *it* (though not all uses of personal pronouns) must be derived from a copy of its antecedent by a transformation which applies to a structure containing two identical embedded sentences and replaces one of them by *it*. Consider now the sentence

(2) Fred isn't going to marry Susan, even though the fortune-teller predicted it.

The *it* would generally be taken as standing for *Fred is going to marry Susan*,[2] which means that in the derivation of (2), the pronominalization transformation must apply to a structure containing two copies of whatever underlies *Fred is going to marry Susan*. Under the proposal of Fig. 2, (2) would have a deep structure containing two copies of such an embedded sentence, but under the proposal of Fig. 1 it would not. Thus, the proposal of Fig. 2 allows the pronominalization transformation that figures in (1) to apply in the derivation of (2) in such a way as to correctly associate it with its semantic structure, whereas the proposal of Fig. 1 does not allow any known formulation of pronominalization which would give a uniform treatment of the occurrence and interpretation of *it* in (1) and (2). This treatment of negation makes the further prediction that a negative clause makes its positive counterpart available to be the antecedent of *it* but a positive clause does not make its negative counterpart available to be the antecedent of *it*. This prediction seems to be borne out by the facts: the *it* of

(3) Fred is going to marry Susan, even though the fortune-teller predicted it.

cannot refer to the proposition that Fred isn't going to marry Susan (unless, of course, that proposition has been mentioned earlier in the discourse; in that case, it is the earlier mention and not the first clause of (3) that provides the antecedent of *it*).

The above argument[3] relies heavily on the notion of CONSTITUENT STRUCTURE, which is indicated in the various diagrams by lines.[4] The reasons for taking syntactic representations to be TREES rather than STRINGS are first, that the transformations that associate underlying and surface structures function in terms of units (which can in principle be of arbitrarily great internal structure) such as are

[2] It could be taken as standing for *Fred isn't going to marry Susan* under conditions which would make that interpretation consistent with the use of *even though* e.g. if one believed that Fred did everything in his power to falsify the fortune-teller's predictions.
[3] I have only provided an argument for that one detail of Fig. 2. Later I will provide some reason for labeling *not* as V. Two details of Fig. 2 which I would argue are wrong are the place of *be going to* (which I maintain is, like *not*, the 'main verb' of a higher clause; see Ross 1969b and McCawley 1971a) and the order of the elements of the clauses (the facts of English, combined with some considerations of universal grammar, demand an underlying order in which every V comes first in its clause; see McCawley 1970a, part of the argument of which is summarized in sec. 4 below).
[4] On the notion of tree and its relation to syntax, see McCawley (1968g).

represented by the non-terminal nodes in such structures; for example, the transformation of EXTRAPOSITION optionally moves an embedded sentence to the end of its clause, as illustrated by the following pairs of sentences (in the first sentence of each pair, extraposition has not applied; in the second, it has):

(4) a. That Harry was arrested shocks me.
    b. It shocks me that Harry was arrested.
(5) a. Why Max hit me is not known.
    b. It is not known why Max hit me.

Secondly, different groupings of the same elements are not equivalent (as e.g. Ajdukiewicz took them to be); a transformation may have the effect of changing the grouping of elements, but once it has been changed, it stays changed in subsequent stages of the derivation of the sentence. For example, there is a transformation in English which combines an ' auxiliary verb ' with an adjacent tense element, thus converting the tree of Fig. 3a into that of Fig. 3b.[5]

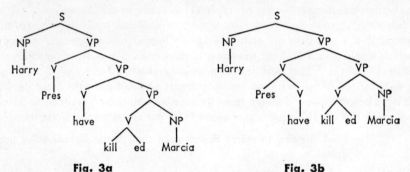

Fig. 3a   Fig. 3b

All subsequent transformations treat Pres+*have* as a unit but do not treat *have* (tenseless)+*kill*+*ed*+*Marcia* as a unit: note the results of the transformations which position the negative element, give rise to question word order, and delete certain repeated items:

(6) a. John hasn't killed Marcia. (*John doesn't have killed Marcia)
    b. Has John killed Marcia? (*Does John have killed Marcia?)
    c. John has killed his wife, and so has Bill. (*...and so does Bill).

The asterisked examples are what would result if these transformations treated *have* as grouped together with *killed Marcia* rather than as grouped together with the present tense element. I maintain that not only syntactic structure but also semantic structure involves the grouping of elements rather than just their linear sequence. In particular, to the extent that ' semantic structure ' will coincide with what has been called ' logical form ', it will have to specify the grouping of elements in order that it be possible to formulate rules of inference

[5] The tree of Fig. 3a is a fairly late stage in the derivation of the sentence *Harry has killed Marcia;* for details of the derivation, see McCawley (1971a).

that work right.   For example, take the following familiar rules of inference:

(7)   a. $p \lor q$ ('$\lor$' is 'inclusive' *or*)

$\quad\quad\quad \dfrac{-p}{q}$ ('$-$' is negation)

$\quad$ b. $\dfrac{p \cdot q}{p}$ ('$\cdot$' is *and*)

If one uses these rules of inference in connection with formulas written according to the usual 'conventions for leaving out parentheses', he cannot simply substitute any string of symbols for p or q and get a valid inference; for example,

(8)   a. $p \lor q \lor r$ $\quad\quad$ $p \cdot q \lor r$

$\quad\quad \dfrac{-p \lor q}{r}$ $\quad\quad\quad\quad \dfrac{}{p}$

are not valid inferences.   The purpose of this example is to show that the grouping of symbols which according to the 'conventions for leaving out parentheses' need not be indicated explicitly continues to function in any use that one makes of the formulas in question: the various rules of inference make reference not just to a string of symbols that has a $-$ or a $\lor$ or a . in the middle but to the negation or the *or*-conjunction or the *and*-conjunction[6] of certain sentences, which is to say that they make reference to the constituent structure of the sentences that they are applied to.   This, incidentally, demonstrates the point which I assumed above, that semantically a negative clause is composed of the negative element plus the sentence that it negates rather than of the negative element plus the pieces that make up that sentence.   In addition, the so-called 'Polish parentheses-free notation', which is often said to eliminate even the restricted use of parentheses which the above-mentioned 'conventions for leaving out parentheses' cannot eliminate, is actually unable to do without some explicit indication of constituent structure if conjunctions of more than two items are allowed, e.g. the formula

(9)   And Or p q r s

would give no clue as to whether the r is bound by the *And* (i.e. And (Or p q) r s)) or by the *Or* (i.c. And (Or p q r) s)).   I will argue later that the proposal that all multi-termed conjunctions be treated as iterated two-term conjunctions is misguided and that in order to allow one to state rules of inference in their fullest generality and to be able to provide the input necessary for the correct application of syntactic rules, a system of semantic representation must involve conjunctions of arbitrarily many terms.   I accordingly conclude that no adequate system of semantic representation can be 'parentheses-free' and will

---

[6] I will use 'conjunction' in accordance with the traditions of grammar rather than of logic and will thus use it to take in what logicians have called 'conjunction' and 'disjunction', which I will refer to as *and*-conjunction and *or*-conjunction respectively.

henceforth assume that the syntactic and semantic structures that I will refer to are trees rather than strings; I will occasionally write proposed semantic structures in linear form, but these strings of symbols are to be taken as merely informal abbreviations for trees.

2. Some Background Material in Syntactic Theory

In this section, I will assume that every sentence[7] has a semantic structure and a surface syntactic structure, both of which are LABELED TREES. (i.e. they specify the grouping of units into larger units and the category membership of those units). I will examine reflexive pronouns in English and on the basis of their behavior draw some conclusions about how semantic structure must be related to surface structure.

Since there are cases in which a sentence with a reflexive pronoun can be paraphrased by a sentence containing something non-reflexive in place of it, e.g.

(10) a. Max_i believes $himself_i$ to be a werewolf.
b. Max_i believes that he_i is a werewolf.[8],

I will assume that the difference between reflexive pronouns and non-reflexive items is not present in semantic structure and thus that a grammar of a language must have rules that relate surface structures with reflexive pronouns to more abstract structures that do not contain reflexive pronouns. Under the assumption that (10a) and (10b) have the same semantic structure, it is clear that semantic structure is not sufficient to determine whether a given item is realized as a reflexive pronoun, since if one interchanges reflexive and ordinary pronouns in (10a-b), the results are ungrammatical:

(11) a.   *Max_i believes that $himself_i$ is a werewolf.
b.   *Max_i believes him_i to be a werewolf.

Evidently, the possibility of using a reflexive depends on whether one avails himself of the option provided by English grammar of moving the subject of certain subordinate clauses into the main clause (Fig. 4), giving such variants as

(12) a.   Max believes that Harry is a werewolf.
b.   Mas believes Harry to be a werewolf.

These examples suggest that the rule for using reflexive pronouns is that (as proposed in Lees and Klima 1963) a reflexive is used in place of one of two coreferential NP's if they are in the same clause. I have already shown that the condition ' in the same clause ' does not refer to the clauses of semantic structure.

[7] It will develop that I should be talking about sentence tokens rather than sentence types. A ' semantic structure ' will thus specify not the ' meaning ' of a sentence but the 'content' of a token of a sentence, e.g. *It's raining* will have different ' content ' depending on when and where it is said.
[8] I will use paired subscripts to indicate presupposed coreferentiality. The fact that (10b) and other examples also allow an interpretation in which the indicated coreferentiality relations do not hold is of no relevance to the arguments presented here.

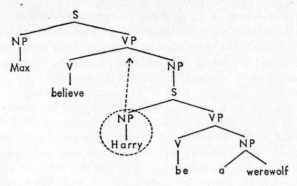

Fig. 4

It likewise does not refer to the clauses of surface structure.   To see this, note first that infinitive expressions act like separate clauses in not generally allowing reflexives whose antecedent is outside the expression:

(13) a.   *$Harry_i$ forced Susan to kiss $himself_i$.
      b.   *$Harry_i$ wants Susan to kiss $himself_i$.
      c.   *Fred promised $Margaret_i$ to kiss $herself_i$.
      d.   *Cynthia seems to me_i to like $myself_i$.
      e.   *$Agnes_i$ believes John to have insulted $herself_i$.

However, there are also sentences in which a reflexive in an infinitive expression does have its antecedent outside that expression:

(14) a.   Harry forced $Susan_i$ to denounce $herself_i$.
      b. $Harry_i$ wants to kill $himself_i$.
      c. $Fred_i$ promised Margaret to wash $himself_i$.
      d. $Cynthia_i$ seems to me to admire $herself_i$.
      e.   Agnes believes $John_i$ to have shot $himself_i$.

The sentences which allow reflexives have either had a NP which is coreferential

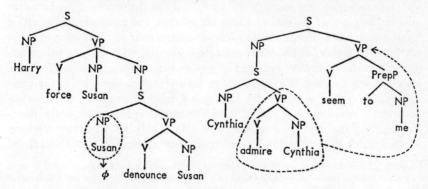

Fig. 5

with the reflexive deleted (a, b, c) or been subjected to a transformation that moves either the reflexive or its antecedent into a higher clause (d, e), as illustrated in Fig. 5.   While (13a-c) have likewise undergone the deletion of a NP and (13d-e) a movement of material into the main clause, the difference is that in (14a-e) the reflexive and its antecedent were in the same clause prior to the application of that transformation, such is not the case with (13a-e).   These facts indicate that the rule for using reflexives has to do with the structure of these sentences prior to the deletion or movement in question.   The rule cannot simply be based on the surface structure of the sentences, since the ungrammatical (13c) and the grammatical (14a) have exactly same surface structure except for the choice of nouns and verbs.   The fact that *force* and *promise* show different patterns in the use of reflexives is the result of their having different conditions for the deletion of the subject of the embedded sentence: the subject of the embedded sentence is deleted if it is coreferential with the indirect object of *force* or if it is coreferential with the subject of *promise*.   Thus, the conditions for using reflexives have to do with something intermediate between semantic structure and surface structure.   The conception of grammar which I will assume in what follows is one in which the rules relating semantic structure to surface structure (henceforth called *transformations*) virtually all have to do with intermediate stages between semantic structure and surface structure.   Using the term DERIVATION to refer to a sequence of trees that lead from semantic structure to surface structure, each transformation may be thought of as a specification of how a certain stage of a derivation may ('optional transformation') or must ('obligatory transformation') differ from the next stage.[9]

The discussion of exx. (10)–(14) has touched on an important aspect of the way in which transformations interact with each other.   I have shown that in the derivation of (10a), raising must apply before reflexivization, and that in the derivation of (14e), reflexivization must apply before raising.   This, however, does not mean that there is no restriction on the order in which reflexivization and raising apply: when two transformations are such that one applies earlier in some derivations and the other applies earlier in other derivations (as is the case with reflexivization and raising), the two classes of derivations differ as to the relative 'heights' of the clauses which are affected, and an application of either transformation to a 'lower' clause takes precedence over an application of either of them to a 'higher' clause.   For example, in the derivation of (14e), reflexivization affects the subordinate clause and applies before raising, which affects the main clause.   In cases like (10a), where both transformations affect the same clause, they apply in a fixed order, in this case, raising first and then reflexivization.   Such considerations lead to the proposal that at least some of the transformations of the language form what Chomsky (1965) called a CYCLE: a system of rules which have a fixed order governing their application to any one clause

---

[9] Lakoff (1970b) has adduced several examples where, unlike the cases discussed here, a rule must mention non-consecutive stages of a derivation, e.g. cases where two consecutive stages are allowed to differ in some way only if certain conditions are met at some third stage of a derivation.

and such that the application of any of them to a 'lower' clause precedes the application of any of them to a 'higher' clause. A demonstration that not all transformations of English belong to a cycle is given in Ross (1967a) and is reported in slightly revised form in McCawley (1970a). The conception of a grammar which Ross arrived at (and which I assume here) is that the transformations form two systems: a cycle, whose rules interact in the manner just described, and a system of post-cyclic transformations, which interact in a somewhat simpler manner: they have a fixed order, and all applications of each of them precede all applications of the next one. While little of the material to follow will be incomprehensible without an understanding of this conception of how transformations are ordered, there will be a couple of places where I have occasion to mention the notion of cycle.

3. On the Notion 'Generalization'

My sweeping statement that in all respects where deep structures proposed within the framework of *Aspects* have differed from semantic structure they can be shown to be wrong crucially depends on a notion that is worth devoting some time to, namely that of ' (linguistically) significant/valid generalization '. Many of the arguments against putative deep structures are based on demonstrations that they make it impossible to give a single rule which covers all cases where a phenomenon occurs and that they thus ' miss the generalization '. As an example,[10] compare two analyses of imperative sentences such as

(15)   Shut the door.

In the one analysis, the sentence is treated as having an underlying subject *you*, which is deleted by a transformation.[11] Under such an analysis, the reflexive pronoun in

(16)   Wash yourself.

and the deletion of the subject in the embedded clause of

(17)   Promise Harry to wash yourself.

arise by the same rules that create reflexives and delete embedded subjects in declarative sentences. Under the second analysis, which no one to my knowledge has seriously proposed, imperatives have no underlying subject, a reflexive pronoun is introduced in place of a noun phrase which either is coreferential to an earlier NP in the same clause or is second person and in the main clause of an imperative sentence, and the subject of the sentential complement of

---

[10] The treatment of ' generalization ' which I present here is largely due to David M. Perlmutter.

[11] Since the semantic structure of an imperative will presumably have to indicate that it is an order or request to the person it is addressed to to do the action in question, the approach taken here lets one avoid having a special rule to delete *you* and to subsume that deletion under the general principle of deletion which was alluded to in the discussion of (14a).

promise is deleted when it is coreferential with the subject of *promise* or when it is second person and *promise* is the main verb of an imperative.   The fault with the second proposal is that it treats the reflexivization and deletion in (16–17) as if they had nothing to do with coreferentiality, as if it were purely accidental that in imperatives reflexivization of NP's in the main clause and deletion of the subject of the complement of *promise* affect second person items rather than, say, first person plurals or expressions denoting baseball players or expressions denoting an even number of objects.   According to the first proposal, (16–17) illustrate the interaction of several extremely general rules of grammar; according to proposal two, (16–17) illustrate rules specific to imperatives which only by coincidence have an effect similar to that of some much more general rules of English.

A more topical example of an argument that one analysis captures a generalization which another misses is the argument which rejects the deep structures proposed in *Aspects* for NP's (according to which a NP such as *every philosopher* or *many Armenians* is present as such in deep structure) in favor of an alternative in which, as in most modern proposals for 'logical structure', quantifiers are outside of the clauses that they appear in in surface structure, and, since *every philosopher* and *many Armenians* are constituents in surface structure and indeed can be shown to be NP's, there is a transformation of QUANTIFIER LOWERING, which attaches the quantifier to one of the NP's which is indexed by the variable that it binds.

The proposal of an external source for quantifiers makes it possible for exactly the same rule that introduces reflexives into quantifier-free sentences to account for where reflexives occur or do not occur in sentences with quantifiers, e.g. Geach's celebrated examples

    (18)   a.   Every philosopher contradicts himself.
             b.   Every philosopher contradicts every philosopher.

and likewise for exactly the same rule which deletes the subject of an embedded sentence in a quantifier-free structure to account for where deletion takes place or does not in sentences containing quantifiers, e.g.

    (19)   a.   Every American wants to be rich.
             b.   Every American wants every American to be rich.

It makes no sense to treat (18b) as differing from (18a) in having a deep structure with non-coreferential tokens of *every philosopher* where (18a) has coreferential tokens of *every philosopher*, in the way that transformational grammarians have often treated

    (20)   a.   Harry kicked himself.
             b.   Harry kicked Harry.

as differing through (20b) having a deep structure with two non-coreferential

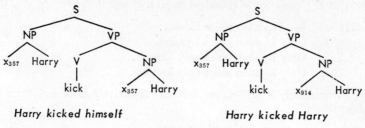

Harry kicked himself   Harry kicked Harry

Fig. 6

tokens of *Harry* where (20a) has coreferential tokens of *Harry*, as in Fig. 6.[12] Since the two surface tokens of *every philosopher* in (18b) refer to the same set of philosophers (to the extent that it makes sense to speak of them referring at all), it is nonsense to speak of them as non-coreferential. Thus, the types of deep structure proposed in *Aspects* give no clue as to how one could assign different deep structures to (18a-b) nor how one could formulate a rule of reflexivization that would apply in the derivation of (18a) but not that of (18b). The proposal that quantifiers originate outside of the clauses that they are manifested in has no such difficulties: taking Fig. 7a-b as a first approximation to the deep struc-

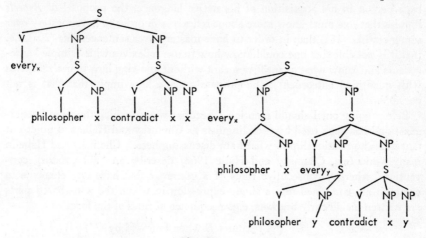

Fig. 7

tures of (18a-b) (they will be modified considerably in sec. 5), the derivations yield exactly the correct outputs, without any revision of the reflexivization rule being necessary, under the assumptions (which are well supported) that reflexivization and quantifier lowering are in the cycle. In McCawley (1970f),

[12] While Chomsky proposed the use of referential indices in *Aspects*, neither there nor anywhere else has he ever drawn a tree that exhibited them explicitly. Thus, Fig. 6 is drawn in accordance with what Chomsky said in *Aspects* about indices but is not modeled after any diagrams that appear there.

I show that the presence of reflexives in (21a, c) and their absence in (21b, d):

(21)   a.   Only Lyndon pities himself.
       b.   Only Lyndon pities Lyndon.
       c.   Only Lyndon pities only himself.
       d.   Only Lyndon pities only Lyndon.

follows automatically if (21a-d) are derived respectively from structures along the lines of[13]

(22)   a. $Only_x$ (Lyndon, Pity (x, x))
       b. $Only_x$ (Lyndon, Pity $(x,$ Lyndon))
       c. $Only_x$ (Lyndon, $Only_y$ $(x,$ Pity (x, y)))
       d. $Only_x$ (Lyndon, $Only_y$ (Lyndon, Pity (x, y)))

and reflexivization and the rule which combines ' Only ' with the corresponding NP (I suspect that that rule can be taken in in a generalized formulation of quantifier lowering) are both in the cycle, with the ' Only '-rule ordered before reflexivization.

It should be emphasized here that the arguments under discussion are concerned not merely with considerations of ' elegance ' but have in principle empirical consequences: if some analogue to the rules of a grammar is learned by a person in his acquisition of his native language, the proposal of *Aspects* implies that one must know more about reflexives in order to have mastery over sentences like (18a) than in order to have mastery over sentences like (20a), i.e. that it is possible that one could know how to use reflexives with ' simple ' antecedents and know what quantifiers meant without knowing how to use reflexives with quantified antecedents; the proposals made here imply that that is not possible.

Before going on, I should mention a peculiar way in which the term ' generalization ' has been used by such linguists as Chomsky and Halle and point out that it has no relationship to what I am discussing here.   Chomsky and Halle in many works (e.g. Chomsky and Halle 1968) describe an ' abbreviatory convention ' whereby consecutive rules of a grammar that have any elements in common are combined into a single expression in which the non-shared parts are written inside curly brackets, e.g. a sequence of rules of the form

$$A \rightarrow B \mid \underline{\hspace{1cm}} C \quad (`A \text{ becomes } B \text{ when followed by } C ')$$
$$A \rightarrow D \mid \underline{\hspace{1cm}} E$$

is abbreviated to

$$A \rightarrow \begin{Bmatrix} B \mid \underline{\hspace{1cm}} C \\ D \mid \underline{\hspace{1cm}} E \end{Bmatrix}$$

While they speak of this notation as ' expressing a generalization ', I can see no

---

[13] I do not mean in (22a-d) to suggest that ' Only ' is semantically primitive. Whether it is derived from a combination of semantically more primitive elements or not has no effect on reflexivization.

justification for that locution.   Indeed, curly brackets are applicable only in
cases where I would normally speak of 'missing a generalization', e.g. the
analysis of sentences like (16–17) which I ridiculed above, whose rules for introducing the reflexive element -*self* could be combined by curly brackets into the
expression

$$\text{Attach } \textit{self} \; / \begin{Bmatrix} \text{NP}_i \; \text{X} \; \text{NP}_i \\ \#\text{V} \; \text{X} \; \text{NP}_{2\text{pers}} \end{Bmatrix} \underline{\quad\quad}$$

Curly brackets would be equally applicable in the absurd case suggested above,
in which reflexivization affected not NP's which are second person but NP's which
denote baseball players.   Curly brackets have been described accurately by
Lakoff as 'a formal device for expressing the claim that no generalization exists'.
I will henceforth ignore curly brackets on the grounds that all rules in which
they have been employed either are sequences of unrelated rules which purely
by accident have parts in common or are simply wrong.

4.   On the Non-Equivalence of Some 'Notational Variants'

I have already mentioned several cases in which linguistic facts argue for
a 'deep structure' which in the respect at issue agrees with what can be demonstrated on the basis of logical considerations to be the 'logical structure' of the
sentence.   There are, however, many cases where there are alternative proposals
for logical structure which no facts of logic allow one to choose between.   For
example, as far as logic is concerned, it is a matter of taste or of convenience
with regard to ulterior (e.g. mathematical) motives whether one uses 'Polish'
notation, in which predicates precede their arguments and 'operators' precede
that which they combine, or 'Italian' notation (to coin a much needed term,
whose choice is based on the proportion Łukasiewicz: predicates first :: Peano:
predicates second) in which a predicate appears after its first argument[14] and
'connectives' such as *and*, *or*, and *if-then* (but generally not quantifiers) are
written between the things that they connect.

While the choice between such alternatives may be purely arbitrary when
viewed purely from a logician's point of view, it often ceases to be so if one takes
'logical structure' to be not merely the input to logical rules of inference but
also the input to a system of syntactic transformations which relate the content
of a sentence to its surface syntactic structure in a given language.   Different
proposals for 'deep structure' have different implications as to what system
of transformations is needed to relate them to the corresponding surface structures, and facts about surface structures in a language in combination with
universal principles concerning what transformations are possible in a language
and how they may be organized often allow one to reject a proposal for 'deep

[14] This statement suggests more uniformity than actually exists.   Many logicians who
write a 2-place predicate between its argument write a 1-place predicate before its argument, and there is no consistent 'Italian' tradition for predicates of more than 2 places.

structure' on the grounds that it conflicts with otherwise valid universals about transformations. In particular, there is an argument of this type (McCawley 1970a) that English requires deep structures with the verb at the beginning of the clause rather than the verb-second order that appears in all prior transformational literature on English except only for the work of Fillmore. If in fact ' deep structure ' can be identified with semantic structure and if the argument just alluded to is valid, then an adequate semantic representation (at least for English) has the form of ' Polish ' rather than ' Italian ' notation. Before sketching an argument for underlying verb-first order in English, two points should be made. First, my reference to universal principles about transformations presupposes that one of the goals of linguistics is to provide as tight as possible a characterization of what a ' possible grammar ' is. Rather than allowing a transformation to be any mapping at all of trees onto trees, one must exclude from the class of possible transformations all types of transformations which cannot be shown to be demanded by the facts (rather than just consistent with the facts) of some language: the fact that a system of transformations correctly associates semantic structures to surface structures in a given language does not justify calling the transformations it contains ' possible transformations '. One of the arguments for underlying verb-first order in English is based on the fact that while it is possible to formulate transformations that correctly associate semantic structures to surface structures regardless of whether semantic structures have verb-first or verb-second order (obviously, if there is a system of transformations that correctly associates semantic structures of the one kind to surface structures, there is also a system of transformations that would do the same for semantic structures of the other kind, namely a system of transformations consisting of the first system of transformations preceded by a transformation that moves the verb from first to second position or vice versa), the proposal of verb first order allows much tighter constraints to be imposed on the class of ' possible transformations ' than does the proposal of verb second order. Secondly, it is an open question whether considerations of the syntax of other languages would lead one to make the same choice between ' equivalent ' systems of semantic representation as do considerations of English syntax. For example, I know of nothing in Japanese syntax that would give any reason for setting up any order of constituents other than that with the verb at the end of the clause. Indeed, in McCawley (1970a), I stated that there appear to be two distinct underlying word-order types, namely verb first and verb last. An alternative worth considering is that there really is a common semantic structure for all languages, namely one in which the verb is unspecified as to its left-right orientation with respect to its arguments, and that languages differ as regards rules for imposing an order on partially unordered structures. However, to date no facts about English or Japanese have been adduced which provide any evidence for an underlying structure in which the verb is unspecified as to orientation with respect to its arguments, nor against such structures. The argument which is to follow is really an argument that if semantic structures are oriented trees, English must have underlying verb-first order.

If English has verb-first order in semantic structure, there will have to be a transformation which changes that order into the surface verb-second order, or at least, that does so in those clauses which have verb-second order: the proposal of underlying verb-first order allows one to say that the verb-first order of yes-no questions comes about through the non-application of the transformation just mentioned rather than through the application of a rule that changes NP-V-X into V-NP-X. If there is a transformation which changes verb-first order into verb-second order, then the transformations which apply before it apply to structures having verb before subject and those which apply after it apply to structures having subject before verb (except in the questions, etc. to which the rule does not apply). The hypothesis of underlying verb-first order can thus be confirmed or disconfirmed by determining which transformations are significantly different if they apply to structures with verb first rather than verb second (there are, of course, many transformations for which either the position of the verb is totally irrelevant, e.g. extraposition and reflexivization, or involves only a trivial difference in the formulation of the transformation, e.g. quantifier lowering—if, as I argue below, quantifiers should be assigned to the category V (='predicate'), then quantifier lowering will move the quantifier to the right if its input has verb first but to the left if it has verb second) and determining whether the transformations which are significantly 'simpler' if they apply to verb first structures must apply before all the transformations which are singificantly 'simpler' if they apply to verb second structures. This in fact turns out to be the case. The transformation which forms passive clauses moves only one NP if it applies to verb first structures but moves two NP's if it applies to verb second structures; the transformation which inserts the *there* of existential clauses need only insert the *there* if it applies to verb first structures but must in addition move the subject from before the verb to after the verb if it applies to verb second structures; three transformations which move material out of a subordinate clause (the 'raising' transformation illustrated by example (12b) and two others that have not been discussed here) move it to the left regardless of the role that the subordinate clause plays in the main clause if they apply to inputs with verb first order but with verb second order they must move material to the left when the subordinate clause is the object and to the right when it is the subject of the main clause. These transformations precede the few transformations which are at all 'simpler' if they apply to verb second structures, e.g. PARTICLE SEPARATION, which (usually optionally) moves the 'particle' of a composite verb such as *look up* and *kick out* after its object, as in[a]

(23)   He looked the price up.
(24)   They kicked the beggar out.

The 'simplicity' to which I alluded above is of greater significance than just the formulation of the rules in question, since the versions of these rules which apply to verb second structures happen to be the best examples of certain rule types (e.g. transformations which perform more than one 'elementary operation and transformations which have a non-uniform effect on the things that they apply to) which now can probably be done away with entirely. Thus, if English (and, presumably, all other languages with surface verb second order) is analyzed as having underlying verb first order, the notion ' possible transformation ' can be much more tightly constrained than would otherwise be the case.[b]

5. Conjoining and Quantification

It may seem strange to call the argument presented in the last section an argument that English requires ' Polish ' and not ' Italian ' semantic representations, since the argument said nothing about ' logical operators ' such as negation, quantifiers, and ' connectives ', which are what all of the fuss about Polish notation has been about. I in fact maintain that these are all V's (predicates) and that the above argument in fact covers their orientation as well as that of things that it is less unsettling to hear called predicates. I take the position that things must be assigned to the same category unless one is forced to do otherwise and that (as pointed out by Lakoff 1965; see also Bach 1968) most traditional category distinctions (e.g. the verb / adjective distinction) can be viewed as a difference in the applicability of some transformation or other to items which combine in the same way with other things and which are otherwise subject to the same transformations (e.g. the difference between verbs and adjectives is that adjectives but not verbs are subject to a transformation which inserts the copula *be*). Negation combines with other elements of semantic structure in the same way as do some things which are manifested as verbs in the ordinary sense, e.g. the *happen* of

(25)　Two plus two happens to be four.

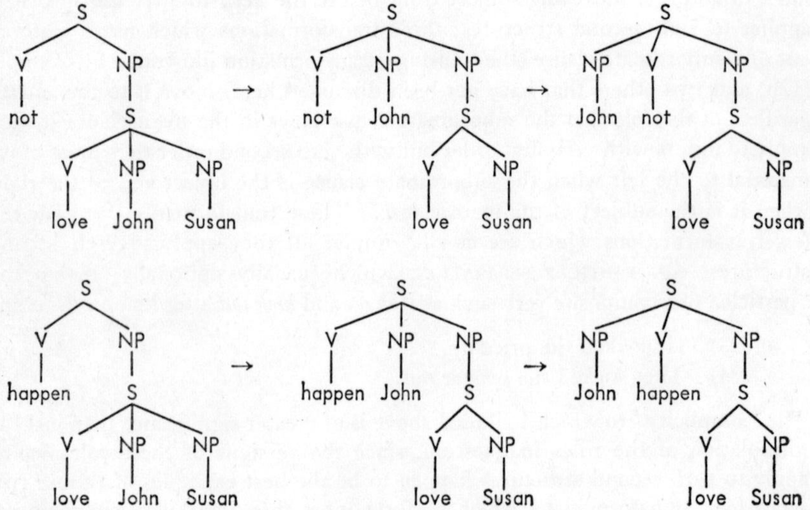

Fig. 8

In either case the item in question combines with a sentence to yield a sentence (i.e. is of Ajdukiewicz's type *s/s*); in either case the element triggers a transformation which moves the first NP of the embedded sentence into the main sentence (Fig. 8). The difference between the syntax of *not* and *happen* appears simply to be that English has transformations which prevent *not* from getting the verbal inflections that English morphology does not allow it to have: if there is an ' auxiliary verb ' present, it is put before *not*, as in *Harry can't swim*, and otherwise *do* is inserted as a semantically empty bearer of verbal inflections, as in *I don't like eggs*. There are languages in which the negative element is morphologically a verb (e.g. Finnish) or an adjective (e.g. Japanese). In both Finnish and Japanese, a sentence meaning *Harry wants to drink beer* and a sentence meaning *Harry doesn't drink beer* have the same surface structure except for the choice of ' want ' or ' not ': in Finnish, ' want ' and ' not ' are both inflected as verbs and are followed by an infinitive, and in Japanese, ' want ' and ' not ' are both inflected as adjectives and appear compounded with the main verb of their complement. The policy which I have adopted regarding the labeling of nodes localizes the difference between English, Finnish, and Japanese as one of morphology plus those syntactic rules which owe their existence to morphological details of the language. I will thus henceforth take the labeling of the negative element as V to be fairly adequately justified and hence take the arguments of the preceding section as applying also to the underlying orientation of negation relative to what is negated. The remainder of this section will be devoted to a somewhat tentative and incomplete analysis of quantifiers and coordinating conjunctions (I will have nothing to say about the one other item which generally figures in a discussion of ' Polish ' notation, namely ' if . . . then ') in which I will show that at least two putative underlying structures for coordination are consistent with what is known about coordination and a large variety of putative underlying structures for quantifiers are consistent with what is known about quantification, but that there are also some facts which support the conclusion that coordination and quantification are the same thing, that only one of the possibilities for the underlying structure of conjoined sentences and only one of the possibilities for the underlying structure of quantified sentences are consistent with that conclusion,'and that the elements which underlie both quantifiers and conjunctions under that analysis (e.g. the same element underlies both *one* and exclusive *or*) are in a configuration which makes it natural to label them ' V '.

The first step in this argument is a demonstration that an adequate system of semantic representation must allow coordination of arbitrarily many sentences at a time, rather than the coordination of two terms at a time, which logicians have generally confined themselves to. The use of the English word *or* that most closely matches the logician's ' exclusive *or* ' yields a true sentence if and only if exactly one of the conjuncts is true; for example, the presupposition of a question such as

(26) Did Andy study physics, chemistry, or geo ⟍ logy? (⟍ denotes fall in pitch)

is that Andy studied exactly one of the three subjects. While exclusive *or* satisfies the ' associative law '

(27) $(p \vee_e q) \vee_e r \equiv p \vee_e (q \vee_e r)$, ($\vee_e$ is ' exclusive' *or*)

which is often given by logicians as justification for ' leaving out parentheses ' in multi-termed conjunctions, the result of iterated binary conjoining with $\vee_e$ is a sentence which is true not only if exactly one of the conjuncts is true but if any odd number of them are (to my knowledge, the only logician to mention this point in print is Reichenbach 1947). Thus, if semantic representation is to contain a conjunction which matches the ' exclusive ' use of English *or*, that conjunction will have to be allowed to combine with arbitrarily many conjuncts: iterated binary conjoining (indeed, iterated *n*-or-less-ary conjoining, for any specific *n*) of a set of conjuncts has different truth conditions form the result of conjoining them all at once with the English word *or* in its ' exclusive ' sense. Moreover, I am reasonably sure that there is no language with a conjunction which fits the truth table of iterated binary exclusive *or*, i.e. is true when an odd number of its conjuncts are true but false when an even number of them are true. Since there is no known way in which the combinatory possibilities of exlusive *or* in semantic structure differ from those of *and* and inclusive *or*, presumably these too would then have to be allowed to combine with arbitrarily many conjuncts rather than with just two. This conclusion is confirmed by the fact that[15]

(28) a. And (p, q, r)
      b. And $(p, \text{And } (q, r))$
      c. And $((\text{And } (p, q), r)$

although they have the same truth conditons (namely, are true when all three of p, q, r are true and false otherwise), correspond to different conceptions of what the various conjuncts have in common, and allow different surface realizations in English, e.g.

(29) a. Tom voted for Cleaver, and he voted for O'Dwyer, and Bill voted for O'Dwyer.
      b. Tom voted for Cleaver, and he and Bill voted for O'Dwyer.
      c. Tom voted for Cleaver and O'Dwyer, and Bill voted for O'Dwyer.

Ross (1967a) has proposed a treatment of conjoining in transformational grammar which fits quite closely the conclusions just drawn. He has deep structures of the form

(30)

---

[15] I write And(p, q, r) rather than p And q And r, since I have in mind the combination of three terms with a single ' operator ' and the latter formula misleadingly suggests that there are two ' operators '.

and derives the surface forms of sentences with underlying conjoined clauses through the following transformations:

(i) Conjunction reduction, which replaces a conjoined structure whose conjuncts are identical except for one term by a simple structure which has a conjoined constituent in place of that term (Fig. 9a, b);

(ii) Conjunction distribution, which attaches a copy of a conjunction to each of its conjuncts, e.g. the tree of Fig. 9b is converted into that of Fig. 9c.

(iii) Various rules of conjunction deletion. In English, the first conjunction in the output of conjunction distribution is deleted except when it is replaced by *both* or *either*, which Ross takes to be positional variants of *and* and *or* respectively, and there is the option of deleting all but the last copy of the conjunction (i.e. either *tennis, and golf, and football* or *tennis, golf, and football* is a possible output).

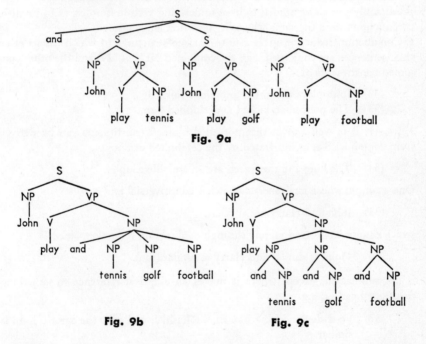

Fig. 9a

Fig. 9b   **Fig. 9c**

There must be a rule of conjunction reduction since there are sentences such as

(31) John has been named vice-president and seems pleased with himself.

in which the conjuncts do not correspond to coherent pieces of semantic structure and arise only through the action of transformations. Conjunction distribution must have the effect indicated because English conjunctions are pronounced as part of the same phrase as the following conjunct (i.e. it is possible to make a

pause before the conjunction but not after it) and because there is only one
' degree of freedom' in the choice of conjunctions in a single conjoined structure:
if one of the conjuncts in a conjoined structure has *and* before it, all the other conjuncts must have either *and* or a positional variant of it (*both* or zero) before
them.[16]   Ross conjectures that all languages have conjunction reduction and
conjunction distribution and that the differences between conjoined structures
in different languages reside in what rules the language has that delete conjunctions or replace them by positional variants and in whether conjunctions precede
or follow the conjuncts.   He notes that in clear cases of languages with underlying
verb first order, conjunctions precede conjuncts, and in clear cases of languages
with underlying verb last order (e.g. Japanese, in which a pause can generally
be made after but not before a conjunction), conjunctions follow conjuncts.
This correlation between the order of verbs and the order of conjunctions is
partially explained by the conclusion to be drawn below that conjunctions are
predicates and is strengthened by the fact that in verb second languages, which
presumably can all be argued to have underlying verb first order, as in English,
conjunctions work the same way as in verb first languages.

Conjunction reduction gives rise to surface structures in which things other
than sentences are conjoined, e.g. the conjoined NP's of (29) and the other conjoined constituents of

(32)   John plays the guitar and sings folksongs.
(33)   The policeman kicked and clubbed Sam.

However, it is well-known that not all conjoined constituents can be derived
from conjoined S's, as illustrated by the celebrated example

(34)   The king and the queen are an amiable couple.

One example whose analysis is somewhat controversial is

(35)   John and Harry are similar.,

which cannot be derived merely through conjunction reduction, since

(36)   *John is similar and Harry is similar (too).

is ungrammatical, except where it makes an elliptical reference to something
mentioned earlier, e.g.

(37)   Fred does nothing but smoke hashish and play the sarod; John is
         similar.;

this kind of interpretation of (36) is irrelevant to the point under discussion.
It is occasionally proposed (Gleitman 1965) that (35) is derived from a conjoined
structure which also underlies

(38)   John is similar to Harry and Harry is similar to John.

---

[16] This does not exclude the possibility of one of the conjuncts in a conjoined structure
being itself a conjoined structure, as in *I talked to Tom, and either Bill or Dick, and Harry.*

via a transformation which creates reciprocal pronouns

(39)   John and Harry are similar to each other.

and a transformation which deletes reciprocals (and any attached preposition) after certain verbs and adjectives.   However, that analysis fails when the subject had more than two conjuncts: as Goodman (1951: 125) has pointed out, the proposition that any two members of a group are similar does not imply that the members of the group are similar, since a member of a group might be similar to each other member in a different respect and there thus might be no similarity shared by all the members, e.g. Tom and Dick might be similar by virtue of looking like Humphrey Bogart, Dick and Harry might be similar by virtue of being confirmed wife-beaters, and Harry and Tom might be similar by virtue of being connoisseurs of pornography, but there might be nothing significant which all three have in common.   Quang (1969) cites another case where a conjoined noun phrase cannot be derived by Gleitman's proposal without setting up a source which is true under different conditions:

(40)   John and Louise kissed.

cannot be derived from the same source as

(41)   John and Louise kissed each other.,

since (40) may be a report of a single kiss in which both John and Louise participate actively, whereas (41) must be a report of at least two events, one or more in which John is the agent and one or more in which Louise is the agent.

Consequently (as concluded in Lakoff and Peters 1969), there must be some source for conjoined constituents besides the conjoined sentences which provide the source for the conjoined constituents that are derived by conjunction reduction.   However, the range of conjoined constituents that cannot be derived from conjoined sentences via conjunction reduction (and/or other transformations) is rather small: the conjoined constituent is always a conjoined NP, and the conjunction is always *and*.   An apparent counterexample to the first of these claims is the sentence

(42)   I have often eaten pizza and been sick an hour later.,

which has what appears to be a conjoined VP but is not paraphraseable by

(43)   ?I have often eaten pizza, and I have often been sick an hour later.

However, (42) is a problem only if one accepts the analysis (Chomsky 1965) in which auxiliary verbs originate within the clause where they appear in surface structure; under the alternative analysis (Ross 1969b, McCawley 1971a) in which auxiliary verbs (including tenses) originate as the verbs of higher clauses, (42) is derived from an underlying structure containing the embedded conjoined clause ' I eat pizza at t and I be sick one hour later than t ', which undergoes conjunction reduction before I is raised into the higher clause which provides the *have* (and the still higher clause which provides the present tense).   Some apparent counterexamples to the second claim are

(44) I want a Cadillac or a Mercedes.
(45) A camera or a pair of binoculars is permitted.
(46) Nixon or Humphrey is a frightening choice.

(44–5) are obviously different in meaning from

(47) I want a Cadillac or I want a Mercedes.
(48) A camera is permitted or a pair of binoculars is permitted.,

and the corresponding sentence in the case of (46) is incoherent:

(49) *Nixon is a frightening choice or Humphrey is a frightening choice.

I maintain that in each of these cases there is an embedded sentence which has undergone conjunction reduction and whose verb (and perhaps more) has then been deleted.   That sentences with *want* and a non-sentential object are derived by the deletion of either *have* or *get* from a sentential object is confirmed by the existence of sentences such as

(50) I want a Cadillac by tomorrow.,

which contains an adverb which does not modify the verb *want* but rather the verb which I claim has been deleted.   It is even possible to say[17]

(51) He wanted a Cadillac by tomorrow.,

in which *by tomorrow* occurs with a past tense verb; this situation does not occur unless the verb is one (such as *want*) which allows one to derive an apparently 'simple' clause from an underlying structure containing an embedded clause that has a time adverb.   A similar piece of evidence supports the claim that (45) involves a deleted *have*: in

(52) A camera or a pair of binoculars is permitted in one's cabin baggage.,

the locative adverb specifies not the place where the permission is given but part of what is permitted (namely, to have a camera or a pair of binoculars in one's cabin baggage).   In (46), it is not clear what has been deleted (possibly (46) comes from something like [[[one choose Nixon]$_s$ or [one choose Humphrey]$_s$]$_s$ be a frightening choice]$_s$), but the following fact supports the claim that pieces of an underlying embedded sentence have been deleted.   In

(53) Nixon and Agnew or Humphrey and Muskie is a frightening choice.,

the verb must be in the singular, although a subject in which plural items are conjoined with *or* normally takes plural number agreement:

(54) Nixon and Agnew or Humphrey and Muskie have / *has been elected.

Note that, as pointed out in Ross (1969c), a sentential subject takes singular

[17] This example is based on a related example of Masaru Kajita's.

number agreement, even when deletion transformations reduce it to a plural
noun phrase:

(55)   Susan is dating several boys, but which boys isn't / *aren't known.

These two restrictions on ' underivable ' conjoined structures are connected
with the following observations (McCawley 1968c): (i) in all environments where
a conjoined NP is allowed, a simple plural NP is also allowed, e.g.

(56)   Those men are similar.,

(ii) there are certain verbs and adjectives which do not admit a singular subject
(e.g. *similar*), and (iii) even a plural noun phrase will not do as subject of such
a verb or adjective unless it denotes a set of two or more things: *scissors, trousers,*
etc. are grammatically plural regardless of the number of pairs of scissors, etc.
being referred to, and the difference in grammaticality between

(57)   Joe and Fred each bought a pair of trousers; the trousers are similar.
(58)   *Joe bought a pair of trousers; the trousers are similar.

has to do with whether *the trousers* refers to one pair or to more than one.   My
conclusion was that the restriction which *similar*, etc. impose on their subjects is
that the subject purport to refer to a set of two or more individuals.   Thus the
NP's which meet such a condition are those which can be used to refer to a set,
either by describing its members (plural NP) or by enumerating its members
(conjoined NP with *and*).   I thus conclude that the conjoined constituents which
cannot be derived from conjoined sentences are precisely those which are used
to enumerate the elements of a set and that conjoined constituents in surface
structure have exactly two sources in semantic structure: sentential conjunction
and description of sets by enumeration.   I will provisionally represent the latter
by a portion of semantic structure in which a NP-node dominates a sequence of
NP-nodes and will treat *and* (the only possible conjunction) as to be inserted by
a transformation, e.g.

(59)

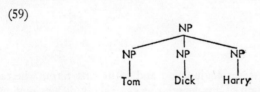

Having concluded that semantic representation should involve pieces like
(59), a slight revision of Ross's underlying structure for conjoined sentences
now presents itself: rather than a conjoined structure with n conjuncts being
represented as an $(n+1)$-ary branching structure (the conjunction on the first
branch and the n conjuncts on the second through $(n+1)$-th branches), it could
be represented as a binary branching structure: on one branch the conjunction,
and on the other branch NP which enumerates a set of n sentences:

(60)

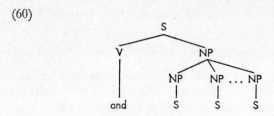

At this point it is hard to see any linguistic evidence which would choose between (60) and (30), since conjunction distribution (whose formulation would be only trivially different under the two proposals) would give the same output in either case and thus any such evidence should have to relate to a stage of a derivation prior to conjunction distribution. One small piece of evidence for (60) is provided by sentences such as

(61)   Either John is an idiot, or you are lying, or both.,

in which *both* refers to the set of sentences enumerated in the preceding part of the sentence; however, the facts relating to the possibility of pronouns, etc. referring to the sets of sentences involved in the proposal of (60) do not give the kind of evidence that would provide a clear case for (60), since ordinary pronouns generally are not possible:

(62)   ??Either John is an idiot, or you are lying, or both of them.
(63)   *John said that Amsterdam was in Liberia and Los Angeles was in Finland, and I disagreed with one of them.

One somewhat unusual piece of evidence that I can offer for (60) relates to the formulation of rules of inference in logic. Logicians are generally content to formulate rules of inference that are sufficient to cover the inferences that are desired, regardless of whether these rules of inference are formulated ' in fullest generality '. A number of commonly encountered rules of inference are in fact special cases of more general rules of inference that could be formulated. For example,

(64) $\dfrac{\text{And } (p, q)}{p}$

makes reference to a two-term conjunction and to its first term, whereas in fact from an *and*-conjunction of any length one can validly deduce any one of its conjuncts. One might try to formulate that rule of inference as

(65) $\dfrac{\text{And } (p_1, p_2, \ldots, p_n)}{p_i \ (1 \leq i \leq n)}$

but here the condition $1 \leq i \leq n$ is tacked on in such a way as to leave its status unclear. Since it really amounts to the premise that p_i is one of the conjuncts that appears in the overt premise, (65) can be reformulated as

(66) And M

    p belongs to M

    ———————

      p,

where M is used to denote a set of sentences. Similarly, the proposal of (60) allows the rule

(67) p

    ———

    $p \lor q$

to be reformulated in the more general form

(68) p

    p belongs to M

    ———————

      Or M.

Later, I will show that if sets of propositions are allowed to be defined by means other than enumeration, (66) and (68) remain valid and take in as special cases some familiar rules of inference relating to quantifiers.

In section 2, I presented an argument that quantifier must originate outside of the clauses which they appear in in surface structure. The tree which I drew there as a suggestion of the source of quantifiers is only one of a large number of possibilities which are consistent with that conclusion. An obvious possibility to consider is an underlying structure matching the analysis which Russell and numerous logicians have given to quantifiers, in which universal and existential quantifiers are one-place operators and e.g.

(69) a.   All Armenians are transvestites.

      b.   Some Armenians are transvestites.

would be derived from respectively

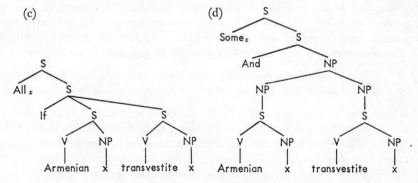

Note that if quantifiers are one-place operators which combine with a S, the ‘connective’ in the S cannot be the same for ‘All’ as for ‘Some’. While the logical structure of (69b) can reasonably be proposed to be Some$_x$ (x is an Armenian and x is a transvestite), i.e. at least that expression is true when (69b)

is true and false when (69b) is false), the logical structure of (69a) cannot possibly be All$_x$ (x is an Armenian and x is a transvestite), since that expression is made false by the fact that J. Edgar Hoover is not an Armenian, regardless of whether any Armenians are transvestites. Similarly, while (69a) can reasonably be suggested to have the logical structure All$_x$ (x is an Armenian $\supset$ x is a transvestite), where $\supset$ is 'material implication' (i.e. $p \supset q$ is true if p is false or q is true), (69a) surely does not have the logical structure Some$_x$ (x is an Armenian $\supset$ x is a transvestite), since that expression is made true by the fact that J. Edgar Hoover is not an Armenian, regardless of whether any Armenians are transvestites. One difficulty with this proposal is that it does not provide for the existential presupposition that sentences with quantifiers other than *any* have in ordinary English: not only is

(70)   All unicorns have accounts at the Chase Manhattan Bank.

infelicitous because of violation of the presuppostion (for which *all* is responsible) that there are unicorns, rather than being (as the more mathematically minded logicians often claim) 'vacuously' true, but the sentence

(71)   Some egg-laying mammals have webbed feet.

is odd if used in a discourse in which the existence of egg-laying mammals has not yet been established; (71) can be used to convey the information that there are mammals with webbed feet but (if one is playing fair) not to convey the information that there are egg-laying mammals, i.e. if one were to use (71) in order to convey that information, he would be engaging in an act comparable to surreptitiously handing a person a note that said 'You are supposed to already know that there are egg-laying mammals; don't give any indication that you didn't know'. In the case of the universal quantifier, it is possible to get the existential presupposition into a structure like (69) by taking the embedded 'connective' to be not the material implication which Russell used but rather something corresponding to the English *whenever*, which does have the existential presupposition needed.[18] However, I know of no such stratagem for getting the existential presupposition into the underlying structure of existential clauses. A more serious difficulty with (69) is provided by sentences like

(72)   At least some Americans want Nixon to invade New Zealand.
(73)   Some, if not all, Americans want Nixon to invade New Zealand.

If *some* combines semantically with the conjoined sentence 'x is an American and x wants Nixon to invade New Zealand', *at least* in (72) should refer to a scale on which the different things that that sentence can be combined with appear and (73) implies that *all* is on that scale; but *all* does not combine with 'x is an American and x wants Nixon to invade New Zealand' in the sentence

(74)   All Americans want Nixon to invade New Zealnd.

---

[18] I am grateful to Östen Dahl for this observation.

Lakoff (1965) has proposed an alternative underlying structure for quantifiers which matches the surface structure of such slightly archaic sentences as

(75)   The students who want Nixon deposed are many.,

in which a quantifier is predicated of a NP whose relative clause provides the eventual main clause:

(76)   Many students want Nixon deposed.

While this analysis is plausible in the case of quantifiers which refer to the (absolute or relative) number of individuals with a certain property, it is much less so in the case of *all, every, each, any,* and *some.* The implausibility which I find here does not have to do with the ungrammaticality even in archaic-sounding English of

(77)   *The philosophers who contradict themselves are every.,

etc. (as will be clear from the analyses presented above, I have no objection to underlying structures in which an item appears in a position where the corresponding English word is not allowed in surface structure) but has rather to do with the idea that ' everyhood ' is a property of a set of philosophers. That it is not is shown by the fact that if the set of philosophers who contradict themselves happens to be identical with the set of wife-beaters who smoke pipes, one cannot deduce from (18a) that

(78)   Every wife-beater smokes a pipe.

Thus, if ' the set of philosophers who contradict themselves ' is involved in the semantic structure of (18a), more than just that set and the quantifier will have to appear, e.g. *every* might be a relationship between a set (e.g. the set of all philosophers) and a putative subset (the set of all philosophers who contradict themselves) which exhausts the whole set.

While I have no substantial objection to the analysis suggested in the last sentence, I see no obvious advantage which it has over another proposal that has been made, that a quantifier is a relation between two sentences (rather than between two sets defined by those sentences), as I proposed in McCawley (1970c):

(79)

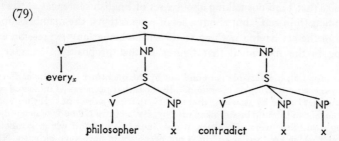

One thing that might be adduced as an advantage of the former proposal over the latter is that the former, by using set construction operations, provides a more natural account of the existential presupposition of quantified sentences: the pre-supposition is simply that the 'subject' of *every*, etc. denote a non-empty set. However, that is no argument, since under the former proposal, the 'object' of *every* is also given by a set description, and that set not only is not presupposed to be non-empty but can indeed be asserted to be empty:

(80)   No philosopher contradicts himself.

Thus, under either proposal, the existential presupposition does not follow from the structure proposed but must be imposed as a condition that one but not the other argument of the quantifier must meet.

There is another possible underlying structure for quantifiers, a somewhat wild one, which I will argue is correct and which in fact automatically provides for the existential presupposition. Under this analysis, a quantifier is predicated not of a set of individuals but of a set of propositions, e.g. in the case of (18a), *every* would be predicated of the set of all propositions 'x contradicts x' for which x is a philosopher. Under the assumption that a NP which defines a set by definite description has as its immediate constituents a NP (which gives the 'general term' of the set) and a S (which gives the conditions which the vari-able(s) in that expression must meet for the corresponding 'value' of the general term to be in the set), the semantic structure of (18a) is[19]

(81)

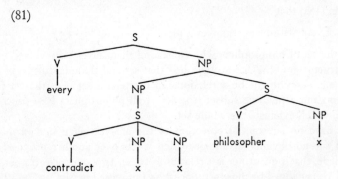

I emphasize that I am not talking about a set of English sentences of the form 'NP contradicts (him)self' but about a set of propositions, the membership of a proposition in the set having nothing to do with whether any expression exists for referring to the individual that figures in that proposition. Under this

[19] Under this proposal, the variable is bound not by the quantifier (as in the earlier pro-posals) but by the set-construction operation. In the earlier proposals, I indicated which variable a quantifier bound by attaching that variable to it as a subscript. It thus appears as if (81) is deficient and should be supplemented by, say, an extra NP node which indicates what is being quantified over. However, if one knows beforehand which symbols are 'constants' and which are 'variables', it is not necessary to have such an extra NP (or for that matter, to have subscripts on quantifiers under a proposal of 'restricted quantifica-tion' such as that embodied in (79), though such subscripts can not be dispensed with in a proposal of 'unrestricted quantification' such as would be involved in (69)), since it is then

proposal, the existential presupposition is simply the presupposition that the set of propositions be non-empty (the only way that it could be empty is for there to be no x such that 'x is a philosopher' is true, i.e. for there to be no philosophers), and the proposal allows that presupposition to be treated as a special case of a principle whereby all sets mentioned in semantic representations are presupposed non-empty;[20] that principle is illustrated by the oddity of the sentences

(82) a. Harry is an expert on the prime numbers between 32 and 36.
      b. Harry is an expert on the operas of Johannes Brahms.,

which are odd because they mention a set which is known to be empty.

The strongest case for this last proposal comes from the fact that it is essentially the only possible analysis which allows one to treat quantifiers and conjunctions as special cases of the same thing, differing only in whether the set of sentences that is involved in either case is defined by enumeration or by a definite description, and certain facts which argue that quantifiers and conjunctions in fact are the same thing. I first note that if universal quantifiers are identified with And and existential quantifiers with Or, then when applied to sets of sentences defined by definite descriptions, the generalized rules of inference proposed above yield familiar rules of inference having to do with quantifiers; for example, (66) includes the familiar

(83) $\text{All}_{x\,:\,f(x)}\ g(x)$
      $f(a)$
      —————
      $g(a)$,

since the first premise of (83) consists of And applied to the set of all propositions $g(x)$ for which $f(x)$ and the second premise gives the condition under which $g(a)$ is in that set; thus (66) covers such classical cases as 'All men are mortal; Socrates is a man; therefore, Socrates is mortal'. Similary, (68) includes the rule of existential generalization as a special case. That rule, when stated in terms of

possible to state a principle which will decide whether variables are being employed 'coherently' and, if so, decide which variable each set-construction operation binds. Specifically, the 'condition' of any set-construction operation must contain exactly one variable which is not contained in the 'condition' of any 'higher' set-description operation (that variable is then the variable which the set-description operation binds), and that variable must also occur in the 'general term' of that set-description operation. Regardless of whether semantic structures explicitly indicate which variable each set-description operation (or quantifier) binds, it will be necessary (at least from a linguist's point of view) to have something like that principle, so as to exclude as semantically ill-formed a putative semantic structure in which a variable is bound by more than one quantifier (all$_x$(some$_x$ (x lives in Tucson))) or in which the 'condition' does not involve the bound variable ('for all x such that Philadelphia is in North America, x is allergic to cucumbers) or in which the 'general term' does not involve the bound variable ('for all x such that x is a hydrogen molecule, Beethoven's fourth symphony is in Bb major'). The first clause of the principle excludes the first two kinds of anomaly, the second clause the third kind.

[20] I emphasize that I am speaking of the language of ordinary speakers of English, not the language of mathematicians.

'restricted' quantification[21] would take the form

(84) $g(a)$

  $f(a)$

  _____

  $\text{Exists}_{x\,:\,f(x)}\ g(x)$

whose second premise is the condition for $g(a)$ to be a member of the set of all $g(x)$ for which $f(x)$, and whose conclusion is Or applied to that set.

One syntactic reason for identifying *and* with universal quantifiers and *or* with existential quantifiers has been called to my attention by Quang Phuc Dong, who notes that curses may be conjoined with *and* but not with *or*, and allow *and* and universal quantifiers but not *or* or existential quantifiers in their 'object':

  (85) Goddamn Nixon and/*or fuck Laird.
  (86) Goddamn Nixon and/*or Laird.
  (87) Fuck all/(every one)/*some/*one of those imperialist butchers.

Quang's observation appears to be a special case of a more general restriction on performative verbs: sentences with a performative verb can be conjoined with *and* but not with *or* and allow *and* and universal quantifiers but not *or* or existential quantifiers in their subject and indirect object:

  (88) I promise you that I'll help you, and/*or I assure you that you won't have any trouble.
  (89) I promise you and/*or Harry that I'll empty the garbage.
  (90) I promise all/(every one)/*one/*some of you that I'll stop kicking my dog.
  (91) My partners and/*or I promise that we'll help you.
  (92) All/(every one)/*one/*some of us promise(s) that we'll/he'll help you.

Also, while

  (93) I promise that I'll help every one of you.

has a scope ambiguity (either it is a single promise which is fulfilled by helping every one of the persons to whom it is adressed, or it is several simultaneously made promises, one for each of those persons, to help him),

  (94) I promise that I'll help one of you.

only allows an interpretation as a promise which is fulfilled by helping one of the persons to whom it is addressed. These facts would all follow from a restriction that a performative verb is allowed to appear in the complement of And but not

[21] The more familiar version of existential generalization has to do with 'unrestricted quantification':

  $g(a)$

  _____

  $\text{Exists}_x\ g(x)$

in the complement of Or.[22]

There is at least one language, namely Japanese, in which some universal quantifiers involve the same morpheme that is used for *and* and some existential quantifiers involve the same morpheme which is used for *or*. Universal quantifiers are formed from an indefinite pronoun plus *mo* (e.g. *itumo* ' always ', *dokomo* ' everywhere ') except that suppletive forms appear in place of some of the expected combinations (*minna* ' everyone ', *zenbu* ' everything '), and existential quantifiers are formed from an indefinite pronoun plus *ka* (e.g. *ituka* ' sometime ', *dokoka* ' somewhere '); *mo* is used for the *and* of sentence conjunction[23] and *ka* is used for *or*. *Mo* and *ka* appear as suffixes but with *mo* following case markers and *ka* preceding them, regardless of whether they are used as conjunctions or quantifiers: *Tookyoo ni mo Oosaka ni mo* ' both in Tōkyō and in Ōsaka ', *doko ni mo* ' everywhere (locative) ', *Tookyoo ka Oosaka ka ni* ' in either Tōkyō or Ōsaka ', *doko ka ni* ' somewhere (locative) '.

In addition, the kinds of ' selectional restrictions ' that predicates impose on their arguments are such that if there were no elements of the type that I claim *and/all* is, that fact would be a gap that would require explaining: there are predicates which require that their subject denote a set (e.g. *similar*) and predicates which require that their subject be sentential (e.g. *not* or *imply*), and there is nothing to exclude the possibility of a predicate which imposes these two restrictions simultaneously. Moreover, if conjunctions are analyzed as in (60) but quantifiers are not treated as being the same as conjunctions, conjunctions would have a selectional restriction of a type otherwise unknown: a restriction that a set-denoting NP define that set by enumeration.

Facts about the use of *respective* and *respectively* also provide evidence for identifying *and* with a universal quantifier. Transformational grammarians have generally treated sentences like

(95)   John and Harry gave Susan and Alice respectively candy and flowers respectively.

from an underlying conjoined structure by means of a generalized version of conjunction reduction which allows the conjuncts to differ in more than one constituent and creates conjoined constituents at all the places where the original conjuncts differ, as in the derivation of (95) from a structure which also underlies

---

[22] I wish to include words such as *Goddamn* (which Quang 1969 calls ' quasi-verbs ') among performative verbs. While they fail some of the familiar tests for performativehood, e.g. they do not admit *hereby*, they certainly seem to fit the defining characteristic of performative verbs, namely that of specifying the illocutionary force of the sentence in which they appear.

[23] Japanese has a variety of morphemes which can be translated as *and*. *Mo* appears as a suffix to a NP but represents sentence conjunction, e.g.

Nedan mo yasukute, sina mo ii.   ' The price is low and the quality is good '.
Taroo mo Ziroo mo dekaketa.   ' Both Taro and Jiro went out '.

In conjoined NP's which are not derived by conjunction reduction, a different conjunction is used:

Taroo to Ziroo to ga dekaketa.   ' Taro and Jiro went out (together) '.

(96)   John gave Susan candy and Harry gave Alice flowers.

In place of each of the conjoined NP's in (95) it is possible to get a plural NP with *respective* instead of *respectively:*

(97)   John and Harry gave their respective girlfriends candy and flowers respectively.

(98)   John and Harry gave Susan and Alice respectively their respective lollipops.

(99)   Those boys gave Susan and Alice respectively candy and flowers respectively.

(100) John and Harry gave their respective girlfriends their respective lollipops.

(101) Those boys gave Susan and Alice respectively their respective lollipops.

(102) Those boys gave their respective girlfriends candy and flowers respectively.

(103) Those boys gave their respective girlfriends their respective lollipops.

Since *respective* and *respectively* may co-occur in the same sentence (exx. 97–102), one cannot say that *respectively* arises through a transformation unless he is also willing to let *respective* arise through the same transformation, since otherwise one would have to treat *respectively* as arising differently in (97–102) than it does in (95), which is absurd.   But what about (103), which contains only plural NP's and *respective*? If *respectively* is created by a conjunction-reduction transformation, then the *respective*'s of (103) will also have to arise through that same transformation, since otherwise the *respective*'s of (103) would have to arise in a different way from those of (97–102), which is absurd.   While one might want to propose that NP's like *those men* are derived from conjoined singular NP's that differed in reference (i.e. from *that man₁ and that man₂* or from *that man₁ and that man₂ and that man₃* or from any of the infinitely many other such expressions), there are sentences like (103) for which that stratagem cannot be employed:

(104) The approximately 50 boys that I talked to gave their respective girlfriends their respective lollipops.

(104) not only can not reasonably be derived from a conjoined source but could hardly be given a semantic representation other than one in which a universal quantifier whose ' range ' is denoted by *the approximately 50 boys that I talked to* is applied to the propositional function *x gave x's girlfriend x's lollipop.*   Therefore, whatever mechanism is responsible for the introduction of *respective* and *respectively* must treat clauses conjoined with *and* the same way that it treats universally quantified clauses.

Having said that, however, I am not much closer to an explicit description of where *respective(ly)* comes from.   An obvious proposal to make (and which I in fact made in McCawley 1968c) is that sentences with *respectively* are really quantified rather than conjoined structures but involve functions defined by enumeration rather than functions given be general expressions such as ' x 's girlfriend ', e.g. to represent the semantic structure of (95) as

(105)   All$_{x\,:\,x\text{ belongs to }\{\text{John, Harry}\}}$ x gave $f(x)$ $g(x)$, where f is defined by ' f (John)=Susan, f (Harry)=Alice ' and g by ' g (John)=candy, g (Harry)=flowers '.

However, that proposal is open to a really overwhelming objection, namely that the ' values ' of the functions that it requires can perfectly well be transformationally derived constituents, i.e. constituents which do not exist at the stage of the derivation (semantic structure) which (105) is supposed to correspond to, e.g.

(106)   John and Harry respectively have been arrested for smuggling pot and happen to be in jail for indecent exposure.

The facts that I have just presented create a major dilemma, and while I am not prepared to give a detailed resolution of that dilemma, I am prepared to offer a program that I think will eventually resolve the dilemma and in the process further confirm my claim that quantifiers and conjunctions are the same thing. One thing that has been missing from my observations so far about *respective(ly)* is a consideration of cases where the *respective(ly)* construction may not be used even though the conjoined structure which (according to the ' classical ' treatment of *respective(ly)*) it ought to correspond to is perfectly normal, e.g.

(107)   a.   The score is tied and Yastrzemski is at bat.
          b.   *The score and Yastrzemski are tied and at bat respectively.
(108)   a.   The sun is shining and the birds are singing.
          b.   *The sun and the birds are shining and singing respectively.
(109)   a.   Truman was President and the war was almost over.
          b.   *Truman and the war were President and almost over respectively.

The cases where *respective(ly)* is good are cases where the conjoined constituents not merely have the same ' grammatical function ' in the input to the putative transformation but also have the same ' pragmatic function ', in the sense that (96) can be used to report several instances of ' a boy giving a girl a present ', where ' a boy ' corresponds to a role in this general formula which is filled by *John* in one case and by *Harry* in the other case, but (107a) cannot be described as reporting several instances of anything like, say ' something doing something ', which has a constituent matching *the sun* in the one case and *the birds* in the other.   There is a type of sentence in which the relation between ' general formula ' and ' specific cases ' is made explicit, using such words as *for example*, *namely*, *specifically*, and *in particular ;* the cases in which such a sentence is possible appear to be exactly the cases in which *respectively* may be used:

(110)   Several boys gave their girlfriends presents; for example, John gave Susan candy and Harry gave Alice flowers.

(111)   *Several things were doing things; for example, the sun was shining and the birds were singing.

(112)   Two of my friends are in trouble; specifically, John has been arrested for smuggling pot, and Harry happens to be in jail for indecent exposure.

The last point is closely connected with Wierzbicka's (1967b) observation that (contrary to not only popular belief but the explicit statements of many linguists and logicians) not just any clauses of the same ' type ' can be conjoined and that many of the standard examples which have been given of conjoined clauses are abnormal because of there not being any ' general ' proposition of which the conjuncts can be taken as special cases, e.g.

(113)   *Plato currit et Sortes est albus.

(114)   *I wrote my grandmother a letter yesterday and six men can fit in the back seat of a Ford.

In the case of (107–9), there are ' general ' propositions of which the conjuncts can be taken as special cases, say, ' two conditions relating to the progress of the game prevailed ', ' two phenomena are making the atmosphere pleasant ', ' two conditions relating to international politics prevailed ', but in none of these cases can a plausible ' general ' proposition be found which is exemplified by the conjuncts and which contains a constituent matching the inadmissible conjoined constituents of the (b) sentences.   I thus propose that an adequate analysis of conjoining must make crucial use of the ' general ' propositions which Wierzbicka proposed, that in fact the underlying structure of a conjoined sentence must specify what ' general ' proposition the conjuncts exemplify, and that conjunction reduction in the generalized version discussed in connection with (95) is dependent on the conjuncts not merely having the same ' syntactic form ' at the point where conjunction reduction applies (and (106) appears to leave no alternative to having some kind of conjunction reduction transformation apply in the derivation of sentences with *respectively*) but also on the conjoined constituents which the transformation creates corresponding to constituents in the ' general formula '.   If this program for the investigation of conjoined structure leads where I conjecture it will, it will show conjoining and quantification to be identical in an even stronger sense than I had proposed above: not only will both be predicated of sets of propositions, but in both cases the semantic structure will have to contain an expression giving the ' general form ' of the members of that set, the difference being whether all propositions of that form come into consideration or only specially designated ones.

6.   Concluding Remarks

The main point of this paper has been that considerations of either logic alone or linguistics alone leave one having to make a large number of highly arbitrary choices in choosing among the various alternative proposals that could be made for the semantic structure of various sentences but that if considerations of both logic and linguistics are employed together, the range of possibilities for semantic structure is drastically narrowed, though not so drastically as to eliminate everything from consideration, i.e. the linguist's concerns and the logician's are consistent with each other. The resulting picture of semantic structure is different in many respects from what either linguists or logicians are used to operating with, and I have found the experience of starting with a linguist's conception of semantics and proceeding in the direction of these conclusions mind-expanding.

One thing which linguistics may contribute to logic is stimulation to study the logical properties of items that logicians generally ignore (e.g. is it valid to argue ' Goddamn all imperialist butchers; Nixon is an imperialist butcher; therefore, goddamn Nixon'?) and to consider the more mundane items such as conjunctions in connection with the full range of things which they combine with (e.g. the conjoined epithets which figured in one of the arguments above; if the *and* of that argument is the same *and* that figures in conjoined declarative sentences, as it surely is, one cannot get away with reducing *and* to truth tables, although one might, *pace* Prior, be able to get away with reducing it to rules of inference).

I should also emphasize that no account of quantifiers can be considered adequate unless it covers a much broader range of quantifiers than just the three (*all, some, one*) which I considered. One major defect in the above treatment is that I have treated all 'universal' quantifiers as if they were semantically the same; see Vendler's ' Each and every, any and all ' (1968) for a highly insightful account of the ways in which those four words differ. In the case of *several, many, five*, etc., I conjecture that their use as ' existential quantifiers ' is a combination of a ' pure ' existential quantifier which asserts the existence of a set with a description of the size of that set; however, I have neither a proposal for the the details of such an analysis nor any linguistic facts which provide any support for it. One matter that could conceivably be the undoing of my proposal that quantifiers and conjunctions are the same thing is the fact that there are no conjunctions corresponding to *several, many, five*, etc. nor to such things as *all but one, almost all, at least seven*, and *at most ten*. What I have said above should be taken with at least a dash of soy sauce until someone succeeds in explaining in a manner consistent with my proposals the lack of a conjunction *shmor* which yields a true sentence if and only if at least two of its conjuncts are true.

[a] Berman (1973) shows that my reference to 'the few transformations which are simpler' is an exaggeration. See fn. *k* to ' English as a *VSO* language '.
[b] Bach (1971) argues that the set of possible transformations can be constrained equally tightly if all languages have underlying verb-first order. He thus proposes that Japanese differs from German and Amharic not in its basic word order (which he takes to be verb-first for all three) but in whether the transformation that moves the verb to the end of a clause is post-cyclic (German, Amharic) or in the cycle or even pre-cyclic (Japanese) and whether it affects only subordinate clauses (German) or all clauses (Amharic, Japanese).

19. William Dwight Whitney as a Syntactician[*]

This paper is a sequel to an earlier paper on Whitney (McCawley 1967c) in which I argued that his practise in the *Sanskrit Grammar* was a consistent application of a phonological theory according to which the phonological rules of a language formed a cycle (which differed from Chomsky and Halle 1968's conception of cycle only in that Whitney began the application of the cycle on the morphemes themselves rather than on the lowest non-terminal nodes, as in Chomsky and Halle) and each rule served to eliminate a phonologically inadmissible combination of segments (including boundaries). I noted that in one instance where Whitney has been criticized (by Halle 1962: 57-8) for having superfluous rules because he failed to order his rules, Whitney's rules were forced on him by the theory which I attributed to him and were not (as Halle's discussion suggests) simply the result of ineptness on Whitney's part.

In this paper I will be concerned with Whitney's conception of syntax, to the extent that it can be recovered from his works. As with his conception of phonology, I know of no explicit statements on his part as to what rules are and how they interact and can only rely on his practise and on the arguments that

[*] This paper was written for Kachru et al. (editors), *Papers in linguistics in honor of Henry and Renee Kahane.*

he gives in favor of his analyses when (which is not often) he gives arguments. My conclusions will be much more tentative than were my conclusions about his conception of phonology, since his practise in syntax seems much less consistent and explicit than in phonology. I will nevertheless be able to present at least as good a case for regarding Whitney as a transformational grammarian as can be made for so regarding Jespersen.

The works of Whitney's which I will be primarily concerned with are his *Essentials of English Grammar*, the *Compendious German Grammar*, and the *Practical French Grammar*. The German and French grammars were college textbooks, the English grammar a high-school textbook. I will have nothing to say about the *Sanskrit Grammar*, since it appears to give a less systematic account of syntax than do the three works mentioned and since what it does say about syntax is buried in discussions of Sanskrit morphology and thus rather hard to ferret out.

Whitney's syntactic practise is ‘ traditional grammar ’ as that was characterized in Percival's important unpublished paper ‘ On the historical source of immediate constituent analysis ’. Percival describes traditional grammarians as largely ignoring immediate constituent structure and operating in terms of dependency relations between pairs of words. For the traditional grammarian, the ‘ subject ’ of a clause was a noun rather than a noun phrase and the ‘ predicate ’ was a verb rather than a verb phrase. Occasionally the term ‘ complete subject ’ was used to denote the noun phrase of which the ‘ subject ’ was the head, and likewise the term ‘ complete predicate ’ to denote something often larger than what a modern transformational grammarian might call a verb phrase: the ‘ predicate ’ proper plus its object(s) and all adverbial expressions that modified it. However, generally only relations between words and not relations between constituents would be discussed, e.g. *very* in *a very tall man* would be said to modify *tall*, *tall* would be said to modify *man*, and the existence of such an item as *very tall* or *a very tall man* would not even be recognized. Thus, traditional grammarians operated in terms of relations such as are indicated in the linear diagram of Fig. 1a rather than the tree diagram of Fig. 1b. One systematic deviation from this policy of speaking of relations between words rather than relations between constituents is that traditional grammarians allowed

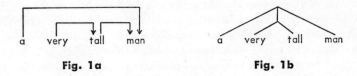

Fig. 1a   **Fig. 1b**

a clause to play the same kinds of roles that a single word could play, e.g. be the subject of another clause or modify a noun. Some typical examples[1] in Whitney

[1] In quoting from Whitney's English, French, and German grammars, I will use the letters E, F, G followed by the section number.

are:

   'An adjective is often limited by a noun (or pronoun) dependent on it' (G145),

which he illustrates with *ledig aller Pflicht* 'free from all obligation', in which, by implication, it is the noun *Pflicht* rather than the noun phrase *aller Pflicht* that limits *ledig*.

   'Between the preposition and its following governed noun may intervene the various limiting words which are wont to stand before a noun '(G381.2).
   'The meaning of the verb may be filled out by an object-noun' (E406b).

It is only within this framework that it makes sense to speak of a pronoun as standing for a noun.

   Aside from the many cases where he speaks of a clause 'modifying' or 'qualifying' a noun or verb or 'filling out' a verb (as its object), references to constituents containing more than one word are rare in Whitney. One example is his discussion of German word order, where he says that 'a single connected member of the predicate' may be 'remove[d] to the head of the sentence' (G431e), which he illustrates by comparing the grammaticality of such examples as *Dort, hinter diesen Fenstern, verträumt' ich den ersten Traum* 'There, behind these windows, I dreamed my first dream' to the ungrammaticality of such examples as **Seinen Kindern aus der Stadt brachte ein Landsmann fünf Pfirsiche* 'To his children from the city a peasant brought five peaches', in which *seinen Kindern aus der Stadt* is not 'a single connected member of the predicate'; his choice of words here, 'member of the predicate', which suggests constituent structure, is unusual: I know of no other place where he speaks of a 'member' of anything.

   Whitney thus did dependency grammar rather than immediate constituent grammar. To make clear just what kind of dependency grammar he was doing, let me list the ways in which his grammatical practise differs from the kind of dependency grammar described in Hays (1964) and in the mathematical work by Gaifman on which Hays drew:

  (1) As mentioned above, Whitney allowed a clause to have a dependency relation to a word of the next higher clause, whereas Hays speaks of one word of the subordinate clause (always the verb, as far as I can tell) as depending on some word in the higher clause

  (2) Where Hays considers the subject to be dependent on the predicate, Whitney treats their relation as something outside of the dependency framework. Whitney's grammar can be interpreted in a strict dependency framework by taking each clause to contain an extra element (call it, say, 'predication') which subject and predicate are dependent on and saying that this ideal element of 'predication' can itself stand in a dependency relation to a word of a higher clause. It will be seen later that this suggestion matches very closely the diagrams of the parsing exercises of *Essentials of English grammar*.

  (3) Whereas Hays has a single relation of 'dependency', Whitney distinguishes between the relation of 'modifying' or 'qualifying' and the

relation of ' filling out ' or ' completing '; I presume that Whitney would have described the ambiguity of Chomsky's example *John decided on the boat* in terms of *on* ' modifying ' *decide* in the one reading and ' filling out ' *decide* in the other reading.

(4)   Whereas Hays allows a word to depend on at most one other word, there are cases where Whitney talks of a word depending on two other words, as (E406b) when he discusses a predicate adjective as both ' filling out ' the verb and ' qualifying ' either the subject or the object; for example, in *He planed the board smooth*, *smooth* both fills out *plane* and qualifies *board*.

(5)   Whereas Hays allows only continuous dependency structure, i.e. allows only dependency structures in which a word *A* which depends on a word *B* can be separated from *B* only by words which depend ultimately on *A* or *B*, Whitney allows ' discontinuous ' dependency structures.   For example, he treats an extraposed relative clause (G439.5) as qualifying its head noun, even though the intervening material does not depend on either the relative clause or the noun, e.g. . . . *als der Deckel von der Schachtel genommen wurde, in der sie lagen* . . . ' when the cover was taken from the box in which they lay . . . ', in which the relative clause *in der sie lagen* depends on the noun *Schachtel* but the intervening material depends on neither.

(6)   Whitney treats coordination as involving no dependency relation and treats prepositions and conjunctions as not having dependency relations themselves but mediating dependency relations between other words.

It should be noted at the outset that Whitney is immune to many charges that are often leveled at traditional grammarians.   Regarding the charge that traditional grammarians are overly concerned with writing and ignore speech, it should be pointed out that in the morphological section of *Essentials of English grammar* Whitney discusses phonological alternations which are not reflected in writing, for example, the voicing of [s] to [z] in *house/houses* and the voicing of [θ] to [ð] which Whitney observes in the plurals of *oath* and *path*, and the conditions under which the plural ending is pronounced [s], [z], or [ɪz] (E123–4). He mentions some purely orthographic alternations, e.g. that between *y* in *lady* and *ie* in *ladies* (E124d), but his discussion of them is set in very small type. Regarding the charge that traditional grammarians engaged in prescriptive grammar rather than descriptive grammar, it should be pointed out that whether a person does prescriptive grammar is completely independent of whether he also does descriptive grammar, and good traditional grammarians such as Whitney did both: they both describe what people actually say and, when they feel so inclined, express value judgments about different ways that something is said or might be said: ' Grammar does not at all make rules and laws for language; it only reports the facts of good language, and in an orderly way, so that they may be easily referred to, or learned, by anyone who has the occasion to do so ' (E12). As an example of the highly perceptive observations that Whitney made about what people actually say, note his observation that ' where an object is said to have more of one quality than of another, the phrase with *more* alone is used: thus, *the news was more true than pleasant* (not *truer than pleasant*) ' (E200).ᵃ Here Whitney clearly is not castigating dolts who say *truer than pleasant* (to my knowledge, no native speaker has ever said that) but simply recording what people actually do.

At a couple of places, Whitney says things that suggest a view of the goals and the central problems of syntax that is not far removed from that found in Chomsky's *Syntactic Structures*. He observes that sentences do not result just from putting words together:

'We cannot produce a sentence by stringing together words of one sort only: for example
    sun tree ink;   shines writes went;
    the this yonder;   good golden bright.
Nor, again, can we take words of different sorts at haphazard out of a dictionary or spelling-book, and make of them sentences—even foolish or false sentences.   Thus
    the with golden brightly away;
    shines over is toward tall never.' (E23)

Whitney thus appears to take as his goal distinguishing grammatical combinations of words from ungrammatical combinations rather than just providing commentary on the grammatical ones. He also suggests that he was aware that there are infinitely many grammatical sentences and that recursive processes which are repeatable without limit are responsible for there being infinitely many grammatical sentences:

'A dependent clause may have another clause dependent on itself, and this again another, and so on: for example,
I went into the garden where the grass was wet with the dew that lay upon it.
This is the dog that worried the cat that killed the rat that ate the malt that lay in the house that Jack built '. (E425)

Whitney did not lay any particular emphasis on this observation, not, I conjecture, because he did not consider it of importance but because he found it so obvious.

The various rules that Whitney gives and those details of his discussion of examples which can be taken as implying rules divide into rules of two types, which match quite closely the base rules and transformations of Chomsky's work. His statements about what may occur in a sentence have to do not with surface structure but with some level of underlying structure. He defines a sentence as ' a combination of words having completeness in itself as the expression of a thought ' (G426) and states that it is composed of a subject and a predicate, to which he adds, ' That a thought cannot be signified or communicated without the combination of a subject and a predicate is not claimed; but only that this combination is the full and regular mode of expression, the norm to which all expressed thoughts may be reduced, or of which they may be regarded as variations '. He thus treats imperatives as having subjects which are not expressed rather than as not having subjects: ' The pronoun-subject of a verb is sometimes omitted. (a) The subject of the imperative 1st and 2nd persons is always omitted . . . ' (F148). It is noteworthy that he speaks here of a *pronoun* subject; since he stated three pages earlier that a verb agrees in person and number with its subject, I conjecture that his reason for this is that the imperatives to which he refers have agreement markers of the first and second persons and that an overt subject of the first or second person would generally be a pronoun.[2]

The rules for what elements a clause may contain are essentially definitions of categories in terms of (underlying) dependency relations:

'a.　The original elements of the sentence are the subject-noun and the verb.

b.　The meaning of the verb may be filled out by an object-noun; also by a predicate adjective or noun (qualifying either the subject or the object); or it may be modified by an adverb.

c.　A noun in any construction in the sentence may be qualified by an adjective; an adjective, by an adverb; an adverb, by another adverb.

d.　A noun may be made to qualify another noun, adjectively [sic], by being put in the possessive case, or by being joined to the noun by a preposition; it may be made to qualify a verb or adjective or adverb, adverbially, sometimes in the objective case simply, but usually by means of a preposition.' (E 406)

They are stated in terms of 'simple' indicative declarative main clauses, of which other clauses are 'variations'. His treatment of interrogative and imperative clauses involves element of an understood higher clause such as appears in Ross's (1970a) performative analysis:

' Sentences are of three fundamental kinds, *assertive, interrogative,* and *optative* (or *imperative*) . . . Of only the first of these can it be truly said that it involves the predication of something of a subject. The relations of the three to one another are best developed by reducing them to the common form of dependent clauses, expressing what is affirmed, inquired, or desired by some definite speaker. Thus, we say of another, *er behauptet, dass du ihn liebst* " He asserts that thou lovest him "; *er fragt (will wissen), ob du ihn liebest* " He asks (wants to know) whether thou lovest him "; *er verlangt, dass du ihn liebest* " He requires that thou love him ". When, now, we come to speak in our own persons, we change *ich behaupte, dass du mich liebst* " I maintain that thou lovest me " into *du liebst mich,* the assertion of the assertion being usually a quite unnecessary formality; *ich will wissen, ob du mich liebst* " I wish to know whether thou lovest me " becomes *liebst du mich* " Lovest thou me? ", the wish to know being intimated by arrangement and tone; and *ich verlange, dass du mich liebest* " I require that thou love me " is changed into *liebe du mich* " Love thou me! ", the desire or demand being expressed by arrangement, tone, and appropriate verbal form. That is to say, the usage of the language has established modes of expression by which the speaker can signify his desire to know, or his request or command, directly, without putting it necessarily, as he may do optionally, into the form of an assertion '. (G427a)

I will digress here into a description of the parsing procedure found in the exercises of *Essentials of English grammar,* which fits well the conception of a grammar involving transformations and base rules that I attribute to Whitney. The first exercise consists in having the pupil identify the subject, predicate, complete subject, and complete predicate in various examples. The pupil is to

[2] Generally, though not always. Whitney mentions first or second person expressions consisting of a pronoun conjoined with a full noun phrase, e.g. *mon ami et moi* (F146).

draw a vertical line separating the complete subject and complete predicate and to underline the subject and predicate proper, e.g.

The <u>rain</u> | <u>falls</u> from the cloud.

Whitney adds the instruction, ' In order that the sentences may be properly divided into subject and predicate, they should, if necessary, be rearranged, the words being put into the more usual order ' (p. 22); I will return later to the question of what he means by ' usual ' in this passage.   He illustrates this with such examples as

Now fades the glimmering landscape on the sight.,

which he says should be treated as

The glimmering <u>landscape</u> | <u>fades</u> now on the sight.

Actually, undue significance should not be attached to Whitney's reference to ' rearrangement': this by itself is not so much evidence that Whitney had transformations (the inverses of the ' rearrangements ') as that traditional grammarians attached little importance to word order.   The vertical line which appears in the examples serves not only to indicate the division into complete subject and complete predicate but to go proxy for the whole clause when the clause is dependent on something else or when clauses are coordinated, as in the following example, in which the placing of the *but* between the two vertical lines indicates that it is the clauses that are coordinated:

    <u>we</u> | <u>laughed</u> loudly
       but
    <u>they</u> | <u>were</u> silent.

The vertical line is what I had in mind in my earlier remark about an ' ideal element ' of ' predication '.   Coordination and subordination are both indicated in Whitney's diagrams by putting the relevant items one above the other, where the items can be either single words or the vertical strokes which correspond to whole clauses.   Since Whitney speaks of conjoined verbs in discussing the example *He came and saw it* (E327), it might appear at first glance that this system would be incapable of representing the difference between conjoined verb phrases (as in that example) and actual conjoined verbs, as in *He produced and directed that movie*.   However, the difference can actually be represented by making use of multiple dependency relations such as Whitney uses elsewhere: in the first example, *it* is the object only of *saw* whereas in the second example, *that movie* is the object of both *produced* and *directed*.   My guess that Whitney would so analyze the latter example is confirmed by his use in the French grammar (F145) of the plural *subjects* in speaking of what I would call a conjoined subject.

The parsing exercises in the first four chapters involve only the devices discussed so far.   In the exercises of chapter 5, Whitney takes up much more detailed parsing.   Here he introduces the notion of parsing a *word* (actually, an occurrence of a word in a sentence), by which he means giving three kinds of information about it:

'A.   What *Kind* of word it is.   This implies telling: **1.**   What part of speech it is; **2.**   To which of the various classes and subclasses into which that part of speech is divided it belongs . . .

B.   What is its grammatical *form*.   This implies telling: **1.**   Whether it is simple, or derivative, or compound; **2.**   If it is an inflected word, what is its form as such: that is, of what number, case, person, tense, mode, or degree it is . . .

C.   What is its *construction*: that is, what part it plays in the sentence to which it belongs, in what way it is combined with other words to make up the sentence . . .' (p. 62).

He supplements his earlier instructions on parsing by saying that one is to parse each word before any words that qualify it.   He illustrates this with the sentence *My brother laid the paintings on John's writing-desk*, in which he first parses *brother*, saying that it is the subject of *laid* (I mention here only the third of the three types of information that Whitney's parsing calls for[3]); then *my*, which he says qualifies *brother*, then *laid*, which is the predicate, having *brother* for its subject; then *paintings*, which is the object of *laid;* then *the*, which is an adjective modifying *paintings;* then *writing-desk*, which is joined by *on* to *laid;* then *John's*, which is an adjective qualifying *writing-desk;* and finally *on*, which is a preposition joining *writing-desk* to *laid*.

In the parsing exercises for chapter 6, which have to do with relative pronouns, Whitney makes clear that when he instructed the pupil to rearrange the words into their 'usual order' he did not mean the order in which one would most likely say the words of that clause but the order which is most usual for the clauses in the language as a whole, i.e. 'subject-verb-object-adverb' order, even when rules of the language forbid that in surface structure.   He says that 'in order to help the scholar to realize what part the relative [pronoun], notwithstanding its position, really bears in the making up of the sentence', the relative clause in *the man whom we saw* must be rearranged to *we saw whom*, even though this 'makes the clauses seem strange and unnatural'.   His diagram is as follows, with the brace indicating that the position of the one word above the other is significant, i.e. that *whom* is connected to *man*:

$$\left.\begin{array}{l}\text{the man} \\ \text{we } | \text{ saw whom}\end{array}\right\} |\text{ is gone}$$

He includes under 'rearrangement' of things into their 'usual order' the restoration of two words whose content is fused into a single word; he thus diagrams *I cannot imagine what you are talking about* as

$$\left.\begin{array}{l}\text{I } | \text{ cannot imagine that} \\ \text{you } | \text{ are talking about which}\end{array}\right\} \text{what}$$

In like manner (p. 97), he decomposes the *what* of *what pupils are here came early* into *those . . . who* and treats the *which* of *we know to which class they*

---

[3] The first two types of information are generally what one would expect, though there are occasional surprises, as when Whitney calls the *the* of *the more the merrier* an adverb.

belong as a relative pronoun replacing the article of *class:*

those pupils⎞ | came early   we | know the class⎞
            who⎠ | are here   they | belong to which⎠

The following illustrate his diagrams for other kinds of subordinate clauses (p. 204):

(a)   We | hear the clock   (b)
            as   That | is certain.
      it | tolls the hour.   it | has tolled |
(c)   I | do not know whether
                    it | has tolled

Note the vertical orientation of the words and strokes: *as* connects the whole clause *it tolls the hour* to the verb *hear*.

The three works under discussion abound in remarks which suggest transformational derivations: references to understood elements and rules for getting ' derived ' word order from a more ' basic ' word order, though it should be kept in mind that (unlike his treatment of Sanskrit phonology) his discussions of English, German, and French syntax appear to contain no explicit examples of intermediate stages of derivations. There are especially many examples of references to elided or understood elements. For example,

' Sometimes an adverb, by an elliptical construction (as representing the predicate of an adjective clause), stands as adjunct to a noun: as *der Mann hier* ' the man here ' . . . , that is, " the man who is here ", (G110.2).

Note that for Whitney *hier* is still an adverb in this example, even though it modifies a noun, and ' adverb ' is defined as something which modifies a verb, adjective, or adverb; this supports my contention that Whitney's statements of what may depend on what amount to ' base rules ' which state what dependencies may hold in underlying structures, even though different dependencies may arise through ellipsis. Similarly,

' Very often, an adverb of direction with the auxiliary takes the place of an omitted verb of motion: thus *sie können nicht von der Stelle* " They cannot [stir] from the place ' . . . Other ellipses, of verbs familiarly used with these, or naturally suggested by the context, are not infrequent: thus, *was soll ich* " What am I to [do]? " . . . The auxiliary is thus often left with an apparent object, really dependent on the omitted verb ' (G259. 2–4).

In discussing rules for the subjunctive in German, he says that ' The verb upon which the clause of indirect statement depends is sometimes unexpressed, being inferred from the connection; thus, ' *Die Lateiner wurden hart verfolgt, weil jener sie zu sehr begünstigt habe* " The Latins were severely persecuted because [it was claimed that] he had favored them too much " ' (G333.3d). One case where intermediate stages in a transformational derivation are at least implied is his discussion of *un singulier homme que ce roi* 'A singular man, this king ', which he gives as an example of his statement that ' In elliptical expressions, the *que* remains, even when the *ce* and the verb are omitted '; this comes directly after his having said ' Very commonly, a logical subject—whether a word, a phrase, or a clause—that follows the verb is anticipated by the indefinite or impersonal *il* or *ce* with the verb . . .   The logical subject is then sometimes preceded by *que* as a sort of correlative to the grammatical subject *ce*' (F147b); the elision to which Whitney refers thus takes place on a structure which he himself seems to regard as derived from something more basic.

Whitney treats conjunction reduction as a kind of ellipsis, which he illustrates by giving precisely the kind of example that shows it not to be just ellipsis:

these are dark [woods, these are] gloomy [woods, these are] unfrequented woods. (E485)

He evidently really means ellipsis here, since the examples of conjunction reduction appear together with examples of gapping:

He is present, she [is] absent.

While his conception of how an underlying conjoined sentence is related to a surface structure with conjoined constituents has ludicrous implications for derived constituent structure, Whitney's observations about what can be derived by conjunction reduction are extremely insightful.   He not only points out that there are sentences with conjoined constituents which cannot be derived by conjunction reduction, e.g. *We thought Tom and Dick and Harry a noisy trio* (which was apparently well known in the 19th century; see Silvestre de Sacy 1824 and Pinneo 1852), but makes the really valuable point that in such sentences the conjunction must be *and*: ' Such combinations with any other conjunction are only rare and irregular ' (E488).   It is unfortunate that Whitney gave no example of ' combinations with another conjunction '; possibly what he had in mind was something like *Grant or Greeley is a horrible choice.*

A clear example of a rule deriving a non-basic word order from a more basic one is found in Whitney's discussion of German word order: ' The prefix stands before the verb in the infinitive and both participles, but after it in all other simple forms . . .   But if, by the rules for the arrangement of the sentence, the verb is transposed, or removed to the end, it comes, even in the simple forms, to stand after its prefix, and is them written as one word with it: thus, *als ich diesen Morgen fruh zu studieren anfing* "As I began to study early this morning "[4] (G299.2).

There are many places where Whitney discusses one sentence in terms of a related sentence, though in most cases it is difficult to decide whether Whitney conceives of them as transformationally related.   He describes the relative pronoun of a non-restrictive clause as ' having nearly the value of *and* with a personal or demonstrative pronoun or adverb: thus,

I gave him some bread, which he ate; . . .

Here *which he ate* is equivalent to *and he ate it*' (E437).   He speaks of apposi-

---

[4] Whitney treats *anfing* in this example as transformationally derived but does not so treat the participle of sentences such as *Ich habe angefangen, zu studieren.*   This is presumably because in the former case but not the latter there is a ' more basic ' surface structure clause in which the prefix is separate from the verb.

tions as 'implying' predications: 'Thus, in *My friend the hunter carries his weapon, a rifle, on his shoulder*, we have the nouns *friend* and *weapon* limited or described by the addition of *hunter* and *rifle*. There are implied in the sentence the two assertions that *my friend is a hunter* and *his weapon is a rifle;* but they are only implied, not actually made' (E375). Here it is not clear whether this should be interpreted as a rule for what a noun may be qualified by, plus a rule for the semantic interpretation of such a structure, or a rule for deriving nominal adjuncts from sentential adjuncts. He speaks of *We paid the wages* as involving a direct object and *We paid the man* an indirect object, on the basis of the fact that a parallel sentence with two objects, *We paid the man the wages*, has an unambiguously indirect object corresponding to the object of *We paid the man* and an unambiguously direct object corresponding to the object of *We paid the wages* (E367); however, it is not clear whether Whitney regarded either of the two sentences as elliptical. There are some interesting cases of discussion of morphologically complex words and paraphrases which distribute their meanings over two or more words:

'In *He made the stick straight*, the adjective *straight* qualifies the object *stick*, by becoming a kind of addition to the verb *made*, defining the nature of the action exerted on the stick. We may say instead *He straightened the stick*. Here the adjective is, as it were, taken into the verb, and becomes a part of the assertion made by the verb alone' (E369).

'Taking *sing* in the usual sense, we should never speak of 'singing a throat'; but we may say *I sang my throat hoarse*, meaning " I made my throat hoarse by singing ". And, in like manner,

She wrings the clothes dry;

The lightning struck him dead;

They planed the board smooth;

where *wrings dry* means 'makes dry by wringing'.

If Whitney understood the longer sentences as more basic than the shorter ones, his analyses are essentially those of Lakoff (1965) and Binnick (1969). Note also the following observations (Whitney 1883: 39–40):

A case of kindred character . . . is that by which a noun or adjective (or its equivalent) is made directly predicative to an object noun. Examples are, *I make him a ruler, I make it black*. That the logical value of the words *ruler* and *black* in these little sentences is that of predicates to *him* and *it* respectively, is past all question. The fact appears from every test that can be applied, in the way of transfer into other and equivalent forms of expression: 'I cause that *he* be a *ruler*' (change to a subordinate substantive clause with its regular subject and predicate); 'I cause *it* to be *black*' (change to accusative-subject with an infinitive copula and following predicate); 'it is made black' (change to passive form, with object turned into subject, and the adjective, etc. becoming an ordinary predicate to it as such); and so on. The predicate word is also often absorbable into the verb itself: thus, 'I blacken it'; which is analogous to 'I fell it', i.e. 'I make it fall'—one of the points of contact between denominative and causative formations. That is to say, *fell* is analyzable into *fall*, as the material part of the predication, and a copula of causation instead of the ordinary copula of existence; and *blacken*, in like manner, into the same copula with the adjective *black*, as the material of predication.

In several cases, Whitney supports his conclusions by citing facts of exactly the same types that recent transformational grammarians have cited in support of similar conclusions. He argues that in German sentences such as *Ich höre euch jeden Tag preisen* ' I hear you praised every day ', ' the real object of the infinitive [has been] transferred to the governing verb ' on the grounds that ' that object, when designating the same person or thing with the subject of the verb, is expressed by the reflexive instead of the personal pronoun: thus, *er wollte sich nicht halten lassen* " He would not let himself be held " ' (G343.5c). In other places he cites facts upon which such an argument could be based, though it is not fully clear that he intends such an argument to be understood. For example, in discussing English sentences with NP plus infinitive which he says ' are equivalent to ' corresponding sentences with a *that*-clause, e.g. *He believed his friend to have been wronged*, which he says ' is equivalent to ' *He believed that his friend had been wronged*, he points out that the ' subject of the infinitive ' can be turned into the subject of a passive: *His friend was believed by him to have been wronged* (E449) and that a predicate pronoun in the infinitive is in the objective case (*We knew it to be him*, E451) even though Whitney's English would have a nominative in e.g. *We knew that it was he*. These two facts provide evidence that *his friend* in *He believed his friend to have been wronged* is the surface object of *believe* even though it is the logical object of *wrong* and thus that its derivation involves the movement of a constituent of the subordinate clause into the main clause.

One characteristic of what I have been calling Whitney's underlying forms which is worth dwelling on is that they are composed of clauses, each of which is a possible surface structure of an indicative main clause, as regards both grammatical relations and word order. Recall in particular footnote 4, where I pointed out that Whitney treated *anfing* but not *angefangen* as transformationally derived, the difference between the two cases being that in only the former was there a corresponding main clause in which the verb was separate from the particle. This seems to be a common characteristic of traditional grammarians, who often come to grief when analyzing a construction that they wish to regard as ' derived ' but whose putative source would involve a clause that did not match any possible surface structure; a striking example of this is found in Pinneo (1852), who attempted[5] to reduce all constructions to a small number of ' basic ' constructions (e.g. to reduce all infinitives to *that*-clauses and relative clauses) but took passives to be ' basic ' when there was no constituent available to serve as subject of the ' underlying ' clause that he wanted to set up, even when, as in the following example (p. 194) he is forced to take a passive relative clause to underlie an active infinitive:

He has this hope to solace him.
He has this hope with which he may be solaced.

I would attribute to Whitney the following implicit (and probably not consciously held) conception of syntax. A grammar consists of two kinds of rules: *base rules*, which generate dependency trees, each clause of which has the

[5] I am grateful to Carolyn Nygren for rediscovering Pinneo and calling the relevant passages to my attention.

form of a ' basic ' declarative main clause (i.e. ' non-basic ' structures such as
extraposed clauses are not generated by the base rules); and *transformations*,
which make whatever obligatory adjustments in clauses as are demanded by their
environments (e.g. move the verb to the end in German subordinate clauses)
and introduce optional variations (e.g. extrapose clauses or delete performative
verbs with their subjects).   Had Whitney treated examples of greater complexity
and cited intermediate stages, it might be possible to argue that his syntax, like
his phonology, was one big cycle, i.e. that rules adjusting structures to allowable
surface forms would apply first to innermost constituents, then to larger constituents, etc.; that conclusion would explain why his underlying clauses take the
form of possible surface clauses, just as the corresponding conclusion in phonology
explains why his underlying forms contain only segments and sequences of segments which can occur in surface phonology.   However, in phonology Whitney
cites numerous intermediate stages of derivations in which he has divided the
form into immediate constituents and those constituents have already undergone
the phonological rules, whereas he cites no such clear examples in syntax.

[a] See ' Qualitative and quantitative comparison in English ' for an example of the ' dis-
covery ' of this fact in 1964.

20. Interpretative Semantics Meets Frankenstein[*]

This paper is a reply to Katz's 'Interpretative semantics vs. generative semantics', which, as my title[1] suggests, was directed not against a theory that anyone subscribes to but against a monster that was put together out of pieces of several corpses. Before taking up Katz's arguments, it would be worthwhile to give a thumbnail sketch of the theory that he claims to be attacking, which the reader may supplement by consulting such works as Lakoff (1970a, b), McCawley (1970c, in press *a*), and Postal (1970). The term 'generative semantics' is applied to a theory of grammar which has evolved out of that of Chomsky (1965), from which it differs in a number of major respects, of which the following had already appeared in papers to which Katz refers and other papers of that vintage. (1) Semantic structures are claimed to be of the same formal nature as syntactic structures, namely labeled trees whose non-terminal node-labels are the same set of labels that appear in surface structure. (2) The notions of a 'deep structure' which separates syntax from semantics and a distinction between 'transformations' and 'semantic interpretation rules' are given up in favor of a single system of rules which relates semantic structure and surface structure via inter-

[*] This paper first appeared in *Foundations of Language* 7. 285–96 (1971).
[1] My title parodies that of an Abbott and Costello film only because there is no Marx Brothers film whose title lends itself to an appropriate parody.

mediate stages which deserve the name 'syntactic' no more and no less than
'semantic'.   (3) It is held that the rules needed to determine what a grammatical
sentence may mean are also needed to determine what is grammatical at all.   (4)
A grammar is taken not to generate a set of surface structures but a set of derivations, and to consist of a set of 'derivational constraints': constraints on what
combinations of elements may occur in semantic structure, on what combinations of elements may occur in surface structure, and on how different stages of
a derivation may differ from each other.   Subsequent papers have argued that
it is necessary to allow derivational constraints to mention non-consecutive
stages of derivations and have elaborated and clarified the notion of semantic
structure and its relation to logic and provided reasons for taking 'semantic
structure' to be the level of linguistic structure to which logical rules of inference
apply (so that it can appropriately be called 'logical structure'), provided that
'logic' is taken in a sense which is broad with regard to what it covers (i.e. its
scope includes not only 'inference' but other relations between the contents of
sentences, not only the study of 'declarative' sentences but of the full range of
sentences in natural languages, and not only the logical properties of *and*, *or*, *not*,
if, *all*, and *some*, to which logicians have been unduly attached, but the logical
properties of all elements of content) and narrow with respect to the linguistic
constraints on the entities that are recognized (e.g. rather than 'atomic predicates' being allowed to be arbitrary functions, as in the work of most logicians,
the existence and atomicity of putative 'atomic predicates' must be linguistically
justified).   I will use the term *natural logic* (following Lakoff) to refer to 'logic'
in this sense.

Katz claims to be defending a theory of transformational grammar which involves a level of 'deep structure' as distinct from 'semantic structure' and a
system of 'semantic interpretation rules' as distinct from the inverses of transformations.   Curiously, little of his paper is devoted to attempts at justifying
either of these dichotomies.   Katz characterizes 'deep structure' as " a level of
syntactic structure for which the best account is a set of phrase markers K that
satisfy the conditions: (5) K is the full input to the transformational component
of the grammar . . .   (6) K is the full input to the semantic component of the
grammar . . . " (221).   This characterization of 'deep structure' gives no way
of telling what the deep structure of anything is unless it is supplemented by
a fairly precise characterization of what the 'transformational component' and
'semantic component' of a grammar do.   Since all that Katz says about them
is that their outputs are surface structures and semantic representations respectively and that the semantic component " must be a function F that is both
compositional in that F determines the semantic representations of a constituent
(including a sentence) from the semantic representations of its subconstituents,
and *general*, in that, for any constituent of the langauge, F recursively determines
the semantic representations assigned to it, with respect to the description the
constituent receives in the syntactic component " (225), his characterization of
'deep structure' is consistent with both the position that the 'transformational
component' is empty (and thus that 'deep structure' is identical to surface

structure) and the position that the ' semantic component ' is empty (and thus that ' deep structure ' is identical to semantic structure), which are two only terminologically different versions of the principal claim that he is arguing against. However, Katz's actual assumptions about ' deep structure ' are in fact richer than the characterization of it which he attributes to himself. Indeed, he assumes all the characteristics of ' deep structure' which he castigates Lakoff (1968 a) for taking to be defining characteristics, and gives ' proofs ' of them which purportedly have (5)–(6) as their premises but in fact have their conclusions for their premises. For example, in his ' proof ' that (5)–(6) imply that lexical insertion must take place at deep structure, Katz assumes that all the lexical items of a sentence must be present in the input to the semantic interpretation rules. I am at a loss to see how Katz could claim that (5)–(6) imply that lexical insertion must take place at deep structure, since he has clearly seen Gruber (1965), which operates in terms of a level of deep structure which satisfies (5)–(6) and whose ultimate elements are not lexical items but semantic units (which, however, were not combined as in semantic structure, so that Gruber needed a system of semantic interpretation rules to relate his pre-lexical deep structure to semantic structure proper). Likewise, in his ' proof ' that (5)–(6) plus ' methodological considerations of the sort that have always been part of the development of generative grammar ' imply that selectional restrictions must be stated in terms of deep structure, Katz surreptitiously inserts the adjective ' syntactic ' before the expression ' selectional and co-occurrence restrictions ', thus assuming not only the division of a grammar into a syntactic part and a semantic part but that the selectional restrictions to which Lakoff referred must be stated in terms of the syntactic part of the grammar, and treats the absurd proposal that selectional restrictions must be stated in terms of surface structure as if it were the only alternative to the proposal that they must be stated in deep structure.

Katz divides (6) into the two pieces: (7) " The semantic component is an interpretative system that operates on phrase markers independently generated by the syntactic component to assign them a compositional semantic interpretation ", and (8) " The phrase markers on which the semantic component operates are just those in K " and states that " in the present context, (8) is not at issue. The issue centers around (7), which expresses the doctrine of interpretative semantics " (222). What Katz says implies that his arguments are a defense equally of his version of ' interpretative semantics ', which accepts (8), and that currently held by Chomsky, which rejects it. However, (5)+(7) says even less about what deep structure is than does (5)+(6) (=(5)+(7)+(8)) and thus leaves an adherent of (7) with even less of a basis on which he might argue that a level of deep structure is necessary. When Katz dismisses the arguments by generative semanticists that lexical insertions can not all take place at the same stage of derivations and that certain familiar transformations must apply before certain lexical insertions by saying, " free interspersal of lexical insertion is also not a point of controversy between the theories of generative and interpretative semantics ", he is (at least for the moment) taking ' the theory of interpretative semantics ' to be something so vacuous that no ' points of controversy ' between it and any other theory are imaginable; by contrast, Chomsky, who rejects (8), accepts the claim that all lexical insertions occur together (which even Katz recognizes can not be ' proven ' from (5) plus (7)) and thus avoids vacuity.   Katz's elaboration of the remark just quoted contains some gross inaccuracies.   His statement that " Grammars fashioned on the model of generative semantics could restrict lexical substitution to a pretransformational stage " makes sense only when interpreted as meaning that a grammar in which all lexical insertions occur at the level of semantic structure would fit his definition of ' generative semantics '; Katz overlooks the fact that the actual assumptions of generative semanticists, which include the assumption that the operands of a transformation are constituents and the assumption that lexical insertions are transformations and thus subject to the latter constraint and all other valid constraints on transformations, imply that lexical insertions cannot all occur at the level of semantic structure, since there are lexical items which incorporate elements of meaning that do not all fit together into a single constituent of semantic structure, e.g. the word *kill*, which Katz discusses.   Katz's statement that " Grammars fashioned on the model of interpretative semantics could allow interspersal of operations inserting lexical items among transformational operations.   If grammars of the latter type were to allow interspersal, the semantic component would have to apply to some phrase markers outside of K, viz. to those derived phrase markers where lexical items not appearing in the underlying phrase markers make their appearance " repeats the gratuitous assumption that semantic interpretation rules must have lexical items in their inputs.

While Katz refrains from defending his assumption that lexical insertion takes place at deep structure, he presents a defense of his assumption that selectional restrictions must be stated in terms of deep structure and his additional claim that syntactic categories can not be identified with semantic categories.   This defense is a criticism of my argument (1968c) that selectional restrictions must be stated in terms of semantic structure.   Katz states that there is no need to consider my arguments for the claim that " any piece of information which may figure in the semantic representation of an item may figure in a selectional restriction ", since " if sound, it supports interpretative and generative semantics alike " (235).   Evidently, by ' supports ', Katz simply means ' is consistent with ', since it makes no more sense to speak of a respect in which deep structure is unnecessary as supporting the claim that deep structure is necessary than to speak of the demonstration that combustion products are heavier than what is burned as supporting the phlogiston theory.   Katz thus allows selectional restrictions to be stated in terms of arbitrary semantic properties of an item but claims that selectional restrictions may in addition make reference to non-semantic properties and to properties (semantic or not) of deep structure.   In the discussion of a selectional restriction which I had said must be stated in terms of the semantic property of denoting a name rather than the syntactic property of ' properness ', namely the restriction on what the second object of *name* may be:

They named their son John.

*They named their son that/some/one boy.

They named their son something outlandish.

Katz says that the restriction should be stated in terms of a feature [+Proper]: " The point McCawley misses is that a constituent can be marked [+Proper] without being a proper noun " (236–7). Katz is apparently using [+Proper] to denote the semantic property to which I referred, and the one fact which he cites to justify calling this feature syntactic, namely the choice of interrogative pronoun in

What/*Who(m) did they name their son?

is irrelevant, since (Lakoff, 1969) choice of pronouns in English is made on the basis of assumptions about the individuals which they refer to or over which they range rather than any properties of lexical items.ᵃ   A more interesting objection to my position by Katz is his claim that there are pairs of items which are semantically identical but have different selectional restrictions. For example, he maintains that

(i)   footwear

(ii) articles of wearing apparel for the feet

are semantically identical but differ in the restrictions that they impose on a determiner, which e.g. may be *much* in the case of (i) but not (ii) and may be *seven* in the case of (ii) but not (i).   However, Katz's statement that (i) and (ii) are identical in meaning is not as obviously true as Katz makes it out to be.   Indeed, upon a few moments reflection it becomes obvious, at least to me, that they differ in meaning in the same way as do *footwear* and *articles of footwear* or *wearing apparel for the feet* and *articles of wearing apparel for the feet*, i.e. the meaning of (ii) involves the proposition that what is referred to is individuated but the meaning of (i) does not.   It is of course easy to jump to the conclusion that they are identical in meaning, since existing footwear is individuated in the same way that feet are.   A more interesting case of this type (not cited by Katz) is provided by the English words *wheat* (mass noun) and *oats* (plural) and their German equivalents *Weizen* (plural) and *Hafer* (mass noun) respectively.[2,b] However, in this case the number seems to be an idiosyncracy of morphology (like the plural in *trousers* and *scissors*), and these items appear all to have the same selectional restrictions.   There are in fact some well-known cases which may refute the strong form of the claim that selectional restrictions are semantic, i.e. the claim that selectional restrictions have to do *only* with semantic structure and have nothing directly to do with lexical items, i.e. that all selectional violations are category mistakes.   For example, *essen* and *fressen* may be semantically identical except for *essen* but not *fressen* imposing a restriction that its subject ' be human '.   However, it is not clear that they refer to the same *kind* of eating (which verb do you use in reporting a well-mannered chimpanzee's eating something with a knife and fork?), and if not, they are no counterexample.   Even if

---

[2] I am grateful to John Robert Ross for calling this example to my attention.

there are counterexamples to the strong form of the claim,[3] I know of no counterexample (and Katz has provided none) to the weaker claim that a selectional restriction imposed by an item (whether by a lexical item or by a semantic item) is a presupposition about what an item in semantic structure purports to denote.

Katz also states that " the features [—Common] and [+Common] [by which Katz evidently means what he called [+Proper] and [—Proper] on the preceding page] clearly function in syntactic selection, since they determine the co-occurrence of nouns with certain determiners and relative clauses " (238).   Rather than offering any justification for this claim, he treats it as too obvious to deserve comment and goes on to argue that the proper/common distinction does not correspond to any semantic distinction.[4]   However, the analysis that Katz assumes for determiners (which is apparently that of Chomsky (1965): determiners are present in deep structure as constituents of NP's and nouns which head a NP are subcategorized as to what other material may go into the NP with them) is by no means the only feasible analysis, and there are so many competing analyses of relative clauses that I cannot even tell which of them Katz has in mind.   The absence of quantifiers before proper nouns follows from three propositions that are generally accepted by generative semanticists: that quantifiers originate as predicates of higher clauses (as in Figure 1, which shows the structure that I argue (in press a) to underlie *All men are mortal;* see Lakoff (1970a) for a related though significantly different proposal and for arguments for an external source for quantifiers) and are moved into their eventual NP's by a transformation that adjoins them to an occurrence of the corresponding variable, that common nouns are underlying predicates, and that proper nouns (pace Quine) are not.   I am not in the position of being able to say that the absence of articles before proper names (leaving aside of *the Hague, the Bronx,* and river names) follows from existing claims of generative semanticists, since generative semanticists have so far said nothing of significance about articles (and interpretative semanticists

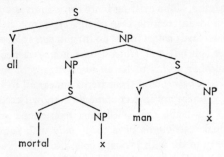

Fig. 1

[3] Abundant material which may well provide many such counterexamples is found in Leisi (1967).

[4] Katz attempts to prove this claim by arguing for a conclusion which, if it were true, would actually disprove it.   His statement, " Thus, we can conclude that a proper noun, and hence the proper-common distinction, does not carry semantic import " (239), suggests that for Katz the something-nothing distinction carries no semantic import.

have done little about articles beyond summarizing some obvious facts about surface cooccurrence); however, I see nothing in principle which gives an analysis such as Katz accepts (plus God knows what semantic interpretation rules) any advantage over an alternative in which articles are inserted by transformations that are sensitive to prior mention of the thing referred to and to certain existence and uniqueness presuppositions, with the absence of articles befor proper names in English (as opposed to Modern Greek) being a restriction on one of those transformations rather than on how things may be combined in deep structure. The impossibility of a restrictive relative clause modifying a proper noun would follow from any analysis in which the head noun of a relative clause construction originates as an underlying predicate (e.g. *a girl who I like* coming from a structure like that of Fig. 2) and in which common nouns but not proper nouns are underlying predicates.

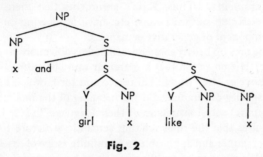

Fig. 2

One important issue which Katz touches on is that of whether syntactic and semantic structures are of the same formal nature, which generative semanticists argue is the case and have presented as evidence that the syntax/semantics dichotomy is invalid. Katz describes the claim that semantic structures are trees[5] as 'trivial'. His remark that " The utility of such apparatus seems to be a very general matter insofar as trees (or parenthesization) are relevant in every subject where hierarchical structure has to be described, e.g. in the case of biological taxonomies, genealogy, electronic circuitry, etc." suggests that he does not know what a tree is, since the circuit diagrams and genealogical diagrams which he evidently has in mind may contain loops and thus are not in general trees. While not quite as trivial as Katz says it is, the claim that semantic structures are trees is relatively trivial unless combined with claims about what may appear as labels in those trees, and generative semanticists have some highly specific claims as to what labels may appear on the nodes of a semantic structure, in particular, the claim that exactly the same labels for non-terminal nodes are needed in semantic structure as in surface structure. Katz attributes to generative semanticists the claim that constituents of semantic structure " can be properly categorized as nouns, noun phrases, verbs, verb phrases, adjectives, and so on " (233), an attribution which evidently results from Katz's combining the claim of the

[5] See McCawley (1968g) for discussion of the sense of ' tree ' intended here.

last sentence with his own conception of what node labels are needed in surface structure.   However, Katz surely has seen works such as Lakoff (1965) and Bach (1968), which argue that the verb/adjective/noun distinction has nothing to do with non-terminal node labels, that verbs, nouns, and adjectives all belong to a single underlying category (which Bach called ' contentive', and Lakoff, in accordance with the position that ' verb ' is the ' least marked ' of the three categories, called ' verb ').   The paper of mine (1967b) which Katz quoted was not very explicit as to what non-terminal node labels were necessary, but more recent papers by Lakoff and me have made explicit the claim that only three non-terminal node labels (S, NP, V) are needed and that these categories match in slightly broadened form categories used by logicians : S corresponds to the use of ' sentence ' in the terms ' closed sentence ' (='proposition ') and ' open sentence ' (=' propositional function '), V to ' predicate ' (taken as including ' operator '), and NP to ' argument '.   Thus, Katz's arguments that there is no semantic property characterizing surface nouns, etc. have no bearing on any claim ever made by any proponent of generative semantics.

Finally, let me take up briefly some miscellaneous objections by Katz to generative semantics.   His objection that a grammar must be ' compositional ' in the sense quoted above or else " it will fail to account for how speakers with a small finite storage capacity can understand the meaning of the indefinitely large (and theoretically infinite) set of sentences of their language " (242) is preposterous: this ability requires that the rules relating semantic structure to surface structure be finite in number and applicable to an infinite range of cases but says nothing about whether there must be the division of grammar into syntactic and a semantic part which Katz's definition of ' compositional ' presupposes.   Equally preposterous is Katz's objection that a generative semanticist requires some kind of semantic interpretation rule to tell whether the structure from which he would derive *John killed Bill* " represents the proposition that John killed Bill, the proposition that Bill killed John, the proposition that both were killed, or the proposition that both are killers " (248).   The structure to which Katz refers[6] contains a predicate ' Cause ', whose arguments are ' John ' and a sentence (Become (Not (Alive (Bill)))); both ' John ' and ' Bill ' have unambiguous roles in that structure, and the information that Katz's ' projection rule ' would derive from it is already there explicitly.   Not much less trivial is Katz's objection that generative semantics requires rules that interpretative semantics does not, viz. rules like

V → (Cause)
V → (Become)
. . .
N → (John),

[6] The tree which Katz ' quotes ' contains one spurious constituent, namely that which Katz labels 'Aux '.   While the article of mine (1968d) to which Katz refers does not indicate where the tense would originate, I have argued elsewhere (1971a) that tenses are verbs (and thus that there is no such constituent as 'Aux '; in this connection see also Ross (1969)) and have indicated that the tense would originate ' higher ' than where the tree that Katz attributed to me has it.

which would specify what ultimate items can occur in semantic structure. Generative semantics does in fact require rules saying that in semantic structure a node labeled V may dominate a node labeled CAUSE, etc.; however, these rules are not context-free, as Katz has them, but must indicate e.g. that CAUSE takes two arguments, one an index and the other a sentence, and that NOT takes a single argument, which must be a sentence. However, such rules serve to do what any grammar must do, namely to exclude sentences such as

*Tom caused.
*Tom caused the vice-chancellor.
*Tom caused the vice-chancellor the explosion.

while allowing

Tom caused the explosion.

One can do without such rules, if at all, only at the expense of incorporating some analogue of them into rules which may occur at some later stage of derivations, e.g. deep structure. The issue here is not whether certain rules are needed but what stage of a derivation ' strict subcategorization ' (in the sense of Chomsky (1965)) has to do with.

Katz's argument that " generative semantics type grammars cannot account for cases of semantically anomalous sentences which are syntactically well-formed " is of appreciably more interest than the objections just discussed but still does not stand up. Katz does not take up explicitly the question of whether the status of ' semantically deviant ' sentences is to be decided purely on the basis of grammar or on the basis of grammar plus logical rules of inference, but his treatment of sentences such as *John sold his after-image to Robert* makes clear that he holds the former view. My reaction to that sentence is that the source of its oddity is that selling involves transfer of ownership and that an after-image is something that it makes no sense to speak of someone's owning; the same oddity appears more directly in *Robert owns John's after-image*. I take the position that such oddities consist in nothing more nor less than contradictions between presuppositions, not presuppositions of the words of the sentence per se but of semantic elements that are incorporated into them (e.g. the ' own ' that is incor-porated into *sell*), and that not only grammar but indeed the whole of logic is in-volved in determining when such a contradiction exists. For example, the oddity of the discourse

John looked at his jacket and then at his reflection. Both of those things are waterproof.

(which is the same oddity as in Katz's example *John's reflection is waterproof*) cannot be shown to exist without applying the rule of universal instantiation to the second sentence (thus concluding that ' m is waterproof ', where m is the second of the two things) and deriving a contradiction from the presuppositions of that clause and ' m is John's reflection ', which comes from the first sentence. Thus, Katz is technically right that " generative semantics type grammars cannot account for cases of semantically anomalous sentences which are syntactically well-formed ", but that is no objection: an adequate account of such sentences requires interaction between grammar and (natural) logic, and Katz has exhibited no defect in the grammar which generative semantics can provide for natural logic to interact with.   Another objection that Katz makes in this connection is based either on an equivocation with the word ' generate ' or on nothing at all. Katz says that the generative semanticist's only ' way out ' of the problem that he has just posed is to " design the semantic component[7] to generate two sets, one a set of representations of fully meaningful senses of sentences, and the other, a set of representations of non-senses, including various degrees of conceptual garble " (255).   This passage may be a rare instance in which Katz (who is usually careful about the distinction) uses ' generate ' in the sense of ' cause to come off the assembly line of a sentence factory ' rather than in the mathematical and linguistic sense of ' specify what the members of __ are '.   If a grammar is a set of constraints on derivations, then many subsets of that grammar will also define classes of derivations (generally a larger class of derivations than that de- fined by the whole grammar).   Thus, if selectional restrictions are in fact to be treated wholly within grammar and if each selectional restriction is itself a derivational constraint, then both the whole grammar and the subset of the grammar obtained by omitting the selectional restrictions define classes of derivations.   To put the same point slightly differently, given a grammar and a putative derivation, one could tell whether the derivation satisfies all the rules of the grammar, whether it satisfies all the rules but some selectional restrictions, etc.   However, that fact is of no more significance than the fact that a grammar containing a number-agreement rule not only defines the class of all well-formed derivations but also the class of derivations which are well-formed except for incorrect number agreement.

[a] This is an overstatement.   As I pointed out in ' The role of semantics in a grammar ', there are lexical items (e.g. *scissors, trousers*) which are idiosyncratically plural and which not only take plural number agreement but require pronouns of which they are the an- tecedent to be plural.
[b] *Weizen* turns out really to be a masculine singular.   Thanks a lot, Haj.

[7] Katz's choice of terminology is confusing, since linguists (including Katz elsewhere in the same paper) have hitherto used ' semantic component ', if at all, to refer to a system of rules that specify what semantic structures correspond to what syntactic structures.   The rules to which he refers here are more analogous to the ' base rules ' of Chomsky's *Aspects* than to its ' semantic component '.

21. Prelexical Syntax[*]

Abstract. The 'generative semantic' conception of grammar, which rejects the familiar syntax/semantics and transformation/semantic-interpretation-rule dichotomies and treats the relation between content and surface form as mediated by a single system of 'derivational constraints', is sketched informally and illustrated, with special attention given to (i) the notion of 'possible lexical item' and interlinguistic differences as to what lexical items are possible, (ii) cases where an adverb modifies a semantic constituent that is not directly represented in surface structure, and (iii) verbs that refer to means and instruments.

This paper treats the questions of what kinds of rules are needed to specify how the content of sentences is related to their surface form and and of how those rules interact with each other. There is fairly general agreement that the surface structure of a sentence is appropriately represented by a labeled tree, i.e. that the surface structure of a sentence consists not merely of a sequence of morphemes but of the larger units which those morphemes are grouped into and that the category membership of those units is significant. There is no general agreement as to the nature of semantic structure; but I will maintain that the content of a sentence token is likewise appropriately represented as a labeled tree, though the ultimate units of a semantic structure will not be morphemes but rather some kind of semantic units. The semantic units which are encoded in a lexical item need not be all together in semantic structure, as they would be if the conception of the content of a lexical item as a bundle of feature specifications were correct. For example, the elements of meaning encoded by the word *persuade* in a sentence such as

* This paper was read at the 22nd Annual Roundtable Meeting, Georgetown University, March 11, 1971, and first appeared in the Georgetown University *Monograph Series on Languages and Linguistics* 24. 19–33.

(1)   Sally persuaded Ted to bomb the Treasury Building.

are combined semantically with different constituents of semantic structure.
Assuming for the moment that it is correct to speak of *persuade* as contributing
notions of 'doing', 'causing', and 'intending' to the content of (1), those
notions are not combined in a homogeneous fashion.   (1) does not make reference to disembodied intention but to intention on Ted's part; it does not
make reference to disembodied 'doing' but to Sally's doing something; and it
does not make reference to disembodied causation but rather to Sally's action
causing Ted to intend to bomb the Treasury Building.   The elements of content to which I have been referring are not features of the sentence but are relations between items of content that figure in the sentence, and to specify the
semantic structure of a sentence, it is necessary to not merely indicate which
such elements are present but also indicate what items those relations relate.
A tree diagram such as[1]

(2)

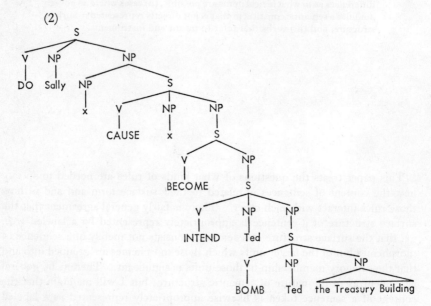

accomplishes that.
    The relationship between (2) and any syntactic 'deep structure' for (1) that
has been proposed by those who accept a dichotomy between syntax and seman-

---

[1] Capitalization is used to distinguish semantic elements from corresponding morphemes.
I have ignored the semantic structure of the various NP's.   I have also snuck into (2) an
item which did not appear in the above discussion, namely 'BECOME', which appears as
a consequence of my claim (McCawley, in press *b*) that the notion of 'causing' which is
relevant here is a relation between two events rather than between an event and a state;
Ted's intending to bomb the Treasury Building is a state, and its coming to be the case
that he intends to bomb it is an event.   Regarding the verb-first order of the nodes of
these trees, see McCawley (1970a).

tics, which I do not, is extremely complicated.   However, the relationship between *persuade* and (2) is far from arbitrary and has much in common with the
relationship between other verbs and the semantic structures of clauses of which
they are the main verb.   The elements of meaning that are encoded in *persuade*
are ' DO ', ' CAUSE ', ' BECOME ', and ' INTEND ', each of which is the
main predicate of the complement of the preceding one in (2).[a]   There are many
other verbs which encode two or more predicates, each of which is the main
predicate of the complement of the preceding one.   For example, *kill* encodes
' DO CAUSE BECOME NOT ALIVE ' and *apologize* encodes ' REQUEST
FORGIVE '.   The common characteristic in the relationship of each of these
verbs to the semantic structures which it is used in expressing can be captured in
the form of a rule which relates stages in a derivation that leads in steps from
semantic structure to surface structure, specifically, a rule that allows the predicate of a clause to be adjoined to the predicate of the next higher clause.
Successive application of that rule to (2) would convert it into[2]

(3)

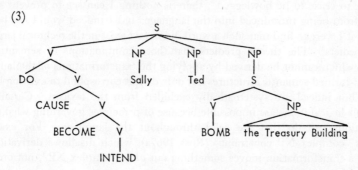

which contains a constituent ' DO CAUSE BECOME INTEND ' which corresponds to the verb *persuade*.   I note that this rule, which is known as Predicate-raising, does exactly the same kind of thing as do the ' adjunction transformations ' of syntactic studies that assume a distinction between syntax and
semantics, only it does it to a structure whose ultimate elements (or at least,
some of them) are not morphemes but semantic units.   It remains to be seen
that all combining of elements of meaning into lexical items can be reduced to
the interaction of a limited number of transformations of the types (permutation,
copying, adjunction, deletion, insertion) which are normally recognized.   Finding
a system of transformations that yield combinations of semantic material which
are exactly the possible lexical items of English is a program of research of which
so far only fragments have been carried out.   However, the hypothesis that an
adequate grammar of any language will involve such a system of transformations
currently appears to me to be the only approach to linguistic structure that has
much chance of providing an explanation of the contribution of individual lexical

---

[2] The subject of BOMB is missing from (3), since Predicate-raising is in the cycle, and thus
Equi-NP-Deletion would have applied to the INTEND-clause before INTEND was
adjoined to BECOME.

items to the content of sentences in which they appear.

In the last paragraph, I used the term ' possible lexical item '. This term is worth dwelling on before I proceed. Since Predicate-raising and the various other transformations that combine semantic material can interact in an infinite number of ways, there is an infinite number of combinations of semantic material that they can yield, although only a finite number of them correspond to actual lexical items of English. The theory that I am sketching here predicts that those combinations which can be derived by Predicate-raising, etc. but to which no actual lexical item of the language corresponds are accidental gaps in the lexicon: combinations of semantic elements which purely by accident do not correspond to any existing word and for which a word could be introduced if the need arose. One example of such an accidental gap is the combination of semantic elements which could arise if the constituent ' Bill is alive ', which I said was contained in the semantic structure of *John killed Bill*, were replaced by ' Bill is bowlegged '; while there is to my knowledge no English word meaning ' cause to cease to be bowlegged ', there is nothing I can see to prevent such a word from being introduced into the language, and I indeed would not be surprised if I were to find that such a word did in fact exist in the technical jargon of orthopedists. The theory predicts that those combinations of semantic elements which cannot be derived by applying the transformations of the language to well-formed semantic structures not only do not correspond to existing lexical items but indeed are systematically excluded from the lexicon. Certain impossible lexical items are impossible because of principles governing what transformations can do that are valid throughout the language. For example, Ross's ' complex NP constraint ' (Ross 1967a), which disallows derivations in which a transformation moves something out of a ' complex NP ', not only explains why one cannot say

(4) a. *How many movies have you met the man who directed?
     b. *Which official do you believe the rumor that Phil plans to assassinate?

but also explains why there is no lexical item meaning ' kiss a girl who is allergic to ', i.e. why there is no word *flimp* which appears in sentences like

(5) *Bert flimped coconuts.

that would be paraphraseable as ' Bert kissed a girl who is allergic to coconuts '. The impossibility of *flimp* follows from the fact that any application of the transformation needed to combine ' a girl who is allergic to ' with ' kiss ' would cause the derivation to violate the complex NP constraint. There appear also to be impossible lexical items whose impossibility follows not from some general principle that would exclude the transformations needed to derive them but rather from the details of what prelexical transformations the language happens to have. Here what I say is highly tentative, since I do not have a clear picture of what the relevant transformations are, but there are systematic differences between Japanese and English as regards what lexical items are possible. For example,

Japanese but not English has compound nouns whose elements each have their own reference, e.g. (examples from Chaplin and Martin 1967):

(6)   a.   Ano tihoo wa *kansyo* dotira mo hidoi ' In that region, the *heat and cold* are both severe '.

  b.   Yoku nite iru *oyako* desu ' It is a *parent and child* who resemble each other a lot '.

  c.   *Koosi* o kubetu suru ' We distinguish *public and private* '.

While English has compound nouns that are paraphraseable by a coordinate structure, e.g. *secretary-treasurer* and *radio-phonograph*, the two parts of the compound have the same reference: a *secretary-treasurer* is a single individual who is both secretary and treasurer.   However, Japanese *oyako* refers to one individual who is *oya* ' parent ' and another who is *ko* ' child '.   If my judgment that this fairly common compound type in Japanese is systematically excluded in English is correct, then Japanese and English differ in the way in which they allow coordinate structures to be combined into a single lexical item.

 I should also note that prelexical transformations include not only transformations which combine semantic material into possible lexical items, but also perfectly ordinary transformations such as Equi-NP-Deletion and *there*-insertion.   One piece of evidence that Equi-NP-Deletion applies prelexically is that *apologize* has Equi-NP-deletion under identity with its subject rather than its indirect object: in

(7)   a.   Tom apologized to Sue for kissing Lucy.,

the deleted subject of *kiss* is *Tom*, not *Sue*.   If *apologize* has the semantic structure proposed by Fillmore (1971), namely

(7)   b.   *x* apologizes to *y* for S=REQUEST $(x, y, \text{FORGIVE } (y, x, \text{S}))$,

then the subject of the lowest sentence would be deleted under identity with the indirect object of FORGIVE.[3]   But since the indirect object of FORGIVE is identical to the subject of REQUEST and thus to the subject of *apologize*, there appears to be Equi-NP-Deletion under identity with the subject of *apologize*:

(7)   c.

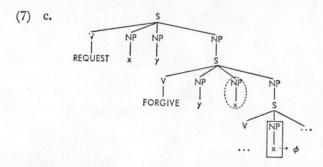

---

[3] This statement rests on the assumption that Equi-NP-Deletion is in the cycle.   For an elementary treatment of the notion of ' cycle ', see the first section of McCawley (1970a).

I have so far said nothing about the important topic of how one justifies putative semantic structures.[4]   One important type of evidence that can be offered
in support of a hypothesized constituent of a semantic structure is the possibility
of having an adverb that modifies that constituent rather than any constituent
that is present in surface structure.   Consider, for example,

(8)   a.   The door opened, and then I clósed it agàin.
      b.   *The door opened, and then I kícked it agàin.
(9)   a.   I closed the door temporarily.
      b.   *I kissed Susan temporarily.
(10) a.   I lent Tom my bicycle until tomorrow.
      b.   *I showed Tom my bicycle until tomorrow.

Again in (8a) does not modify the whole clause *I closed it* but rather the clause
' it is closed ' which would be posited in an analysis of the transitive verb *close*
as the causative of the stative adjective *closed*. (8a) presupposes that the door was
once closed but does not presuppose that I or anyone else had ever closed it before.   By contrast, *kick* is not open to an analysis as a causative of anything, and
the clause *I kicked the door again* only allows an interpretation which presupposes
that I had kicked the door before; (8b) is odd because *again* is not in a context
which would provide grounds for that presupposition. (9a) confirms the analysis
of transitive *close* as a causative of the stative adjective *closed:* what (9a) asserts
to be temporary is the door's being closed, not my action in closing it.[b]   For there
to be derivations of sentences like (8a) and (9a) within the framework adopted
here, it is necessary that there be a transformation which may apply before predicate raising and which raises ' adverbial ' elements over certain predicates:

(11)

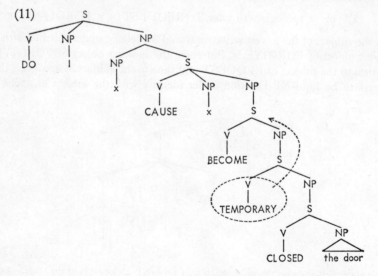

[4] A fairly detailed treatment of this topic is found in McCawley (in press *b*).

If this approach is correct, then the distribution of *temporarily* will be predictable without reference to idiosyncracies of any lexical items: it will appear in those sentences which are derivable from a well-formed semantic structure (thus, one in which ' TEMPORARY ' is predicated of something that can coherently be said to be temporary, i.e. either a state or an activity) by moving adverbs and combining predicates in the ways that the grammar allows.   Similarly, *until tomorrow* will occur in those sentences that are derivable from a structure containing a clause which *until tomorrow* can coherently modify and which allow it to be moved into the appropriate higher clause.   (10a) provides evidence that *lend* encodes a structure containing ' POSSESS ': *until tomorrow* in (10a) gives the time during which Tom's possession of my bicycle is to take place, not the time during which the lending takes place.   The analysis of *until tomorrow* as originating in a clause ' Tom possess my bicycle until tomorrow ' also explains why *until tomorrow* can occur in a clause with a past tense verb in (10a), even though it normally requires the tense of its clause to be future:

(12)   a.   *Jack stayed in his room until tomorrow.
       b.   Jack will stay in his room until tomorrow.

By the same token

(12)   c.   The sheriff of Nottingham jailed Robin Hood for four years.

is ambiguous as to whether *for four years* modifies the whole clause (in which case it would refer to repeated jailings) or modifies the ' Robin Hood be in jail ' part of the semantic structure that would be set up under the analysis of the verb *jail* (Binnick, 1969) as ' cause to be confined in jail '.   There is an interesting syntactic correlate to the property of modifying a clause which disappears through its main verb being incorporated into another verb, namely that such adverbs cannot be moved to the beginning of the clause.

(13)   Again I closed the door.

can only refer to a second action of closing the door, not to merely the door's being again closed:

(14)   Temporarily I closed the door.

if possible at all, can only be a past habitual (e.g. I worked temporarily as a doorman) and cannot refer to my making the door be temporarily closed;

(15)   *Until tomorrow I lent Tom my bicycle.

is ungrammatical; and in

(16)   For four years the sheriff of Nottingham jailed Robin Hood.

for four years can only be the period over which the sheriff (repeatedly) jailed Robin Hood, not the sentence which Robin Hood was to serve.   The analysis proposed here at least distinguishes the preposable adverbs from the nonpreposable ones, and, depending on details of the adverb-raising transformation that are not yet worked out, it may even explain why adverbs that modify part of the meaning of a word cannot be preposed.   Keyser (1968) argues convincingly that adverb-preposing moves an adverb to a position on the same ' level ' of IC-structure.   Adverbs originate in the clause immediately above the clause that they modify.   If adverb-raising makes an adverb a constituent of the next-higher clause, then after adverb-raising, an adverb which modifies a piece of the meaning of the main verb of a clause will be lower in the tree than an adverb modifying the whole clause would be.

I turn now to a topic, the fragmentariness of my understanding of which may or may not reflect inadequacies in my theory, namely verbs that make reference to means and instruments.   I will discuss especially *hammer* and *nail*. First, a word about the relation between those verbs and the homophonous nouns. Hammering need not be done with a hammer, but nailing has to be done with nails:

(17) a.   He hammered the nail with a rock.
      b.   *He nailed the proclamation to the door with rivets.

Thus, the meanings of the verb *hammer* and the noun *nail* must be more basic than those of the noun *hammer* and the verb *nail*.   In what follows, I will treat the meanings of the verb *hammer* and the noun *nail* as if they were unanalysable, since, while the verb *hammer* at least is surely analysable into more basic predicates having to do with striking and repetition, whatever internal structure they may have plays no role in what follows here.

Besides the transitive verb *nail*, there is also something that looks like its past participle

(18)   The proclamation is nailed to the door.

but really is not, since something is nailed to the door just as long as there are nails through it that hold it to the door, regardless of whether anyone nailed it. If the nails had just appeared out of the blue through divine intervention, it would be correct to say that the proclamation is nailed to the door; but it would not be correct to say that God had nailed it there: the latter would be appropriate only if God had assumed material form and driven the nails in by hammering them.   The range of things that can appear with *nailed* is as follows:

(19) a.   The proclamation is nailed to the door.
      b.   The boards are nailed together.
      c.   The door is nailed shut.
      d.   The flagpole is nailed at a 45° angle to the wall.
      e.   The boards are nailed into a rectangle.

The items that can appear with *nailed* appear to be any and all items that make up sentences describing a configuration that is maintained thanks to the nails:

(20) a.   The proclamation is on the door.
      b.   The boards are together.
      c.   The door is shut.

    d.   The flagpole is at a 45° angle to the wall.

    e.   The boards are (form?) a rectangle.

The subject of *nailed* must be something whose stability is maintained by the nails; compare (19d) with

    (21)   *The wall is nailed at a 45° angle to the flagpole.

I thus propose that the semantic structure of the sentences (19) is along the lines of:

    (22)

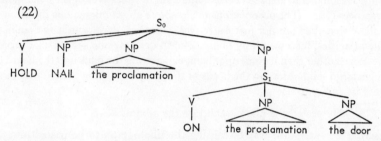

where ' HOLD ' is a three-place predicate relating an instrument, an object to which the instrument is ' applied ', and a state in which the instrument maintains the object.   The prelexical transformations involved in the derivation of (19) are Equi-NP-Deletion, which deletes the subject of S_1 under identity with the object of S_0, and some transformation which combines the instrument, NAIL, with HOLD.   It is tempting to conjecture that there is prelexical passivization here, yielding an intermediate stage of the form ' the proclamation is held by nails on the door ', and that NAIL is then combined with BE HOLD by the same prelexical transformation that combines generic objects with verbs in the derivation of occupation terms such as *dentist*, if one accepts an analysis in which *dentist* encodes a semantic structure containing ' treat teeth '.   The only evidence I know that has any bearing on that conjecture is the fact that not only in *nailed* but in the entire range of such words, the adjective in question consists morphologically of the noun for the instrument plus the past participle morpheme, and the past participle morpheme is the normal accompaniment of the passive construction.   At any rate, there is an apparently productive relationship between nouns denoting instruments that can hold things in a fixed configuration, homophonous transitive verbs, and adjectives that are homophonous but for the extra past participle morpheme:

    (23)   nail, screw, rivet, glue, paste, tack, staple, (paper) clip, pin, skewer, seal, tape, stitch, muzzle, shackle, chain, fetter, gag, handcuff, manacle, strap, lock.

The productivity of this relationship can be captured in a grammar by allowing the transformations sketched above to combine not just complexes of semantic material with HOLD but actual lexical items, and having a rule that would delete HOLD, thus yielding a derived verb homophonous with the original noun.   The transitive verbs appear to allow, besides an agent NP, exactly the same material that the corresponding adjective allows:

> (24) a. He nailed the proclamation to the door.
> b. He nailed the boards together.
> c. He nailed the door shut.
> d. He nailed the flagpole at a 45° angle to the wall.
> e. He nailed the boards into a rectangle.

It is thus reasonable to analyse (24) as some kind of causatives of the corresponding sentences (19).   The observations made above about miraculous insertion of nails show that they are not just causatives.   Indeed, even within the realm of human capacities, it seems funny to use (24a) to describe one's inserting the nails by any means other than hammering them, e.g. getting the nails into the board by putting a large solid object on the heads of the nails and sitting on it.   Similarly, it would be funny to use

> (25) He pasted the photograph into the album.

to describe an outlandish way of causing the photograph to be pasted into the album, e.g. placing the photograph on top of a page in the album and then bombarding it with subatomic particles in such a way that its rear surface turns into paste.   To paste a photograph into an album, one must not merely do something that causes it to be pasted into the album but do a standard kind of thing.   I will leave up in the air the question of how to indicate this notion of ' standard action ' in semantic structure and also the question of whether it may sometimes or perhaps even always be predictable on the basis of other things that an action must be ' standard '.

The range of constituents that can be combined with *hammer* is much broader than the range that can be combined with *nail:*

> (26) a. He hammered the nail into the board.
> b. He hammered the nail through the board.
> c. He hammered the metal smooth/flat/thin/soft/shiny.
> d. He hammered the flowerpot (in)to pieces/smithereens.
> e. He hammered the metal into a cylinder/disk/frying-pan.
> f. He hammered a groove into the metal.
> g. He hammered the dent out of the fender.
> h. He hammered the gold onto the sign.
> i. He hammered the shine off of the fender.
> j. He hammered a hole in(to) the wall.
> k. He hammered a 6-inch disk out of the wall.
> l. He hammered the boards apart.

In all of these sentences, *hammer* is combined with constituents that match the parts of a sentence which describes something that is brought about by hammering the object in the appropriate way:

> (27) a. The nail is in the board.

    b. The nail is through the board.
    c. The metal is smooth/flat/thin/soft/shiny.
    d. The flowerpot is in pieces/smithereens.
    e. The metal is (has become) a cylinder/disk/frying-pan.
    f. A groove is in the metal.
    g. The dent is not in the fender.
    h. The gold is on the sign.
    i. The shine is not on the fender.
    j. A hole is in the wall.
    k. A 6-inch disk is no longer in the wall.
    l. The boards are apart.

Curiously, certain states which can be brought about by hammering an object in the appropriate way cannot be referred to by sentences of the form (26). For example, it is possible to hammer something in such a way as to make it beautiful or ugly or dangerous or safe (by either creating or removing sharp edges); but the following are ungrammatical:

    (28) *He hammered the metal beautiful/ugly/dangerous/safe.

The acceptable adjectives appear to denote ' objective' properties, the unacceptable ones ' subjective' properties. While the adjectives denoting shapes, which surely are ' objective' properties, are unacceptable:

    (29) *He hammered the metal cylindrical/circular/spherical.,

the possibility of sentences such as (26e) suggests that this may be merely a case of suppletion involving adjectives and corresponding prepositional phrases. One weird restriction about which I have nothing to say is illustrated by

    (30) He hammered the rod straight/*bent.,

and one fact which may indicate that my mention of ' objective' properties in connection with (28) is wrong is the ungrammaticality of

    (31) *He hammered the reflection of City Hall off of the fender.,

which may indicate that *hammer* requires a property of the object itself, not of the object in relation to its environment.[c]

Essentially the same range of items appears with the verbs (32), with the qualification that certain combinations are impossible due to the impossibility of performing the action so as to bring about the effect in question, e.g. one cannot sift flour into a disk or to smithereens:

    (32) hammer, file, sand(paper), saw, sift, plane, iron, roll (as with a rolling pin), brush, comb, rake, mop, sponge, pound, knead, beat (eggs), polish, sweep, scrub, wipe.

Under the assumption that the meaning of the verb *hammer* plays the same role in all the sentences of (26), the semantic structure of those sentences would have to be something along the lines of ' x causes S by hammering y ', e.g. ' he causes the metal to become smooth by hammering it '. One interesting characteristic of these sentences is the prepositions that appear in them: *into* in (26f), *out of* in (26g), *onto* in (26h), and *off of* in (26i). These are the same prepositions that occur in sentences referring to motion:

(33) a. He ran into the kitchen.   BECOME IN
      b. He ran out of the garage.   BECOME NOT IN
      c. He jumped onto the table.   BECOME ON
      d. He jumped off of the roof.   BECOME NOT ON

In (26f-i), the *groove, dent, gold,* and *shine* do not move. The one thing that is common to (33a-d) and (26f-i) is that they involve locative relations coming into being (in (26f) it becomes the case that the *groove* is in the metal, and in (33a) it becomes the case that he is in the kitchen) or ceasing to be (in (26g) the dent ceases to be in the fender, and in (33b) he ceases to be in the garage), and the prepositions match the relation that comes into being or ceases to be: *into* is used for the ' in ' relation coming into being, *out of* for its ceasing to be, *onto* for the ' on ' relation coming into being, and *off of* for its ceasing to be. Thus, subject to the qualifications mentioned in connection with (28–31), the range of sentences involving *hammer* and the other verbs of (32) can be predicted on the basis of derivations that I conjecture are along the following lines, although here the analysis is highly tentative. Given a semantic structure such as (34), predicate-raising combines IN with NOT and then combines NOT-IN with BECOME, the resulting combination being realizable as the preposition *out of*. Subject-raising raises *the dent* into S_1, thus making it the derived object of CAUSE, Equi-NP-

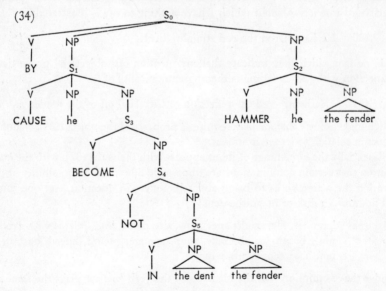

Deletion (as in *He made the metal smooth by hammering it*) deletes the subject of HAMMER, a highly suspect transformation deletes the object of HAMMER under God knows what identity condition with S_3, Predicate-raising combines CAUSE with BY, and a transformation hereby christened Means-incorporation replaces BY-CAUSE by the remaining verb (HAMMER) of S_4.

I have discussed *hammer* and *nail* in the hope of therby making clear what will have to be done to decide on the merits of the conception of grammar that I have sketched here or of any alternative theory. The analysis of *hammer* that I gave requires detailed justification, and I gave none because I so far have none worth speaking of. One kind of justification needed is a demonstration that the various steps into which I decomposed the relation between (26) and their meanings would recur in the relationships of other types of clauses to their meanings; until analysis of other lexical items shows that to be the case (or does the same for an alternative and superior treatment of *hammer*), my claim that the means which a language has at its disposal for combining semantic units into lexical items is a system of transformations will not have much support. In addition, the restrictions on *hammer* noted in connection with (28–31) and the restriction of transitive *nail* to a 'standard action' do not appear to follow from anything in my analysis, and it is not even clear that they can be expressed within my framework. Any analysis which shows these restrictions to follow from something else has a lot going for it.

To adequately account for the relationship between content and surface form, a grammatical theory must provide an answer to the question of how languages allow semantic units to be combined into lexical items, and if some alternative theory which upholds a distinction between syntax and semantics allows a correct answer to be given to that question which the theory sketched above does not, the division of a grammar into syntactic and semantic parts will (at last) receive some justification. I have rejected the distinction between syntax and semantics and between transformations and semantic interpretation rules not so much out of certainty that they are wrong as because they have been assumed gratuitously, they have been applied arbitrarily, and even if they are correct, they can be shown to be correct only on the basis of the consequences of not accepting them.

---

[a] The CAUSE-clause actually is not the complement of DO: it is a relative clause contained within the object of DO. It is not clear to me whether the rule that combines CAUSE with DO is really the same rule that combines each of the lower predicates with the one above.

[b] Since the following sentence is also grammatical:

The door closed, and then I ópened it agàin.,

(8a) says nothing about whether 'open' or 'closed' is more basic, but only that *close* is the causative of *closed* (just as the transitive *open* is the causative of the adjective *open*). The use of *again*, contrary to what I said in the text, is not based on presupposition but on inference. The presupposition of the first clause of (8a) which is of relevance is that the door (prior to the event being reported) was not open, and the fact that that entails that the door was closed is what justifies the use of *again*, regardless of whether the meaning of *closed* can be decomposed into NOT+OPEN.

c See McCawley (1970c) for reasons why *beautiful* really applies not to the object but to the way in which the object is manifested to the senses.

22. Notes on Japanese Potential Clauses[*]

1. There are two principal ways of expressing ' can ' or ' be able ' in Japanese: by the verb *deki-* and by the derivational affix *-e-* (*-rare-* when combined with a vowel stem verb):

> (1) a. Tanaka-san wa oyo'g - u   koto ga deki '- ru.
>   TOP swim PRES COMPL NOM can   PRES
>   ' Tanaka is able to swim '
>   b. Tanaka-san wa oyog - e' - ru.   ' Tanaka is able to swim '
>   swim-can-PRES

This paper is concerned with whether *deki-* is a one-place (' intransitive ') or a two-place (' transitive ') verb and with the status of *-e-*.

I begin with a brief word of clarification about what it would mean to call *deki-* a two place verb. I will have to make reference to sentences without topicization so as to determine what case marker underlyingly precedes the topic marker *wa* (cf. Mikami 1960). While exact analogues to (1a) are somewhat strange, there is no difficulty in getting embedded or interrogative sentences of that form:

* This paper first appeared in *Studies in Descriptive and Applied Linguistics* (Bulletin of the Summer Institute in Linguistics: International Christian University, Tokyo) 5. 18–40. 1972.

(2)   ?Tanaka-san ga oyo'g-u koto ga deki'-ru.

(3)   Tanaka-san ga oyo'g-u koto ga deki'-ru no   wa atarimae da.
                                         COMP TOP natural COP
        ' It is natural that Tanaka can swim '

(4)   Da're ga oyo'g-u koto ga deki'-ru ka.   'Who can swim? '

If *deki-* is a two-place verb, then it is one that takes two nominative NP's
(*Tanaka-san* and *oyo'gu koto* in the case of (1a)), as do *kowa-* ' afraid ' and *zyoo-zu'* ' good at ':

(5)   Bo'ku ga he'bi ga kowa'i no wa atarimae da.
        I NOM snake   afraid
        ' It's natural that I am afraid of snakes '

(6)   Tanaka-san ga ryo'ori ga zyoozu' na   no   wa atarimae da.
                          cooking NOM good-at COP COMPL TOP
        ' It's natural that Tanaka is good at cooking '

The second NP would then be a *koto*-clause whose subject is obligatorily deleted
under identity with the first NP. To say that *deki-* is a two-place verb in
surface structure does not imply that it is a two-place verb throughout derivations: a possibility that must be considered is that *deki-* could be an underlying
one-place verb with a sentential subject (like *atarimae*) but subject to a rule
which moves the subject of that embedded sentence into the main clause (SUBJECT
RAISING), as proposed in Kuroda (1965: 193), making it the derived subject of
deki-. The bulk of the following arguments will provide evidence that *deki-*
is two-place throughout most of a derivation, including surface structure, but
will be non-commital as to whether it is a two-place verb throughout the entire
derivation; then an additional, unfortunately not really airtight, argument will
be given that it is indeed a two-place verb throughout the entire derivation.
    Throughout the bulk of the paper I will assume that case markers are inserted
by rules and ignore the question of how those rules are to be formulated and
at what stage(s) of the derivation they apply, though I will eventually take up
certain details of those questions.   I will in addition ignore topicization except
in one argument.

2.   The first argument that *deki-* is a two-place verb at at least some stage of
a derivation is due to Kuno (1968), who observes that cleft sentences can be
used as a test of constituent structure.   The following examples show that the
' predicate ' part of a cleft sentence must be a single NP:

(7)   a.   Ta'roo ga Zi'roo ni ho'n o yat - ta.
                          DAT book ACC give-PAST
            ' Taro gave Jiro a book '
      b.   Zi'roo ni ho'n o yat-ta' no wa Ta'roo da.   ' It is Taro that gave
            Jiro a book '
      c.   Ta'roo ga ho'n o yat-ta' no wa Zi'roo (ni) da.   ' It is to Jiro that
            Taro gave a book '

    d. Ta'roo ga Zi'roo ni yat-ta' no wa ho'n da. ' It is a book that Taro gave to Jiro.

    e. *Ta'roo ga yat-ta' no wa Zi'roo ni ho'n da. ' *It is to Jiro a book that Taro gave '

    f. *Ho'n o yat-ta' no wa Ta'roo ga Zi'roo (ni) da. ' *It is Taro to Jiro that gave a book '

I am not clear as to what steps are involved in the derivation of cleft sentences; I lean towards the proposal (first suggested in unpublished work on English by Robert Faraci) that they arise by deletions from a structure such as ' The answer to the question (who did Taro give a book to) is (Taro gave a book to Jiro) '. At any rate, whatever rule gives rise to the predicate part of cleft sentences, if *deki-* is a two-place verb at the stage of the derivation where it applies, *oyo'gu koto ga* will be a NP and thus eligible to become the predicate element of a cleft sentence, but *Ta'roo ga oyo'gu koto ga* will not be:

```
                            S
         _____|_____
        NP                  NP                V
      __|___             ___|___              |
     NP     ga          NP      ga          deki-
     |                __|__
   Taroo             S    koto
                     |
                     V
                   __|__
                 oyog-  ru
```

On the other hand, if *deki-* is a one-place verb at the point in the derivation where the deletion (or whatever) in cleft sentences takes place, things will be exactly reversed: *Ta'roo ga oyo'gu koto ga* will be a NP and thus eligible to become predicate element of the cleft sentence, but *oyo'gu koto ga* will not be:

```
                        S
              _____|_____
             NP                    V
          ___|___                  |
         NP      ga              deki-
       __|__
      S     kato
    __|__
   NP    V
 __|_  __|__
NP  ga oyog- ru
|
Taroo
```

The facts about cleft sentences accord with the predictions of the two-place hypothesis. For comparison, cleft sentences based on a clearly one-place structure are included also:

(8)   a.   Ta'roo ga deki'-ru no wa ano kawa' de   oyo'-g-u koto da.
                                  that river INSTR
            'What Taro can (do) is swim in that river'
    b.   *Deki'-ru no wa Ta'roo ga ano kawa' de oyo'-g-u koto da.
    c.   Ta'roo ga ha'ya-ku oki'-ru koto wa mezurasi'-i.
                early   get up   unusual-PRES
            'It's unusual for Taro to get up early'
    d.   *Ta'roo ga mezurasi'-i no wa ha'ya-ku oki'-ru koto da.
    e.   Mezurasi'-i no wa Ta'roo ga ha'ya-ku oki'-ru koto da.[1]   'What is unusual is for Taro to get up early'

Topics must also be constituents (indeed, presumably NP's), and facts about topicization give a second argument for *deki-* being two-place at at least some stage of a derivation:

(9)   a.   Oyo'g-u koto wa Ta'roo ga deki'-ru.
    b.   *Ta'roo ga oyo'g-u koto wa deki'-ru.
    c.   *Ha'ya-ku oki'-ru no wa Ta'roo ga mezurasi'-i.
    d.   Ta'roo ga ha'ya-ku oki'-ru no wa mezurasi'-i.

A third argument is due again to Kuno (1968, 1971c). Certain verbs and adjectives allow their subjects to be put into the dative case. However, the subject can be put into the dative case only if the object is put into the nominative case (which for some of these verbs and adjectives is optional and for others obligatory):

(10)   a.   Bo'ku wa he'bi ga   kowa'-i.
          I   TOP snake NOM afraid-PRES
          'I am afraid of snakes'
    b.   Ta'roo wa he'bi o kowa-ga'r-u.   'Taro is afraid of snakes'
    c.   Bo'ku ni wa he'bi ga kowa'-i.
    d.   *Ta'roo ni wa he'bi o kowa-ga'r-u.
(11)   a.   Tanaka-san wa yaki-soba o tukur- e'-ru.
                                    prepare-can-PRES
          'Tanaka can make fried noodles'
    b.   Tanaka-san wa yaki-soba ga tukur-e'-ru.
    c.   Tanaka-san ni' wa yaki-soba ga tukur-e'-ru.
    d.   *Tanaka-san ni' wa yaki-soba o tukur-e'-ru.

Kuno thus concludes that there must be a rule applying to structures containing two nominative cases and turning one of them into a dative. The two nominative NP's must be in the same clause for this rule to apply, as evidenced by the following instances of nominative cases that are not in the same clause:

---

[1] *No* may be used in place of *koto* as the complementizer in (8e), but in (8c), only *koto* is possible for the complementizer. I have no explanation for this fact.

(12) a. Ta'roo ga/*ni kat-ta   reizo'oko ga kosyoo-sita.
                 buy-dAST refrigerator out-of-order
          'The refrigerator which Taro bought is out of order'
      b. Ta'roo ga/*ni ha'ya-ku oki'-ru no wa mezurasi'-i. 'It's strange
          for Taro to get up early'
      c. Ta'roo ga/*ni Zi'roo ga kat-ta reizo'oko o syuuzen-sita. 'Taro
          repaired the refrigerator that Jiro had bought'

Since the nominative-into-dative rule is applicable to sentences with *deki-*,
the NP which becomes dative must be a clause-mate of *deki-* and *deki-* must
thus have a two-place structure when this rule applies:

(13) Ta'roo ni wa oyo'g-u koto ga deki'-ru.

A fourth argument that *deki-* is two-place at some stage of the derivation is
due to S. I. Harada (personal communication). Harada argues that the rule
which puts verbs and adjectives into the honorific form with *o-* requires that
the subject of the verb or adjective be the person honored:[2]

(14) a. Yamada-sense'i wa o-isogasi'-i. 'Prof. Yamada is busy'
      b. Yamada-sense'i wa tegami o   o-kaki ni   nari-ma'si-ta.
                             letter ACC HON-write DAT become-
                                                      POLITE-PAST
          'Prof. Yamada wrote a letter'
      c. *Ta'roo wa Yamada-sense'i ni tegami o o-kaki ni nari-ma'si-ta.[3]
          'Taro wrote a letter to Prof. Yamada'
      d. Yamada-sense'i ga tegami o o-kaki ni na'ru no wa mezurasi'-i.
                             *o-kaki ni na'ru no wa o-mezurasi'-i.
                             *ka'k-u no wa o-mezurasi'-i.
          'It's unusual for Prof. Yamada to write letters'

In a clause with *deki-*, either *deki-* or the embedded verb or both takes the *o-*
honorific form:

(15) a. Yamada-sense'i wa gu'nka o uta-u koto ga o-deki ni nari-ma's-u.
      b.   o-utai ni na'ru koto ga deki-ma's-u.
      c.   o-utai ni na'ru koto ga o-deki ni
                            nari-ma's-u.
      'Prof. Yamada can sing military songs'

(15b, c) show that *Yamada-sense'i* is the subject of *utaw-* when *o-*honorification
applies to the embedded clause; (15a, c) show that *Yamada-sense'i* is the subject
of *deki-* when *o-*honorification applies to the main clause. This implies first of
all that when *o-*honorification applies to the main clause, *deki-* has a two-place
structure. Secondly, it implies that either *Yamada-sense'i* is the underlying
subject of both clauses (in which case there must be a rule of EQUI-NP-DELETION

[2] Honorification is optional as long as the person to be honored gets honored at least once
per sentence.
[3] If one were honoring Taro, he wouldn't call him Taro but something more dignified.

to delete its occurrence as subject of the embedded clause) or *deki-* is converted from a one-place structure to a two-place structure by a rule of SUBJECT-RAISING, which would then have to be in the cycle and ordered before *o*-honorification: if *deki-* has an underlying one-place structure, *o*-honorification must apply to the lower sentence before subject-raising moves the lower subject into the main clause, and subject-raising must in turn apply before *o*-honorification applies to the higher sentence, since it creates the conditions necessary for the application of *o*-honorification.

The arguments given so far show that *deki-* is two-place at the points of the derivation where various transformations apply (*o*-honorification, nominative-into-dative, the deletion in cleft sentences; it is not clear what underlies topicized sentences, and depending on what account of topics is right, argument 2 may imply that *deki-* is two-place at the very beginning of derivations or that it is two-place when a certain movement transformation applies). It is logically possible that in the course of a derivation *deki-* could be converted from a two-place verb into a one-place verb by a transformation that does the inverse of the subject-raising transformation considered above. However, on the grounds that such a transformation appears to be unknown in any language, I conclude that *deki-* is two-place not only at the points of the derivation referred to above but at all subsequent points of the derivation, surface structure included. It remains to determine whether *deki-* is basically two-place or becomes two-place through subject-raising.

An argument that *deki-* is basically two-place can be made on the basis of facts about selectional restrictions plus some conclusions about what is a possible selectional restriction universally. I take the position (McCawley 1968c, Lakoff 1969) that a selectional restriction is simply a presupposition and that violation of a selectional restriction is a (logical) contradiction between that presupposition and something else in the semantic structure of the discourse,[4] possibly supplemented with relevant factual knowledge. In addition, I accept the conclusion (G. Lakoff, unpublished work) that a predicate only imposes selectional restrictions on the NP's of its clause and that if one of those NP's is a S (a ' complement '), the selectional restriction on that NP must be a restriction on what the topmost verb of that S may be. For example, *try* requires that its complement refer to an action, which (given the conclusion of Ross (1971) that in a clause referring to an action, the topmost predicate is *do*, or rather DO, the meaning of *do*) implies that the topmost predicate of the complement of *try* must be DO.

Subject to a qualification which I will bring up shortly, the surface subject of *deki-* must be an animate being (or beings) and the surface object (the *koto* clause) a description of an action:

(16) a.   *A'me wa hu'r-u koto ga deki'-ru. ' Rain can fall '
           rain   fall

[4] See McCawley (1971c) for an argument that more than one sentence may be involved in a single selectional violation.

     b.   *Ano bakudan wa bakuhatu-suru koto ga deki'-ru.
            bomb   explode
         ' That bomb can explode '
     c.   *Tukimisoo   wa yo'ru sak-u koto ga deki'-ru.
          evening primrose
         ' Evening primrose can bloom at night '

(17)   a.   *Tanaka-san wa Sa'too-syusyoo ni ni-ru koto ga deki'-ru.
         ' Tanaka can resemble Prime Minister Sato '
     b.   *Ta'roo wa Ha'nako o/ga suki' na koto ga deki'-ru.
         ' Taro can like Hanako '

If *deki-* expresses a relationship between an agent and an action type, expressing, say, that agent has the ability needed for the action (which would make *deki-* semantically a two-place predicate), then the ungrammaticality of (16)–(17) will follow automatically, since *a'me*, etc. are not possible agents, and *Sa'too-syusyoo ni ni-ru* is not an action. If *deki-* were a one-place predicate which were predicated of a proposition (e.g. a habitual present such as ' It rains ') and meant, say ' is possible ', (16) ought to be grammatical, since there is nothing semantically incoherent about ' It is possible that it rains ' or ' It is possible for it to rain '.

This of course does not prove that *deki-* is two-place: the alternative considered is hardly the only way in which a predicate could be one-place. One must also consider the possibility that *deki-* is a one-place predicate that requires the topmost predicate of its complement to be DO (though in this case, there is no obvious description of the meaning in English). That proposal would also correctly predict the restriction on the surface subject of *deki-*: since the surface subject of *deki-* would be the subject of the DO, the impossibility of *a'me* as subject of DO would imply its impossibility as surface subject of *deki-*. I suspect that one-place predicates which require DO as topmost verb of their complement canbe excluded universally, since in all clear cases of a verb a with complement whose topmost verb must be DO (e.g. *try* and *force*), the main clause contains another NP and that NP controls obligatory deletion of the subject of DO.

In the meantime, let me try to determine whether the same kind of argument that can be given for the underlying transitivity of *try* can also be given for *deki-*. The principal argument for treating *try* as basically two-place rests on the assumption that passives, or at least, the kind of passives involved in the examples, have essentially the same underlying structure as ' corresponding ' actives; see Kuno (1971b) for arguments that Japanese ' simple ' passives (*Ano sima' wa Ro'siya ni tor-a're-ta* ' That island was taken by Russia '), which are the type relevant here, have essentially the same underlying structure as actives. The sentences

(18)   a.   The sheriff tried to arrest Mark.
     b.   Mark tried to be arrested by the sheriff.

differ in meaning by more than do

(19)   a.   The sheriff arrested Mark.
     b.   Mark was arrested by the sheriff.

Specifically, (18b) but not (18a) implies that being arrested by the sheriff is a goal which Mark was pursuing, and indeed (18b), as noted in Perlmutter (1968, 1970), makes reference not just to the sheriff arresting Mark but to Mark causing the sheriff to arrest him, and is indeed paraphrasable by ' Mark tried to get the sheriff to arrest him '.   These facts are explained by the hypothesis that *try* is an underlying two-place verb which requires Equi-NP-deletion in its complement and that ' get ' is optionally deletable in the complement of *try*.   A similar argument can be given for saying that *deki-* is basically two-place, though it is somewhat simpler, since Japanese apparently has no analogue to the deletion of ' get ':

> (20) a. Keikan wa ya'kuza o ta'iho-suru koto ga deki'-ru.   ' Policemen can arrest thugs.'
>
> b. *Ya'kuza wa keikan ni ta'iho-s-are-ru koto ga deki'-ru.

A further fact that might be cited as evidence for the basic transititity of *deki-* is the grammaticality of sentences such as

> (21) Tanaka-san wa na'n-demo deki'-ru.   ' Tanaka can (do) anything.'

However, it is not completely clear that this fact implies that *deki-* is basically transitive: one cannot dismiss out of hand the possibility that *na'ndemo* is not the complete object of *deki'-ru* but rather the object of a deleted verb *suru* ' do ' in the complement of *deki-*.   If in fact that is what *na'ndemo* is, then (21) is consistent with the one-place analysis of *deki-* that I argued against above.

Now to the qualification that I mentioned above.   In fact, there are some sentences with *deki-* that have a non-agent subject and are grammatical:[5]

> (22) a. Asa'gao   wa a'sa   sika sak-u koto ga deki'-na-i.
>   morning-glory   morning only bloom   can-NEG-PRES
>   ' Morning-glories can only bloom in the morning '
>
> b. Saboten wa sabaku ni hae'-ru koto ga deki'-ru.
>   cactus   desert   grow
>   ' Cactus can grow in the desert '
>
> c. ' Yuu ' wa ' ____ to yuu ' . . . nado no yoo ni ta' no go' ni ziyu'u
>   etc.   like   other   word   free
>   ni tu'k-u koto ga deki'-ru.
>   attach   ' *Yuu* can combine freely with
>   other words, as in ____ to yuu, etc.'

The use of *deki-* in (22) differs materially from that in the examples discussed so far.   Note that two of the arguments for transitivity of *deki-* which I gave earlier fail if sentences like (22) are used:

> (23) a. *Asa'gao ni wa a'sa sika sak-u koto ga deki'-na-i.
>
> b. *Saboten ni' wa sabaku ni hae'-ru koto ga deki'-ru.

[5] I am grateful to Takatsugu Oyakawa for calling (22a-b) to my attention.   (22c) is a sentence which I noticed in Shiraishi Daiji, *Nihongo no idiomu* (Tokyo: Sanseido, 1950).

    c. *' Yuu ' ni wa ' ____ to yuu ' . . . nado no yoo ni ta' no go' ni ziyu'u ni tu'k-u koto ga deki'-ru.

(24) a. *Saboten ga deki'-ru no wa sabaku ni hae'-ru koto da.

    b. *' Yuu ' ga deki'-ru no wa ' ____ to yuu ' . . . nado no yoo ni ta' no go' ni ziyu'u ni tu'k-u koto da.

These facts suggest that *deki-* is not always transitive: that the examples in (22) involve a basically intransitive *deki-* whereas those given previously involve a basically transitive *deki-*. The use of intransitive *deki-* appears to be fairly restricted, but I am not in a position to say what the restriction is.

3. I turn now to the other device which Japanese has for expressing ' can ' or ' be able ', the potential morpheme *-e-* (*-rare-* after a vowel stem). I will argue that *-e-* corresponds to the same element of semantic structure as does transitive *deki-* and that the differences between the derivations of *deki-* clauses and *-e-* clauses are attributable to the rule of PREDICATE RAISING, which lifts the verb out of the complement of *-e-* and combines it with *-e-*,[6] and the difference of constituent structure and clause membership which this step brings about.

    There are of course more differences in surface structure between *deki-* clauses and *-e-* clauses than just whether the verb of the embedded sentence is combined into a single word with *-e-* but not with *deki-*. The three encircled morphemes are present in *deki-* clauses but not in *-e-* clauses:

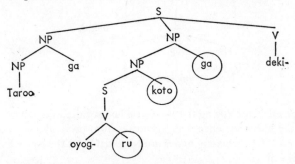

Thus, if the derivations of *deki-* clauses and *-e-* clauses are to be the same up to the stage where predicate raising applies and only to diverge from then on, each of these three morphemes will have to be either present at that stage in both derivations and subsequently deleted in the case of *-e-*, or absent in both derivations and subsequently inserted in the case of *deki-*. I have no extremely strong argument that the three morphemes are inserted by rule (as I conjecture to be the case), but I can offer reasons for finding that conjecture plausible. First, the three morphemes appear to carry no semantic content in *deki-* clauses. In particular, the present tense morpheme of the *koto* clause has no temporal significance, and the substitution of a past tense renders the sentence ungrammatical:

---

[6] The same step occurs in the case of other derivational morphemes, e.g. causative *-sase-*, passive *-rare-*, desiderative *-ta-*.

(25)   *Ta'roo wa oyo'i - da koto ga deki'- ru /de'ki-ta.
           swim-PAST   can -PRES/ can -PAST

I conjecture that *deki-* clauses have a complement in the present tense only because the complementizer *koto* must be preceded by a tensed clause, and the present tense, as unmarked tense, is inserted when a complementizer demands that
an otherwise tenseless clause contain a tense.   In addition, Kuno (1968, 1971c),
elaborating earlier work by Kuroda (1965), has demonstrated that the choice
between *ga* and *o* is predictable, in particular, that the verbs and adjectives which
take a direct object in the nominative case are a semantically definable subset of
' stative ' verbs and adjectives, namely those which express feeling or abilities.
I will assume in what follows that prior to predicate raising, both *deki-* clauses
and *-e-* clauses have structures lacking *ga*, *o*, *koto*, and the embedded present
tense (the tense of the main clause being presumably the underlying predicate of
a higher clause; see McCawley 1971a for arguments that tenses in English are
higher predicates):

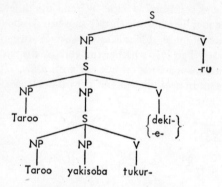

and that after predicate raising the *-e-* clause has acquired the following structure
(the loss of the lower sentence node resulting from principles such as those discussed in Ross 1969a, whereby nodes are removed from the tree when they cease
to be ' functional '):

The same predicate raising transformation that combines *tukur-* with *-e-* also
combines *deki-* or *tukur-e-* with the tense morpheme.
   I offer the following arguments for the existence of an embedded clause in *-e-*

clauses and the underlying transitivity of *-e-*. First, *-e-* is subject to the same selectional restriction on its surface subject as is transitive *deki-*; note in particular that the analogues to (22)[7] are all ungrammatical:

(26) a. *A'me wa hur-e'-ru.
 b. *Tukimisoo wa yo'ru sak-e-ru.
 c. *Asa'gao wa a'sa sika sak-e-na-i.
 d. *Saboten wa sabaku ni hae-rare'-ru.
 e. *'Yuu' wa '____ to yuu' nado no yoo ni ta' no go' ni ziyu'u ni tuk-e'-ru.

Secondly, the complement of *-e-* which I hypothesize must exist since it is the only possible antecedent for the zero pronominalization found in sentences such as

(27) Tanaka-san wa yaki-soba o tukur-e'-ru to it-ta ga, hontoo wa deki'-na-i.
 'Tanaka says that he can make fried noodles, but really he can't.'

The zero pronoun in (27) refers to 'make fried noodles', and for pronominalization to be applicable here, both clauses must contain a constituent corresponding to 'make fried noodles'; but the first occurrence of that constituent would be precisely the complement which I claim *-e-* has. Thirdly, it is necessary that *-e-* have a clause embedded as its complement in order for there to be a constituent which the adverbs in the following examples can reasonably be said to modify:

(28) a. Ta'roo wa zi' o hude de kak-e'-ru. 'Taro can write characters with a brush'
 b. Ta'roo wa gohu'n-kan i'ki o tome-rare-ru. 'Taro can hold his breath for five minutes'

In (28a), *hude de* 'with a brush' is not the instrument of Taro's being able to write but the instrument of his writing, and in (28b), *gohu'n-kan* 'for five minutes' is not the duration of Taro's ability to hold his breath but the duration of his holding his breath. (28a-b) involve the same modification relations as in

(29) a. Ta'roo wa zi' o hude de ka'k-u koto ga deki'-ru.
 b. Ta'roo wa gohu'n-kan i'ki o tome-ru koto ga deki'-ru.,

and if (as seems obvious) *hude de* modifies (*Ta'roo ga*) *zi' o ka'k-u* in (29a) and *gohu'n-kan* modifies (*Ta'roo ga*) *i'ki o tome-ru* in (29b), the same embedded clauses must be present in the underlying structure of (28a-b).

A final piece of evidence for an embedded sentence in *-e-* clauses comes from a consideration of the use of case markers in *-e-* clauses, which seems to involve both case marking on the basis of the embedded clause and case marking on the basis of the main clause. The potential form of a verb which takes an accusative object may have its object in either the accusative or the nominative case:

---

[7] There is no analogue to (16b) because *suru* does not have a potential form: there is no such form as **s-e-ru*, and *sareru* (the *-rare-* form of *suru*) cannot be used as a potential.

(30) a. Tanaka-san wa yaki-soba o tukur-e'-ru.
      b. Tanaka-san wa yaki-soba ga tukur-e'-ru.

If a verb takes an object in any other case, the potential form takes the same case on its object:

(31) a. Tanaka-san wa Nikuson-daito'oryoo ni a't-ta. 'Tanaka met President Nixon'
      b. Tanaka-san wa Nikuson-daito'oryoo ni/*ga a'-e-ta. 'Tanaka was able to meet President Nixon'.

In (30a), the object is treated as if it is the object of *tukur-*; in (30b), it is treated as if it is the object of the derived verb *tukur-e-*, which (being a verb of ability) takes a nominative object; in (31b), the object can only be treated as object of *aw-* and not of the derived verb *a(w)-e*. These facts would be explained by the following hypotheses:
(i)   *-e-* has a complement;
(ii) idiosyncratic case marking (e.g. marking the object of *aw-* as dative) takes place in the cycle;
(iii) after idiosyncratic case marking, the following two rules apply to attach case markers to NP's WHICH DO NOT YET HAVE CASE MARKERS:
      (a) if the verb is a verb of feeling or ability, the second NP in its clause is made nominative,
      (b) (optional) the second NP in the clause is made accusative[8];
(iv) there is an output constraint which excludes structures in which there is a NP that does not have a case marker.
(i) and (ii), plus the restriction of (iii) to NP's that do not yet have case markings, would insure that the object of *aw-* would remain dative regardless of whether predicate raising applies. (i) and (iii) allow the object of *tukur-* to be made accusative when the cycle applies to the embedded clause, and it would remain accusative regardless of whether predicate raising applies; they would also allow the possibility of its not being marked with a case when the cycle applies to the embedded clause, but only after it has become the derived object of *tukur-e-*, in which case it would become nominative by (iii-a).[a]

---

[a] One important fact which I neglected here is that *-e-* but not *deki-* has the additional meaning of 'is permitted':

    Koko ni suwarema'su ka? 'May we sit here?'
    *Koko ni suwaru koto' ga dekima'su ka?

---

[8] Kuno treats accusative marking as obligatory and nominative object marking with *-e-* (and desiderative *-ta-*) as optional and derives (30b) through an intermediate stage of . . . *yakisoba o ga* . . .

Bibliography

Abbreviations used in the bibliography
CLS=Papers from the -th regional meeting, Chicago Linguistic Society.
FL=Foundations of language
IJAL=International journal of American linguistics
Lg.=Language
LI=Linguistic inquiry
MSLL=Monograph series on languages and linguistics, Georgetown University.
PIL=Papers in Linguistics
POLA=Project on linguistic analysis, Ohio State University and the University of California at Berkeley

Annear, Sandra. 1964. Prenominal modifiers. *POLA report* 8. 95–121 (Ohio State University).
Austin, J. L. 1962. *How to do things with words.* Oxford: Oxford University Press.
Bach, Emmon. 1964. *An introduction to transformational grammars.* New York: Holt, Rinehart and Winston.
—— 1968. Nouns and noun phrases. Bach and Harms 1968, 90–122.
—— 1970. Problominalization. *LI* 1. 121–2.
—— 1971. Syntax since *Aspects. MSLL* 24. 1–17.
—— and Robert T. Harms. 1968. *Universals in linguistic theory.* New York: Holt, Rinehart and Winston.
Baker, C. L. 1970. Notes on the description of English questions: the role of an abstract question morpheme. *FL* 6. 197–219.
—— 1971. Stress level and auxiliary behavior in English. *LI* 2. 167–81.
Berman, Arlene. 1974. On the VSO hypothesis. *LI* 5. 1–38.
Bierwisch, Manfred. 1967. Some semantic universals of German adjectivals. *FL* 3. 1–36.
—— and Karl-Erich Heidolph. 1970. *Progress in Linguistics.* The Hague: Mouton.
Binnick, Robert I. 1969. *Studies in the derivation of predicative structures.* University of Chicago Dissertation. Published in *PIL* 3. 237–339 and 519–602 (1970).
Bird, Charles S. 1968. Relative clauses in Bambara. *Journal of West African languages* 5. 34–48.
Birkhoff, Garrett, and Saunders MacLane. 1953. *A survey of modern algebra*, 2nd edition. New York: Macmillan.

Bloch, Bernard. 1946. Studies in colloquial Japanese II: syntax. *Lg.* 22. 200–48. Reprinted in Joos 1958, 154–84.

—— and George L. Trager. 1942. *Outline of linguistic analysis.* Baltimore: Linguistic Society of America.

Bolinger, Dwight. 1965. The atomization of meaning. *Lg.* 41. 555–73.

—— 1967a. Adjectives in English: attribution and predication. *Lingua* 18.1–34.

—— 1967b. The imperative in English. *To honor Roman Jakobson* 335–62 (The Hague: Mouton).

Boole, George. 1854. *The laws of thought.* London.

Brend, Ruth M. 1968. *A tagmemic analysis of Spanish clauses.* The Hague: Mouton.

Bresnan, Joan W. 1971. Sentence stress and syntactic transformations. *Lg.* 47.257–81.

Cantrall, William R. 1969. *On the nature of the reflexive.* University of Illinois dissertation.

Carden, Guy. 1968. English quantifiers. Report NSF-20 of Harvard University Computation Laboratory.

—— 1972. Multiple dialects in multiple negation. *CLS* 8.32–40.

Castañeda, Hector-Neri. 1966. ' He ': a study in the logic of self-consciousness. *Ratio* 8.130–57.

—— 1967. Indicators and quasi-indicators. *American Philosophical Quarterly* 4.85–100.

Chafe, Wallace L. 1968. The ordering of phonological rules. *IJAL* 34.115–36.

Chapin, Paul G. 1970. Samoan pronominalization. *Lg.* 46.366–78.

Chaplin, Hamako Ito, and Samuel E. Martin. 1967. *A manual of Japanese writing.* New Haven and London: Yale University Press.

Chiba, Shuji, 1972. Another case for ' Relative clause formation is a copying rule '. *Studies in English Linguistics* 1.1–12. Tokyo.

Chomsky, Noam A. 1956. Three models for the description of language. *IRE transactions on information theory* 2.113–24.

—— 1957. *Syntactic structures.* The Hague: Mouton.

—— 1962. A transformational approach to syntax. A. A. Hill, *Proceedings of the Third Texas Conference on Problems of Linguistic Analysis of English* (Austin: University of Texas), 124–58. Reprinted in Fodor and Katz (1964), 211–45.

—— 1963. Formal properties of grammars. Luce et al., 323–418.

—— 1964. *Current issues in linguistic theory.* The Hague: Mouton. Also appears in Fodor and Katz 1964, 50–118. (page references in the text are to the reprint).

—— 1965. *Aspects of the theory of syntax.* Cambridge, Mass.: MIT Press.

—— 1966. *Topics in the theory of generative grammar.* The Hague: Mouton. Also appears in Sebeok 1966, 1–60.

—— 1967. The formal nature of language. Appendix to Eric H. Lenneberg, *Biological foundations of language* (New York: Wiley), 397–422.

—— 1970a. Remarks on nominalization. Jacobs and Rosenbaum 1970, 184–221.

—— 1970b. Deep structure, surface structure, and semantic interpretation. Jakobson and Kawamoto 1970, 52–91. Reprinted in Steinberg and Jakobovits 1971, 183–216. (page references in the text are to the reprint).

—— and Morris Halle. 1968. *The sound pattern of English.* New York: Harper and Row.

—— and George A. Miller. 1963. Formal analysis of natural languages. Luce et al. 269–321.

Dahl, Östen. 1971. Tenses and world states. Gothenburg papers in theoretical linguistics, no. 6.

Darden, Bill J. 1971. Diachronic evidence for phonemics. *CLS* 7.323–31.

Davidson, Donald, and Gilbert H. Harman. 1972. *Sematics of natural language.* Dordrecht: Reidel.

Donnellan, Keith. 1966. Reference and definite descriptions. *Philosophical review* 75.281–304. Reprinted in Steinberg and Jakobovits 1970, 100–114.

Dougherty, Ray. 1970. Review of Bach and Harms 1968. *FL* 6.217–31.

Drange, Theodore. 1966. *Type crossings.* The Hague: Mouton.

Ferguson, Charles A. 1971. A sample research strategy in language universals. *Working papers in language universals* (Stanford) 6.1–22.

Fillmore, Charles J. 1963. The position of embedding transformations in a grammar. *Word* 19.208–31.

—— 1965. *Indirect object constructions in English and the ordering of transformations.* The Hague: Mouton.

—— 1966. A proposal concerning English prepositions. *MSLL* 19. 19–34.

—— 1967. Introduction to *Working papers in linguistics* no. 1 (Ohio State University), 1–8.

—— 1968. The case for case. Bach and Harms 1968, 1–88.

—— 1971. Verbs of judging. Fillmore and Langendoen 1971, 273–89.

—— and D. Terence Langendoen. 1971. *Studies in linguistic semantics.* New York: Holt, Rinehart and Winston.

Fischer, Susan. 1967. A late paper on time. Unpublished.

Fodor, Jerry A., and Jerrold J. Katz. 1964. *The structure of language.* Englewood Cliffs: Prentice-Hall.

Geach, Peter T. 1962. *Reference and generality.* Ithaca: Cornell University Press.

—— 1968. Quine's syntactical insights. *Synthese* 19.118–29.

Geis, Michael L. 1970. Time prepositions as underlying verbs. *CLS* 6.235–49.

Gleitman, Lila R. 1965. Coordinating conjunctions in English. *Lg.* 41.260–93. Reprinted in Reibel and Schane 1969, 80–112.

Goodman, Nelson. 1951. *The structure of appearance.* Cambridge, Mass.: Harvard University Press.

Gruber, Jeffrey. 1965. *Studies in lexical relations.* MIT dissertation. Also available from Indiana University Linguistics Club.

—— 1967. Functions of the lexicon in formal descriptive grammars. Santa Monica: System Development Corp. report.

Haiman, John. 1970. Former and latter. Report NSF-24 of Harvard University Computation Laboratory, 129–201.

Halle, Morris. 1959. *The sound pattern of Russian.* The Hague: Mouton.

—— 1962. Phonology in generative grammar. *Word* 18.54–72. Reprinted in Fodor and Katz 1964, 334–52.

—— 1963. O russkom sprjaženije. *American contributions to the Fifth International Congress of Slavists* (The Hague: Mouton), 363–82.

Harman, Gilbert H. 1963. Generative grammars without transformation rules: in defense of phrase structure. *Lg.* 39.597–616.

Harris, Zellig S. 1946. From morpheme to utterance. *Lg.* 22.161–83. Reprinted in Joos 1958, 142–53.

—— 1951. *Structural linguistics.* Chicago: University of Chicago Press.

Hasegawa, Kinsuke. 1968. The passive construction in English. *Lg.* 44.230–43.

Hays, David. 1964. Dependency theory: a formalism and some observations. *Lg.* 40.511–25.

Hofmann, T. R. 1966. Past tense replacement and the English modal auxiliary system. Report NSF-17 of the Harvard University Computation Laboratory.

Horn, Laurence R. 1969. A presuppositional analysis of *only* and *even.* *CLS* 5.98–107.

Huddleston, Rodney. 1969. Some observations on tense and deixis in English. *Lg.* 45.777–806.

Jackendoff, Ray. 1968. An interpretive theory of pronouns and reflexives. Unpublished.

—— 1969. An interpretive theory of negation. *FL* 5.218–243.

—— 1971. Modal structure in semantic representation. *LI* 2.479–514.

—— 1972. *Semantic interpretation in generative grammar.* Cambridge, Mass.: M.I.T. Press.

Jacobs, Roderick A., and Peter S. Rosenbaum. 1970. *Readings in English transformational grammar*. Boston: Ginn.

Jakobson, Roman. 1941. *Kindersprache, Aphasie und allgemeine Lautgesetze.* Reprinted in Jakobson's *Selected writings*, vol. 1, 328–401 (The Hague: Mouton).

—— 1957. Shifters, verbal categories, and the Russian verb. Harvard University (multilithed).

—— 1958. What can typological studies contribute to historical comparative linguistics? *Proceedings of the 8th International Congress of Linguists* (Oslo), 17–25.

—— and Shigeo Kawamoto. 1970. *Studies in general and oriental linguistics.* Tokyo: the TEC Corp.

Jespersen, Otto. 1924. *The philosophy of grammar.* London: Allen and Unwin.

—— 1933. *Essentials of English grammar.* London: Allen and Unwin.

—— 1937. *Analytic syntax.* London: Allen and Unwin.

Jones, Daniel. 1962. *The phoneme: its nature and use.* Cambridge: Heffer.

Joos, Martin. 1958. *Readings in Linguistics.* vol. 1. Chicago: University of Chicago Press.

Karttunen, Lauri. 1969. Pronouns and variables. *CLS* 5.108–16.

—— 1971a. Definite descriptions with crossing coreference: a study of the Bach-Peters paradox. *FL* 7.157–82.

—— 1971b. Implicative verbs. *Lg.* 47.340–58.

Katz, Jerrold J. 1964. Semantic theory and the meaning of ' good '. *Journal of Philosophy* 61.739–66.

—— 1966. *The philosophy of language.* New York: Harper and Row.

—— 1967. Recent issues in semantic theory. *FL* 3.124–94.

—— 1970. Interpretative semantics vs. generative semantics. *FL* 6.220–59.

—— and Jerry A. Fodor. 1963. The structure of a semantic theory. *Lg.* 39.170–210.

—— and Edwin Martin, Jr. 1967. The synonymy of actives and passives. *Philosophical Review* 76.476–91.

—— and Paul M. Postal. 1964. *An integrated theory of linguistic descriptions.* Cambridge, Mass.: MIT Press.

Kaye, Jonathan D. 1971. Selectional restrictions and the Algonquian animate-inanimate classification. *University of Toronto Anthropological Series* 9.80–91.

Keyser, S. Jay. 1968. Review of Sven Jacobson, *Adverbial positions in English. Lg.* 44.357–74.

Kiefer, Ferenc. 1970. *Studies in syntax and semantics.* Dordrecht: Reidel.

Kiparsky, R. P. V. 1965. *Linguistic change.* MIT dissertation.

—— 1968. Tense and mood in Indo-European. *FL* 4.30–57.

Klima, Edward S. 1964. Negation in English. Fodor and Katz 1964, 246–323.

Koutsoudas, Andreas. 1972. The strict order fallacy. *Lg.* 48.88–96.

Kuno, Susumu. 1968. Case marking in Japanese. Unpublished.

—— 1971a. The position of locatives in existential sentences. *LI* 2.333–78.

—— 1971b. The reflexive pronoun and the passive and causative constructions. (Notes on Japanese Grammar no. 23). Unpublished.

—— 1971c. Case marking (Notes on Japanese grammar no. 22). Unpublished.

Kuroda, S.-Y. 1965. *Generative grammatical studies in the Japanese language.* MIT dissertation.

—— 1970. Remarks on selectional restrictions and presuppositions. Kiefer 1970, 138–67.

Lakoff, George. 1965. *On the nature of syntactic irregularity.* Indiana University dissertation. Published 1970 under the title *Irregularity in syntax* (New York: Holt, Rinehart and Winston).

—— 1968a. Instrumental adverbs and the concept of deep structure. *FL* 4.4–29.

—— 1968b. Counterparts, or the problem of reference in transformational grammar. Unpublished.

—— 1969. Presuppositions and relative grammaticality. *Journal of philosophical linguistics* vol. 1, no. 1, 103–16. Also appears under the title ' Presuppositions and rela-

tive well-formedness' in Steinberg and Jakobovits 1971, 329–40.
—— 1970a. Repartee. *FL* 6.389–422.
—— 1970b. Global rules. *Lg.* 46.627–39.
—— 1971. On generative semantics. Steinberg and Jakobovits 1971, 232–96.
—— Abortion a. Deep and surface grammar.
—— Abortion b. Pronouns and reference. Completed parts available from Indiana University Linguistics Club.
—— In preparation. *Generative semantics.* New York: Holt, Rinehart and Winston.
—— and P. S. Peters. 1969. Phrasal conjunction and symmetric predicates. Reibel and Schane 1969, 113–42.
—— and John Robert Ross. 1967. Is deep structure necessary? Available from Indiana University Linguistics Club.
Lakoff, Robin. 1968. *Abstract syntax and Latin complementation.* Cambridge, Mass.: MIT Press.
—— 1969. A syntactic argument for *not*-transportation. *CLS* 5.140–7.
—— 1971a. If's, and's, and but's about conjunction. Fillmore and Langendoen 1971, 114–49.
—— 1971b. Passive resistance. *CLS* 7.149–62.
—— 1971c. Tense and its relation to participants. *Lg.* 46.838–50.
Lamb, Sydney. 1964. On alternation, transformation, realization, and stratification. *MSLL* 17.105–22.
—— 1966a. *Outline of stratificational grammar.* Washington, D.C.: Georgetown University Press.
—— 1966b. Prolegomena to a theory of phonology. *Lg.* 42.536–73.
Langacker, Ronald W. 1968. *Language and its structure.* New York: Harcourt Brace and World.
—— 1969. Pronominalization and the chain of command. Reibel and Schane 1969, 160–86.
Larkin, Don. 1969. Notes on English modals. *Phonetics laboratory notes* (University of Michigan) 4.31–6.
Leech, Geoffrey. 1969. *Towards a semantic description of English.* London: Longmans, and Bloomington: Indiana University Press.
Lees, Robert B. 1957. Review of Chomsky (1957). *Lg.* 33.375–408.
—— 1960. The grammar of English nominalizations. Supplement to *IJAL.*
—— and Edward S. Klima. 1963. Rules for English pronominalization. *Lg.* 39.17–28. Reprinted in Reibel and Schane 1969, 145–59.
Leisi, Ernst. 1967. *Der Wortinhalt.* (3rd ed.). Heidelberg: Quelle u. Meyer.
Lewis, C. I. 1946. *An analysis of knowledge and valuation.* La Salle, Ill.: Open Court.
Linsky, Leonard. 1952. *Semantics and the philosophy of language.* Urbana, Chicago, and London: University of Illinois Press.
—— 1968. *Referring.* London: Routledge, Kegan Paul.
Lightner, Theodore M. 1965. *The segmental phonology of modern standard Russian.* MIT dissertation.
Luce, R. Duncan, Robert R. Bush, and Eugene Galanter. 1963. *Handbook of Mathematical psychology,* vol. 2. New York: Wiley.
Mates, Benson. 1949. Synonymity. *University of California publications in philosophy* 25.201–26. Reprinted in Linsky 1952, 111–36.
Matthews, G. H. 1963. Discontinuity and asymmetry in phrase structure grammars. *Information and Control* 6.137–46.
—— 1965. *Hidatsa syntax.* The Hague: Mouton.
McCawley, James D. 1967a. Edward Sapir's 'phonologic representation'. *IJAL* 33.106–11.
—— 1967b. Meaning and the description of languages. *Kotoba no uchū* vol. 2, nos. 9 (10–18), 10 (38–48), and 11 (51–57).
—— 1967c. The phonological theory behind Whitney's *Sanskrit grammar. Languages*

and areas: studies presented to George V. Bobrinskoy (Chicago: Humanities division of the University of Chicago), 77–85.

—— 1968a.	*The phonological component of a grammar of Japanese.*	The Hague: Mouton.

—— 1968b.	The annotated respective.	Unpublished.

—— 1968c.	The role of semantics in a grammar.	Bach and Harms 1968, 124–69.

—— 1968d.	Lexical insertion in a transformational grammar without deep structure. *CLS* 4.71–80.

—— 1968e.	Review of Sebeok 1966.	*Lg.* 44.556–93.

—— 1968f.	Can you count pluses and minuses before you can count?	*Chicago Journal of Linguistics* (available from University Microfilms, Ann Arbor, Mich.) 2.51–56.

—— 1968g.	Concerning the base component of a transformational grammar. *FL* 4.243–69.

—— 1970a.	English as a *VSO* language.	*Lg.* 46.286–99.

—— 1970b.	Where do noun phrases come from?	Jacobs and Rosenbaum 1970, 166–83.

—— 1970c.	Semantic representation.	Paul M. Garvin, *Cognition: a multiple view* (New York: Spartan Books), 227–47.

—— 1970d.	Similar in that S. *LI* 1.556–9.

—— 1970e.	Review of Jespersen (1937). *Lg.* 46.442–9.

—— 1970f.	A note on reflexives.	*Journal of philosophical linguistics*, vol. 1, no. 2, 6–8.

—— 1971a.	Tense and time reference in English.	Fillmore and Langendoen 1971, 96–113.

—— 1971b.	Prelexical syntax.	*MSLL* 24.19–33.

—— 1971c.	Interpretative semantics meets Frankenstein.	*FL* 7.285–96.

—— 1972.	A program for logic.	Davidson and Harman 1972, 498–544.

—— 1973.	Syntactic and logical arguments for semantic structures.	In Osamu Fujimura, editor, *Three dimensions of linguistic theory* (Tokyo: TEC Corp.), 259–376.

Mikami, Akira. 1960.	*Zoo wa hana ga nagai.*	Tokyo: Kuroshio.

Miyadi, Denzaburo.	1964.	Social life of Japanese monkeys.	*Science* 21.783–6.

Morgan, Jerry L. 1969.	On arguing about semantics.	*PIL* 1.49–70.

Newmeyer, Frederick J. 1971.	A problem with the verb-initial hypothesis. *PIL* 4.390–2.

Palmer, F. R. 1965.	*A linguistic study of the English verb.*	London: Longmans.

Parsons, Terence. 1970.	An analysis of mass terms and amount terms.	*FL* 6.362–88.

Partee, Barbara Hall. 1970.	Negation, conjunction, and quantifiers: syntax vs. semantics.	*FL* 6.153–65.

Percival, W. Keith. 1967.	On the historical source of immediate constituent analysis. Unpublished.

Perlmutter, David M. 1968.	*Deep and surface structure constraints.*	MIT dissertation.

—— 1970.	Surface structure constraints in syntax.	*LI* 1.187–256.

—— 1972.	A note on syntactic and semantic number in English.	*LI.* 3.243–6.

Peters, P. S. 1966.	A note on ordered phrase structure grammars.	Report NSF-27 of the Harvard University Computation Laboratory.

Pike, Kenneth L. 1943.	Taxemes and immediate constituents.	*Lg.* 19.65–82.

Pinneo, T. S. 1852.	*The English teacher.*	Cincinnatti.

Postal, Paul M. 1964.	*Constituent structure.*	Supplement to IJAL.

—— 1966.	On so-called ‘pronouns’.	*MSLL* 19.177–206.

—— 1967.	Linguistic anarchy notes, seriesA: Horrors of identity.	Yorktown Heights: IBM Watson Research Center.

—— 1970.	On the surface verb *remind.*	*LI* 1.37–120.	Also appears in Fillmore and Langendoen 1971, 180–270.

—— 1971.	*Crossover phenomena.*	New York: Holt, Rinehart and Winston.

—— Abortion.	Crazy notes on restrictive clauses.

Putnam, Hilary. 1953.	Synonymity and analysis of belief sentences. *Analysis* 14. 114–22.

Quang Phuc Dong. 1966. English sentences without overt grammatical subject. *Conneries linguistiques* 19.23–31. Reprinted in Zwicky et al. 1971, 3–10.

——. 1969. A note on conjoined noun phrases. *Conneries linguistiques* 17.94–101. Reprinted in Zwicky et al. 1971, 11–18.

Quine, Willard van Orman. 1960. *Word and Object*. Cambridge, Mass.: MIT Press.

—— 1961. Reference and modality. In Willard van Orman Quine, *From a logical point of view* (New York: Harper Torchbooks), 139–59.

Reddy, Michael. 1969. A semantic approach to metaphor. *CLS* 5.240–51.

—— 1971. *Reference and metaphor in human language*. University of Chicago dissertation.

Reibel, David A., and Sanford A. Schane. 1969. *Modern studies in English*. Englewood Cliffs: Prentice-Hall.

Reichenbach, Hans. 1947. *Elements of symbolic logic*. New York: Macmillan.

Rice, Lester A. 1968. Do trees have leaves? Unpublished.

Rosenbaum, Peter S. 1965. *The grammar of English predicate complement constructions*. MIT dissertation. Published 1967, Cambridge, Mass.: MIT Press.

Ross, John Robert, 1967a. *Constraints on variables in syntax*. MIT dissertation. Available from Indiana University Linguistics Club.

—— 1967b. On the cyclic nature of English pronominalization. *To Honor Roman Jakobson* (The Hague: Mouton), 1669–82. Reprinted in Reibel and Schane 1969, 187–200.

—— 1969a. A proposed rule of tree-pruning. Reibel and Schane 1969, 288–99.

—— 1969b. Auxiliaries as main verbs. *Journal of philosophical linguistics* vol. 1, no. 1, 77–102.

—— 1969c. Adjectives as noun phrases. Reibel and Schane 1969, 352–60.

—— 1969d. Guess who. *CLS* 5.252–86.

—— 1970a. On declarative sentences. Jacobs and Rosenbaum 1970, 222–72.

—— 1970b. Gapping and the order of constituents. Bierwisch and Heidolph 1970.

—— 1972. Act. Davidson and Harman 1972, 70–126.

Russell, Bertrand. 1920. *Introduction to mathematical philosophy*. London: Allen and Unwin.

Rutherford, William E. 1970. Some observations concerning subordinate clauses in English. *Lg.* 46.97–115.

Sadock, Jerrold. 1969. Hypersentences. *PIL* 1.283–370.

Schane, Sanford A. 1964. A schema for sentence conjunction. Mitre Corp. report.

Sebeok, Thomas A. 1966. *Current trends in linguistics*, vol. 3. The Hague: Mouton.

Sellars, Wilfred. 1954. Putnam on synonymity and belief. *Analysis* 15.117–20.

Sharman, J. C. 1956. The tabulation of tenses in a Bantu language. *Africa* 26.29–45.

Silvestre de Sacy, Antoine Isaac. 1824. *Principes de grammaire générale*, 5th ed. Paris.

Smith, Carlota. 1961. A class of complex modifiers in English. *Lg.* 37.342–65.

Stampe, David L. Abortion. Yes, Virginia.

Stanley, Richard. 1967. Redundancy rules in phonology. *Lg.* 43.393–436.

Steinberg, Danny D., and Leon A. Jakobovits. 1971. *Semantics: an interdisciplinary reader*. London and New York: Cambridge University Press.

Stockwell, Robert P., J. Donald Bowen, and John W. Martin. 1965. *The grammatical structures of English and Spanish*. Chicago: The University of Chicago Press.

Strawson, P. F. 1950. On referring. *Mind* 59.320–44. Reprinted in Strawson 1971, 1–27.

—— 1952. *Introduction to logical theory*. London: Methuen.

—— 1964. Identifying reference and truth values. Theoria 30. 96–118. Reprinted in Strawson 1971. 75–95.

—— 1971. *Logico-linguistic papers*. London: Methuen.

Teller, Paul. 1969. Some discussion and extension of Manfred Bierwisch's work on German adjectivals. *FL* 5.185–217.

Thorne, J. P. 1966. English imperatives. *Journal of linguistics* 2.69–78.

Trager, Edith C. 1960. *The Kiowa language: a grammatical study.* University of Pennsylvania dissertation.

Uhlenbeck, E. M. 1967. Some further remarks on transformational grammar. *Lingua* 17.263–316.

Vendler, Zeno. 1967a. Effects, results and consequences. Vendler 1967c, 147–71.

—— 1967b. Each and every, any and all. Vendler 1967c, 70–96.

—— 1967c. *Linguistics in philosophy.* Ithaca: Cornell University Press.

Voegelin, C. F., and Florence M. Voegelin. 1967. Anthropological linguistics and translation. *To honor Roman Jakobson* (The Hague: Mouton), 2159–90.

Warshawsky, Florence. 1966. Reflexives. Unpublished.

Weinreich, Uriel. 1966. Explorations in semantic theory. Sebeok 1966, 395–477.

Wells, Rulon. 1947. Immediate constituents. *Lg.* 23.81–117. Reprinted in Joos 1958, 186–207.

Whitney, William Dwight. 1877. *Essentials of English grammar.* Boston: Ginn.

—— 1883. The varieties of predication. *Transactions of the American Philological Association* 14.36–41. Reprinted in Michael Silverstein, *Whitney on Language* (Cambridge, Mass.: MIT Press, 1971).

—— 1887. *A practical French grammar.* New York: Holt.

—— 1888. *A compendious German grammar,* 6th edition. New York: Holt.

—— 1889. *Sanskrit grammar,* 2nd edition. Cambridge, Mass.: Harvard University Press.

Whorf, Benjamin Lee. 1965. *Language, thought, and reality.* Cambridge, Mass.: MIT Press.

Wierzbicka, Anna. 1967a. Mind and body from a semantic point of view. Unpublished.

—— 1967b. Against conjunction reduction. Unpublished.

Wundt, Wilhelm. 1900. *Völkerpsychologie,* 1. Band, 2. Teil. Leipzig: Wilhelm Engelmann.

Yuck Foo. 1969. A selectional restriction involving pronoun choice. *Conneries linguistiques* 17.102–103. Reprinted in Zwicky et al. 1971, 19–20.

Ziff, Paul. 1965. What an adequate grammar can't do. *FL* 1: 5–13.

Zwicky, Arnold M. Jr. 1966. On context-sensitive recognition and related matters. Unpublished.

——, Peter H. Salus, Robert I. Binnick, and Anthony L. Vanek. 1971. *Studies out in left field: defamatory essays presented to James D. McCawley.* Edmonton: Linguistic Research Inc. .

Index

Authors

Subjects

Rules

Words

388 Index

shackle 351
shall 87
she 68
sibling 181, 252
shift 353
similar 79, 273, 305
sister 252
skewer 351
slap 135
small boy's school 102
so 210
so-called 242
some 197, 249, 255, 309
specifically 317
sponge 353
spouse 53
staple 351
stitch 351
straighten 330
strap 351
strike 135
suicide 254
surgeon 194
surprise 134
suru 367
sweep 353
-ta- 365
tack 351
tape 351

tell 85, 163
temporarily 349
than 3
there 299
time 90
to 6
together 82
trächtig 58
trousers 307, 337
try 176, 362
twice 89
under surveilance 254
until 225, 349
very 28
very few 91
vice versa 237
victim 198
want 104, 143, 149, 156, 212, 280, 306
warm 64, 96
Weizen 337, 342
wheat 337
when 32
whenever 310
where 32
whether 32
while 32
will 31, 87
wipe 353
yellow 9